MORE THAN MEDALS

MORE THAN MEDALS

A HISTORY OF THE PARALYMPICS AND DISABILITY SPORTS IN POSTWAR JAPAN

DENNIS J. FROST

CORNELL UNIVERSITY PRESS
Ithaca and London

This book was published with the assistance of the Wen Chao Chen Chair of East Asian Social Sciences Endowment at Kalamazoo College

First published 2020 by Cornell University Press

Printed in the United States of America

Library of Congress Cataloging-in-Publication Data

Names: Frost, Dennis J., author.
Title: More than medals : a history of the Paralympics and disability sports in postwar Japan / Dennis J. Frost.
Description: Ithaca [New York] : Cornell University Press, 2020. | Includes bibliographical references and index.
Identifiers: LCCN 2020011140 (print) | LCCN 2020011141 (ebook) | ISBN 9781501753084 (hardcover) | ISBN 9781501753107 (pdf) | ISBN 9781501753091 (epub)
Subjects: LCSH: Paralympic Games—History. | Sports for people with disabilities—Japan—History. | Athletes with disabilities—Japan—History. | Sports tournaments—Japan—History.
Classification: LCC GV722.5.P37 F76 2020 (print) | LCC GV722.5.P37 (ebook) | DDC 796.04/56—dc23
LC record available at https://lccn.loc.gov/2020011140
LC ebook record available at https://lccn.loc.gov/2020011141

*To my students,
who not only inspired this project but also constantly
remind me how exciting it can be to uncover history*

Contents

FIGURES

ACKNOWLEDGMENTS

As I worked on this project, I was constantly reminded that I was never truly researching and writing on my own. A lengthy list of individuals and groups have provided assistance in some way, from anonymous grant application readers to the efficient photocopy workers at the National Diet Library. Although I am indebted to them all, it is simply not possible to mention everyone here. For those I omit, I can only apologize for the lack of formal recognition and express my all-too-inadequate appreciation for their help.

Carrying out research on Japan is an expensive and time-consuming undertaking, and this book would not exist without the generous institutional and financial support I received from its very earliest stages. A Xavier University Summer Fellowship helped me launch this project, and the funds available because of the Wen Chao Chen Endowment associated with my position at Kalamazoo College, along with a well-timed sabbatical leave, were instrumental in bringing the book to completion. At various points, I was fortunate to receive external support as well, including a grant from the GLCA Fund for the Study of Japan, an NEH Summer Stipend, an NEH Fellowship for Advanced Social Science Research on Japan, and an IIE Fulbright Fellowship.

In Japan, many people assisted me throughout my research. Lee Thompson served as my sponsor at Waseda University during my sabbatical and also arranged for me to share my work and gain invaluable feedback at Waseda's Sports Science Research Workshop. The staff at Waseda's international office arranged for my affiliation, housing, and even a convenient, quiet office. The Japan-U.S. Educational Commission staff made my time as a Fulbright Fellow all the more productive and enjoyable with their quick and accommodating efforts to address any concerns from me or my family. Staff from both the Japan Para-Sports Association (previously known as the Japan Sports Association for the Disabled) and the Ōita International Wheelchair Marathon took time out of their busy schedules to assist me and helped me gain access to key resources. Fujita Motoaki and Watari Tadashi generously shared research materials with me, and both have performed a service to the field with their detailed and groundbreaking work on disability sports. Josh Grisdale and Michael Gillan Peckitt also shared resources, and for years to come I will continue to make use of the online materials that they developed. The staff at the Nippon Foundation's Paralympic Support Center flew me to Tokyo to share my work at a symposium and, even more importantly, have played a pivotal role in developing a community of scholars and specialists working on sports and disability in Japan and beyond. The events that they organize and the materials that they continue to share and make available online are fundamentally reshaping the field.

I owe a special debt to those who agreed to sit for interviews or meet to discuss their involvement with the sporting events studied here. Asō Manabu, Kyōya Kazuyuki, Suzaki Katsumi, and Yamaguchi Ichirō participated in extended interview sessions. Although my discussions with Matthew Davis, Peter Hawkins, Katayama Takaki, Chino Eto, Kudo Norifumi, and Gotoh Keiko did not involve formal interviews, the insights each shared in our conversations provided me with critical insights. Yotsutani Natsuko, from Taiyō no Ie, merits particular mention: she arranged my interview with Suzaki Katsumi and literally opened the door to the archives at Taiyō no Ie, providing me access to materials unavailable anywhere else. Similarly, my work would have been incomplete without the assistance of Kashihara Tomoko, a member of the Kobe FESPIC alumni group, who not only welcomed me into the group on two occasions but also facilitated my introductions to both Yotsutani Natsuko and Asō Manabu.

I also benefited immeasurably from the support and advice of several colleagues outside Japan. Gregory Pflugfelder and William Kelly offered advice and assistance at various points in the project. My longtime mentor Jim Huffman was the first to read the entire manuscript. The book is undoubtedly stronger for his feedback, and I am better for his encouragement and ongoing friendship. I am grateful to participants in the Midwest Japan Seminar, as well as audiences at several other talks; their questions and comments shaped many sections of the work in beneficial ways. Portions of chapter 1 were originally published in the *International Journal of the History of Sport* in 2012 and in the *Asia-Pacific Journal of Sport and Social Science* in 2013, and Taylor & Francis granted permission for their use in the book. To access the original articles in these journals, visit https://www.tandfonline.com/. My anonymous reviewers provided kind words and useful insights for revision. I am also thankful that my editor Roger Haydon agreed to take my call that day. His patience, support, and timely feedback made a difficult process more than manageable and resulted in a much improved work. Ange Romeo-Hall and Mary Ribesky and their respective teams repeatedly exceeded my expectations as the manuscript moved through the editing process. I am particularly indebted to Gail Naron Chalew for her thorough and astute copyediting and to Kate Mertes for assistance with the index.

Many colleagues, friends, and family members supported me throughout this project, but I owe special thanks to a few: Tobias Barske, Valerie Barske, Mark Bookman, Mark Edington, Reto Hofmann, Robin Kietlinski, Kathryn Lightcap, Aaron Miller, Helen Macnaughtan, Thomas Mullaney, David Obermiller, Lee Pennington, Jennifer Robertson, Mathew Thompson, and Yuki Taketani Thompson. My colleagues at Kalamazoo College were also a regular source of inspiration and support.

Finally, I want to acknowledge those who lived with this book for the better part of a decade. My sons Dominick and Xander helped me celebrate each step of the process and made research in Tokyo a family affair in more ways than I can count. To my wife, Kelly, I owe far more than I could begin to express here. Without her help reading drafts, editing, compiling bibliographies, proofreading, and relocating our family halfway around the globe, this book would still be nothing more than notes and some files on my desktop. Thank you for everything.

Abbreviations

1989NFKT	1989 nen Fesupikku Kōbe Taikai Soshiki Iinkai
ANA	All Nippon Airways
APC	Asian Paralympic Committee
CPISRA	Cerebral Palsy International Sports and Recreation Association
CSR	corporate social responsibility
D1KK	Dai 1kai Kyokutō Minami Taiheiyō Shintai Shōgaisha Supōtsu Taikai Jikkō Iinkai
DVS	Deutschen Versehrtensportverbandes
FESPIC	Far East and South Pacific (Games / Movement)
FINS	FESPIC Information System
IBSA	International Blind Sports Federation
ICC	International Coordinating Committee
IOC	International Olympic Committee
IOSD	International Organizations of Sports for the Disabled
IPC	International Paralympic Committee
ISMGF	International Stoke Mandeville Games Federation
ISOD	International Sports Organization for the Disabled
JOC	Japanese Olympic Committee
JPSA	Japan Para-Sports Association
JSAD	Japan Sports Association for the Disabled
KSSSTUI	Kokusai Shintai Shōgaisha Supōtsu Taikai Un'ei Iinkai
NAOC	Nagano Olympic Organizing Committee
NAPOC	Nagano Paralympic Organizing Committee
NPBK	Nagano Para Bora no Kai
NPTKTSI	Nagano Pararinpikku Tōki Kyōgi Taikai Soshiki Iinkai
NSSSK	Nihon Shintai Shōgaisha Supōtsu Kyōkai
NYD	Nakamura Yutaka Den Kankō Iinkai

OCA   Olympic Council of Asia
OKKMTJ   Ōita Kokusai Kurumaisu Marason Taikai Jimukyoku
PAJ   Paralympians Association of Japan
PE   physical education
WVF   World Veterans Federation

NOTE FROM AUTHOR

Even without the challenges of translation, writing about disability always involves difficult and imperfect choices in relation to language and terminology. For a study that is interested in questions of representation, language is foundational, and I sought to be conscientious about word usage throughout, taking into account both historical usages and how I translated them. In some instances, this approach resulted in terminology that may seem particularly jarring to readers today. For instance, Tokyo's first Paralympics were also known as the International Stoke Mandeville Games for the Paralysed, an official name that uses phrasings that have fallen out of use for understandable reasons. In most cases, however, my sources consistently employed the Japanese term *shōgaisha*, a word used to characterize people with a wide variety of disabilities. In deciding how to translate this word, I considered both the rationale for "people-first" language and the critiques of this approach; in part because many athletes placed particular emphasis on their status *as athletes*, in most instances I use people-first language. Where other usages were more common at the time or more reflective of the original Japanese, such as "wheelchair racers," I do not employ people-first terminology.

In referring to sports, I tend to render the Japanese term *shōgaisha supōtsu* as "disability sports," instead of "adapted sports" or the International Paralympic Committee (IPC) preferred phrasing of "para-sports." In part, I feel that "disability sports" captures the original Japanese best. I would also suggest that disability sports are actually a subset of adapted sports, and contrary to what the IPC might like everyone to believe, para-sports do not, in fact, encompass all disability sports. Because disability sports have long relied on a variety of systems for classifying athletes for competition, in most cases, specific references to classification are kept to a minimum here, but when addressed, most employ the terminology relevant to the time, even if the language has since changed.

To make the work as accessible as possible, Japanese words are kept to a minimum in the main body text, but when provided, the long vowel sounds in Japanese words or names are marked with macrons, except for well-known place names. Personal names for all Japanese individuals, including authors, are given in the standard Japanese form with the family name listed first, unless they were written otherwise in a quoted source. As this book entered the final stages of the publication process, the COVID-19 pandemic led to the unexpected postponement of the 2020 Tokyo Olympics and Paralympics, and as of this writing, the possibility of outright cancellation remains. Although most of *More than Medals* addresses content from well before 2020, the final chapter in the book focuses on various planning and organizational efforts undertaken to host the 2020 Games. Regardless of the ultimate outcome, such efforts were already exhibiting impacts in Japan before the Games were slated to arrive, and their long-term effects remain to be seen.

MORE THAN MEDALS

Introduction

The Paralympic Movement in Japan:
An Imperfect Success Story

> The success of the Paralympics is really the key to the
> success of the overall Games here. I believe putting
> weight on hosting a successful Paralympics is more
> important than a successful Olympics.
>
> Governor Koike Yuriko, 2017

As Tokyo prepared to make history in August
2020 by becoming the first city in the world to host the International Paralympic Games on two occasions, countless organizers, athletes, promoters, volunteers, and politicians lent their enthusiastic support. Many expressed their expectations that the 2020 Paralympics would be an inspirational success, raising awareness and ultimately leading to improvements in the lives of those with disabilities in Japan. Tokyo governor Koike Yuriko exemplified such enthusiasm and hope when she spoke to the Foreign Correspondents' Club in August 2017 about the upcoming Games. Her striking statement that "putting weight on hosting a successful Paralympics is more important than a successful Olympics" was instantly picked up and circulated as a ringing endorsement of the Paralympic Movement and its benefits.[1] Whether or not this was a case of political hyperbole, Koike's declaration three years before the 2020 Games put everyone on notice that for her, Tokyo, and Japan more generally, the Paralympics mattered—perhaps even more than the Olympics.

Less than sixty years earlier in Japan, the situation could not have been more different. In early 1961, a small group of Japanese organizers began discussing the possibility of holding the 1964 Paralympic Games in Tokyo. At the time, the very notion of hosting any athletic competition for individuals with disabilities—let alone an international event deemed on par with the Olympics—would have struck many in Japan as ludicrous. Government

1

support and institutions promoting disability sports were lacking, and very few people in Japan seemed aware that such sports existed. No Japanese athletes had ever participated in Paralympic events, and even medical professionals tended to scorn the idea of sports for those with disabilities. It was no small achievement, then, that a few years later Japan became the third country, and the first outside Europe, to host the Paralympics, bringing Japan's first Paralympic Games to Tokyo in November 1964.

As Tokyo prepared to host the Olympic and Paralympic Games for a second time, organizers for 2020 were able to point to a rich history of involvement in the Paralympic Movement beginning with these efforts in the 1960s. In the years since, the establishment of new institutions, events, and forms of support allowed Japanese athletes with disabilities to compete in a range of domestic and international sporting competitions, often with marked success. As Japan constructed its domestic disability sports environment and continued engaging at the international level, the country also took leading roles in promoting these sports in the Asian region and beyond, especially through events like the FESPIC (Far East and South Pacific) Games and the Ōita International Wheelchair Marathon. Particularly in the wake of the 1998 Winter Paralympics in Nagano, disability sports events and their athletes in Japan garnered a degree of popular attention and support that would have been unimaginable for Japanese advocates in the 1960s. Governor Koike's seemingly wholehearted embrace of the Paralympics, then, is just one more example of how different the present situation in Japan is compared to just a few decades earlier. This book tells the story of how this dramatic transformation came about.

As the first comprehensive English-language study of the impact of the Paralympic Movement outside a Euro-American context, *More Than Medals* addresses histories of individuals, institutions, and events that played important roles in the development of the Paralympics and disability sports in Japan but remain little known or explored. Asking how and why Japan engaged with international movements as it developed domestic approaches to disability sports, this book focuses on discourses and practices surrounding five international sporting events held in Japan for athletes with disabilities: the 1964 Paralympics, the FESPIC Games, the Ōita International Wheelchair Marathon, the 1998 Nagano Winter Paralympics, and the 2020 Summer Games. Most narratives of Japan's past have overlooked these events entirely, and the combination of language barriers and limited access to resources has prevented scholars of the Paralympic Movement from studying their histories as well. This book aims to change that.

While understanding the institutional histories of sporting events for those with disabilities is important in its own right, I also argue that the influence of such events has extended well beyond the playing field. Because of their international scope and media prominence, the events examined in the following chapters have had disproportionate impacts on approaches to and understandings of disability in Japan. Sporting events in Japan's postwar era (1945–present) have repeatedly served as forums for promoting new policies, pushing international ideals, fostering improved awareness, or seeking to address a variety of concerns expressed by individuals with disabilities. Providing new insights on the culturally and historically contingent nature of disability, this book demonstrates how these sports events and especially representations of their athletes have challenged some of the stigmas associated with disability while reinforcing or even generating others. Whereas organizers in 1964 linked the Paralympics to efforts to promote changes in rehabilitation techniques in Japan, the efforts to use the Games to promote changes in approaches to disability were equally—if not more—apparent in the lead-up to Tokyo's second Paralympics. Koike's emphasis on the Paralympics, for instance, was intertwined with her understandings of Japan's future social and infrastructural needs. As she observed at that same press conference in August 2017, "In Tokyo and Japan we have an aging society, and it is clear there will be more and more people who will be requiring the use of wheelchairs or canes in coming years. Preparing for the Paralympics is preparing for Tokyo's aging population. The challenge of an aging city is a common theme all developed countries will be facing." She continued, "In the case of Tokyo we take the Paralympics as an opportunity to prepare for these coming challenges and how to make the city fully accessible to people with disabilities or other special needs." Koike also explained how her experiences trying out a wheelchair herself on some of Tokyo's non-barrier-free sidewalks left her even more motivated "to eliminate the uneven paving of Tokyo's streets and make them accessible and welcoming to match the hospitality provided by the people of this great city."[2] Given that uneven pavement and sidewalks have little to do with medal counts, it is readily apparent that Koike's support of the Paralympics was about much more than highlighting Japan's prowess in sports. Her commitment to disability issues was also clear: the Tokyo government under her watch launched a concerted effort to improve the city's accessibility. Examinations of these sorts of policies, as well as legal reforms, institutional materials, media reports, biographical sources, direct observations, and interviews with Japanese organizers and athletes, allow me to highlight some of the profound, although often ambiguous, ways in which sports have shaped how disability has been perceived and addressed in Japan from the 1960s through the present.

An Abbreviated History of Disability in Japan

To examine the impact of disability sports events within and beyond the sporting realm, the chapters that follow seek to situate those events in their larger sociohistorical contexts. That said, because many readers may be unfamiliar with the broader history of disability in Japan, it will be helpful to offer a few words here on that topic. A detailed study of disability history in Japan is well beyond the scope of this introduction, but I take solace in the fact that a number of recently published works now make that history more accessible to non-Japanese-speaking audiences. Many of these works are cited in the notes and included in the bibliography for readers interested in exploring such issues further.

As with many societies around the world, we have limited information about the experiences of people with disabilities in early Japan. There are references to people with disabilities in early legal codes (ca. 700 CE) and historical accounts of elites, but we have little sense of how these references reflected the situation on the ground for others. It is more apparent that some of the ideas associated with early religions in Japan have had long-term impacts on perceptions of disability. As Karen Nakamura noted, early Shinto's approach to disability seemed to mix treatments of it as either a disruptive form of impurity or as a sign of something special, perhaps even lucky. Buddhist teachings tended to represent any sort of impairment as a sign of karmic retribution for wrongs committed in a past life by either the parents or the individual. Although much has obviously changed in Japan since these systems of belief first took root, strains of these earlier ideas are still visible in later periods.[3]

During the Middle Ages (ca. 1200–1300 CE) some Buddhist monks and temples became well known for taking in people with various disabilities or health ailments, and the era also saw the emergence of famous itinerant blind bards, as well as groups of visually impaired people practicing massage or acupuncture. In the early modern period under the Tokugawa Shogunate (1600–1868), many of these groups for the blind were able to take advantage of the peace and stability of the era to establish formally recognized guilds.[4] Other records from this period tell us that individuals with disabilities simply went about their lives in their home villages, with some gaining limited access to education through private "temple schools" in their communities.[5] But the increasingly urbanized Tokugawa era was also infamous for its short-lived, carnivalesque, and commercially driven *misemono* shows. Some of these shows were simply exhibits of rare or unusual objects ranging from camels to telescopes. Other *misemono* were more akin to "freak shows," displaying all manner of variations of the human form. This latter type of show continued well into the 1870s, at which point the freak shows were phased out as part of broader reforms in Japan's modern era. The frequency with which the early Paralympics in Japan were linked to these earlier *misemono* suggests, however, that they lived on in popular memory well into the twentieth century.[6]

After the fall of the Tokugawa in 1868, a number of individuals in Japan's newly centralized and rapidly modernizing state engaged in efforts to expand educational opportunities for children with disabilities, inspired in part by what Japanese travelers had observed abroad. Some of the earliest schools, set up in the late 1870s and '80s, served both deaf and blind students. The first school for students with intellectual disabilities was established in Nagano Prefecture in the 1890s, and specialized schools for those with limb or other physical impairments were founded in Tokyo in the 1930s. It is worth noting that many of these schools included some form of physical education in their curricula, laying the groundwork for developments in disability sports in the postwar era.[7] Beyond the realm of education, Japan's official approach to individuals with disabilities was premised on what might be described as benign neglect. Regulations were established in the late nineteenth century for providing "relief" to a wide range of people, including those considered to be disabled, but well into the 1930s the primary focus was on private assistance as the best means to support people with disabilities, even disabled military personnel.[8]

Japan's escalating war in the East Asian region, particularly after 1937, would transform governmental approaches to disability. As in many other societies, many of these changes in Japan were geared specifically to meeting the needs of war-wounded soldiers. Lee Pennington's work on wounded Japanese servicemen shows that these measures included not only new treatments and forms of financial support but also an emphasis on rehabilitation and fostering positive imagery of wounded servicemen.[9] As noted in chapter 3, sports were integral to several of these efforts, a part of disability sports history in Japan that is just now being uncovered.

Following Japan's surrender in World War II, the Allied Occupation (1945–1952) oversaw a thorough revamping of the expansive wartime social welfare system, including the implementation of the nation's first laws explicitly addressing support for those with disabilities.[10] Nevertheless, over the following decades, private care, especially by family members, remained the norm for most individuals with a disability. The early phase of Japan's disability rights movement is often dated to the 1960s, around the same time that Japan began its engagement with the Paralympics. At that point, many activists were parents or caretakers, who increasingly drew on the language of human rights as they pushed for more support or improved care facilities for their children. In the 1970s people with disabilities themselves became more engaged in activism, partly in response to horrific conditions in "model" residential facilities. Arguably the most famous activist organization during the postwar era was Aoi Shiba no Kai (Association of Green Grass). As a group for people with cerebral palsy, it had roots in the prewar period, but became more politically active in the 1960s. In the 1970s a new generation took charge of Aoi Shiba no Kai, and the organization began directly challenging popular assumptions about disability and activism by pursuing a radical, confrontational approach. It saw part of its mission as exposing problems and drawing attention to ableism in Japan.[11]

By the 1980s the disability rights movement in Japan had generally shifted from awareness raising and resistance to a focus on living independently within communities, rather than in institutions. As outlined in chapter 4, during the last decades of the twentieth century, activists in Japan drew inspiration from the Independent Living Movement and other disability-related movements abroad to continue pushing for changes in domestic approaches to disability. These years also overlapped with international movements connected with the United Nations that have continued to spark legal and policy changes in Japan as recently as 2013.[12] Since the turn of the twenty-first century, the focus of Japanese disability advocacy has shifted overwhelmingly to issues of accessibility and equal opportunities, measures that are inextricably tied to Japan's current concerns about a rapidly aging society with a shrinking workforce.[13] What role the Tokyo 2020 Paralympics will ultimately play in Japan's still unfolding story of disability remains to be seen, but it is clear that these Games were coming to a country with an already complex history of disability and disability rights activism.

Positioning

Despite the important role the Paralympic Movement and disability sports have played in Japan, their history has received minimal scholarly attention, particularly in English. In part, this research gap stems from the fact that this history falls between fields of study that have traditionally not overlapped: Japanese studies, disability studies, and sports studies. Until recently, research in Japanese studies has tended to overlook both disability and sports, and language barriers have made it difficult for scholars who focus on disability or sports in other contexts to gain access to materials about Japan. As noted earlier, a diverse set of recent and ongoing English-language studies about disability in Japan are beginning to change that situation, and the same is true for sports studies.[14] Yet at most only a handful of articles and official reports in English have examined aspects of Japan's engagement with the Paralympics.[15] Much of the research in Japanese on disability sports is focused on contemporary issues, on particular sports, or on providing introductory descriptions of the Paralympics and disability sports to general audiences.[16] By offering a more comprehensive examination of the role of sports in shaping Japanese approaches to disability at both the official and popular levels, my study complements these existing works while helping bridge some of the gaps in these different research fields. Of course, no single work can do everything, so a few comments will be helpful here to address the specific goals, approaches, and limitations of this book.

First, I feel it is important for readers to know how I came to study the Paralympics in Japan, especially as an American who is currently nondisabled. Before immersing myself in this topic, I was like many people in that I was vaguely aware that the Paralympics existed, but had never seen them and knew little about their history. My academic curiosity, however, was piqued when a student in my "Sports in East Asia" class in 2006 asked if she could include information on the 1998 Nagano Paralympics in her presentation on the Nagano Olympics. At the time, I was completing a dissertation on the history of sports celebrity in Japan and was embarrassed to realize that I had not even known about this large international event. How was that possible? Some preliminary research revealed one answer: except for scattered media reports, there was little information on hand to read about it, even in Japanese-language scholarship.

As I concluded my first book project on sports celebrity and began exploring new topics in Japanese history, I returned to this question of the Paralympics, making my first research trip to Japan in the summer of 2011. Around the same time that I was initiating this new project, the younger of my two sons was starting to express interest in joining other children in athletic activities. He had been born with spina bifida, resulting in various long-term impairments, which led us to look beyond school sports or other local youth sports programs. In part because of my growing familiarity with disability sports, we searched for local options and were fortunate to discover that we lived near a rehabilitation hospital with a vibrant sports program. My research made me more passionate about finding the best ways to support and develop such opportunities for my son and others; in turn, his experiences encouraged me to look more closely at the role of disability sports in Japanese society.

In 2017, my work on this project also provided our family with the chance to live in Tokyo for six months. As we traversed the city, visited other areas in Japan, attended multiple disability sports events, and carried out our daily lives in a place that I thought I knew well, doing so with someone using a wheelchair taught all of us something new about disability in both Japan and our home in the United States. Many of those experiences directly informed my observations of Tokyo's preparations for the 2020 Paralympics discussed in chapter 5. This combination of the personal and the academic made my research for this project rewarding and at times confounding, but I believe that the resulting book is the richer for it.

At its most basic, my goal in this work is to introduce the history of the Paralympics and disability sports in Japan to a broader audience. Although the book will enhance understandings of postwar Japanese history more generally, it sheds particular light on the crucial place of disability-related issues—and disability sports—in social welfare debates and policymaking. From worries about low employment rates for those with disabilities in the 1960s (and well beyond) to ongoing anxieties about meeting the needs of Japan's aging population, concerns related to disability have been a recurring theme in the postwar era, and they have repeatedly molded—and in turn been molded by—Japan's engagement with the Paralympic Movement. The following pages show that disability sports have played, and continue to play, a far more significant role in this process of mutual molding than has been acknowledged to date.

I would note, however, that this study is not simply a tale of success or progress, nor does it offer criticism for criticism's sake. Approaches that have proven effective, such as Ōita's ability to maintain its annual wheelchair marathon through four decades, are acknowledged as potential models. Likewise, when shortcomings become apparent, as in the case of Nagano's and Tokyo's struggles to achieve truly barrier-free environments, highlighting them can serve as a first step in addressing such issues for Japan and elsewhere. In studies on mega-events, scholars in sports studies have generally focused on the economic, political, or environmental impacts of these large-scale sporting events; however, by shifting the attention to questions of accessibility and inclusion, the chapters that follow offer new insights on such events, demonstrating that they have proven a mixed blessing for people in Japan with disabilities.[17] Sporting events have certainly generated significant public discussion aimed at improving policies and changing popular understandings, but for a variety of reasons examined here, these changes have not always been fully realized. By sharing both the benefits and limitations of using sporting events to effect change in Japan, it is my hope that this work will be useful for others who are seeking to understand how experiences with the Paralympic Movement can be leveraged to maximum benefit in resolving lingering inequalities and removing barriers associated with disability.

Indeed, another of my goals is to raise awareness in disability studies and sports studies of research on Japan, because both fields have tended to concentrate on Euro-American contexts. By focusing on disability sports in Japan, this study offers a critical reminder that such "universals" as the body, disability, and sports are interpreted and addressed in culturally and historically specific ways. The shifting categories of athletes eligible to participate in the Paralympics are a case in point, and as I show here, Japan has been instrumental in generating those shifts at multiple points, particularly in the FESPIC Games and the Ōita International Wheelchair Marathon. With sixty years of active involvement with the Paralympics, Japan has made multiple contributions to the broader movement and can offer many insights to the international community on the advantages and pitfalls of using sports to promote change. Yet, until now, Japanese experiences have remained largely absent from scholarly discussions of the Paralympics and their impact.

This book, however, does more than simply introduce a non-Western perspective. Because sports have played a central role in shaping how societies understand the human body, my examinations of the ways in which disability sports have challenged—and at times reinforced—normative perceptions of the body contribute to ongoing efforts to interrogate the social construction of disability. In particular, the analyses of evolving representations of athletes in Japan help explain the roots and resilience of stereotypes that continue to influence understandings of disability today. As seen in chapter 1, stereotypes like the "super-crip" are closely linked to the goals and approaches of Paralympic promoters and cannot be attributed solely to the media or an uninformed public. But the media, too, play a key role, and my attention to media coverage and especially its evolution over time in chapter 4 offers new insights on how seemingly minor choices about which elements of a sports event to feature can have a profound impact on broader social perceptions of disability.

Because this study investigates Japan's interactions with the international Paralympic Movement, it embraces—even necessitates—transnational and comparative perspectives. Quite simply, disability sports in Japan cannot be understood without taking into account a variety of external factors, policies, and ideas, ranging from internationally sanctioned rehabilitation techniques to United Nations campaigns. In developing my analyses of disability sporting events in Japan, I drew insights from a number of works addressing the Paralympics in other contexts. The Ōita International Wheelchair Marathon, for instance, offers an excellent example of Laura Misener's "para-sport leveraging framework," in which local advocates have used the annual event to promote accessibility, volunteerism, and positive images of individuals with disabilities.[18] Danielle Peers's work on disability and inspirational discourses in Canada served as a critical comparative frame for my examinations of athletes' experiences and personal narratives in chapter 5.[19] Several of the following chapters also suggest that the "Paralympic paradox" described by David Purdue and P. David Howe in connection with more recent Paralympic events and athletes has deep roots in Japan.[20] In these and several other cases, this book seeks to build on such works while introducing the Japanese case into dialogue with existing scholarship on the Paralympics.

Not least of all, *More Than Medals* makes the case for viewing disability sports in a broad historical context.[21] At a time when activists, the United Nations, and the International Paralympic Committee are actively promoting "Sports for Development" in countries around the world, it is critical to understand the benefits and challenges of earlier efforts to promote change through sports. In many ways, the history of disability sports in Japan can be seen as a success story, but it is a complex—and often imperfect—success meriting careful examination.

I would be remiss, at this point, if I did not also acknowledge the limitations of this work. For one, the focus on large-scale international events that is central to this study means that I am not able to offer similar attention to a host of other forms of sports or physical activities that people with disabilities in Japan have pursued at various points. In part, my focus stemmed from the availability of archival resources. Even the records for some of the earlier international events explored here are scattered and spotty, so it is not surprising that the history of disability sports at the grassroots level in Japan is not well documented. Moreover, a study of such activities in contemporary Japan would have necessitated a different and probably multi-sited approach that would have dramatically expanded the scale and scope of the project. Many of the same points would apply to a work seeking to explore sports in Japan's specialized schools for those with disabilities. Along similar lines, it is important to note that several major international disability sporting events held in Japan are omitted here, not least of all the Special Olympics, which are discussed briefly in chapter 4. All of these topics merit full-length studies of their own, and it is my hope that this book may serve as a useful starting point for future research.

I must also admit that the focus on events has resulted in less emphasis on athletes, perhaps especially in comparison with my first book on Japanese sports stars. As a work about sports, this book does reference athletes at various points and offers several observations on evolving official and popular representations of athletes in a general sense. The final chapter gives the most focused attention to athletes, providing brief accounts of five Japanese Paralympians. Yet even these accounts are not full biographies, and they can only begin to capture the remarkable diversity of athletes' experiences with disability sports in Japan since the 1960s. Here, too, I am optimistic that future scholars will be able to examine the experiences of athletes in greater detail, and I will be pleased if this book proved beneficial in their efforts to do so.

Finally, even though this book argues that Japan's engagement with the Paralympics has had a profound impact beyond the playing fields, I must confess that it can be remarkably difficult to assess such impacts in concrete terms. Changes in perceptions and attitudes prove particularly challenging to measure given the lack of relevant data gathered before or after most events, and even in more clear-cut cases like modifications to the built environment, it can be hard to determine exactly how, why, or when these changes occurred. In the following chapters, I try to be as clear as possible about how and why I am assessing these impacts. If readers on occasion find these evaluations overly cautious, I can only ask for forgiveness, because I would rather hedge than overstate. In the end, even if we cannot verify every potential impact, I firmly believe that readers will agree that the Paralympics and disability sports more generally have played critical roles in postwar Japan, roles that have gone underappreciated for long enough.

CHAPTER 1

Tokyo's Other Games
The Origins and Impact of the 1964 Paralympics

> That it has been possible to hold the 1964 International Stoke Mandeville Games for the Paralysed in Tokyo is due greatly to the understanding of our Japanese friends, who had the vision to recognize the significance of these Games not only as an important sports Movement but as a beam of hope for disabled people all over the world. The Japanese Organizing Committee, under the Chairmanship of Mr. Y. Kasai, have undertaken their great task with an enthusiasm, efficiency and generosity which commands our admiration and gratitude. It is gratifying to know they have had the full support of their Government and many leading Japanese organizations.
>
> Ludwig Guttmann, 1964

In his words of welcome to the competitors in what became known as the Tokyo Paralympics, Ludwig Guttmann, founder of the Stoke Mandeville Games for the Paralysed, offered high praise for the vision and enthusiasm of the host country. Four years earlier, however, when the Paralympic Games concluded in Rome on September 25, 1960, a mere handful of people in Japan were aware of their existence, and even though preparations for the 1964 Tokyo Olympics were already underway, few people in Japan or elsewhere would have believed that Tokyo would *ever* host this international sporting event for athletes with physical disabilities. At the time, Olympic venues were not required or even expected to host the Paralympics, and Japan was not a country renowned for progressive treatment of the disabled. Indeed, many in Japan dismissed the very notion of sports for those with disabilities as a preposterous and even dangerous idea.[1] Yet only a few years later, Japan became the third country—and the first outside Europe—to host the Paralympic Games.[2] This chapter explores how this remarkable turn of events came about.

With Tokyo's selection as the host for the 2020 Olympic and Paralympic Games, the city was set to be the first in the world to hold the International Paralympic Games on two occasions, a development that inspired increased interest in Japan's earlier experience hosting the Paralympics.[3] Despite this renewed attention and the obvious significance of the 1964 Games to the history of disability sports more generally, Japan's first Paralympic Games have remained little known, especially for those without access to Japanese-language materials.[4] Japanese accounts themselves tend to fall into two categories: official or institutional reports and general overviews of the Tokyo Paralympics; both focus almost exclusively on key organizers whose vision and effort helped overcome various obstacles to bring the Paralympics to Japan.[5] Although these individuals played pivotal roles, closer consideration of the events leading up to the Games reveals a more complex picture involving intersecting personal, local, national, and transnational actors and motivations, all of which culminated in intense pressure to hold the Games in Tokyo immediately following the Summer Olympics.

In the end, the 1964 Tokyo Paralympics attracted hundreds of athletes, thousands of spectators, widespread media attention, and major sponsorships. They were widely hailed as a success and credited with giving "hope, courage, and self-confidence to Japan's physically disabled."[6] As the first Paralympic Games held outside Europe, they also had a profound impact on the emerging Paralympic Movement by demonstrating its growing international appeal, strengthening its association with the Olympic Games, and promoting an expanded multi-disability approach to disability sports. Nevertheless, analyses of the Games themselves and especially the ways in which Paralympic organizers sought to present them in Japan point to the need for a more nuanced understanding of their impact that goes beyond simple claims of success and progress.

Given the relatively limited nature of existing scholarship on the Tokyo Paralympics, it is not surprising that there has not yet been proper attention to how these Games, and especially their participants, were represented in Japan. Studies of more recent Paralympic coverage have highlighted the importance of close examinations of such representations, because it has become increasingly clear that the amount of attention these events receive can be less significant than the ways in which the Games and their athletes are portrayed. As a number of scholars have demonstrated, representations of Paralympic athletes, especially those appearing in the mass media, have often relied on images and descriptions that reinforce medicalized understandings of disability. Athletic involvement and achievement have tended to be framed in terms of "overcoming" disability through sports, a reductionist approach that presents

Paralympians as victims who warrant pity or as "super-crips" who merit attention because they have not allowed their disability to prevent them from pursuing and achieving success.[7] Research has also shown that nationalism, gender, forms of impairment, and the types of sport also play a significant role in shaping representations of disability sports.[8]

As explored later in the chapter, the representations of athletes participating in the 1964 Tokyo Paralympics share several similarities with those from more recent disability sports events. But analyses of the materials associated with the 1964 Games also offer insights that go beyond adding a "non-Western" perspective to the existing scholarship. For one, an examination of what the Japanese public was seeing in the early 1960s serves as a useful reminder that the representations we often encounter today have a history. Because Japan was among the earliest countries to host the Paralympics and did so at a time when few in the country were familiar with disability sports, the Tokyo Games provide a unique vantage point for exploring how a large population was introduced to the Paralympic Movement and its ideals. In other words, a study of these Games can help explain how patterns of representation and stereotypes took shape.

The history of the Tokyo Paralympics clearly demonstrates that the perceptions and approaches that Paralympic organizers adopted were pivotal in shaping these early representations. Their emphasis on sports as a means of rehabilitation ultimately helped re-inscribe preexisting medicalized views of the disabled body, views particularly apparent in official reports and promotional commentaries. At the same time, disability advocates and Paralympic athletes were able to take advantage of the prominence of the Tokyo Paralympics to articulate and display alternate understandings of disability to a large audience, laying the groundwork for Japan's domestic disability sports movement and a broader, gradual shift in perceptions of disabled athletes in postwar Japan. At the core of these efforts was a form of co-constitution, a negative nationalism of sorts, that praised the "brightness" of foreign Paralympians while at times demeaning Japanese athletes to highlight the flaws in Japanese approaches to disability in an attempt to initiate changes. Although these efforts ultimately seem to have helped foster such changes, they also complicate any effort to see the Tokyo Paralympics as a clear-cut "beam of hope for disabled people all over the world."[9] Analyses of the writings of Paralympic promoters from the periods before, during, and after the 1964 Paralympics also make it clear that for many, the significance of the Paralympics as a "beam of hope" was also secondary to their role as an arena for evaluating Japan's standing in the global community.

"The De Coubertin of the Paralysed"
Looks to Japan

Before turning to an examination of the Tokyo Paralympics themselves, it will be useful to situate them in the broader history of the Paralympic Movement, which in 1964 was still in its earliest stages. Without a doubt, Ludwig Guttmann, the man Pope John XXIII once described as "the De Coubertin of the paralysed," is a critical figure in that early history.[10] Guttmann, a respected Jewish neurologist, hospital director, and full professor of neurology, fled Nazi Germany in 1939 and resettled in England. After he spent several years at Oxford University, the British government commissioned him in 1943 to be the director of the newly established National Spinal Injuries Unit at the Ministry of Pensions Hospital, Stoke Mandeville, which was located roughly 65 kilometers outside London. Guttmann's well-documented activities as director at Stoke Mandeville and his revolutionary emphasis on movement and activity for people with severe spinal injuries quickly led to the integration of sports as a critical component of his patients' total rehabilitation programs.[11]

Competitive sports were part and parcel of Guttmann's approach at Stoke Mandeville from the beginning, but the origins of the Paralympics are often dated to July 29, 1948, when Guttmann helped organize the first Stoke Mandeville Games. What began as a small public archery competition between two teams of paraplegics quickly became an annual tradition. With each passing year, the Stoke Mandeville Games (which used varying names during these early years) attracted more competitors and added new sports. In 1952, a Dutch team participated, making the Stoke Mandeville Games truly international.[12]

As many, including Pope John XXIII, have observed, Guttmann's Stoke Mandeville Games were often associated with the Olympic Movement. Whether intentional or fortuitous, the first Stoke Mandeville Games occurred in 1948 on the same day as the opening ceremony for the London Olympic Games.[13] Throughout the early years of the Stoke Mandeville Games, Guttmann repeatedly referenced the Olympic Movement, citing it as both an inspiration and a goal: he hoped paraplegics would one day compete in the Olympics. After the International Olympic Committee awarded the Fearnley Cup to the International Stoke Mandeville Games "for actions in keeping with the true spirit of Olympism," Guttmann and other organizers began exploring the possibility of holding the ninth International Stoke Mandeville Games in Rome immediately following the 1960 Olympics.[14] The result of their efforts, an event that is now officially recognized as the first Paralympic Games, involved nearly 370 athletes from twenty-two countries competing in twelve different events and using many of the same facilities that the Olympic athletes had used only a few weeks before.

With the success of the Rome Paralympics and the ongoing growth of the annual Games held at Stoke Mandeville, it might seem only natural that Guttmann and other organizers of those Games would look to Tokyo, the host for the next Olympics, as the site for the thirteenth International Stoke Mandeville Games. In fact, one brief English-language account describing the origins of the Tokyo Paralympic Games notes that Guttmann was "keen to stage the Games again at the same venue as the Olympic Games in 1964, in Tokyo."[15] Another account comments specifically on the "self-assurance" of Stoke Mandeville organizers and their widespread belief that the "International Games really could be exported to any country."[16]

Japanese sources reveal much less optimism. In 1960 there was, in fact, very little reason for anyone, including the organizers in Rome, to believe that Tokyo would be willing or able to host the Paralympics. For one thing, no Japanese athletes or official observers had ever participated in or attended the International Stoke Mandeville Games. Although the International Paralympic Committee website claimed that support for Guttmann's plan to hold the Paralympic Games in Tokyo "was boosted by the positive reactions of Japanese observers who visited the 1960 Games in Rome," the sole Japanese who actually witnessed these Games was Watanabe Hanako, whose presence at the Paralympics appears to have been partly accidental; she was there because she was married to the chief of the Rome bureau for Japan's Kyōdō News Service.[17] Fortunately, Watanabe was also a scholar of labor and welfare policies, and she took an avid interest in the Games.[18] She reportedly spoke with Guttmann about the possibility of holding a similar event in Tokyo, but this discussion was certainly not an official commitment.[19] Perhaps it goes without saying, but a conversation with an enthusiastic individual spectator hardly seems like the best foundation for planning a major international sporting event in a foreign country. There is also good reason to suspect that Guttmann may have been skeptical of Watanabe's statement of interest. Only a few months earlier, in February 1960, Nakamura Yutaka, a 32-year old doctor from southwestern Japan, traveled to Stoke Mandeville to observe the facilities and study Guttmann's methods. According to Nakamura, Guttmann greeted him rather harshly: "So you're Japanese? Several Japanese have come here already. All of them have said that they want to imitate what we are doing here, and then they go back to Japan. So far, not one of them has followed through and done it." Nakamura acknowledged that Guttmann's statement was probably accurate, and Watanabe herself indicated that Guttmann had offered similar complaints when she spoke with him about her interest in bringing the Paralympics to Japan.[20] If Guttmann had so little faith in Japan's medical professionals, the very people who would seem most likely to share his ambitious goals, it raises an important question: Why was he so "keen" to hold the International Stoke Mandeville Games four years later in a country that seemed to have minimal interest in or commitment to sports for the disabled?

In many respects, Guttmann's desire to hold the Games in Tokyo makes perfect sense; these Games were simply the next logical step in his broader agenda. If the Paralympics were to continue to grow, develop, and gain prestige, then they had to go to Tokyo: they had to follow wherever the Olympics led. It also seems plausible, given Guttmann's record, that Japan's seeming lack of interest in disability sports itself would make it a particularly appealing host site. He was certainly not one to avoid a challenge, and if the Paralympics could be held successfully in Tokyo, it would demonstrate that the Stoke Mandeville Games could, in fact, be exported anywhere—even outside Europe or to countries without a strong history of involvement in disability sports. Moreover, Guttmann's encounters with the various Japanese doctors who had visited Stoke Mandeville pointed to latent interest in his approaches to sports and rehabilitation. A large-scale event such as the Paralympics could garner greater attention for his ideas and help them take root in Japan.

Japanese source materials also indicate that Guttmann and his Stoke Mandeville Games were not the only forms of disability sports attracting attention in Japan in the years before the first Tokyo Games. Sporting events in Japan for those with hearing impairments dated from 1918, and those for the visually impaired were launched in the 1920s. Many of these events were local or national events tied to Japan's specialized schools for visually or hearing impaired students, and they seemed to have had only limited connections to international organizations or developments. In that sense, these early examples of sports events shared similarities with localized events hosted for other disability groups in places such as Tokyo, Saitama, and Nagano in the years following World War II.[21] Recent archival discoveries and scholarship have also revealed a variety of sports events organized during the war for Japan's veterans with disabilities, an intriguing and still developing story examined further in chapter 3. All of these events suggest that Guttmann was pitching his particular disability sporting event to a country with more exposure to disability sports than it might first appear.

In fact, by the early 1960s, a handful of Japanese medical experts interested in rehabilitation had established relationships with specialists outside of Great Britain who were actively promoting sports for those with disabilities other than spinal injuries.[22] Japanese organizers of the 1964 Games seem to have been in regular contact with a group of specialists that included Gerd Brinkmann, Hanz

Lorenzen, and Norman Acton, who eventually became head of the International Sports Organization for the Disabled (ISOD).[23] In July 1963, at Acton's urging, Japan dispatched a team of athletes to participate in what various Japanese sources identify as the First International Sports Festival for the Disabled held in Linz, Austria.[24] Unfortunately, this early sports festival, which was likely the world's first international multi-disability sports event (though one that did not include athletes with spinal cord injuries), appears to have attracted little scholarly notice, so further consideration of its relationship to the Stoke Mandeville Games must await further research. That said, Japanese participation in Austria highlighted the fact that Tokyo's would-be organizers were willing to engage with any and all forms of disability sports, an approach that would, as outlined later, result in a structure for the Tokyo Paralympics unlike any previous Stoke Mandeville Games.

It is also apparent that the years leading up to the Tokyo Games were marked by simmering tensions in the emerging disability sports movement. Details are murky, but these tensions reached a boiling point during the June 1963 meeting of the International Working Group for Disabled Sport, where unspecified events launched a dispute between Guttmann and Gerd Brinkmann, who was serving as president of the Deutchen Versehrtensportverbandes (DVS), the organization that represented Germany at the Stoke Mandeville Games. The dispute proved serious enough that Guttmann resigned from the Working Group and the DVS opted to boycott the 1964 Stoke Mandeville Games in Tokyo.[25] These behind-the-scenes tensions and Japanese organizers' manifest interest in potentially competing approaches to disability sports both point to the distinct possibility that Guttmann and other promoters of the Stoke Mandeville Games were experiencing added pressure in the early 1960s to ensure that *their* Games were represented in Tokyo. Whatever the case may be, it is clear that Guttmann wanted to hold the thirteenth International Stoke Mandeville Games in Tokyo, but as he acknowledged as the Games began in 1964, his goals and plans were ultimately dependent on the actions and interests of those in Japan.

From Zero to Paralympics in Four Years

On the Japanese side in 1960, the prospects for the 1964 Paralympics did not look promising. Very few people even seemed aware of the existence of the Stoke Mandeville Games, and broader familiarity with disability sports was lacking at nearly all levels. There were no institutions, official or otherwise, in place for organizing an event of this sort in Japan. Even if the Paralympics were smaller and more informal than they are today, hosting them in Tokyo was going to be a monumental, and uncertain, undertaking. Among many other tasks, would-be organizers needed to establish new organizations, create basic public awareness, gain at least tacit approval from national and local leaders, generate funding, find and train Japanese participants, and, certainly not least of all, plan and host the Paralympic Games themselves—all in less than four years and at a time when attention and resources were overwhelmingly focused on preparations for the 1964 Olympics. An examination of how and why Japanese organizers decided to pursue these tasks offers insights into institution building and especially the ways in which several individuals mobilized existing social networks, the media, and the symbolic power of the imperial family to pursue their agendas.

According to official accounts as recorded in both the organizing committee's *Official Report on the Tokyo Paralympic Games* and the *Twentieth Anniversary History* of the Japan Sports Association for the Disabled, the 1964 Games were rooted in a series of events that occurred in early 1961. In February, Okino Matao, a disabled navy veteran and director of the Japanese branch of the World Veterans Federation (WVF), received materials about disability sports from the head office in Paris. Interested in bringing greater attention to the topic in Japan, Okino joined with Hieda Masatora, the head of the National Disability Rehabilitation Training Center, to translate the materials and prepare a 157-page booklet titled "Sports for the Disabled."[26] Hieda's interest in disability sports was not new; during a 1953 conference in Copenhagen, he acquired some written materials on the topic, including those by Hanz Lorenzen, one of the pioneers of multi-disability sports in Austria and West Germany. While visiting Europe in 1957, Hieda also observed a regional sporting event for the disabled in Hamburg, West Germany, an experience that inspired him to share what he learned after he returned to Japan, which may explain why Okino reached out to him in particular.[27] Despite their interest in promoting sports for the disabled, neither Okino nor Hieda expressed a desire to host the Paralympics at this point. Discussions about that possibility, however, soon followed.

On April 13, 1961, at a workshop on disability rehabilitation training, Watanabe Hanako gave a presentation about her experiences at the Rome Paralympics, and Okino followed with a talk titled "Elevating Sports for the Disabled in Japan." Details about these presentations remain vague, but based on references to the discussions that followed, it is clear that at least one of them raised the possibility of hosting the Stoke Mandeville Games in 1964. Although Watanabe's name largely disappears from official accounts soon after this meeting—a reflection of the male-dominated nature of the organization recording the history of this event—she undoubtedly played a pivotal role. According to Hieda, Watanabe later provided him and Okino with introductions to Ludwig Guttmann, and her personal connections to labor and welfare scholars, as well as the media, would have been useful to any nascent organization looking to gain publicity.[28] Watanabe would continue to be an active supporter of the Paralympics, publishing frequently on the role that disability sports could play in improving Japanese approaches to disability. Her later advocacy aside, as the sole Japanese observer of the Rome Games, her firsthand knowledge would have been an invaluable resource in the early planning stages.

That is not to say, however, that Watanabe's and Okino's presentations translated into an instant commitment to the Games. Several of those present at the April workshop raised concerns about funding and the difficulty of hosting such an event without any institutions in place to do so. Dazai Hirokuni, who was attending as head of the Health and Welfare Ministry's Social Welfare Bureau, allegedly suggested, "This is great news for the disabled, but preparing to host [the Paralympics] will be a real problem. Why don't we just see today's meeting as the first steps in the right direction?"[29] In other words, Dazai had no problem with the promotion of disability sports, but was not ready at that point to commit himself and, by extension, the Japanese government. He, and many others, needed to be convinced that holding these Games in Tokyo was both possible and worthwhile.

Unfortunately, some of the earliest attempts to forge the necessary institutions proved less than successful. In May 1961, Okino attended the international congress for the WVF in Paris, where he met with Guttmann. After returning to Japan, Okino held an informational meeting at which attendees agreed to form an organization for promoting disability sports in Japan, but remained reluctant about hosting the Paralympics.[30] According to the official account from the Japan Disabled Veterans Association, those present felt that Japan needed to start by promoting disability sports at home before hosting an international event.[31] In line with that approach in August 1961, representatives from twenty-four groups that worked with the disabled population formed the Association for the Promotion of Sports for the Disabled. With the bulk of its meetings focusing on bureaucratic minutiae, this organization proved ineffective, taking little concrete action toward achieving its mission.[32]

Just as early organizational efforts appeared to have stalled, a series of events reinvigorated the movement and sparked a new round of institution building. First, on October 22, 1961, Ōita Prefecture, located approximately 1,000 kilometers from Tokyo on the island of Kyushu, hosted Japan's first competitive sporting event for the disabled. Organized by Dr. Nakamura Yutaka and

Hirata Atsushi, a prefectural government official, this groundbreaking event employed rules and approaches associated with international sports organizations, demonstrating that disability sports could work in Japan, despite the widespread belief to the contrary. Then, in March 1962, Iimuro Susumu, an executive officer from the Lions Clubs International, contacted Terada Muneyoshi, who was affiliated with the Asahi Shimbun Social Welfare Organization, and informed him that if Japan were going to host the Stoke Mandeville Games, the Lions Clubs would provide "across-the-board support."[33] The next month, Terada and several other social welfare leaders and rehabilitation specialists met at the offices of the Asahi Shimbun Newspaper Company, where they drafted a definitive plan of action that would bring the Paralympics to Japan. Those present agreed that they should work actively with the Lions Clubs, that they should launch a Preparatory Committee composed of a small core of selected individuals, and that the International Games held in Tokyo should be a multi-disability event, including athletes with paraplegia, blindness, hearing impairments, and other physical challenges. Immediately after this meeting, Terada shared these plans with several officials from the Health and Welfare Ministry, who on hearing that the Games would include participants with a range of disabilities, offered their full-fledged approval of the plan to establish a Preparatory Committee. Having secured the blessings of these officials, Terada and Ishijima Haruyuki, who was affiliated with the NHK Public Welfare Organization, began using their institutional contacts to notify relevant individuals about their plans, and on May 10, 1962, twenty-one individuals met to form the official Preparatory Committee.[34]

Although Japan's hosting of the Games themselves was still far from guaranteed, the creation of this committee in 1962 marked the country's first official step toward that goal. Compared to only a year earlier, the changes in the level of both governmental and nongovernmental support the effort received were striking, especially given that one of the officials now giving his full-fledged approval was Dazai, whose lack of enthusiasm for hosting the Games had been readily apparent in early 1961. Clearly something had changed.

For one, the idea of hosting the Paralympics had proven to be more than the fleeting dream of a handful of enthusiasts; supporters continued to organize, events continued to be held, and more and more people seemed to be taking notice of disability sports, which raises a second key difference. By 1962 individuals and groups outside the medical or rehabilitation fields, including the Lions Clubs, the Asahi Shimbun Social Welfare Organization, and the NHK Public Welfare Organization, were expressing an interest in bringing the Paralympics to Japan.

The official accounts remain largely silent on the factors that motivated such groups to offer their support, though recollections from participants suggest that Ujiie Kaoru, the deputy director of the National Center for the Disabled, and Dr. Nakamura Yutaka both played key roles in lobbying for support from nongovernmental groups.[35] As for the Lions Clubs, the organization's long-standing commitment to the visually impaired may offer some explanation, and support for disability sports also fit well with the health- and welfare-oriented missions of both of the other organizations.[36] Regardless of their specific motivations, the support from all three of these organizations promised significant benefits for the would-be organizers of the Paralympics. As an established institution with branches throughout Japan, the Lions Clubs could serve as a conduit for fostering popular awareness and raising much-needed funds. The other two organizations offered social networks of their own, but perhaps more importantly, they provided links to national media outlets: the *Asahi* newspaper and the NHK radio and television networks. With this increased popular, institutional, and media backing, the emergence of official support seems less surprising.

In addition to increased support of various sorts, one of the other key developments associated with the creation of the Preparatory Committee in 1962 was the explicit commitment to hosting the Paralympics as a multi-disability international sporting event. At that time, there was no precedent for such an event; the Rome Games, like all the International Stoke Mandeville Games before them, had only included athletes with spinal injuries. Unfortunately, available sources do not reveal who proposed this approach for Tokyo's Games or why they did so. Given the connections between some of the organizers and promoters of multi-disability sports in Europe, it seems feasible that some in Japan and perhaps abroad saw the Tokyo Games as an opportunity to unify disability sports by combining Guttmann's established approach with the multi-disability formats championed by Lorenzen, Acton, and others associated with the emerging ISOD. For instance, Nakamura's biographers suggested that by 1962 he was convinced by his interactions with Lorenzen to approach Guttmann about the need to provide more sports-related opportunities for other disability groups. The tantalizingly vague nature of the references to these interactions makes it difficult to determine whether they preceded or followed plans unfolding in Tokyo.[37] The Japanese commitment to hosting a multi-disability event may also have reflected the agendas of such groups as the Lions Clubs, which had pledged their support, or of others that might be inclined to do so if the event involved a broader spectrum of athletes with disabilities. We might also speculate that this approach was a possible manifestation of pressure—whether actual or perceived—from the Health and Welfare

Ministry to hold an event serving a larger disabled population. Evidence of such pressure can be seen in a July 1961 *Yomiuri shimbun* newspaper article about the possibility of holding the Paralympics in Tokyo. Along with details about the purpose of the Games and the earlier, largely unsuccessful efforts to promote them in Japan, the article quoted an unnamed ministry source stating that even though it could not presently agree to host a "Paralympics only for those with spinal cord injuries," the ministry wholeheartedly supported the development of "sports for all disabled" in Japan and was planning to study the issue further in the coming year.[38] Given these public pronouncements, it makes sense that Terada made a particular point of mentioning the multi-disability element to Health and Welfare Ministry officials when seeking their approval. Opening the event to more participants would seem to satisfy any number of stakeholders. Although the specific reasons behind this early Japanese commitment to hosting a multi-disability event remain unclear, it ultimately gave the Tokyo Paralympics a structure unlike any before or since.

As significant as the establishment of the Preparatory Committee was, in many ways its primary purpose was to create another committee: the official, government-sanctioned committee for organizing the Paralympics themselves. As a first step in that process, the Preparatory Committee members sought out a new leader, Kasai Yoshisuke, who was serving as chair of the Association for the Promotion of Social Welfare. As a former Health and Welfare Ministry official, Kasai was almost certainly selected because of his background and the influence that came with it. In particular, during the Allied occupation following World War II, Kasai was instrumental in the conversion of military rehabilitation centers to civilian use and was also closely involved in the drafting and implementation of the 1949 Law for the Welfare of Physically Disabled Persons.[39] Despite these credentials, Kasai appears to have had little previous interest in or exposure to disability sports before the summer of 1961, when he witnessed a sports event for the disabled while visiting Germany. The very fact that one of the key leaders in Japan's disability sports movement had minimal familiarity with such sports before 1960 exemplifies the challenges facing efforts to bring the Paralympics to Tokyo. As chairman of the organizing committee, Kasai quickly overcame this initial lack of familiarity and would frequently serve as the public face for the Tokyo Games in both official and popular venues. He continued to be a tireless promoter of disability sports long after the Games ended.[40]

With a new, influential leader in place, the Preparatory Committee set to work on two other immediate goals: working with the Lions Clubs to begin raising funds and sending a Japanese team to compete at the annual International Stoke Mandeville Games in England less than two months later. On

May 30, 1962, members of the committee attended the annual Lions Clubs Governors' Convention where they shared pamphlets and information about the Paralympic Games and asked the regional governors to encourage their local members to assist in fundraising. In July, the committee achieved its second goal when two men from Ōita Prefecture became the first Japanese athletes to participate in the International Stoke Mandeville Games in England.[41]

According to the official accounts, because the Preparatory Committee had minimal resources at the time, the Asahi Shimbun Newspaper Company and NHK agreed to serve as guarantors, which enabled the committee to secure a loan from a bank in Ōita to fund the trip of the two-member Japanese team. In the end, these somewhat risky financial moves proved worthwhile. Even before their departure in mid-July, Japan's first delegation to the International Stoke Mandeville Games attracted widespread media coverage, which often explicitly mentioned the possibility of hosting a similar international sporting event for disabled athletes in Tokyo. In early August the recently returned athletes and several members of the Preparatory Committee also met with members of the imperial family, including Crown Prince Akihito, who expressed his hopes that the Paralympics would be held in Tokyo two years later. As part of the barrage of press coverage associated with these meetings, several newspapers featured photographs of the athletes demonstrating their skills for the crown prince and princess.[42] In addition to securing the blessings of Japan's imperial family, at a press conference, Prime Minister Ikeda Hayato, Health and Welfare Minister Nishimura, and Labor Minister Ōhashi also expressed their desires to see the Games in Tokyo, pledging "as much assistance as the government could possibly provide."[43]

Although it is too simplistic to see these events in August 1962 as the turning point when the dream of hosting the Paralympics in Japan became a reality, they do represent a critical moment in that process. The Japanese athletes gained more media attention in July and August alone than the organizers had achieved in nearly two years. Perhaps understandably, given its formal and informal association with the Preparatory Committee, the *Asahi* newspaper offered especially detailed coverage, including interviews with the athletes and reports on their performances in England.[44] The fact that Prime Minister Ikeda allegedly informed one observer that these events marked "the first I've ever heard that they hold an Olympics for the disabled" suggests just how important this expanded media coverage was.[45]

Although it remains unclear how the meetings with imperial family members came about, it seems likely that committee members, and perhaps Kasai specifically, mobilized their social connections to establish what proved to be a long-lasting and critically important link between the Paralympics and the imperial household. Associations with the crown prince, in particular, practically guaranteed the Games increased media attention. At a moment when the ruling conservative party in Japan, led by Prime Minister Ikeda, was looking to revive the influence and prestige of the imperial family, the potential power of the crown prince's expressions of support should not be underestimated.[46]

While Kasai and other members of the Preparatory Committee continued to cultivate support and funding, they turned their attention to the establishment of the formal Organizing Committee. On February 12, 1963, members unanimously approved the charter creating the Organizing Committee for the Paralympic Games, and on April 5, 1963, the Health and Welfare Ministry authorized its incorporation.[47] On May 14, 1963, the Organizing Committee hosted a two-hour public convocation that attracted more than 700 people and included musical performances, speeches, a film of the Rome Games, and several exhibitions of disability sports. The event culminated in a public declaration of the intent to host the Paralympics in Tokyo one year later.[48] Only a day earlier, on May 13, Kasai sent a formal notification to Guttmann and the International Stoke Mandeville Games Committee about the Japanese intention to host the Games immediately after the Olympics. Guttmann's reply, received several weeks later, expressed his excitement about developments in Japan and indicated that the Japanese request would be discussed and presumably approved at the International Committee's meeting in July.[49]

As exciting as these events must have been for all involved, the ultimate success of the Games remained uncertain, perhaps especially on the financial front. Despite the ongoing attempts of organizers to solicit funds from Japanese business and financial leaders, their efforts proved frustrating in large part because many of Japan's corporations and businessmen were already committing significant resources to the upcoming Tokyo Olympics.[50] Gradually, as planning for the Games continued, the financial situation for the Paralympics stabilized. The Lions Clubs, for instance, contributed nearly 7 million yen in September 1963, and a month later, a 12.5 million yen donation from the Japanese Automobile Manufacturer's Association subsidized the purchase of nine new buses, adapted for wheelchairs and equipped with lifts, costing 25 million yen. These contributions were soon followed by 20 million yen from the national government, 10 million yen from the Tokyo metropolitan government, and nearly 48 million yen from the Japanese Bicycle Promotion Association, the organization that oversaw professional bicycle racing, a popular gambling sport in Japan.[51] Smaller donations also came from schools, local groups, and individuals throughout Japan. The Japan Bartenders' Association created special Paralympic "Goodwill Boxes" for collecting individual donations from bars and cabarets all over the country, producing more than 3 million yen in total.[52] By the end of the Games, fundraising had proven so successful that a small surplus remained, providing a base for the ongoing development of disability sports in Japan after the Paralympics.[53]

Alongside its fundraising activities, the Organizing Committee also continued to promote Japanese participation in disability sports at home and abroad. In July 1963, seven Japanese athletes traveled to Europe, five to participate in the First International Sports Festival for the Disabled in Linz, Austria, and the other two in the International Stoke Mandeville Games. Several members of the Organizing Committee accompanied the athletes to observe the Stoke Mandeville Games, gather resources, and meet with the International Stoke Mandeville Games Committee, which formally approved Japan's plan to host the Paralympics the following year.[54] After their return, participants again received an audience with the crown prince.[55] Organizing Committee members were also involved in planning Japan's first National Sports Meet for the Disabled held in Yamaguchi Prefecture on November 10, 1963. In contrast to the earlier prefectural sports meet in Ōita in 1961 and a similar meet held in Okayama Prefecture in November 1962, the event in Yamaguchi involved nearly 500 athletes from throughout the country and used the same facilities as the annual National Sports Festival (Kokutai), which Yamaguchi had hosted only a week earlier.[56] After the Paralympics, involvement in similar national and international sporting events for people with disabilities remained a primary commitment for many members of the Organizing Committee.

With the Paralympics themselves only a year away, organizers also began planning in earnest. Everything from the refereeing of sporting events to the accessibility of athletes' housing had to be addressed. In September 1963, Kasai met with Satō Eisaku, the government minister in charge of organizing the Tokyo Olympics, and finalized arrangements for the use of the Olympic facilities for the Paralympics. In November, the Organizing Committee established ten subdivisions tasked with arranging particular elements of the Games, such as translation, promotion, and management of the Athletes' Village. Each of these subdivisions was in turn paired with a relevant nongovernmental organization, which assumed responsibility for completing any assigned duties.[57] Without the direct assistance of this army of organizational volunteers, it is difficult to imagine that Kasai and others, no matter how ambitious they might have been, could have organized the Games at all.

In February 1964 the Health and Welfare Ministry dispatched the first of several official notifications to all prefectural and municipal governors about the Paralympics, which among countless other details, included information on the recruitment of Japanese athletes for the event.[58] Two months later, the

Organizing Committee extended formal invitations to thirty-one countries and thirty-nine organizations.[59] Guttmann's visit to Japan in June spurred the final push, as organizers busily finalized daily itineraries, planned menus, designed uniforms, trained volunteer translators, arranged transportation, and planned necessary modifications to the Olympic Village, modifications that would have to wait to be made until after the conclusion of the Olympic Games.[60] With athletes scheduled to arrive on November 5, 1964, the Olympic Committee handed over control of the Olympic Village on November 1, leaving fewer than five frantic days and nights to construct ramps and modify bedrooms, bathrooms, and other facilities to make them wheelchair accessible.[61] The team from Argentina arrived a day earlier than expected, and by November 7, almost all of the foreign athletes had arrived at the Athletes' Village.[62] The International Stoke Mandeville Games had come to Tokyo.

Nakamura Yutaka: A View from the Margins

When looking at the names of the twenty-one individuals who founded the Preparatory Committee in 1962, the affiliation of one member, Nakamura Yutaka, appears oddly out of place on a list consisting mostly of members representing national welfare or disability organizations, government agencies, or institutions based in Tokyo.[63] Nakamura Yutaka was from the national hospital in Beppu, a city in Ōita Prefecture, a thousand kilometers from Tokyo. What was this man doing on a committee of selected individuals devoted to bringing the Paralympics to Tokyo? Details from the official accounts of the Games offer a simple explanation: the previous year, Nakamura and Hirata Atsushi had organized the country's first competitive sports event for athletes with disabilities in Ōita. As important as this path-breaking sporting event may have been, however, it was only one example of Nakamura's involvement with the Paralympics and disability sports more generally. Exploring Nakamura's role in the organization of the 1964 Games, a role largely obscured in official accounts, complicates our understanding of how these Paralympics came about. Whereas institutional and official sources privilege the center, implying that change radiated outward from Tokyo, Nakamura's story offers a view from the periphery, demonstrating how strategic actions at the local level could effect changes at the center.

A native of Beppu, Nakamura had pursued a specialty in orthopedics with a particular focus on rehabilitation. In 1958, at the age of 31, he became head of orthopedics at the national hospital in Beppu.[64] According to his own writings, Nakamura had given little thought to the role that sports might play in rehabilitation until 1960, when the Health and Welfare Ministry sent him on a six-month overseas trip to study rehabilitation facilities and practices in the United States and Europe.[65] One of Nakamura's fellow doctors from Kyushu had earlier translated some of Ludwig Guttmann's writings into Japanese, enabling Nakamura to learn about his work; therefore, Nakamura included a visit to Stoke Mandeville on his itinerary.[66] Nakamura's experience at Stoke Mandeville appears to have been transformative. Fascinated by Guttmann's "sports before surgery" approach, Nakamura repeatedly expressed amazement at Stoke Mandeville's success: after six months of treatment, 85 percent of patients with spinal injuries experienced at least some level of rehabilitation, with many leaving the hospital and returning to society.[67]

Perhaps motivated by Guttmann's criticism of the Japanese failures to implement what they had learned on their visits to England, Nakamura returned to Japan in August 1960 committed to incorporating sports into Japanese rehabilitation practices as quickly as possible. However, when Nakamura approached his colleagues in Beppu and surrounding areas about having their patients participate in sporting events, most were adamantly opposed. Some openly ridiculed the idea, stating that no real medical professional would suggest such a thing. In the views of many doctors, sports would simply undo all the rehabilitative work they had achieved, and putting the disabled on public display at a sporting event was the moral equivalent of showing off "freaks" at a circus.[68]

The reluctance on the part of Nakamura's colleagues almost certainly reflects general attitudes toward disability sports in Japan at the time. But there was also something else going on. Nakamura, a young doctor, was seeking to introduce a new foreign technique in a region of Japan long famous for its medically efficacious hot springs (an issue examined more fully in chapter 3). Nakamura's foreign-inspired emphasis on exercise and sports not only challenged more traditional Japanese methods involving hot springs treatments and massage but also threatened to undermine one of the factors that made Beppu and its surroundings an attractive location for rehabilitation facilities.[69] Sports for the disabled, unlike hot springs treatments, could be used and developed anywhere.

Despite the resistance he encountered, Nakamura forged ahead, convinced that a local sporting event in particular would demonstrate the viability of Guttmann's approach. With almost no facilities, institutional support, personnel, or equipment available, Nakamura spent the next several months meeting with local disability organizations, physical education (PE) instructors, and medical specialists. With the support of Hirata Atsushi, head of the Ōita Prefecture Department of Social Welfare, Nakamura's efforts culminated in the First Ōita Prefectural Sports Meet for the Disabled, held on October 22, 1961.[70]

In retrospect, the groundbreaking nature of this event—Japan's first competitive disability sports event conducted using international rules and guidelines—is easy to see. At the time, however, Nakamura recalled that, with the exception of those who might have had a vested interest in rehabilitation issues, few in Japan seemed to take notice, and many dismissed the event as simply the "hobby of a quirky, back-country doctor."[71]

In addition to its significance as a "first" in Japan, the Ōita sports meet proved critical to Nakamura's involvement in the Paralympic Movement for two specific reasons. First, the general response to the sports meet convinced Nakamura that disability sports were going to make little headway in Japan unless they could generate national publicity, and only Japan's participation in an international event, like the Stoke Mandeville Games, was going to do that.[72]

Second, the Ōita meet attracted the notice of would-be Paralympic organizers in Tokyo. The July 1961 *Yomiuri* article about the possibility of holding the Paralympics in Tokyo had mentioned the planned sports event in Ōita as a promising development in Japan's quest to host the Paralympics, so Nakamura's work was not as unrecognized as he seemed to think. However, up to this point, Nakamura appears to have had little formal contact with people or activities in Tokyo, so in this sense, the Ōita sports meet served to draw him into early organizational efforts at the center. But it is critical to note that Nakamura did not wait for people to come to him. Fueled by his newfound commitment to hosting the Stoke Mandeville Games in Tokyo after the Olympics, Nakamura made a whirlwind visit to the capital city in early 1962 with the express purpose of selling these Games to would-be Paralympic supporters, including Terada Muneyoshi from the Asahi Shimbun Social Welfare Organization. According to Terada's recollections, Nakamura had taken the night train to Tokyo and was preparing to return to Beppu that same evening. His unexpected visit was prompted by concerns that reluctance on the part of the Health and Welfare Ministry would spell the end of efforts to host the Paralympics. After explaining the goal and broader significance of the Games, Nakamura argued that the only hope for the Tokyo Paralympics lay with leadership from groups like the Asahi Shimbun Social Welfare Organization. And Japan could not afford to fail. Not hosting this event in 1964, Nakamura contended, "would give lie at an international level to the notion that Japan is a modern welfare state."[73] Struck by Nakamura's fervor, Terada vowed his support and later provided Nakamura with a venue for sharing his ideas with others, interactions that ultimately led to Nakamura's membership on the Preparatory Committee that formed in May 1962.[74]

Nakamura's growing enthusiasm about the Paralympics explains not only his involvement on the Preparatory Committee but also the committee's role in sending a Japanese team to the Stoke Mandeville Games in England in July 1962. It was Nakamura who first proposed the idea, which must have seemed far-fetched to many of his fellow organizers at the time. The Games were less than two months away, Japan had few athletes who might be able to compete, and the new committee had no funds to pay for the team's trip anyway. Perhaps realizing the potential media attention that would result, the committee's new leader, Kasai, agreed with Nakamura that sending a Japanese team was "a priority," regardless of the funding situation.[75] As it turned out, Nakamura was also instrumental in securing the funds for the trip. The lack of sponsors at the time led Nakamura—rather than the Preparatory Committee itself, as official accounts imply—to approach the bank in Ōita about a loan, which was eventually secured because of the backing of NHK and the *Asahi* newspaper. Even with this loan and a donation from the British Overseas Airway Corporation that covered roundtrip airfare for one, Nakamura was forced to sell his own automobile to pay for the team's trip to England.[76] In the end, both of the athletes and two of the other three delegates, including Nakamura, came from Ōita Prefecture, a clear reflection of the prefecture's, and by extension Nakamura's, pioneering role in the development of disability sports in Japan.

A year later Nakamura and several athletes from Ōita once again traveled to Europe to participate in the international games held in both Austria and England. Several members of the recently established Organizing Committee, including Kasai, joined them in July 1963, and by that point funding was less problematic. Recounting his experiences at the Stoke Mandeville Games in 1963 when Japan's bid to host the Paralympics was formally approved, Kasai later commented, "If it hadn't been for Nakamura, we would have had nothing but problems."[77] According to Kasai, Nakamura's familiarity with the staff and facilities, his knowledge of the Games themselves, and especially his relationship with Guttmann proved invaluable. "Without Nakamura," Kasai observed, "the Paralympics might not have happened."[78]

Two Games in One: Tokyo's 1964 Paralympics

At 10 o'clock in the morning on November 8, 1964, four thousand spectators, including Crown Prince Akihito and Crown Princess Michiko, gathered at Ota Field in the Olympic Village to witness the opening ceremony for the Tokyo Paralympics. The ceremony, intentionally modeled on the spectacular Olympic Ceremonies held a month earlier, began with a colorful, flag-waving procession of 369 athletes from twenty-two countries. Following speeches from Guttmann and Kasai, Crown Prince Akihito, in his capacity as "Patron of the

Games," offered words of welcome and praise. Noting his sincere respect for the International Stoke Mandeville Games, the crown prince also expressed his wish that the honor of hosting these Games in Tokyo would provide Japan's disabled with hope and encouragement. At that point, Aono Shigeo, one of the Japanese athletes, took an oath on behalf of all the Games' participants, as five hundred doves were released into the sky. With the conclusion of these festivities, the crown prince and princess descended from their royal box to greet and offer words of encouragement to the athletes who had come to Tokyo from around the world.[79]

Two hours later the Games were underway, and over the course of the next five days, male and female athletes with spinal injuries competed in more than twenty events, including several newly added wheelchair races. Reflecting the comprehensive planning efforts of the Games' organizers, special meals and parties, evening entertainment, shopping, and sight-seeing trips complemented the sporting events. Throughout the Games, several members of the imperial family—Crown Prince Akihito and Crown Princess Michiko, Prince and Princess Hitachi, and Empress Kōjun (unaccompanied by Emperor Hirohito)—attended the athletic events, attracting particular media attention. Finally, on November 12, after words of praise and thanks from Kasai and Guttmann and the ceremonial departure of the crown prince and princess, the closing ceremony concluded with the recession of the athletes bearing their countries' flags. Soon thereafter athletes began their journeys home.[80] The Games had ended, but not completely.

Indeed, one of the more curious elements of the Tokyo Paralympics was their structure. The International Sports Meet for the Disabled, as it was officially known in Japanese, was a two-part event. Part One, referred to in Japanese as the "International Sports Meet," was the five day-event just described, the thirteenth iteration of the International Stoke Mandeville Games. Part Two of these Games, called the "National Sports Meet," began on November 13 and concluded a day later. This two-day event attracted 480 participants hailing from all 46 of Japan's prefectures and Okinawa, which was still occupied by the United States at the time. Despite its name, organizers of the National Meet had also invited athletes from Europe, and a team from West Germany competed as "special participants."[81]

Unlike the initial International Sports Meet, which followed the Stoke Mandeville Games' parameters and featured only athletes with spinal injuries, the second part of the meet was a multi-disability event that appears to have been organized with little direct input from outside Japan.[82] With more than thirty-four sporting events for men and women with a wide range of disabilities, the National Sports Meet added a layer of complexity to the planning efforts that in later years would play a role in other potential host sites' decisions to decline the Paralympics.[83] The structure adopted for these Tokyo Games reflects the commitment to hosting a multi-disability event that was apparent in some of the earliest organizational efforts. Though it does appear that some in Japan and elsewhere might have been interested in holding a single, rather than a split event, the plan for a two-part event was apparently already settled by the time Kasai wrote to Guttmann officially announcing Japan's intent to host the Paralympics.[84] In a sense, it was the perfect plan. It did not threaten to alter the approach of the Stoke Mandeville Games themselves, and it addressed Japanese desires to serve a larger portion of the disabled population. Yet the Games were clearly not equal in length or prestige, and as a result, the National Sports Meet attracted far less attention.

Ultimately, several aspects of the Tokyo Games, including their structure, would prove significant in the history of the Paralympics. For one, these Games marked the first attempt to directly link differing approaches to disability sports at the same venue. Tokyo's approach was both unprecedented and groundbreaking, and it was not until 1976 that official joint international games were held.[85] Even though they would have other official names for years to come, media and popular references before and during the Games in Tokyo helped standardize the usage of the name "Paralympics," particularly in Japan. Contrary to the wishes of Guttmann, Kasai, and many others, the 1964 Paralympics would also be the last International Stoke Mandeville Games held in the Olympic host city until the 1988 Seoul Games. As it turned out, the Games could be held in Japan, but they could not, in fact, be exported anywhere.

The National Meanings of a Transnational Movement

Continuing in his role as patron of the International Sports Meet for the Disabled, the crown prince helped open the National Sports Meet portion of the Games, declaring that this event offered "an excellent opportunity to improve our nation's inadequate understanding of disability and strengthen our interest."[86] Clearly intended to be inspirational, his message to participants about the significance of the Games also hints at two facets of their ultimate impact in Japan. On one hand, the Paralympics were linked to the promotion of sports for the disabled, activities that came to be seen as a means of improving the lives of individuals with disabilities and changing social perceptions of disability more generally. On the other hand, these Games offered a chance to assess Japan's global standing, especially—though not exclusively—in relation to the nation's approach to disability. In other words, the 1964 Paralympics, much like the Tokyo Olympics, were more politically significant than they appeared to be on their surface.

The largest impact of the Tokyo Games came, not surprisingly, in the realm of sports. Soon after the Paralympics ended, the organizing committee was dissolved and replaced by the Japan Sports Association for the Disabled (JSAD), a national organization led for many years by Kasai Yoshisuke. With the support of this new association, national and local sports meets for athletes with a range of impairments became regular events, and increasing numbers of Japanese began competing and winning abroad.[87] As explored in chapters 2 and 3, Nakamura Yutaka, like Kasai, continued his commitment to the promotion of disability sports both at home and abroad, playing a pivotal role in the establishment of the regional Far East and South Pacific (FESPIC) Games for the Disabled and the Ōita International Wheelchair Marathon. Within months of the Paralympics, Nakamura also began implementing his plan to establish what became Taiyō no Ie (Japan Sun Industries), a factory in Beppu specifically created to employ individuals with disabilities.[88]

Given such developments it seems understandable that many saw the Paralympics as a grand success in improving the lives of individuals with disabilities. Looking at other aspects of the Games reveals a more complex picture, however. For instance, the time crunch involved in preparing to serve as host meant that the Tokyo Games had little impact on the city's infrastructure. Unlike more recent Paralympics where the creation of barrier-free environments and transportation has been a key component of the host-city bidding process, Tokyo after the 1964 Games was as inaccessible as it was before them.

Perhaps even more importantly, these Games, because of the many "firsts" they involved, helped shape Japanese understandings of disability sports and disability more generally. Although we cannot, of course, know how all Japanese interpreted these events, we can explore the ways in which those events were presented. The structure of the 1964 event, for example, played a perhaps unintended role in shaping how disabled athletes were portrayed. Even though far more Japanese athletes with disabilities participated in the National Sports Meet, their efforts received much less official and popular attention than the more spectacular and prestigious international component. It is therefore not enough to say that the Tokyo Paralympics shaped Japanese perceptions of disability; understanding the impact of the Games necessitates a more careful exploration of who was being represented, who was doing the representing, and what those representations suggested about those with disabilities.

Selling the Paralympics

The process of representing athletes with disabilities in Japan began long before the crowd of four thousand spectators gathered on November 8, 1964, to observe the opening ceremony of the Tokyo Paralympics. Given the general lack of awareness about the Paralympics in Japan before this point, those seeking to bring the Games to Tokyo faced a difficult task, one that required them to make a case both for the importance of the 1964 Games and for the need to continue developing sports for the disabled in their aftermath.

Naturally, part of making that case involved educating the public about the event and its participants via the mass media. A more thorough examination of such popular media representations is provided in chapter 4, but it bears noting here that the 1964 Games—and the International Sports Meet portion in particular—generated far more Japanese media coverage than might be expected given the state of disability sports in Japan at the time. The major urban dailies, sports newspapers, a mix of regional papers, and the NHK public television network all covered the event, with some offering extensive commentary, multiple photographs, and, in the case of NHK, live coverage. Even a cursory glance at the leading dailies in Japan reveals that the "spectacular" elements of these Games—their international nature, their ceremonies, and the involvement of imperial family members—generated far more attention than the athletes' achievements or the broader social issues that organizers hoped the Paralympics would address. Reflecting a pattern that has only recently begun to change in Japanese newspapers, much of the coverage of the 1964 Paralympics appeared not in the sports sections but on the society pages.[89] The Paralympics and disability sports were being treated as human interest or health-and-welfare stories, not "real" sports. The distinction between sports and disability sports apparent in media coverage of the Tokyo Games reflected the approach of organizers, like Kasai, Nakamura, and others, who explicitly emphasized the rehabilitative purpose of sports for the disabled.[90] In all these ways, the extensive media coverage generated by the Tokyo Paralympics serves as an important reminder that the amount of publicity can be less important than its content.[91]

It is also clear that such coverage was no accident, having been actively pursued and cultivated by Paralympic supporters. Well aware of the benefits of media attention, organizers established a large publicity subcommittee in early 1963, which was charged with reaching out to major newspapers, magazines, broadcast networks, and governmental publications, including those from some 630 cities across Japan. Leaving few potential publicity outlets uninformed, subcommittee members also provided Paralympic-related materials to labor unions, women's groups, youth organizations, 420 major companies, 320 cultural or educational organizations, and 80 industry publications. The subcommittee established a particularly close relationship with the reporters' club connected with the Ministry of Health and Welfare, a less-than-surprising development considering the ministry's oversight of disability-related issues and its support for the Tokyo Games. During the Games themselves, subcommittee members sought to maximize coverage by offering almost free media access to all areas and events as long as it did not interfere with the competitions underway.[92]

As the work of this publicity subcommittee suggests, Paralympic organizers did not leave media coverage to chance. Of course, they could not ultimately control how the media covered the Games, but that did not stop them from attempting to direct coverage toward their own agenda of "raising societal awareness and understanding about disability issues and generating discussion about promoting rehabilitation policies."[93]

The combination of such behind-the-scenes publicity work and the media prominence of figures such as Kasai and Nakamura points to the need to understand how the organizers themselves conceptualized and talked about the Games and their participants. Unfortunately, original records related to the earliest history of the Paralympic Movement in Japan remain scarce. However, a number of official reports outline early organizational efforts and document the success of the 1964 Games, and when examined together with promotional pamphlets, event programs, the speeches and writings of Paralympic supporters, and a documentary film produced by the NHK Public Welfare Organization, these official and semi-official sources offer good indications of how and why those interested in promoting the Paralympics sought to do so.

Not surprisingly, materials used to introduce the Tokyo Games highlight efforts to address the general lack of awareness of disability sports in Japan at the time by placing emphasis on the rehabilitative purpose of the Paralympics. One of the earliest official pamphlets, "The International Sports Meet for the Disabled (An Explanation)," dates from 1963. It outlines the history of the Games, their relationship to the Olympics, and the origin of the name "Paralympics" (a combination of *para* from paraplegia and *lympics* from Olympics); yet it devotes less than a page to listing plans for the actual event, with minimal clarification of the distinctions between the Games' two parts. Well over half of the pamphlet's eleven pages are devoted to explaining why it is "extremely important to incorporate sports as a means toward rehabilitation" and how several countries—Germany, England, and Greece, but not Japan—had already done so with great success.[94] The pamphlet ends by noting that "even Pakistan and Indonesia are implementing disability sports," an implicit critique of Japan's slow start.[95]

Distributed by the publicity committee in 1964, a second pamphlet, "Paralympic Tokyo 1964: The International Sports Meet for the Disabled," follows a similar approach, framing the Paralympics as a means for improving Japan's engagement with beneficial international trends in rehabilitation. This pamphlet provides much more information about the upcoming Games, including specifics on the types of competitions and the selection process for Japanese athletes; yet most of its content (twelve of eighteen pages) juxtaposes details on existing disability-related policies, facilities, and statistics in Japan with first-hand reports from Kasai, Lorenzen, and two Japanese athletes that describe the situation abroad. For instance, in Takazaki Ken'ichi's account of his experiences as a participant in the 1963 disability sports event in Linz, talk of sports proves secondary to glowing praise for Austrian society's treatment of those with disabilities.[96] Similarly, Andō Tokuji's report from his time competing at the 1963 Stoke Mandeville Games describes England as a place that is "easy to live in as a disabled person," and he ends his brief essay with a sentiment clearly shared by Paralympic organizers: "I can't stop hoping that our country will become that kind of country as soon as possible."[97] In case readers had any doubts about how to go about achieving this goal, the pamphlet's other essays and comments made it apparent that the answer lay in Japan's adoption of new approaches to rehabilitation, approaches modeled on these European countries where sports had helped make "disabled people feel very bright."[98] Although it remains unclear exactly who would have been reading these kinds of promotional pamphlets, their writers left little doubt that disability sports were critical to Japan's future.

Perhaps intended to supplement the official Japanese-language programs that included little more than dates, times, and locations, the glossy Japanese leaflet distributed during the Paralympics themselves seems to have targeted a broader audience than the earlier promotional pamphlets. Using a question-and-answer style, the colorful, double-sided leaflet offered simple explanations of the Games' history, purpose, and format, interspersed with multiple photographs of individuals with disabilities engaging in athletic competition. Even without the detailed comparisons with Europe in the pamphlets, the leaflet authors made it clear that the Paralympics were a form of rehabilitation that Japan needed to embrace, as exemplified by the response to the question, "What are the Paralympics for?": "The social rehabilitation of the physically disabled. . . . Sports are one means for attaining this sort of rehabilitation, and therefore, each country is seriously promoting these kinds of events."[99] Along similar lines, the leaflet described the various sports competitions of the Games, but informed readers, "For the Paralympics, the goal wasn't about winning competitions."[100] This comment was almost certainly intended to reinforce the rehabilitative purpose of the Games while preempting potentially unrealistic expectations about athletic performances (perhaps especially those by Japanese athletes) raised by the recent Olympics. It also unintentionally brought to the surface underlying tensions in the emerging Paralympic Movement. Organizers in Tokyo and elsewhere were intent on distinguishing their Games— which had clearly defined rules, countable medals, and honored victors—from mere recreational events, yet promoters' tendency to view and market the Paralympics as medically and socially beneficial compelled them to downplay these very same sport-like elements. Disability sports were sports, but they were clearly being portrayed as different from sports for the able-bodied.

These sorts of mixed messages were echoed in the official *Photograph Collection from the Tokyo Paralympic International Sports Meet for the Disabled*, published in the immediate aftermath of the Games. The collection provided an annotated visual record of the athletic competitions themselves, along with substantial coverage of the preparations leading up to the Paralympics and their ceremonial elements. Although images of athletes with disabilities have often been rightfully critiqued for problematic patterns of representation, the photos used here were remarkably diverse.[101] A mixture of active and passive shots depicted both men and women of different national and ethnic backgrounds, displaying a whole range of emotional expressions. The collection also featured athletes with a wide variety of physical disabilities, and in fact, among the official materials produced before, during, or after the Games, the photo collection offered the most detailed attention to the athletes who participated in the National Sports Meet portion of the event, coverage that still amounted to roughly half that given to the International Meet.[102]

Images of the sports themselves tended to be grouped by event, with surrounding text that highlighted how the pictured athletes competed and why the particular sporting activity would be medically efficacious. In that sense, these annotations diverged little from other official sources with their emphasis on the rehabilitative purpose of the Games. For instance, the comments introducing the photographs from competitions at the International Sports Meet portion directly referenced modern Olympic founder Pierre De Coubertin's famous statement: "The important thing in the Olympic Games is not to win, but to take part." They continued, "De Coubertin's words are perhaps even more appropriate for the Paralympics. The point of the Paralympics as a competition for the disabled is not to strive for records, but for them to participate in the competition, and in so doing improve their abilities and encourage each other."[103] Yet readers who continued examining the photos of athletes from both the international and national sections of the Games would learn that a significant portion of those pictured had earned medals for their victories. For a sporting event that was not about winning, those telling the story of Tokyo's Paralympics certainly seemed intent on documenting winners.

In contrast to the photo collection in which athletes with a variety of disabilities featured prominently, one of the more striking aspects of the organizing committee's *Official Report on the Tokyo Paralympic Games* is the relative absence of those with disabilities, winners or otherwise. To be sure, general references to the physically disabled or to forms or indicators of disability abound, and the report opens with eight pages of photographs, including several images of athletes competing at the Games. However, the rest of the 271-page report incorporates the words of only two Japanese athletes and a formal statement from the British team, all of whom had been involved with the international portion of the Games.[104] In the section explaining key events before the Games, the reference to Japanese athletes participating in the International Stoke Mandeville Games for the first time ever in 1962—an obvious turning point in the history of the Paralympic Movement in Japan—provides no information on the athletes' names, their sports, or their results. This section does, however, include specifics on how the trip was financed and shares quotes describing the responses of the crown prince and the prime minister after the athletes returned home.[105]

The second delegation of Japanese athletes who traveled to Europe in 1963 to participate in two international sporting events receives slightly more attention, including a small chart listing their names, home prefectures, ages, occupations, and form of disability. The focus quite clearly is on the fact that these people were disabled, not that they were athletes with disabilities, because once again, the report provides no indication of what sports these participants actually did while abroad. Yet it does share the names of organizers who traveled to Europe with the Japanese team and offers details about their participation in the international meetings held in conjunction with these sporting events.[106] The absence of concrete information about the athletes' experiences in this section of the report is even more noteworthy, because such details would have been readily available. Only a few months earlier, the publicity subcommittee's own promotional pamphlet had used firsthand accounts from athletes participating in each of these 1963 events to advertise the real-world benefits of disability sports.[107]

Despite the groundbreaking nature of the National Sports Meet portion of the 1964 Paralympics and its large number of participants, the official report also gives surprisingly little attention to these competitions or their athletes. It is mostly limited to documenting the ceremonies, including transcripts of speeches from Kasai and the crown prince. Were it not for photos at the beginning and the list of results at the end, the vast majority of Japanese participants at the Tokyo Paralympics would almost be entirely absent from the Game's official report. These sorts of omissions and the detailed documentation of bureaucratic minutiae, meeting schedules, and commentary from various section heads or volunteers that make up the vast majority of the official report, could easily be dismissed as a peculiarity of the genre, but they also reflect more general approaches and attitudes of the organizers. These Games were being organized for—not by—individuals with disabilities.

By all accounts, the early organizational efforts were initiated and dominated by medical professionals and individuals associated with government agencies or national welfare and disability groups, and only a few of them were individuals with a disability. Moreover, the most visible supporters featured in the report and in promotional efforts more broadly were nondisabled men such as Kasai and Nakamura. On one hand, this was hardly unique or surprising. Many of the so-called pioneers of disability sports around the world, including Guttmann, were nondisabled individuals interested in promoting rehabilitation; indeed, Japan's far-from-progressive attitudes toward disability in the 1960s would have made it especially challenging for individuals with disabilities to promote sports entirely on their own. On the other hand, the dominance of nondisabled promoters before, during, and after the Paralympics did little to challenge paternalistic views of the disabled as individuals incapable of acting without the help of the able-bodied. I do not mean to imply that these organizers were not genuinely interested in improving the lives of Japan's disabled population. It seems clear that they were, but in their earnest efforts to do so, they crafted a story that sometimes gave greater attention to themselves than the population they aimed to serve.

Indeed, the prominence of certain promoters in some of the official materials threatened to overshadow the intended focus of the event, the athletes. For instance, in the documentary produced by the NHK Public Welfare Organization, only three athletes (two of them Japanese) are named; in contrast, Guttmann, Kasai, Nakamura, four Japanese celebrities who participated in a promotional autograph event before the Games, and several members of the imperial family all receive both name recognition (even the "royal box" in the stands gets a special mention) and extended screen time.[108] Similarly, the official English-language program for the Paralympics includes twelve photographs: three depicting members of the imperial family, one of Guttmann, one of Kasai, one of an Organizing Committee event, and two of the Paralympic venues, leaving only four photos focusing on athletes.[109]

In many respects, the star of the Paralympics was Japan's crown prince. The very first photo in the English program portrays him in his role as the "patron" of the Tokyo Paralympics, and he was often the first one mentioned in speeches during the Games, usually with words of profound gratitude. The prince's actions—and those of other imperial household members—received particular attention in the press and in many of the post-Games materials. The official report, for example, included a special section marked with a distinctive border that detailed every instance of imperial involvement during and after the Games; this section largely duplicated information recorded elsewhere in the report.[110] As noted earlier, the link between the crown prince and the Paralympic Movement in Japan was not new or the result of mere happenstance, having been mobilized early on to provide maximum publicity for the Games. After seeing so many images of the crown prince and hearing or reading the words of praise and appreciation that organizers offered him in their speeches and official words of welcome in the program, one could easily reach the conclusion that he himself was a central attraction and that his patronage was a special gift to the disability sports movement.[111] Strategically, seeking imperial patronage made perfect sense, especially because the crown prince proved to be an important long-term ally in the effort to promote sports for the disabled in Japan. But because many of the official materials seem to place particular emphasis on his patronage or on the mere presence of imperial family members at the Games (none of their comments or words of welcome are recorded in the documentary or shared in the programs), one is left to wonder whether the crown prince's support was being interpreted more generally at the time as advocacy or as charity for the disabled.

Rehabilitation Games

In his own words of welcome at the opening ceremony for the International Meet, which are recorded in the official report, Crown Prince Akihito did express an interest in fostering change for those with disabilities. Not surprisingly given the setting, his speech focused on sports as the means by which many of the participants had "recovered their health" and achieved their rehabilitation or, more literally, their "return to society."[112] The crown prince was not alone in his views on the potential benefits of the Games. Impressed with results that they were seeing or hearing about from abroad, such organizers as Kasai, Nakamura, and other promoters who shared similar medical or social welfare backgrounds focused on rehabilitative potential as a primary selling point of the Paralympics and sports for the disabled. As Kasai wrote in an article he published in the Ministry of Health and Welfare's official bulletin in December 1964, Japan's previous experience with sports for the disabled had been limited to "recreational field days" that were "far removed from sports aimed at rehabilitation that can build up the body and inspire confidence and courage."[113] Only a few months before, on the eve of the Games, Kasai had offered a similar argument to a much broader readership during an extended interview he gave for the mainstream magazine, *Asahi Weekly*.[114] In the foreword to the official report on the games, Kasai expanded on these general points, insisting that disability sports aimed for transformation: they were meant to "build up the strength of disabled individuals, so that they could regain confidence in that strength and their abilities, and in so doing find the bright hope and courage that would allow them to alleviate their disability complex. As Dr. Guttmann has said, 'Do not focus on what has been lost; live to the fullest with what remains.'"[115] For Kasai and others, promoting sports as a rehabilitative tool was not only a new and arguably superior technique from abroad but also a means of improving the social welfare of Japan's disabled population in general, a goal clearly expressed in the founding charter of the Paralympics Organizing Committee.[116] Watanabe Hanako, who had been among the earliest promoters of the Tokyo Paralympics, echoed these ideas in her post-Paralympic article for the weekly newsletter of the Japan Labor Study Group. Referring to the oft-mentioned six-month rehabilitation rate in Europe and the United States, Watanabe argued that the real significance of the Paralympics lay in their demonstration for the general public that participation in sports was an inseparable element of getting those with disabilities integrated back into society and back to work.[117]

Advocates like Watanabe and Kasai often acknowledged that changes were necessary in Japanese society to allow individuals with disabilities to pursue sports, but supporters' approaches tended to shift the focus of rehabilitation back onto the individual. The preface to the promotional pamphlet from 1964, for example, cited the importance of governmental and private efforts to promote rehabilitation, but pointed out that Europe and America were increasingly turning to sports for the disabled because "the most important thing is that the disabled individuals themselves first develop confidence in their bodies."[118] Later in this same pamphlet, Kasai pointed to a similar conclusion he had reached based on what he saw abroad: increasing financial support and improving social services were certainly necessary, but even before that Japan needed to establish sports and job training opportunities "to give the disabled themselves health and confidence."[119] In a context where people were just beginning to learn about disability sports, it is not difficult to see how these sorts of efforts to sell the Games, and especially organizers' overwhelming, and internationally rooted, emphasis on sports as *the* primary means of rehabilitation, could lead to the notion that all disabled individuals could overcome their impairments if they were only willing to work for it. In other words, official organizational approaches and ideas played a central role in the emergence of a version of the "super-crip" stereotype, fostering the problematic notion that athletes with disabilities merit particular attention because they have not allowed their disability to prevent them from becoming successful.

Organizers' focus on rehabilitation also tended to reinforce preexisting medicalized views of the disabled. Several of Nakamura's writings on the Games were published in medical journals, and reflecting their intended audience, they tended to rely on specialized language to outline the specific benefits or dangers associated with particular sporting activities. Like some of the earlier promotional materials, Nakamura's medically oriented writings also tended to deemphasize competition in sports for the disabled.[120] As a physician, Nakamura's tendency to frame the Paralympics along medical lines seems understandable, but he was hardly unique in this approach. Among the various official materials, the NHK Public Welfare Organization documentary offers some of the most concrete examples of this emphasis.[121] Although we know that the film was produced in coordination with the public broadcast network NHK, most other details about its origins and intended use remain unclear. However, with its detailed descriptions of how the various events were intended to affect the athletes physically, emotionally, or socially, it seems likely that the documentary was targeting potential advocates for disability sports among various professionals already working with Japan's disabled population. This film was a recruitment or educational tool, rather than a source of entertainment for the general public.

After an opening shot of airplanes and narration noting that a new group of foreign athletes has arrived in Japan in the days soon after the Tokyo Olympics, the voiceover for the film explains the origins of the name "Paralympics" and reveals the intended purpose of the Games—leaving no doubt that they are first and foremost a form of rehabilitation for the physically disabled. These opening scenes also include the seemingly obligatory references to the amazing rehabilitation rates in Great Britain, coupled with images of the British team members smiling and interacting cheerfully at the airport and on their way to the Olympic Village.

After breaking to Ōita Prefecture's Beppu National Hospital, the film offers its first glimpse of Japan's own athletes who are engaged in their final practices before leaving for the Games; here the narrator provides the first specific indication of how sports can aid such individuals. In contrast to most of the foreign athletes who are said to be in the workforce already, the documentary points out that all of the Japanese participants are coming to the Games from hospitals or other health care facilities; then it proceeds to explain that, for the Japanese athletes shown on screen, "practicing with their impaired bodies is certainly not easy, but one by one their faces light up with joy as they realize that they can do it if they try." In the next scene depicting the arrival of the Japanese team members in Tokyo, the narrator once again offers a statement on sport's transformational impact on Japan's athletes:

> From Hokkaido in the north, to Kyushu in the south, the 53 athletes selected from throughout the country, including two women, began gathering in Tokyo one after another. Only a year ago, some among them were bedridden, and some had withdrawn into themselves because of the loneliness of their isolation from society. Ranging in age from 20 to 46, they have learned sports, and it is only through sports that they have become so bright.[122]

The next several minutes of the documentary offer shots of the Games' facilities, glimpses of numerous social interactions between the athletes, and more extended coverage of various ceremonies, with the opening ceremony naturally receiving the most time. At approximately the nineteen-minute mark, the forty-five-minute film shifts its focus to the athletic events themselves, and for the next eighteen minutes most of the footage—with the exception of a short scene depicting the empress's arrival at the Games—is dedicated to displays of wheelchair races, field events, ping pong, weightlifting, snooker, basketball, swimming, fencing, and archery. With each new sport, the narrator provides a brief explanation of how wheelchair athletes perform it. Each of these mini-lessons invariably includes highly detailed descriptions of the specific physiological improvements the sports are intended to promote and the skills that athletes can gain by performing them. As the athletes on screen race, throw, swim, shoot, swing, lift, win, and lose, observers are reminded over and over that this athletic event is really a form of treatment and recovery. Taking into account the sociohistorical context in which this documentary was produced, one where disability sports promoters in Japan needed to convince many doubtful colleagues in the medical and social welfare fields that such sports were safe, beneficial, and internationally sanctioned, the medicalized approach and rhetoric in the film are understandable and undoubtedly helped foster improvements in the lives of many Japanese with disabilities. That said, the official emphasis on sports as a rehabilitative tool, especially apparent in the documentary and other official materials, simply recast would-be athletes as another kind of medical patient. They might be out of the hospitals, but their bodies were still being subjected to a uniquely medicalized gaze, one that reinforced, rather than challenged, understandings of disability as an individual health issue.

Living the Bright Life

The rehabilitative emphasis so apparent in the documentary and other official representations of disability sports proved appealing to Japan's Paralympic promoters in part because many of them saw their own nation's approach to disability at the time as inherently flawed, especially after learning about the experiences of individuals with disabilities outside of Japan. Overcoming what many saw as a dramatic gap between Japan and the West necessitated the adoption of Euro-American methods and views of disability, a process that could only happen if people in Japan, especially rehabilitation specialists, government officials, and social welfare advocates, were aware of the flaws in the Japanese system. As Nakamura Yutaka concluded after his first attempt to promote disability sporting events in Ōita, one of the only ways to create national awareness quickly was to engage in international events.[123] In this sense, participating in the Stoke Mandeville Games and, more importantly, bringing those Games to Tokyo would serve both to indict and to correct existing Japanese approaches to disability. The goal for Nakamura and other promoters of disability sports, then, was to shame Japan into action. In practice, what this approach involved was the repeated, and clearly reductionist, juxtaposition of foreign and Japanese methods and athletes. Although national humiliation can be a powerful motivating force for change, the process of comparing "bright" foreign athletes with their Japanese counterparts generated an overly simplified picture of life for those with disabilities in both Japan and the West.[124]

While the Tokyo Paralympics were widely hailed as a success, Nakamura saw something different. As he put it, "The foreign athletes were strong, and their complexions were bright. But the Japanese athletes were weak, with dull complexions. There was more to this contrast than a difference between those actively involved in sports and those not. It reflected a difference in daily lives."[125] For Nakamura, the Paralympics served as a clear indication that his nation's approach to disability was woefully lacking, and his evaluations seemed more the rule than the exception. In her post-Paralympic essay, for example, Watanabe Hanako offered an extended analysis of successful rehabilitation practices in Italy that she had learned about during the Games. She concluded her essay with a call for a more humane labor policy in general, adding harsh words about Japanese labor policies and policymakers who, she suggested, would almost certainly reject outright the kinds of methods and policies proving so successful in Italy. With repeated positive references to Italy, Finland, England, and the "various developed nations" (*senshin shokoku*), Watanabe left little doubt that, in terms of its treatment of the disabled, Japan was not in that group. This implicit criticism would have had particular resonance at the time, because much of Japan's Olympic and Paralympic hopes had been tied up in the idea that the nation was on the rise.[126] Watanabe offered a similar critique in another essay published soon after the Paralympics in the mainstream magazine, *Women's Friend*. Here, Watanabe lamented the persistence of discriminatory attitudes and actions toward those with disabilities in Japan. She ended her essay with an observation that a truly democratic society would embrace the opportunities for promoting rehabilitation that the Paralympics had demonstrated.[127] Aono Shigeo, one of only two athletes to have his words featured in the official report, offered an even more explicit critique. Observing that he was "not alone in wondering where the brightness of the foreign athletes came from," Aono cited the different national welfare systems and the stability of life that the foreign athletes benefited from, and he concluded that "there is too big a gap between the current situation in Japan and that of the developed nations."[128] Although Aono expressed his own joy about the opportunity to participate in the Games, the Paralympics shone a light on problems in Japan that he was all too familiar with.

Like Watanabe, Nakamura, and Aono, Kasai Yoshisuke's views on the success of the Tokyo Paralympics were tempered by his awareness of how conditions in Japan compared with those abroad. In his interview with the *Weekly Asahi*, he described Japan as ten years behind the West in terms of its understanding of and approaches to those with disabilities, and many of his writings sought to highlight this gap.[129] Writing for the Health and Welfare Ministry bulletin, he pointed out that "in England, 95% of the disabled were rehabilitated and working at a job, but regrettably, in our country, we have not even reached 50%."[130] Perhaps because of the shocking disparity they reflected, these or similar figures served as regular talking points for Kasai and many other Paralympic promoters. Kasai acknowledged that the problems in Japan were multifaceted, but he proposed a twofold solution clearly modeled on what he had seen during his time in Europe: increased promotion of sports for the disabled and the development of comprehensive rehabilitation programs that combined treatment, sports, and job training. According to Kasai, Japan could not simply allow the recent attention to disability-related issues to end with the Paralympics: "Because the disabled from various countries have brightly and cheerfully displayed the results of their training before our very eyes, and they have shown us that they can do such things, I cannot stop hoping that by seizing this opportunity, Japan's disabled can achieve rehabilitation quickly and brightly."[131] In Kasai's view, the Paralympics had highlighted the problems, and now it was up to Japanese policymakers and rehabilitation specialists to respond with a new, internationally inspired approach. Failure to do so would leave Japan's disabled people languishing in the dark.

Even the crown prince seems to have shared such concerns. In the days following the Games he hosted a meeting to congratulate the members of the Organizing Committee on their accomplishments, but according to the official report, he began with an implicit criticism of the Japanese system: "Watching the recent Paralympics, I noticed that the foreign athletes were much brighter and had better bodies. I know that unlike the Japanese athletes, who tended to come from hospitals or health care facilities, the majority of the foreign athletes had already returned to society. I think that foreign rehabilitation is going well."[132] Although he stopped short of actually saying that Japanese practices were failing, he really did not have to. Everyone in the room already knew, and they responded not with a defense but with a pledge to pursue change.

Perhaps not surprisingly given its repeated appearance in many of the comments from Paralympic supporters and participants, "brightness" proved to be a recurring idea in the NHK Public Welfare Organization documentary as well.[133] The very first use of the term appears in connection with the arrival of the British athletes, whose "bright smiles" seem only natural, because viewers are informed that Britain has an exceptionally high rehabilitation rate (here given as 90%), and that the British team consists entirely of fully employed members of society. This portrayal of the cheerful British athletes heading for the Athletes' Village in Yoyogi serves as a foil for the next scene where viewers see the Japanese athletes for the first time, but not before getting a clear indication of their location: an extended shot of the sign marking the entrance to Beppu National Hospital. This image, combined with the narration, shows clearly that Japan's athletes are inferior to their British counterparts. The Japanese team members are not employed members of society; they are still hospital bound; and as noted previously, they are only beginning to experience some joy as they realize they are able to engage in sports. Whether intentional or not, the depiction of the Japanese athletes at the hospital, when combined with the next scene showing the Japanese team's arrival in Tokyo, constructs a sort of mini-narrative: the Japanese Paralympians start in hospitals (unlike the British team who start in society), begin learning sports, travel to the Games, and finally become "so bright."

It is also critical to note here that this scene offers the only use of the word "bright" in direct relation to the Japanese athletes. Although the Japanese athletes are frequently depicted in the film smiling, laughing, and otherwise competing and interacting in ways that seem to differ little from their foreign counterparts who appear in many of the same scenes, these representations are not labeled as bright. During the footage of the opening ceremony, for instance, the event itself is described as bright, and there is a reference to the bright faces of all present, but this description is belied by the shots of the Japanese team, whose serious, staid expressions do not seem to reflect the narrator's comment that they are all "delighted that they are able to participate in the Games." When the film moves into the coverage of the sporting events themselves, the notion of brightness and enjoyment takes second place to depictions and images of the hard work involved in sports' rehabilitative benefits, as discussed earlier.

In contrast, as the film nears its end, brightness returns, but notably, the Japanese athletes disappear entirely. Following a group identified only as "foreign athletes" on a trip to a Japanese department store, the film shows these athletes—most of whom are being pushed by members of Japan's Self-Defense Force—cheerfully interacting with shop clerks, tossing balls, trying on caps, and making purchases, activities that seem to reflect the narrator's observation that "no matter where they go, their brightness is unwavering." The final moments of the film, which depict the foreign athletes making their way to the airport and boarding their planes, exude a sense of appreciation to the foreign athletes (their countries of origin no longer specified) for showing Japan the potential outcomes of rehabilitation. Not surprisingly, the film ends with a call to pursue brightness in Japan: "Even though the Games have ended, and the athletes have left Japan and returned home, for us, we cannot allow the Paralympics to end. When each and every disabled person in Japan bears a bright smile like those of the foreign athletes, only then can we say for the first time, that the true Paralympics has begun." Although sports might have helped Japan's own Paralympians "become so bright," apparently the documentary makers and many of the Paralympic promoters did not yet find them bright enough to serve as icons for the future of sports for others with disabilities in Japan. For that future to become a reality, only outside, foreign models would do.

Given the state of disability sports in Japan before the Paralympics, the comparisons between Japanese and foreign athletes in the documentary and in other official sources seem both understandable and strategically advantageous. For one thing, what we see in the case of disability sports reflects a broader process of co-constitution that has, at various points, proved critical to the promotion of sports in Japan more generally. Experts and promoters have often looked abroad to diagnose and correct perceived problems at home.[134]

Furthermore, there certainly were very real differences between some of the Japanese athletes and their foreign counterparts, especially those coming from countries with more established programs for disability sports. Some of these differences would have been particularly apparent during the athletic competitions, where Japanese athletes generally fared poorly in terms of victories. Even though many promoters deemphasized the competitive aspect of the Paralympics, many of these same people saw the disparities in athletic performance as a key way to highlight and then address more fundamental differences in the countries' approaches to rehabilitation. As Nakamura put it in one of his medical journal essays, "The positive or negative results of the wheelchair competitions were a direct reflection of the levels of a country's medical rehabilitation and its wheelchairs."[135] In this sense, documenting differences in athletic success at these Games was critical to helping Japan diagnose its problems and would serve as a baseline for measuring future improvement.

Other potential differences between the foreign and Japanese athletes, such as greater independence and a more positive attitude, would have been and continue to be harder to measure in any objective way. That said, there are moments captured in the film or other reports from the Games, where the independence of the foreign athletes surprised the nondisabled volunteers (often members of the Self-Defense Forces) preparing to assist them in some way. Such instances served to highlight the potential benefits of these comparisons. Writing for the Health and Welfare Ministry bulletin, for instance, Terada Muneyoshi of the Asahi Shimbun Social Welfare Organization described seeing two female athletes from London flag a taxi and go out shopping on their own in Tokyo. For Terada and presumably some of his readers, the scene he witnessed completely surprised him and brought home the fact that Japanese society needed to change its approaches to and views of people with disabilities.[136]

Even with its highly medicalized approach, the Tokyo Games did demonstrate to a wide audience that people with disabilities, including those in Japan, were more than patients stuck in hospitals. They could be athletes living, working, playing, and going out on their own. As exemplified by the extensive media coverage they generated and the ongoing promotion of disability sports in their aftermath, the 1964 Paralympics and the differences they made apparent served as an unprecedented means of raising popular and official awareness about the current status of Japan's largely overlooked disabled population. The Games also drew attention to the possibility of providing new methods for helping them succeed. Organizers would have been foolish to miss the opportunity of the Paralympics to seek change by pointing out some of these differences.

At the same time, it is hard not to see the repeated juxtaposition of the "bright" foreign athletes with the less bright or even "dark" Japanese competitors as a negative and stereotypical representation. On the foreign side, these comparisons not only gloss over the stark differences in approaches to disability among the various countries represented at the Games but also fail to distinguish between the varying experiences of people with different types of impairment in those countries. Tellingly, the oft-cited rehabilitation and employment statistics that organizers used to highlight Japan's gap with the West make no such distinctions for either side. The descriptions of foreign athletes also overlook the self-selected nature of those who chose to compete in Tokyo. Traveling to Japan would have been an expensive and challenging undertaking for anyone, and those who decided to make the trip to Tokyo were probably less representative of the disabled populations in their home countries than many of the comparisons seemed to suggest. Such comparisons also rely to a great extent on the omission of details and depictions of the Japanese athletes. We are never told, for instance, if any of the Japanese athletes took advantage of their time in Tokyo to do some sightseeing or whether they, too, were given regular assistance from an army of volunteers, which would have made it much easier (and potentially enjoyable) for them to navigate the far from barrier-free environment in Tokyo. The National Meet component of the Games, which featured many more Japanese athletes than the International Stoke Mandeville Games, also remains strikingly absent from most of these comparisons, precisely because it did not involve large numbers of foreign athletes. When no one sees you, it will be hard for people to know whether you are "bright" or not. Based on the official materials few, if any, of these athletes measured up to any of the foreigners, and if Japan's athletes could not measure up, what might that suggest about other individuals with disabilities? Perhaps the most problematic aspect of these comparisons, then, is the suggestion (sometimes explicit) that a relatively small, probably unrepresentative, and inaccurately depicted group should become the measure of success for Japan's disabled population as whole. Even though promoters were clearly interested in using these comparisons to press for societal, governmental, and medical changes, they simultaneously seem to have produced a dark image of people with disabilities and set a standard that would have made it difficult for many in Japan to overcome that image.

Goodwill Games

As important as the Games were for those interested in improving Japan's approaches to disability, for many, Japan's hour on the Paralympic stage was equally, if not more, significant because of its potential for promoting international goodwill (*kokusai shinzen*). The official Japanese cabinet report on the upcoming Paralympics, for example, cited two explicit goals for the Games: promoting social rehabilitation for the physically disabled and contributing to international goodwill.[137] With a range of people from Guttmann to Prime Minister Ikeda commenting on this perceived benefit of the Games, it would be easy to dismiss this notion as high-minded, but ultimately empty, rhetoric.[138] However, closer consideration of the historical context suggests that promoting international goodwill was, in fact, a pressing concern in Japan. As studies have shown, the 1964 Tokyo Olympics were widely viewed as a critical venue for literally re-presenting Japan to the rest of the world less than twenty years after World War II. The Japan of the Tokyo Games was a peaceful, high-tech, rising economic power ready to take its place among the world's great nations. Conservative leaders in Japan also used the Olympics as an occasion to revive such symbols of nationalism as the emperor, the flag, and the national anthem, symbols that had been associated with Japan's wartime aggression only a few decades earlier.[139]

The Tokyo Paralympics, emerging from this same historical and cultural milieu, proved no less important as a tool for reviving national symbols and bolstering Japan's international prestige.[140] Indeed, viewed in this light, the crown prince's oft-mentioned involvement with the Paralympics reflected more than a personal commitment on his part; it was a carefully cultivated and highly politicized link designed to benefit both the Games and the international reputation of Japan's future monarch. The Paralympics also served as an ideal arena for promoting the new postwar Japan committed to peace and international goodwill. Voluntarily agreeing to organize an international event that only two other European countries had ever hosted was the perfect way for the nation to demonstrate such a global commitment, particularly because the Paralympics were seen as serving an especially "humane" international purpose.[141]

Adding to the sense that Japan should, or perhaps even must, host the Paralympics was the fact that the previous host had been Rome, another city using the Olympics to help negotiate a postwar return to the global community. After all, if Italy had volunteered to host the Paralympics and Japan did not, what would that say about Japan? We might recall, here, Nakamura's warning to Terada about the potential damage to Japan's international reputation should the country fail to bring the Games to Japan. The world was watching, which meant that failure to host the Paralympics and learn from them was not an option that Japan could afford to take.

In the end, of course, Japan did host the Paralympics with marked success. As this chapter has shown, that success and even the very possibility of hosting the Games had never been guaranteed. Driven by diverse agendas, individuals such as Guttmann, Kasai, Nakamura, Watanabe, and a host of others harnessed existing organizational networks, the power of the media, and the prestige of Japan's imperial family to help an emerging transnational movement take root in Japan in a remarkably short period of time. Ultimately, the Tokyo Paralympics had an undeniable—if multifaceted and not always progressive—impact on Japan and the Paralympic Movement. As the following chapters demonstrate, the 1964 Games proved to be a foundational moment for Japan's engagement with disability sports both at home and abroad. Even though Tokyo's Paralympics in 1964 have been long overlooked, their significance cannot be ignored.

Chapter 2

Lost Games

The Far East and South Pacific (FESPIC) Games for the Disabled, 1975–2006

> The achievements of [the] FESPIC Federation in the development of sports for people with disabilities shall be recognized.
>
> Dr. Chang Il Park, 2010

On December 1, 2006, FESPIC disappeared. To be more accurate, with the closing ceremony of the ninth FESPIC Games hosted in Kuala Lumpur, Malaysia, the FESPIC Federation formally merged with the Asian Paralympic Council to become the new Asian Paralympic Committee (APC), and future sports events hosted by this new committee became known as the Asian Para Games. The terms of the merger agreement, several years in the making, specified that FESPIC's pioneering role in promoting disability sports in the region and its more than thirty years' worth of history would be "recognized" and "reflected in the merged organization's constitution."[1]

Given such plans, it seems unlikely that anyone could foresee the extent to which the FESPIC Federation and its Games would fade from popular and institutional memory in the years since 2006. Internet searches for FESPIC in both English and Japanese, for instance, produce brief Wikipedia entries and only a handful of other webpages, most of which include less than a page of incomplete explanation. With the exception of official reports on selected individual Games, original documents related to the federation's more than thirty-year history have proven extremely difficult to access despite initial plans to digitize FESPIC documents.[2] Perhaps not surprisingly then, academic work on FESPIC is limited at best.[3] Turning to the organization explicitly tasked with recognizing FESPIC's role, the APC, a search of its official website in early 2019 produced only six hits for the word "FESPIC," and most were news releases mentioning the FESPIC Games as a precursor for the Asian Para Games, with no further explanation.[4] As specified in the merger agreement, FESPIC's role was mentioned in the APC's original constitution, but the revised version from November 2018 contains no such references.[5] The history section of the APC website begins with the creation of the Asian Paralympic Council in 2002 and fails to provide a single reference to FESPIC or even the merger that created the APC.[6]

It would be easy enough to fault the APC for forgetting, intentionally or not, a significant piece of its own institutional history, but FESPIC's absence from the organization's website and from collective memory more generally raises a number of important issues that merit greater attention. To appreciate why these seemingly lost Games matter, it is essential to understand what the FESPIC Movement was, how it developed, and what it sought to do. The Far East and South Pacific Games for the Disabled, more commonly referred to in English and Japanese as FESPIC (*fesupikku*), were first held in Ōita Prefecture in 1975. Dr. Nakamura Yutaka, who had played a pivotal role in bringing the 1964 Paralympics to Tokyo, was one of the key organizers of this event. It explicitly aimed to promote greater awareness about and opportunities for athletes with disabilities in Asia and the South Pacific, a goal that dovetailed with Japan's efforts to reassume a postwar leadership role in the region. With the success of the first Games, a regional movement was born, and they were ultimately hosted by different countries on nine occasions until they were replaced by the Asian Para Games in 2010. Although the FESPIC Games were initially envisioned as simple rehabilitation-oriented events that could be held even in countries that lacked established programs in disability sports, they became increasingly complex and geared toward elite competition, generating new challenges and tensions. Such trends began to emerge with the 1989 FESPIC Games held in Kobe, Japan. By offering an examination of the origins and development of the FESPIC Games, with attention to the role of Japanese organizers in Ōita and Kobe, this chapter highlights the FESPIC Movement's place in Japan's history of disability sports, thereby serving as a step toward giving it the recognition it deserves within and beyond Japan.

At the same time, exploring FESPIC's relationship with the Paralympic Movement, and especially the FESPIC Federation's absorption by the new APC, serves as an important reminder that the development of the Paralympic organizations we see today was never a forgone conclusion. From their earliest days, the FESPIC Games posed challenges to the larger Paralympic Movement, fostering important changes in the process. The establishment of the APC offers a case study of regional efforts to come to terms

with the emerging International Olympic Committee/International Paralympic Committee (IOC/IPC) juggernaut in international sports. Although
not inevitable, formal integration with the IPC proved increasingly unavoid-
able for organizations like FESPIC, producing underexamined consequences
for disability sports in the region, including changes in regional boundaries
and shifts in organizational goals and ideals. For better or for worse, when
the FESPIC Games disappeared in 2006, certain approaches and opportunities disappeared with them. Like the lost FESPIC Games, these losses, too,
need to be recognized.

Finally, the striking lack of attention that the FESPIC Games have received,
even as disability sports in general have slowly generated wider notice, un-
derscores the need to understand why some events have a larger impact than
others. The earliest FESPIC Games struggled to gain recognition outside their
local areas, and throughout their history they seemed to face a significant prestige gap. Explorations of their history also point to the need to move beyond
commonly held assumptions that hosting such events automatically equates
to long-term legacies. Indeed, if the larger history of a movement like FES-
PIC can be nearly forgotten, it seems especially prudent to document how and
why the impact of such events are remembered or not.

The Origins of a Movement

According to a variety of personal accounts, the history of the FESPIC Movement began with little fanfare—and no formal documentation—as a series of
informal discussions during the third Paralympic Games held in Tel Aviv, Israel, in 1968, followed by another set of conversations during the fourth Paralympics in Heidelberg, West Germany, in 1972. Even though they provide few
specifics, references to these preliminary discussions reveal one of the keys to
the emergence and development of FESPIC: Dr. Nakamura Yutaka. As seen
in the previous and the succeeding chapters, it would be difficult to overstate
Nakamura's role in the history of disability sports in Japan, and this is equally
true for the FESPIC Movement.

Nakamura's own writings about his conversations in Israel when he was
captain of the Japanese Paralympic team in 1968 indicate his enthusiasm about
the idea of launching an international sporting event for those with disabilities in the Asian region. From Nakamura's perspective, Japan needed to assume a leading role in establishing a new set of games that would make
disability sports accessible for those living in the less economically developed
countries of Asia. He also sought to expand on the existing Paralympic ap-

proach by inviting athletes with a wider variety of physical impairments.[7] Encouragement from Australians, Koreans, and others during the 1972 Paralympics only served to fuel his initial interest.[8] Writing in 1975 after the first FESPIC Games, Nakagawa Kazuhiko, one of the Japanese officials involved with the 1972 Heidelberg Paralympics, recalled a string of comments by Nakamura reflecting his growing excitement about the prospects of organizing this event: "'We could do it!' 'I'd really like to do it!' 'If we used Taiyō no Ie, surely we'd have enough rooms and venue spaces.' 'I'd like to re-create the Tokyo Paralympics!' 'We should see about planning this!'"[9] In other words, the seed for the FESPIC Games had been planted.

Unfortunately, others involved in the promotion of sports for those with disabilities in Japan proved less enthusiastic. Nakamura noted that many people, including Kasai Yoshisuke, head of the Japan Sports Association for the Disabled (JSAD), initially dismissed the idea as unrealistic given the region's political instability and economic challenges.[10] For his part, Kasai cited not only his own reluctance but also the Ministry of Health and Welfare's concerns about the potential cost of such an event. Yet as Kasai observed, Nakamura was not the type of person to let such concerns stop him. Once he decided on a course of action, he pursued it wholeheartedly; monetary and other issues were always secondary concerns, much to the chagrin, Kasai noted, of government officials.[11]

In the face of resistance at the national level, Nakamura adopted a different tack, seeking support at both the local and the international level first. Beginning with Taiyō no Ie, the company he established in 1965, Nakamura announced at the 1973 year-end board of directors meeting that he wanted to host an international sports meet in Ōita Prefecture as part of the ten-year anniversary celebrations for the company.[12] In other cases, Nakamura linked the soon-to-be FESPIC Games with the celebration of the planned construction of a sports center for the disabled in Beppu, as well as recognition of the fact that the Ministry of Health and Welfare had designated Beppu as one of only six model social welfare cities in Japan.[13] Thanks in no small part to his prominence in the region, an issue explored in greater detail in the following chapter, Nakamura's efforts to build support for these Games in Ōita benefited from his local reputation and political connections. In February 1974, Nakamura held multiple meetings with prefectural government staff, leading to the establishment on February 18 of a preparatory committee for hosting the first FESPIC Games in Ōita. Reframing the event as a local affair with an international component was a clever marketing technique, one that proved to be a trademark of later FESPIC Games as well. As Nakamura himself observed, unlike the Paralympics this was not "national business."[14]

At the same time that he was building support for the FESPIC Games on the ground in Ōita, Nakamura was also seeking international backing, including making inquiries to Australia and sending a formal letter dated February 15, 1974, to Sir Ludwig Guttmann, the head of the International Stoke Mandeville Games Federation. Nakamura's letter sought Guttmann's blessing for establishing the new "Pan-Pacific Sports Games" as a way to celebrate local events in Ōita and promote disability sports in the broader region.[15] Guttmann's response, dated February 20, 1974, congratulated Nakamura on the local achievements and largely affirmed his support of Nakamura's plan, though he explicitly noted that "it would be a fundamental mistake to mix these Games with the Games of other disabilities."[16] Guttmann also expressed concern that using the name Pan-Pacific might generate confusion, because of its similarity to the name of the Pan-American Games, which also included countries on the Pacific Ocean. Guttmann's suggested regional name, the Far East and South Pacific, would eventually become part of the new Games' name and the source of the commonly used acronym FESPIC (Far East and South Pacific).

Although it seems likely that Nakamura was in regular contact with officials in Tokyo throughout this early planning stage, there are presently no records of any such interactions, and it was only after he had already secured both local and international backing that Nakamura and other representatives from Ōita officially took his plan to Tokyo, meeting with officials from the Ministry of Health and Welfare and JSAD on March 22 to iron out the details of supporting and sponsoring organizations, venues, time frames, and the list of invitees. A month later Nakamura traveled to Singapore for the first FESPIC planning meeting, where he met with Mr. C. Goh and Dr. Robert Don from Singapore and Dr. John Grant and Mr. Graham Pryke of Australia. Among other key decisions, participants at this international meeting drafted a list of invited countries. During the next few months there were many organizational and sponsorship meetings in Ōita and Tokyo. Finally, on October 8, Nakamura met in Singapore with representatives from Australia, New Zealand, Indonesia, and Singapore to draft and approve a constitution for the new FESPIC Federation. Four days later he was back in Ōita when Kasai and the head of the rehabilitation section of the Ministry of Health and Welfare both visited the city to inaugurate the First FESPIC Games Executive Committee. This new committee was now charged with organizing—in less than seven months—what was to become the first-ever international event hosted by Ōita, as well as a trailblazing event in the history of disability sports.[17]

Organizational and logistical hurdles aside (and there were many as noted later), the greatest challenges facing these new FESPIC Games stemmed directly from the very issues that had been previously raised as obstacles, namely regional politics and economics. Promoting international goodwill and overcoming boundaries of all sorts were among the oft-mentioned goals for FESPIC from the beginning, but the Games understandably proved unable to escape the reality of their geopolitical moment. For instance, North Korea, North Vietnam, and Taiwan (which was no longer recognized internationally as the official government of China) were all notably absent from the list of twenty-four invitees. South Vietnam, China, Laos, and the Khmer Republic were all invited to the first FESPIC Games, but domestic politics and in several cases, ongoing wars prevented these countries from sending participants to Ōita.[18]

Nakamura seemed to be particularly disappointed by China's lack of participation, despite the personal letters of request he sent to both Mao Zedong and Zhou Enlai after a group of Chinese studying sports had visited Taiyō no Ie. When he did not receive any response (which would not be surprising given the political situation in China at the time), Nakamura followed up with the Chinese Embassy, only to have his request for Chinese participation summarily dismissed with the claim that "the disabled do not play sports in China."[19]

In contrast, South Vietnam initially promised to send four participants, and the Games organizers had already dispatched funds to pay for their travel to Japan. When the individual serving as their point of contact in South Vietnam committed suicide after Saigon fell, organizers were unable to establish contact with the potential participants or anyone else under the new government.[20] Clearly, the early 1970s were not the ideal time to launch any sort of regional event in Asia, let alone one that aimed to promote sports for those with disabilities.

FESPIC organizers could do little to counter the negative impacts of political instability in the region. They could and did, however, find ways to address financial barriers to participation. Overcoming such barriers was a primary motivation for establishing the FESPIC Games in the first place, and many of the tactics, goals, and structures that organizers used to maximize participation in the first Games in Ōita became central elements of the larger FESPIC Movement. Both before and after these Games, Nakamura in particular adopted a missionary's zeal in promoting the gospel of sports for those with disabilities in the FESPIC region. In doing so, he never failed to highlight the financial and social challenges present in Asia and the ways in which FESPIC could help overcome them.[21]

One of Nakamura's key talking points was the gap in access to disability sports between developed and developing nations, a category that included many of the countries in Asia. As Nakamura pointed out, international sporting events for the disabled such as the International Stoke Mandeville Games or the Paralympics were almost all based and held in Europe or North America. Combined with the difficulties of long-distance trips for those with disabilities, travel expenses made it virtually impossible for people from developing nations in Asia to participate in these events. Even a cursory survey of the lists of participating countries at such events bears this out, and increased Asian participation in the Paralympic Games eventually became a point of pride for FESPIC organizers.

Travel costs, however, were not the only issue. At the time of the first FESPIC Games, a majority of countries in the region lacked the sort of rehabilitation or social welfare systems that could maintain and promote disability sports. For many people who were living with disabilities in such environments, meeting basic needs and dealing with social stigma were far more pressing concerns than preparing to compete in an international sports event. Japan, Australia, and New Zealand had more developed social welfare programs, as well as established track records in disability sports competition, but they were the exceptions in the region. In Nakamura's view, the lack of such programs was a problem to which FESPIC could be the answer.

Nakamura's vision, one shared by others in the region, crystallized in the initial constitution for the FESPIC Federation, which went into effect in October 1974. Although the constitution and structure of the organization were subject to revisions over the next thirty-plus years, the values articulated in this first charter continued to serve as the federation's polestar. Thus the "Aims and Objects" section of the constitution, the second longest in the entire document, merits quoting in full:

The aims and objects of the games are to

a) promote the general interest and welfare of the handicapped peoples of the member countries through participation in sports events and activities.
b) deepen the mutual understanding and the friendship of the handicapped of the member countries.
c) maintain and strengthen the remaining functions of the handicapped.
d) develop research and study techniques in relation to the rehabilitation of handicapped people.
e) exchange information and material relating to handicapped people as a means for providing further assistance to them in rehabilitation.
f) create and continue to hold regularly games, sports competitions involving handicapped peoples of the member countries.

g) acquire, print, publish, and circulate such books, brochures and any other writing as may be conducive to the attainment of and the furtherance of the aims and objects of FESPIC.
h) co-operate, act in conjunction with or affiliate with any other body in respect of any matters or games which may be deemed to be in accordance with the aims and objectives of FESPIC and to do all things incidental thereto.
i) establish good relations with champions and athletes and their respective organizations.[22]

It is telling here that the hosting of sporting events was not anywhere near the top of the list, coming in sixth of nine aims. Even though this document established a new regional sporting event, the event itself was only a means to an end. This new organization and its Games were *not* focused on sports as competition or even sport for sport's sake. The ultimate goal was the promotion of social welfare and rehabilitation in member countries "through the participation in sports events and activities."

In adopting this approach, the FESPIC Federation reflected not only the times but also the backgrounds of its organizers. Much like those who organized the 1964 Tokyo Paralympics, most of FESPIC's founders were nondisabled men with backgrounds in medicine or social welfare services. Having seen the effects of promoting sports for the disabled in their own societies, these organizers were thoroughly convinced of the benefits of the rehabilitation-through-sports approach. They were also committed to using the resources at their disposal to assure that others in the region had similar opportunities.

Echoing many of the post-Paralympic analyses discussed in the previous chapter, FESPIC promoters frequently referenced Japan's experience as an implicit model for possibilities in the region. In the narratives they employed, the exposure to European and American athletes at the Paralympics had not only inspired Japan's athletes but also jump-started Japan's mostly nonexistent disability sports programs and prompted changes in social attitudes and rehabilitation practices. With ten years of development in disability sports since the Tokyo Games, Japan was now in a position, and perhaps even duty bound, to take up the mantle of leadership and foster change for the rest of Asia.

To be sure, such historical references were fraught with potentially misleading oversimplifications, as well as striking similarities to earlier imperialist pan-Asian discourses, but the primary lesson that Nakamura and others seemed to draw from the Tokyo experience had to do with the benefits of exposure. As Nakamura repeatedly asserted, there was meaning in having even a single participant represent a country at the FESPIC Games.[23] For athletes from developing nations who were encountering disability sports often for the first time, these Games would help them realize and maintain their "remaining functions," as the constitution put it, ideally improving their lives in the process. At the same time, deepening "mutual understanding" with those who had already benefited from sports and observing the social welfare situation in places like Japan would alert these athletes and any accompanying officials to the gaps in their systems at home and inspire them to pursue change. In this sense, the Games were also a chance to demonstrate Japan's level of development to both foreign and domestic participants, as reflected in comments by Japanese participants and coaches on the shortcomings they had witnessed outside Japan. Where Japanese athletes had been portrayed as "dark" in connection with the Tokyo Paralympics, now they were the ones exemplifying brightness. The fostering of friendships, development of research, sharing of resources, and circulation of information called for in FESPIC's constitution were all meant to help athletes from other parts of Asia brighten their lives and change their societies.

Of course, the benefits of exposure to disability sports as exemplified by the Japanese Paralympic case were meant to extend well beyond the participants themselves. By giving athletes with disabilities the opportunity to compete as representatives of their nations at an international sporting event, FESPIC organizers sought to awaken governments and entire societies to the fact that individuals with disabilities were far more than victims, charity cases, or invalids: they were people who could contribute to their societies if they were given the opportunity to do so. Although systemic change would require more than a single event, FESPIC, like the Paralympics that inspired them, would ideally serve as a tool for transforming social perceptions of and approaches to disability throughout the region.

Reflecting the larger goal of generating exposure, several of the provisions in FESPIC's constitution were crafted to facilitate participation for the widest possible range of athletes. The "Rules for FESPIC Games" section, for example, includes a distinction between rules that would govern the paraplegic or quadriplegic athletes and those that applied to athletes with other forms of impairment. Given the complex classification system in Paralympic sports events today, the reference to different categories of rules for FESPIC does not appear all that remarkable, but if one considers Guttmann's earlier explicit warning to Nakamura about avoiding the "fundamental mistake" of including participants with different types of disabilities, the implications of this seemingly simple distinction are immediately apparent. From its inception, FESPIC was a multi-disability, international sporting event.

At the time this approach was unique, though not entirely unprecedented, as noted in chapter 1. In fact, as described by Ujiie Kaoru, an official with JSAD, the initial design of the structure of the first FESPIC Games was similar to that of Tokyo's event: it involved both an international and a local section, though both were meant to be held simultaneously. The international part would feature only wheelchair athletes, whereas the local one would include athletes from Ōita with a variety of physical disabilities. The specific timing remains unclear, but at some point before the drafting of the constitution in October 1974, requests to participate from foreign athletes without spinal cord injuries led organizers to modify the initial plan and open the event to athletes with a variety of physical impairments.[24] The end result was arguably the first truly multi-disability, international sporting event, but one that was perfectly aligned with existing Japanese approaches to disability sports, because Japan's annual National Sports Meet for the Disabled had been a multi-disability event from its inception in 1965. Perhaps with those experiences in mind, Nakamura had reportedly approached Guttmann multiple times in previous years about the possibility of opening international events like the Paralympics and the International Stoke Mandeville Games to a wider range of disability groups, only to have Guttmann repeatedly dismiss such suggestions as "premature."[25] According to Nakamura, it was only after he witnessed the success of the first FESPIC Games in Ōita that Guttmann acknowledged the viability and benefits of such an approach, a conversion that Nakamura regarded as one of the key legacies of these Games.[26]

The early emphasis on creating a multi-disability event exemplified FESPIC organizers' commitment to broadening the range of possible participants; so, too, did their unique ideal that at least 30 percent of the athletes from each team should be first-time participants in international competition. According to both founding board member Dr. John Grant and former federation president Dr. Hatada Kazuo, the "30 percent novices" ideal was developed at the October 1974 organizational meeting as a way to generate even more exposure for disability sports in the region.[27] This approach clearly reflected the Games' rehabilitation-oriented roots, and the ideal was later incorporated formally into the federation's principles in the lead-up to the third Games in Hong Kong. Despite the trends toward professionalization that came to define the Olympic and Paralympic Games during this period, FESPIC's distinctive approach to participation continued to serve as a guiding ideal for member countries until its dissolution in 2006.

In some respects, the notion of opening the Games to novices also extended to hosting. In the constitution, the section addressing future FESPIC Games provides only the most basic criteria for potential hosts: "The Games shall be held in the country which has advised the Board of its willingness to host the Games." The vagueness of this statement indicates far more than FESPIC's rudimentary organizational structure in 1974 (though that was certainly the case). For one, the founding members of FESPIC were coming primarily from societies with more developed programs in sports for those with disabilities, so organizers probably assumed—correctly, it turned out—that the countries expressing a willingness to host these Games in the immediate future would be their own. At the same time, the lack of any criteria aside from willingness was arguably intentional: organizers wanted to leave open the possibility that any society interested in doing so could serve as a host. As the oft-cited example of Tokyo in 1964 demonstrated, holding an international sporting event for those with disabilities was seen as perhaps the best way to generate exposure and thereby foster change in the society serving as host. Nakamura, in particular, was adamant about his desire to keep these Games as simple as possible so that they could be held anywhere, and he often pointed to the decision to host them in the "countryside" of Ōita rather than a large metropolis like Tokyo or Osaka as a calculated example for future Games. As he put it, "My approach to FESPIC began with the hope that we could hold these kinds of events for people with disabilities in any country, even in a place where we might have to drink coconut juice under palms on a beach. I wanted to create an event where even the poorest nation could serve as a host country."[28] What one observer characterized somewhat critically as the "handmade" feel of the early FESPIC Games thus stemmed from both the challenges this new organization faced and the founders' goals of fostering accessibility and exposure.[29]

Naturally, for FESPIC to be accessible, Game organizers had to find a way to address financial barriers to participation and hosting that had sparked the creation of FESPIC in the first place. It is not surprising, then, that the constitution includes a section titled "Expenses of FESPIC Games," which has the following single provision: "The country member hosting the games shall be responsible for the expenses internally incurred in respect to the [p]articipating athletes, their officials and escorts, together with those expenses involved in the staging of the games." This statement is remarkable as much for its understatement as its ambition. Beginning with Ōita, any host site was agreeing to pay not only for the expected costs of organizing and running the Games but also domestic travel, lodging, and food expenses for an unspecified number of people for an unspecified number of days. Even a smaller scale, "handmade" event would not be cheap for the host, and considering FESPIC's goal of increasing participation in disability sports in the region, it was only going to get more expensive.

Given the widely acknowledged financial disparities in the region, this approach to funding assumed that wealthier member nations in FESPIC would find ways to underwrite the costs of participation for developing countries. In other words, the survival of the FESPIC Games and their ability to pursue, let alone achieve, their goals depended almost entirely on voluntary contributions from particular governments, corporations, NGOs, and individuals. The ultimate success of the first Games in securing such contributions, as well as the continuation and growth of the Games over the following decades, indicated that FESPIC organizers had devised a unique approach that resonated with people in the region.

At the same time, the funding approach outlined in the constitution faced both short- and long-term problems. After hearing from several countries that they wanted to participate but could only do so if funds were provided to cover the costs of traveling to Japan, organizers in Ōita realized that paying for the participants only after they arrived at the Games was not enough. Nakamura had already secured support from local and national governments in Japan to cover the Games and related costs within Japan, but it was unlikely that these governments would be willing or able to contribute additional funds to offset international travel expenses. As noted later, Nakamura ultimately secured the necessary resources with a tactic used previously in Tokyo for the Paralympics: mass fundraising and other private contributions. Similar tactics were used to address another problem that became apparent as the Games continued: the limited availability of proper equipment, including wheelchairs, for the participants.

In the long term, these newly apparent costs, when combined with those already outlined in the constitution, seemed to threaten Nakamura's goal of creating an event that any country could host. After all, if Japan was scrambling to hold the first Games, how could the FESPIC model be sustainable? In the end, FESPIC's track record of not one but nine Games, with several held in countries classified as developing nations at the time, tells us that organizers repeatedly found ways to meet the needs—financial and otherwise—of the Games' participants. That they did so while maintaining the organization's early commitments to making these Games as accessible as possible for people with disabilities in the region makes that accomplishment all the more noteworthy. Yet, the future of FESPIC might have looked very different, indeed, if the first Games in Ōita had not, in the words of Dr. John Grant, "guaranteed that this concept was something worthwhile."[30]

The Inaugural FESPIC Games: Ōita

On May 29, 1975, two chartered All Nippon Airways (ANA) Boeing 727s arrived at Ōita airport from Hong Kong. On board were the majority of the international participants for the first FESPIC Games. The story behind the arrival of these flights in many ways exemplified the logistical, financial, and organizational struggles that went into holding the Games in Ōita. When it became apparent that travel costs were going to be a barrier, organizers reached out to ANA about the possibility of arranging a charter flight direct from Hong Kong to Ōita, since this would be cheaper and more direct than a series of individual flights routed through Tokyo. The airline agreed to offer one plane at a reduced cost of 3 million yen. As the number of participants increased, a single plane proved too small, prompting a request for a second charter. Perhaps understandably, ANA balked, insisting that the costs would be much higher because they would need to reassign a plane from an existing route to meet the request. In what Kasai called "a feat that only Nakamura could pull off," Nakamura proceeded to telephone Diet member and former minister of transportation Hashimoto Tomisaburō to seek his intercession with the airline. In the end, ANA agreed to accept only 6 million yen for the two charters.[31]

The direct international flights to Ōita posed problems in addition to cost. Ōita did not have an international airport, which meant that it did not have the immigrations and customs offices necessary for people to enter Japan. Although Nakamura had suggested that temporary facilities and staff could be arranged to accommodate participants at the Games, this proposal was dismissed out of hand by the Ministry of Justice and the Ministry of Finance. It was only through mobilizing Kasai's connections in the Ministry of Health and Welfare that the relevant ministries were convinced—almost certainly pressured—to relent and create temporary offices in Ōita.[32]

Even as these sorts of logistical and financial concerns were being addressed, it was not an easy task to assure that the participants would actually be on the planes. For one, the political instability in the region raised the potential for unexpected events to prevent travel, as exemplified most clearly by the situation in South Vietnam. Nakamura also reported that it took repeated efforts to establish contact with the relevant parties in many countries, and there were often substantial gaps and lags in communication, a challenge no doubt amplified by the fact that many of the people involved were communicating in non-native languages.[33] Whether it was because of these sorts of communication gaps, the inherent complications of international travel, politics, or something else altogether, the participants from Pakistan and Burma actually missed the charters, and organizer were forced to scramble to find them flights through Tokyo that allowed them to arrive in Ōita in time for the Games.[34] As Nakamura observed somewhat understatedly, organizing this event "necessitated perseverance."[35]

In the end, that perseverance paid off. When the opening ceremony of the first Games convened at 10 a.m. on June 1, 1975, a standing-room-only crowd of more than 25,000 gathered at Ōita City Athletic Stadium to cheer the entrance of 973 participants representing eighteen countries from throughout the Asia-Pacific region. As host, Japan fielded more than two-thirds of the participants, with 207 escorts or officials, 484 athletes from Ōita, and 58 from other prefectures. International participants included 148 athletes and 76 accompanying officials, though nine of the countries had delegations of only 3 people each. In keeping with the ideals of FESPIC, most of these smaller delegations represented developing nations like Bangladesh, Nepal, and Papua New Guinea that were sending teams to an international sporting event for the disabled for the first time; in most cases their participation had been contingent on securing the travel assistance that FESPIC provided.[36] Participants also demonstrated the viability of FESPIC's goal of establishing a multi-disability regional event: both domestic and international teams included athletes with a variety of physical impairments. In addition to Stoke-Mandeville-style events for wheelchair athletes, the Games in Ōita involved competitions for blind and deaf participants, as well as events for competitors with cerebral palsy, amputations, or other conditions that are now classified as *les autres*.

Nakamura is said to have crafted nearly every detail of the opening ceremony so that it would be inspiring without being extravagant, an approach linked to his desire to make it seem both desirable and possible to host the FESPIC Games anywhere.[37] With teams from poorer regions in mind, Nakamura insisted, for instance, that Japanese athletes attend the ceremony wearing everyday clothes, rather than a team uniform. The traditional procession of athletes, complete with internationally themed marching music and Japanese Self-Defense Force personnel carrying national flags, was complemented by a ceremonial torch lighting. In a ritual meant to symbolize both a fighting spirit and friendship, a hearing-impaired athlete from Sri Lanka and another from a local Ōita school for the deaf entered simultaneously from opposite sides of the stadium carrying torches, crossed in front of the main stands, and then circled halfway around the stadium to come together to light a ceremonial torch as music played, fireworks boomed, and the flag for the FESPIC Games was raised for the first time.[38] Two days earlier in a ceremony held on the rooftop of the hotel housing the international athletes, participants from Korea and New Zealand had used glass lenses to light what Nakamura called the "fire of the sun," which then served as the source of the flames for the two torches used at the opening ceremony.[39]

In keeping with the Games' inspirational goals, Nakamura selected Yoshinaga Eiji to offer the athletes' oath. Only months earlier, Yoshinaga, a Taiyō no Ie employee, had been elected to the Beppu City Council, becoming Japan's first elected official in a wheelchair. Fulfilling Nakamura's request from more than a year earlier, Sir Ludwig Guttmann also attended the Games and offered words of welcome at the ceremony. For Nakamura, having the "father of the Paralympics" present at the disability sports event he was hosting in his hometown was clearly a highlight, perhaps especially because Guttmann's involvement in the opening ceremony was a de facto endorsement of FESPIC and its goals. In addition to Guttmann, a number of national and local dignitaries were invited to participate in the opening ceremony, but much like the Tokyo Paralympics, pride of place at the ceremony and the Games as a whole went to Crown Prince Akihito, who together with Princess Michiko spent four days in Ōita during the FESPIC Games. The crown prince had continued, since 1964, to actively support disability sports in Japan, particularly by attending the annual National Sports Meets for the Disabled, which were held in a different prefecture each year. In that sense, his involvement with FESPIC—as well as the treatment his role received in official Japanese-language materials—was not so surprising, nor were his words of welcome strikingly different from his comments eleven years earlier at the Paralympics or those he shared yearly at the National Games. In fact, what seems to have resonated most with participants at the Games was not his speech but the couple's direct engagement with the athletes. Both foreign and domestic athletes and officials commented on the unique pleasure of exchanging greetings with the royal couple or the honor of having them cheer them on in a competition.[40] The crown prince's involvement with FESPIC helped make the Games even more memorable for all involved, which is exactly what Nakamura and other organizers were hoping for.

After the opening ceremony ended, the focus turned to the sporting events until the Games concluded on June 3. The first FESPIC Games featured eight sports with medals awarded in several hundred distinct categories. Venues for the first day were concentrated in Ōita City, and in Beppu for the final two days. In contrast to today's highly regulated events, the competitions in Ōita appear to have been far more open and loosely officiated. As Hatada recalled, the athletes who arrived at the Games were at times not the same ones listed in the original registration materials, and on several occasions athletes would sign up for a new or different event on the spot.[41] Many athletes were participating in disability sports competition for the first time, which meant that they were unaware of the competitions open to them and unfamiliar with the rules as well. In this sense, they were not alone, because some of the officials also lacked expertise in the sports they were tasked with administrating.[42] Although this approach to the Games was perfectly in line with FESPIC's rehabilitation-oriented goals of generating exposure by making disability sports accessible to the widest range of participants, it was unlikely to generate anything close to elite-level performances.[43]

Nevertheless, comments from participants, organizers, and local residents suggest that the Games produced a number of memorable athletic moments. Among the most commonly cited was the running performance of a 13-year-old Nepalese girl dubbed "Suriya-chan" in many Japanese references. Even though she did not meet the minimum age requirement, she was admitted as a special participant, joining another amputee as the only two athletes representing Nepal. Her completion of her race using a pair of crutches elicited widespread praise and multiple photos, making her a literal poster child for these Games and their goals.[44] For Nakamura, the dominant performances of Japan's multiple wheelchair basketball teams were particularly meaningful as a symbol of how far disability sports had come in Japan. Recalling Japan's humiliating 57–7 loss to a team from the Philippines in 1964—a loss all the more shameful because the empress herself had been present—Nakamura recounted his inability to avoid excited outbursts as the basketball team from Taiyō no Ie soundly defeated another team from the Philippines as the crown prince and princess watched. In the end, basketball teams from Japan finished as both champions and runners-up. The medal tally reveals Japanese dominance as well, with Japan winning 249 golds and 539 medals in all, nearly four times as many medals as Australia, the next closest national team.[45] Japan's results no doubt reflected the disproportionate size of the home team, but they also provided a clear indication that unlike the situation in 1964, disability sports had established a strong presence in Japan, especially in Ōita. To be sure, medal tables never convey the whole story, and in this case the criteria for medal categories were especially unclear. However, it is telling, and in many ways representative of FESPIC, that each country participating in these Games went home with at least one medal winner. As a means of exposing people in the region to sports for those with physical disabilities, the first FESPIC Games had made a good start.

With the conclusion of the first FESPIC Games on June 3, 1975, the Game's flag was passed on to Australia, the next host country. Though no one knew this at the time, this flag would be flown at every FESPIC Games until it was taken down for the final time in Kuala Lumpur in 2006.[46] Nakamura used his off-the-cuff English-language closing remarks to remind everyone present at the closing ceremony that the sports they had enjoyed over the past three days were just a means to an end: "Sports are important. However, employment is even more important. Let's work together to promote rehabilitation!"[47] This unambiguous reinforcement of FESPIC's goals officially brought an end to the Games, but before the international athletes left Ōita via their chartered flight on June 6, they were treated to an organized sightseeing trip in the area. Their final day in Japan was dedicated to visiting Taiyō no Ie and other social welfare facilities in Beppu. While the athletes were touring, organizers held a rehabilitation conference in Ōita that led to the establishment of the FESPIC Information Center for the Disabled. Based at Taiyō no Ie, the new Information Center was tasked with publishing news about the Games, disability sports, and rehabilitation in the region.

The study tours, conference, and new Information Center were all integral elements of the larger FESPIC plan to expose people not only to disability sports but also to rehabilitation and social welfare approaches so that they might be inspired to pursue changes at home. In the process, of course, they also highlighted Japan's facilities, and it is worth noting that a number of the international FESPIC participants established ties with Taiyō no Ie either before or after the Games. All of the Korean athletes at the Games, for instance, had arrived in Beppu in late 1974 to spend a year training at Taiyō no Ie. During their time there, they began participating in sports, and after a complicated back-and-forth exchange with the South Korean government, which wanted to assure that these young athletes would not embarrass the nation with their performances, these five teenagers became Korea's only representatives at the first FESPIC Games. In another case, one of the officials with the Indonesian team, Mr. Masgiakhir, became interested in the work of Taiyō no Ie during the Games. With the support of the newly established FESPIC Rehabilitation Fund described later, he and Mr. Slamat, a patient from his rehabilitation facility in Indonesia, arrived in Ōita in December 1975 to spend two months training at Taiyō no Ie.[48] Ten years after its founding, Taiyō no Ie was proving its viability at home. Now, thanks in part to Nakamura's efforts with FESPIC, it was simultaneously gaining regional attention for its approach to improving the lives of those with disabilities.[49] As these examples suggest, the relationship between Taiyō no Ie and FESPIC established during the first Games would continue to play an integral role in the disability sports movement even after the Games themselves moved to other sites.

Another cause for optimism about FESPIC's future became apparent as the final financial accounts for the Games in Ōita were tallied. Funding had been a primary concern from the beginning. Yet the first FESPIC Games ended with a sizable surplus, thanks to organizational penny-pinching, the heavy reliance on volunteers, resourceful approaches to lodging and transportation, official sponsorships, and especially the fundraising efforts of the aptly named Society for Allowing Developing Nations to Participate in FESPIC. Sources documenting specific costs are lacking, but organizers seem to have operated with minimal budgets for organizational expenses to maximize resources for other aspects of the Games.[50] Based on the sheer number of Taiyō no Ie employees and local government staff engaged in chairing or serving on the various organizational subcommittees, it appears that Nakamura and prefectural organizers kept costs down in part by relying on their own employees for staffing instead of hiring new people.[51] Much like the Tokyo Paralympics, FESPIC was heavily dependent on volunteers, ranging from school groups greeting athletes at the airport and Self-Defense Force members carrying flags at the opening ceremony, to translators from the Japanese Red Cross Language Service, and a variety of medical specialists who assisted with classification for competition.

Organizers also found ways to cut costs on key Game-related expenses like lodging and transportation. Lacking both the time and the funds to establish a formal Athletes' Village, they opted to use the Ōita Nishitetsu Grand Hotel to house the international guests. In addition to providing a discounted per-person rate of 5,000 yen, which included three meals per day for eight nights and nine days, the hotel made minor modifications to rooms to make them more accessible. Small tables were installed at wheelchair height in bathrooms to facilitate bathing, and doorknobs were changed to make doors easier to use for those with upper limb impairments. The hotel also served as the final headquarters for the organizing committee and provided venues for reception halls and cultural exchange rooms staffed full-time with volunteer translators.[52]

In terms of transportation, organizers ultimately benefited, as noted earlier, from the initially less-than-enthusiastic support of Japan's major airlines in getting the international athletes to Ōita. For local ground transport, a major hassle and expense for any large event, they relied on the local branch of the Ground Self-Defense Forces, particularly for assistance with unloading and boarding the planes and trips to and from the airport.[53] Just before the Games started, Ōita also took delivery of a so-called social welfare bus, equipped with a lift and an interior designed to accommodate up to seventeen passengers with physical disabilities. At a cost of nearly 10 million yen, the bus seems to have been purchased using funds earmarked for Ōita and Beppu's development as model social welfare cities, rather than from monies linked to the Games. Nonetheless, as the headline of a local news story "The FESPIC Athletes' 'Legs'" revealed, the arrival of the bus just in time for the Games was more than coincidence.[54] A few days later, a second bus, this one a gift from the Japanese Automobile Manufacturer's Association, was delivered to Taiyō no Ie.[55] Although the buses were perhaps the most dramatic—and long-lasting—examples of donations, FESPIC benefited from similar in-kind donations of goods and services from more than seventy companies and individuals throughout Japan, ranging from the local Coca Cola bottler to Sony subsidiaries.[56]

Despite Nakamura's calls to hold the Games as a celebration of Taiyō no Ie's tenth anniversary, he was well aware that the company could never afford to organize this event on its own. Officially, the first FESPIC Games were hosted under the auspices of JSAD and the Ōita Sports Association for the Disabled, with sponsorship from the Ministry of Health and Welfare and the local governments of Ōita Prefecture, Ōita City, and Beppu City. Final funding figures indicated that JSAD provided approximately 54 million yen, a total that included 15 million acquired from the central government and another 29 million from the Japanese Bicycle Promotion Association. Ōita Prefecture contributed 11 million yen, and the cities of Ōita and Beppu gave 5 million each. Combined with an additional 500,000 yen from the Ōita Sports Association for the Disabled and another 300,000 yen from additional unspecified income streams, the resources from official sponsors totaled slightly less than 76 million yen—a generous amount for a new event. Unfortunately, this figure was still 12 million yen short of actual Games-related expenses, not including the more than 12 million needed to cover the costs for international travel for participants.[57]

The financial gap was covered—and exceeded—by a range of voluntary contributions. More than 14 million yen was gathered locally in Ōita, with nearly 7 million of that provided by Taiyō no Ie and its workers. Another 18 million was collected from other areas in Japan and especially from Tokyo. The Society for Allowing Developing Nations to Participate in FESPIC served as the driving force behind these funding efforts. When it became apparent that official sources were going to be inadequate, and especially that athletes from developing nations would only be able to participate with subsidies for international travel, two early supporters of Nakamura's efforts at Taiyō no Ie—radio celebrity and social critic, Akiyama Chieko, and cofounder of Sony, Ibuka Masaru, created this new fundraising organization to support the first Games. Ibuka solicited donations from business circles, and Akiyama worked with volunteer women's groups. She was especially well known for renting booth space and hosting what became annual FESPIC fundraising bazaars at Tokyo's famed Setagaya Boro-Ichi Flea Market, which was held yearly in December. The group's original goal was to raise 7 million yen to cover the travel costs for selected nations to attend the Games in Ōita, but it eventually succeeded in raising more than three times that amount.[58] The donations gathered for FESPIC not only covered the multimillion-yen budgetary shortfall for the Games and the 12 million yen needed for international travel expenses but also left a surplus of more than 8 million yen. This surplus enabled the creation of the FESPIC Rehabilitation Fund to be used to support participation in future Games, as well as other rehabilitation activities in the region.[59] As FESPIC continued to develop, the FESPIC Rehabilitation Fund initiated by these Japanese fundraisers truly became international in nature, and together with various other forms of voluntary contributions, it would prove critical to the continuity of the Games.[60]

From their earliest conversations, FESPIC organizers conceptualized these Games as an international event that would continue to serve the region long after the athletes left Ōita. Indeed, the first FESPIC Games provided a strong foundation for the continuation of the FESPIC Movement, demonstrating that there was interest in promoting disability sports throughout the region that could be mobilized given adequate resources. In particular, organizers' approaches to participation in Ōita modeled not only the viability but also the desirability of creating future multi-disability international events open to all skill levels, a legacy that extended beyond the FESPIC region itself. Guaranteeing the availability of resources to maintain these approaches would continue to pose a challenge for FESPIC organizers, but the generous support that the Games enjoyed in Ōita, and especially the creation of the FESPIC Rehabilitation Fund, suggested the possibility of—and a means for—overcoming these sorts of financial obstacles. Institutionally, the first Games clearly served as a prototype for later events, proving the value of securing both local backing and recognition from key political figures; they also highlighted the potential necessity and effectiveness of relying on nongovernmental volunteers and organizations for support. The establishment of both the Information Center and the permanent office for the FESPIC Secretariat at Taiyō no Ie also provided the movement with a secure base of operations, which could foster and preserve institutional know-how, even as the Games rotated to new sites. The first FESPIC Games may have ended, but the FESPIC Movement was just beginning.

Gaining Momentum: The Early Games

As significant as the first FESPIC Games in Ōita were to the broader movement, they might have proven little more than an interesting footnote in the history of disability sports if the Games themselves had not continued over the next thirty years. The first three Games following those in Ōita reflected disability sports' development as a work-in-progress. With each of these events, the Games as a whole continued to gain institutional momentum, helping ensure their survival despite the unique challenges at each host site. Although it would only be apparent in retrospect, the fifth FESPIC Games held in Kobe, Japan, in September 1989 proved a moment of transition for the FESPIC Movement in several respects. For one, the Kobe Games maintained the core values of earlier events, but set new benchmarks in terms of scale, competitiveness, and organizational complexity, initiating patterns and trends that would continue until the dissolution of FESPIC in 2006. The Games in Kobe were also the last FESPIC events held before the creation of the International Paralympic Committee in late September 1989. The last four FESPIC Games would be characterized by increasing cooperation and integration with the IPC, culminating in the formal end of FESPIC after the ninth Games in Kuala Lumpur.

The difficulties facing the second FESPIC Games, which were held from November 20–26, 1977, in Australia serve as a reminder of just how tenuous the future of FESPIC was early on.[61] The city of Perth, which had hosted the British Commonwealth Paraplegic Games in 1962, was originally slated to host the FESPIC Games in 1977, but after the state government in Western Australia refused to provide funds, organizers scrambled to organize the Games in Parramatta, a suburb of Dr. Grant's home city of Sydney. Much like those in Ōita, the second Games were dependent on a combination of public and private financing, complemented by a heavy reliance on volunteers. Participation in Parramatta was once again heavily subsidized for a number of countries, thanks in part to the FESPIC Rehabilitation Fund, which was reconstituted as an international fund following the second Games.

Despite organizers' efforts to make them accessible, both sports venues and accommodations proved less than ideal, a reflection no doubt of time and monetary constraints. The dormitories at a Masonic school that had closed a few years earlier served as the Athletes' Village but lacked adequate facilities, necessitating significant modifications, including the installation of portable showers and toilets. An asphalt area doubled as the basketball courts and an eight-lane track, which had a downward slope. Officiating, too, continued to be a challenge in Parramatta, because many officials were local volunteers who lacked familiarity with the adapted rules for athletes with disabilities. Despite such shortcomings, with 430 participants from sixteen countries and competitions in thirteen events, the second Games were widely hailed as a positive experience overall and as a success that furthered the growth of the FESPIC Movement.

According to the original FESPIC constitution, the Games were to be held every two years. However, the situation in Australia demonstrated how challenging that could be, even for nations with more established programs in disability sports, especially if those same programs were trying to raise funds to send athletes to the Stoke Mandeville Games or Paralympics. It is not surprising, then, that the original time frame was modified to create a longer gap between FESPIC events. Hong Kong, the host for the third Games held from October 31 to November 7, 1982, appeared to benefit from both the longer time window for preparation and fortuitous timing.[62] In contrast to the previous two sites, Hong Kong had the opportunity to host a smaller-scale international "test event" in 1979. Additionally, both the sports complex and Athletes' Village were brand-new facilities that were being built for other purposes, but because they were slated for completion just before the third FESPIC Games, they were still vacant and therefore available for use during the Games.

In other respects, the situation in Hong Kong echoed that of the previous two Games; the Hong Kong government contributed funds, but the majority of costs were covered—and eventually exceeded—by contributions from nongovernmental sources. The third FESPIC Games seem to have been particularly reliant on volunteers, given that the local government provided no official staffing to help organize or host the event. Characterized once again as a great success, the Games in Hong Kong featured eleven sports and attracted 744 participants from twenty-three countries or regions, including the first teams from Bhutan, China, Macao, the Solomon Islands, Vanuatu, and West Samoa. In addition to introducing several new member states to the FESPIC Movement, the 1982 Games marked the first time that the event operated explicitly under the "30 percent novices" guideline. They were also the last Games carried out under the leadership of Nakamura Yutaka, who passed away unexpectedly in 1984 and was succeeded as leader by Professor Sir Harry S. Y. Fang of Hong Kong.[63]

By all accounts, the fourth Games in Surakarta, Indonesia, presented the FESPIC Movement with its greatest tests to that point. Indonesia had originally offered to host the third Games, but faced complications when the Indonesian National Sports Committee refused to support this proposal.[64] At the end of the Games in Hong Kong, Surakarta, a city known as a social welfare center in Indonesia, was selected to host the next Games from August 31 to September 7, 1986.[65] According to Hatada, updates on the approaching Games from the organizing committee in Indonesia were very slow in coming, which prompted a visit from members of FESPIC's Executive Committee. On his first visit to the proposed host site, Hatada found that the stadium was rotting, the track was not usable for wheelchair races, and the dormitories were unsatisfactory. Despite requests for improvement during this first visit, when Hatada and others returned only months before the Games in March 1986, few changes had been made, and local organizers confirmed that they would not be able to do much more since the government was not providing the necessary funding. Faced with nearly unusable sporting venues, FESPIC leaders considered asking Japanese businesses to provide funds to build a new track, a possibility that Hatada dismissed given the short time frame and the business environment in Japan at the time. The Indonesian government's suggestion that the event should be moved to Jakarta where there were better facilities from an earlier Asian Games was also rejected because of the lack of accessible accommodations there. In the end, FESPIC leaders decided they had little choice but to pave the road in front of the stadium and use that for the wheelchair races, while making do with everything else.[66]

The result was an event that welcomed 834 participants from nineteen countries to compete in thirteen sports but was one that participants seemed to remember less for its competitions and ceremonies than its challenges. And those challenges were copious: a lack of easily accessible transportation, small bunk beds in the military dormitories used as the Athletes' Village, military guards that prevented departures from the Athletes' Village except on the official buses, limited food selections, concerns about safe drinking water, a four-lane wheelchair track (i.e., the newly paved road) that curved downward in the outer two lanes and sloped up at the finish, and many more. To be sure, in accounts of these Games, participants often accompanied their more critical observations with compliments on the thoughtfulness of their Indonesian hosts and praise for these Games as "an important step" for FESPIC.[67] In many respects, the fourth Games demonstrated that the goals of FESPIC could be pursued even in less-than-ideal conditions. But given these experiences, it was probably with some relief that FESPIC members received, and unanimously approved, the formal request to hold the fifth Games in Kobe, Japan, a large, internationally known city with a brand-new stadium and several other updated venues that had been used to host the international Universiade Games only a year earlier.[68] The FESPIC Games were coming back to Japan.

Rescuing FESPIC: Kobe's Games

For the first four FESPIC Games, the key organizers at the host sites had been people intimately involved with the movement since its earliest years. Kobe was different in this and other ways. Official materials suggest that the soon-to-be organizers for the fifth Games began their quest to host the event with minimal knowledge of FESPIC. As the Universiade Games concluded in September 1985, Kobe mayor Miyazaki Tatsuo suggested that the city should build on the success and momentum of this event to hold another international sports event, one for athletes with disabilities. His comments prompted city officials to investigate the limited options available at the time, leading to their discovery of FESPIC and particularly the fortuitous fact that the Federation had not yet designated a site for the fifth Games. Thanks to the added benefit of having ready access to the FESPIC secretariat at Taiyō no Ie in Ōita, organizers in Kobe were quickly able to secure both national and international support for their bid to serve as a host for the FESPIC Games in 1989.[69]

At first glance, Kobe's motivations for hosting the fifth FESPIC Games seemed to reflect little more than the need to find an acceptable event for a political pet project, and given the previous lack of awareness about FESPIC and the rush to host the Games after discovering it, that initial conclusion would not seem too far off the mark. It is, however, important to keep in mind that the FESPIC Games had been more or less pet projects for Nakamura and others from the beginning, projects they had to sell to sometimes skeptical politicians and officials. In Kobe the situation was reversed: officials unaffiliated with FESPIC actively sought out these Games. Whatever the reasons behind it, this was something new for the FESPIC Movement, and the resulting event reflected the change.

For one, organizers in Kobe approached the Games from a different perspective, with their focus understandably on their city, rather than on the FESPIC Movement as a whole. That said, their goals for and approaches to Kobe's Games meshed well with FESPIC's ideals and demonstrated organizers' wholehearted commitment to fostering exposure and accessibility. Like earlier Games, those in Kobe were framed in relation to local issues, with perhaps even more emphasis placed on local benefits. Meant to help commemorate the 100th anniversary of Kobe's founding, the 1989 Games were also explicitly linked to efforts to make the city more livable for the elderly and those with disabilities.[70] Several sporting events were held at the Village of Happiness (*Shiawase no mura*) to highlight its long-planned opening as a comprehensive social welfare complex in 1989.[71] In addition, the goals spelled out for the FESPIC Games called for implementing proposals dating from the late 1970s that had aimed at making Kobe more barrier-free: building additional elevators at train stations, creating more accessible public restrooms, adding curb cuts at crosswalks, and constructing ramps for accessible entrances. By the end of the Games, Hyōgo Prefecture and Kobe City had invested nearly 1.9 billion yen on upgrades for public facilities, and the city took advantage of the Games to encourage privately owned facilities and transportation networks to make similar changes.[72] Reflecting organizers' attempts to maximize the long-term impact of these Games for Kobe and its citizens, the particular emphasis on urban planning and development in 1989 differed from earlier FESPIC events, but certainly did not deviate from the spirit of the movement.

FESPIC promoters had long advocated the use of the Games as a way to improve social understandings of disability. In keeping with that notion, as well as their locally based approach, organizers in Kobe sought to improve their citizen's perceptions of and responses to those with disabilities by maximizing opportunities for people to encounter FESPIC and its athletes. The funding drives, volunteer recruitment, cultural exchange events, media publicity, official ceremonies, and, of course, athletic events were all cast as ways to generate awareness and promote changes that would improve the lives of those with disabilities. In other words, exposure was key, and organizers were intent on exposing as many people as possible to these Games, even if that affected the financial bottom line for the event. Although they discussed the possibility of entrance fees for the opening and closing ceremonies, organizers ultimately rejected the idea as contrary to the history and goals of FESPIC.[73] The opening ceremony attracted a capacity crowd of 60,000, and the closing ceremony another full house with 5,000 spectators.[74] As the Games approached, new cultural events with previously unbudgeted costs of 60 million yen were added to the schedule to promote "international goodwill" and "international exchange."[75] The desire for widespread exposure was also behind the decision to hold the FESPIC Games' first marathon, because it could singlehandedly attract more spectators than most of the other events combined. Dubbed the "Flower of the Games" in official materials, the marathon overcame multiple logistical hurdles, ultimately featuring 114 athletes from twelve countries with an estimated 350,000 spectators lining the route.[76]

If the Games in Kobe were meant to provide benefits to the city and its residents, organizers gave far more than lip service to the FESPIC Movement's broader aim of promoting disability sports in the region. Official goals for the event embraced FEPSIC's 30 percent novices ideal as an essential means for exposing new participants to disability sports, and the Games expanded on this commitment by adding new official and exhibition sports. In addition to the marathon, Kobe's Games included the official sports of wheelchair tennis, judo for the blind, and soccer for those with upper-limb disabilities. At the time, tennis and judo had established track records as adapted sports in Japan, but the soccer team had to be created from scratch, highlighting the fact that FESPIC's potential for creating new opportunities in sports was not limited to developing countries.[77]

In contrast, all five exhibition sports—ground golf, blind ping-pong, rolling volleyball, blind baseball, and twin basketball—featured Japanese athletes competing in events little known outside of (and probably within) Japan. Twin basketball, which remains prevalent today mainly in Japan, offered a case in point; the exhibition game between two teams from the Kobe area introduced the crowd to a version of wheelchair basketball where rule modifications and the addition of a second, "twin" basket situated roughly four feet above the ground allowed athletes with quadriplegia or similar impairments to play competitively, even if they could not shoot for the traditional basket.[78] Although none of these sports seemed to have been picked up by later Games, they were notable for demonstrating how relatively minor adaptations to existing sports could make them accessible for people with a wide variety of physical impairments. Thus, the fifth FESPIC Games continued the process of redefining and expanding the category of athlete, a process that had been central to the movement's earliest goals.

The Kobe Games also proved successful in dramatically expanding regional participation. Using as a model Kobe's recent experience of hosting what had been the world's largest Universiade Games to that point, initial goals called for 1,300 participants from twenty-five countries, numbers promising significant increases from each of the four previous Games. In the end, organizers vastly exceeded these already lofty goals with 1,646 participants from forty-one of the forty-three states in the FESPIC region. As the host, Japan had the largest delegation with 514 athletes and 72 accompanying officials, but they were joined by 700 athletes and 360 officials from abroad—far more international participants than any of the previous Games. Fourteen of the forty-one states joined the Games for the first time. Kobe organizers had managed to redefine the possibilities for participation in FESPIC, and later hosts would face a significantly higher threshold for their Games.[79]

Behind these high numbers lay a number of factors.[80] For one thing, the region's politics had shifted, if not entirely stabilized. States such as Taiwan, Vietnam, Laos, and Mongolia that were previously uninvited or otherwise unable to send athletes were among the first-time participants in Kobe. With the eighth largest delegation of thirty-nine athletes, the Taiwanese team appears to have secured access to the Games by following the so-called Olympic model and participating under the name "Chinese Taipei." Notably, North Korea was also formally invited but did not send a team.

Politics aside, organizers also capitalized on various resources at their disposal to seek out and eventually bring more people to the Kobe Games. An entire subcommittee, staffed primarily by city employees, was devoted to various forms of foreign relations work; according to official reports, from its inception, it had nearly 70 million yen earmarked for its efforts. To help them establish relations with FESPIC's member states, subcommittee members relied on a broad network of contacts that took full advantage of Kobe's standing as a large international city. In addition to more traditional outreach through known sports organizations, consulates, and embassies, the subcommittee used a variety of personal and business connections to distribute English-language information about the Games nearly two years in advance of the event. This informal outreach eventually served as the basis for a more systematic approach in which each member state was assigned a liaison officer, usually a representative of a Japan-based business or group that had branch offices, onsite staff, or other preexisting connections with the given locale. The liaison for Macau, for example, came from a Japanese construction company, whereas the one for Bhutan was from Kobe's local Bhutan Friendship Society. Once the formal invitations were sent out, liaison officers were asked to help guarantee the continued flow of information to and from FESPIC organizers and the member states. Thanks to these and other preliminary outreach efforts, in the first batch of entry forms—sent to Kobe in February 1988 more than a year and a half before the Games—twenty-five countries, including five first-timers, reported that they were planning to send a total of nearly 1,600 participants.

Having achieved their original goals at this early stage, Kobe's organizers could easily have stopped there and still accurately characterized their results as a record-setting accomplishment for the Games. That they did not do so is a testament to their persistence and their commitment to a Nakamura-like ideal that bringing even one more country or a single additional participant to the Games was worthwhile. Over the next several months, they launched a multifaceted approach targeting those states that had yet to commit.

In May 1988, for instance, organizers held a special "South Pacific Conference" in Australia aimed at sharing the most up-to-date information about the Games with both committed participants and the ten states in the area that had not yet responded to the initial invitations. After communications with potential participants revealed a lack of knowledge about disability sports rules and methods, Kobe hosted potential disability sports instructors from Kiribati, Laos, Vietnam, Nauru, the Marshall Islands, and New Caledonia in Japan for five days of training in October 1988. Although the specifics are unclear, it appears that Nauru's involvement in these training days not only led to their participation in the Games but also helped facilitate the establishment of the Nauru Sports Association for the Disabled a few months later. Securing Myanmar's participation involved frequent correspondence via the country's liaison officer and eventually a direct visit from a high-ranking member of the Game's organizing committee in July 1989. Even if Kobe's organizers had not known much about FESPIC initially, these sorts of recruitment efforts indicated that they had taken FESPIC's goals to heart.

Of course, these efforts benefited from the Game's generous foreign relations budget, as well as the fact that participants' costs during the FESPIC

Games themselves were once again going to be covered by the host site. In this case, 185 million yen had been budgeted for accommodations, with additional funds set aside to cover transportation expenses during participants' time in Japan. As with previous Games, however, it was immediately apparent that athletes from developing regions would only be able to participate with additional financial support. To cover these unbudgeted costs, organizers turned to FESPIC's tried-and-true approach of local, nongovernmental fundraising, including the use of 2,800 donation boxes set up throughout the city and in Hyōgo Prefecture. These funding drives served as low-cost PR for the event while eventually raising more than the original goal of 100 million yen.[81]

Using these donated funds, organizers waived all participation fees and paid for the international travel of up to five people each from thirty of the participating states. Among those states, nineteen received additional fee waivers to allow more people to join their teams. Because some regions needed extra time to reach the Games, nineteen countries were given funds to cover their lodging costs en route to Japan. In addition to the disability sports instruction session hosted in Kobe in October 1988, various sporting goods and supplies were provided to seven countries. Realizing that wheelchairs presented prohibitive expenses for many in the region, organizers also asked the Kawamura Cycle company to design and build special "FESPIC" wheelchairs. The resulting chairs were adjustable, lightweight, foldable, and capable of modification for use in sports or daily life. Beginning in August 1988, organizers used donated funds to purchase and dispatch three chairs each to twenty-nine participating countries.[82] These sorts of gifts—and even the participation of many states—would have been unimaginable without generous nongovernmental funding. In that way, the situation in Kobe echoed that of earlier Games, highlighting the FESPIC Movement's continued reliance on various forms of voluntary support in order to achieve its goals.

In many other respects, it is clear, looking back, that the fifth FESPIC Games represented a moment of transition for the FESPIC Movement. Perhaps most obviously, Kobe differed markedly from previous Games in terms of scale. Gone were the days when attracting less than a thousand participants could be qualified as a success. In future Games the number of participants would continue to rise, even as the number of participating states waxed and waned without ever dropping back to pre-Kobe levels. The adoption of new sports at Kobe also represented the start of an upward trend. Kobe's thirteen official sports—a number that did not count the marathon because it was subsumed in the "Athletics" category—was among the largest to date. Parramatta and Surakarta had also hosted thirteen sports, but that number included one-off events like snooker or chess. The additions of tennis and the marathon in Kobe demanded significantly more from a host site, and each of the next four Games would continue to add new sporting events while phasing out others. Reflecting increased participation and opportunities in disability sports throughout the region, these developments aligned perfectly with FESPIC's earliest goals but raised new challenges at the same time.[83]

In particular, more people and more sports meant greater costs for the hosts, and here, too Kobe represented a change. Given the lack of detailed financial reports from earlier Games, as well as the changes in time and place, side-by-side cost comparisons between Kobe and previous FESPIC host cities are not feasible in most cases. There are a number of general similarities, however, between the financial situation in Kobe and that of earlier Games, not least of which were the organizers' oft-expressed desires to keep expenses within reasonable limits—though it seems clear that the definition of "reasonable" differed. In addition to the ongoing reliance on nongovernmental donations to provide travel and other funds for participants, the Games in Kobe made perhaps even greater use of in-kind donations and volunteer labor as ways to cut costs.[84] They also adopted the hotel-as-Athletes' Village approach used in Ōita, housing foreign participants in three private downtown hotels, while Japanese delegates stayed at three other facilities, including the Village of Happiness.[85] As in the past, their ingenuity helped organizers address transportation challenges without incurring exorbitant expenses. Faced with a shortage of lift-equipped buses, Kobe created a portable ramp truck that parked beside the bus, extended one ramp into the bus, another to the ground, and thereby allowed relatively safe and easy access to public transportation.[86]

Despite these general similarities, it is telling that Kobe's organizers rejected previous FESPIC Games as models when preparing their initial budget, turning instead to their experience with the Universiade Games, which had an operating budget of 7.5 billion yen.[87] Final costs for the fifth FESPIC Games came in just under 1.5 billion yen, a figure that excluded international travel costs for participants, infrastructural changes in Kobe, or base salaries for public employees working on Game-related committees. Even without those additional expenses included, budgeted costs in Kobe represented a stunning 1,700-percent increase from the first Games in Ōita. The majority of expenses in Kobe came from three categories: the sporting events understandably proved most costly at more than 340 million yen, whereas roughly 268 million went for the ceremonies and another 235 million for accommodations. In contrast to Ōita where the Ministry of Health and Welfare contributed roughly 20 percent of budgeted income and the local governments added another 28 percent, in 1989 the 40 million yen from national coffers made up less than 3 percent of the total. Hyōgo Prefecture gave 360 million and Kobe

City 720 million yen, which together covered nearly 78 percent of the budgeted costs. The remaining income for Kobe came from JSAD and two new sources, including roughly 46 million from sales of FESPIC-branded products and another 291 million from businesses who paid for sponsorship rights.[88]

Although inflation and the more expensive urban location certainly need to be taken into account, these basic figures leave little doubt that the fifth Games were cheaper than Kobe's Universiade but significantly more costly than earlier FESPIC events. It is worth noting that, despite cost overruns in every budget category, the final outlays did not create sticker shock at the end of the Games. Working from their Universiade model, organizers had anticipated comparable expenses from the beginning. In other words, Kobe was ready and willing to spend a great deal of money on a set of Games that had previously struggled to provide adequate sports venues. Funding concerns would persist throughout the remaining Games, but Kobe's willingness to invest in this event served as a de facto recognition of FESPIC's value and helped transform the Games into a rising sports mega-event, the type of event that future cities might be eager to host as a symbol of their own rise.

The transition to mega-event was also apparent in Kobe's use of branding and official sponsorship. Organizers began crafting the "FESPIC KOBE '89" brand almost immediately after securing the right to host. An official symbol mark was designated in December 1986, two months before the official organizing committee was established.[89] During 1987 and early 1988 contests were held for designing and naming the Games' mascot "Mōta," a horned cartoon cow that was eventually drawn in five different poses by famed manga artist, Tezuka Osamu; official songs, slogans, and posters were ready by May 1988.[90] Of course, earlier Games had their share of such promotional activities; Nakamura, for instance, is said to have monitored the development of imagery and materials for the Ōita Games with a watchful and often critical eye.[91] Symbols, slogans, and the like were all deemed critical as PR tools that could help generate and maintain interest in an event that most people had never heard of.

In Kobe, these same tools were put to use as an essential element of fundraising. Drawing once again on the Universiade model, which had guaranteed exclusive rights and privileges to official corporate sponsors or suppliers, organizers for the 1989 FESPIC Games sought to secure donations totaling 200 million yen from official sponsors, with an additional 100 million yen in in-kind donations from official suppliers. In addition to guaranteed name recognition and advertising space, official sponsors were given the exclusive right to use FESPIC-related symbols on their products and sell relevant goods at events. Suppliers received similar benefits and exclusive rights to develop and sell FESPIC-branded versions of their own goods. Not wanting to exclude additional forms of PR or income, organizers reserved the right to authorize the creation of other FESPIC-branded products that were not already provided by sponsors or suppliers. The end result was an assortment of FESPIC-themed phone cards, tie tacks, letter openers, necklaces, key chains, and a host of other trinkets that sold even better than organizers had anticipated. The small percentages FESPIC received from each of these sales added up, producing the 46 million yen noted earlier. Donations from the eighteen official sponsors and the twenty-one official suppliers, along with those from twenty-four other companies, also exceeded original estimates, aided in part by the organizing committee's designation as a special tax-exempt entity as of September 1988.[92] Companies had been donating to FESPIC from the beginning, but Kobe's approach of turning the Games themselves into a marketable commodity was something new.

Costs and revenues aside, another central difference between the Games in Kobe and their predecessors was their complexity, a further testament to their emerging status as a sports mega-event. Added complexity came in many forms in Kobe. Organizationally, the 1989 FESPIC Games resembled their predecessors on the surface: all such events had to address lodging, athletic competitions, ceremonies, transportation, and the like. But even cursory glances through the highly detailed 500-page official report for the Kobe Games—a report more than 400 pages longer than the one from Ōita in 1975 and nearly double the length of the 1964 Paralympic report—suggest a new level of organizational complexity.

As a case in point, the secretariat for the organizing committee, which started with only four subcommittees in April 1987, was restructured multiple times over the next two years to address developments and challenges as they arose. In the end, the secretariat consisted of fourteen subcommittees, five of which were working specifically on athletic competitions, including an entire subcommittee devoted to the marathon. New staff members from the Kobe City and Hyōgo Prefecture government joined the secretariat on a regular basis, with the last additions in April 1989, sending the total number of secretariat staff to sixty-seven. In total, the organizing committee, its secretariat, and its five technical subcommittees involved nearly 400 people, a figure that does not include the more than 1,800 individuals serving as officials or referees for sporting events during the Games or the 3,593 other official volunteers who contributed more than 10,000 worker days' worth of labor to the event.[93] It is no stretch to characterize Kobe's organizational complexity as unprecedented.

As the number of subcommittees devoted to organizing the specific competitions suggests, increased complexity was also readily apparent in Kobe's athletic events in ways that went beyond the addition of new sports. In part, such changes reflected developments in international sports and disability sports more generally. For instance, the simple statement in the official rules declaring that "doping is forbidden" was clearly an early manifestation of the antidoping efforts that we have come to expect as part of international sports competitions.[94] Rules and classification were also more complicated in Kobe than had been the case previously. In Ōita only two sets of rules were used for competitions, but by 1989, the establishment of new International Organizations of Sports for the Disabled (IOSDs) in the late 1970s and early '80s meant that organizers in Kobe were working with rules and classification schema from four different IOSDs, as well as those from the international organizations associated with soccer and badminton.[95] It is also important to note that the Games in Kobe were being organized and held during a period of increasing, if not always smooth, integration for existing IOSDs, a process that culminated in the establishment of the IPC in September 1989.[96]

Unlike earlier FESPIC events that were organized under sometimes intense fiscal or temporal constraints, the Games in Kobe had both the time and the resources to assure that the sporting events were being conducted in accordance with all of the newest international developments and guidelines. As part of that process, organizers not only worked with JSAD to translate all of the relevant rules from the different IOSDs but also dispatched teams to observe and document procedures and policies at sporting events in Japan and at the 1988 Seoul Paralympics. Training sessions for soon-to-be officials and referees were held throughout the organizing period, and to assure smooth operations, each competition ran a full rehearsal at the official venue in the days immediately before the actual Games.[97] Such efforts helped distinguish the fifth Games in Kobe from the previous four Games, marking a shift from the "handmade" feel of earlier events toward the order, professionalism, and competitiveness associated with the sports mega-event that FESPIC was becoming.[98]

Organizers' approaches to information management and media outreach represented similar professionalism. Operating in a pre-Internet era, the Games in Kobe overcame barriers to communicating among the multiple competition venues and Athletes' Village sites by establishing the FESPIC Information System (FINS), which used a network of fax machines, photocopiers, telephones (hardwired, car, and cellular), pagers, and a central computer system to gather, process, and share information throughout the Games. While not without hiccups, FINS and its staff at the Information Processing Center proved particularly adept at compiling classification data and other details about athletes and providing timely updates on results at the various venues. FINS was especially useful for reporters covering the Games, because it enabled the Information Processing Center to share its official data directly with the Press Center, as well as the three Press Rooms set up at the three largest sports venues. Field reporters were also provided with access to elements of the system to file their onsite reports with the Press Center.[99]

The creation of such special areas and resources for reporters reflected Kobe organizers' particular attention to media relations. Of course, seeking media support was nothing new for FESPIC; several local media outlets had been among the sponsors of Ōita's Games in 1975, but in Kobe the benefits of additional time and resources led to key differences from earlier efforts. From the earliest planning stages for the 1989 Games, organizers' outreach had coupled in-house publicity work, such as the creation of a PR video and the publication of eight FESPIC newsletters, with close interactions with media, including significant print and broadcast media buys in the lead-up to the Games.[100] As the Games approached, organizers worked with the Japanese telephone company NTT to set up an automated telephone information line and gained special government permission to establish a short-term radio station, "FESPIC Kobe FM," which was used to provide updates on events for visually impaired attendees and anyone else within a twelve-kilometer radius.[101]

During the Games, an ID system facilitated easy media access to events, and regular press briefings and interview sessions were organized with athletes; translators were also provided if needed. Aware that many reporters lacked familiarity with disability sports and the athletes competing at Kobe, organizers prepared a pre-Game questionnaire for participants; more than 80 percent of the Japanese delegation and 160 foreign athletes representing twenty-seven countries responded. The responses were translated, compiled, and made available at the Press Center for use in preparing news reports or profile pieces.[102] These sorts of media-friendly gestures and a host of other PR undertakings were part and parcel of organizers' efforts to assure that the widest possible audience would be exposed to Kobe's FESPIC Games.

Similar motivations appear to have driven approaches to various ceremonial aspects of the 1989 Games, which not coincidentally tended to attract particular media attention. Despite repeated observations in the official report that the FESPIC Games needed to avoid ostentation because of their roots as a form of rehabilitation for those with disabilities (a notable misreading of Nakamura's reasoning for pursuing "simple" Games), the budget for the ceremonies alone suggested that organizers in Kobe were working with a different vision from the beginning.[103] To be sure, as early as the first Games, Nakamura had been particularly attentive to the role of ceremonies, ritual, and post-event activities in promoting FESPIC's ideals. Throughout the Games' history the opening ceremonies would remain a key venue for highlighting the FES-

PIC Movement's support, at least in a symbolic sense, from key figures like Japan's crown prince, Australia's prime minister, Hong Kong's governor, and Indonesia's president. All of this held true at Kobe, where participation in the ceremonial events was meant to give large numbers of people a vested interest in the Games and thereby serve as a means for fostering their commitment to the larger FESPIC Movement. Kobe's Games also continued the tradition of imperial patronage for disability sports in Japan. Crown Prince Naruhito, who had recently assumed this role when his father became emperor in January 1989, spent three days in Kobe participating in the opening ceremony and attending several athletic events and an evening reception.[104]

Organizers in Kobe took their Games to a new level, with elaborate ceremonies and an ambitious slate of other FESPIC-related events. The grandeur of the Games in 1989 was foreshadowed by a series of PR events intended to raise awareness of FESPIC; the first two major PR efforts were a ceremony and parade held in December 1987 to unveil the official symbols for the Games. Increasingly elaborate events followed to mark 2 years, 500 days, 1 year, 300 days, 200 days, and 100 days before FESPIC began in Kobe. In line with the goal of exposing people to the Games and their ideals, many of these events featured exhibitions of adapted sports and information sessions, as well as performances and special promotions, like the first sales of phone cards bearing images of the official mascot Mōta.[105] Throughout this period, smaller-scale events, training sessions, and pep rallies were held in neighborhoods and districts throughout the city.[106] In August 1989, FESPIC Festival '89 opened with an evening ceremony and concert that attracted a crowd of 4,500. Over the next fifty-one days, the festival served as an umbrella label for a variety of events, performances, informational displays, and special promotions that reached an estimated 420,000 people.[107] Among the festival events were two disability-related international symposiums targeting specialists: one addressing urban planning and the other related to disaster relief and prevention. As the Games concluded, organizers also hosted a research-based seminar that explored issues related to classification, training, and the best means for continuing to promote disability sports in the region.

In a move clearly intended to celebrate the city of Kobe, as well as Japan's pioneering role in the FESPIC Movement, organizers crafted a particularly elaborate torch relay. One torch, dubbed the "Flame of Happiness," was initially ignited in April 1989 at the opening ceremony for the newly completed Village of Happiness complex. A second, called the "Flame of Friendship," was lit at Taiyō no Ie in Beppu on September 8, 1989. It was then carried via ship to Kobe, where it was joined with the torch from the Village of Happiness and displayed in front of the new municipal building for several days until it was used for the formal opening ceremony torch relay and lighting on September 15, 1989.[108]

The opening ceremony itself featured the requisite flag ceremonies, parade of athletes, welcome speeches, and the like, all of which were complemented—or perhaps even overshadowed—by marching drills performed by 430 students from twelve local schools; a rhythmic gymnastic performance involving 650 college women; a wheelchair dance featuring 58 people; performances of the newly composed FESPIC Fanfare song by 100 students from local schools; the release of 800 birds and 24,000 balloons; a 50-person choral performance of the FESPIC theme song; 1,800 parents and preschool children decorating participants with handmade paper-crane necklaces; a traditional dance performed by 500 members of local women's organizations; five more rhythmic gymnastic performances featuring a total of 4,400 students from local elementary, middle, and high schools; and, last but not least, an early evening fireworks display.[109] Throughout the opening ceremony, 2,500 female high school students sitting in the stadium used handheld cards to create billboard-sized images and spell out different words of welcome. Hosted at a much smaller venue, the closing ceremony was not nearly as grand, but still featured a mix of local and professional performances designed to highlight Kobe's standing as a modern international city.[110] In short, the ceremonies in 1989 were spectacles of the truest sort, bookending an iteration of the FESPIC Games that proved to be far grander in scale and complexity than any before it.

By almost any metric, the 1989 FESPIC Games in Kobe, which ended on September 20, was a success. They had not only attracted more countries and participants than ever before but also witnessed twenty-four world-record performances. The Games had given numerous athletes in Japan and abroad their first tastes of international competition, and several hundred were returning home with new insights about and in some cases resources for pursuing disability sports further.[111] Hundreds of thousands of Kobe citizens had been able to experience some element of the Games in person, and countless more had been exposed to the FESPIC Movement and its ideals for the first time via the media or some form of PR.[112] Thanks to new elevators and other infrastructural changes, Kobe ended the Games as a more livable city for some of those with physical disabilities. Hosting FESPIC had been expensive, but the generosity of the host city and its citizens and the organizational aptitude of the various individuals tasked with overseeing the Games in Kobe had helped turn a struggling event into a more stable, impressive, and even marketable enterprise while managing to fulfill many of the movement's ideals.

All that said, it is equally important to acknowledge the ways in which Kobe's turn as host transformed the Games on the whole. If nothing else, the

1989 Games had raised expectations for future FESPIC events. There were, of course, no provisions declaring that future host sites needed to surpass earlier Games, but failure to at least equal the success of a previous host would almost certainly raise questions. Consequently, the size, complexity, and cost of future Games would mean that only large cities with preexisting, high-quality athletic venues and adequate funding would be able or willing to host. Nakamura's already problematic vision of an event that could be held anywhere was effectively defunct. Yet, longtime FESPIC organizer Fujiwara Shinichiro acknowledged that better facilities and more careful attention to international rules and norms had also made Kobe "the most orderly and competitive Games" to that point, a development that was almost certainly a boon for athletes looking to compete at an elite level.[113]

Future Games would be able to build on this foundation to garner increased international recognition for FESPIC and raise the level of sporting performances in the region. In doing so, however, they would also be faced with the challenge of balancing FESPIC's goals of providing opportunities for new participants in the region with the increasing professionalization and commercialization that were driving disability sports at the international level. In this sense, it is clear in retrospect that the fifth FESPIC Games in Kobe foreshadowed many of the changes and struggles that the FESPIC Movement would face during its last four Games.

FESPIC as Mega-Event: Bigger, Grander, Better?

As the Games in Kobe concluded, the FESPIC Federation flag was passed to leaders from Beijing, China, which had been named as the host for the sixth FESPIC Games, slated for September 4–9, 1994. At that time, China had yet to become the economic superpower it is today, and it had a relatively short track record in disability sports at any level. Having rejected the opportunity to join the Games at their inception, China participated in the FESPIC Games for the first time in Hong Kong in 1982. Between those Games and their designation as a future host site in 1989, several national disability sports organizations were established in China, and national sports meets for individuals with disabilities had been held twice.[114] China had continued its involvement with FESPIC and participated in the Paralympics for the first time in 1984, but there was no denying that China's programs in disability sports were still in the early stages of development. In keeping with FESPIC's ideals, this lack of development actually made Beijing an ideal site, especially because the city had recently hosted the Asian Games, which meant that it would not have any problems providing top-notch sports venues. In the end, the Games in Beijing benefited from widespread local and national support and were generally perceived as proceeding smoothly.[115]

As the largest Games to date, Beijing welcomed 2,081 participants from forty-two countries, including five former Soviet states that joined FESPIC for the first time. Close interaction with and support from the IPC helped assure accurate classifications and high performance levels in the Games' fourteen official sports, where athletes set ninety-eight world records. As in previous Games, Beijing relied heavily on governmental support at the organizational level, complemented by the mass mobilization of volunteers. Indeed, volunteerism and other types of formal engagement with the Games in Beijing dwarfed even Kobe's impressive results; as just two examples, more than 10,000 people participated in the performances during the closing ceremony, and another 16,000 joined fifty-seven cheering teams organized to support different countries during competitions. Thanks in no small part to an aggressive marketing and media campaign, official surveys indicated that more than 85 percent of Beijing respondents expressed interest in the FESPIC Games. However, the observations of the anthropologist Matthew Kohrman, who visited Beijing for the Games, suggest that experiences on the ground among spectators might have involved a lot less enthusiasm and interest than official reports indicated.[116]

Organizers in Beijing also exemplified FESPIC's commitment to meeting the needs of participants. In a particularly striking case, on learning that the wheelchairs for athletes from Vietnam and Indonesia violated the standards for their competition, organizers had new wheelchairs built overnight so that the athletes would be able to compete the next day.[117] A new hotel designed to accommodate individuals with disabilities was constructed to serve as the Athletes' Village, and it was staffed round the clock with some 2,800 volunteers, as well as 250 chefs ready to cook on demand. Despite such efforts, anecdotes from athletes suggest that the facilities and food remained less than ideal.[118]

In keeping with past events, Beijing's organizers offered to cover travel costs for participants who would not be able to attend otherwise, and they donated sixty wheelchairs as well. To aid Chinese efforts to bring more people to the Games, Hatada, who became president of the FESPIC Federation at the conclusion of the 1994 Games, returned to FESPIC's tried-and-true approach of soliciting voluntary contributions. Working with Japanese businesses and the Nippon Foundation, Hatada established a fund that ultimately contributed 20 million yen and more than 250 sports wheelchairs to support the Beijing Games. Similar levels of support were provided to future Games in Bangkok and Pusan.[119] With the closing ceremony on September 10, 1994, China's first and only FESPIC Games ended, but the FESPIC Movement continued, turn-ing its gaze to another first-time host, Bangkok.

Like all of the previous venues, Bangkok had never hosted a large-scale in-ternational sporting event for those with disabilities, but it had welcomed the Asian Games on three separate occasions and was slated to serve as host for those Games again in December 1998, just before the FESPIC Games, which were to be held on January 10–16, 1999.[120] Perhaps understandably the offi-cial report on the Games talks glowingly of their accomplishments, yet other accounts indicate that preparations for Bangkok's Games faced a number of challenges. Although Thailand had been involved with FESPIC from the be-ginning, many of its domestic disability sports organizations were relatively new and struggled with limited support. Both organizers' familiarity with in-ternational regulations and their coordination with potential participating countries were initially lacking as well. Sporting venues were less of a con-cern, but Hatada reportedly had to make special requests that the dormito-ries being built to house the athletes be made accessible for FESPIC's participants, given that construction of barrier-free facilities was not the norm in Thailand at the time.[121] By working closely with FESPIC headquarters (Hatada noted the need for frequent visits), other regional experts, and the IPC, organizers managed to overcome many of these obstacles to hold an event that continued to break new ground, even as it demonstrated new challenges or developments for the FESPIC Movement.

Bangkok's Games welcomed 2,258 participants and, in a first for FESPIC, included additional events for athletes with intellectual impairments as dem-onstration sports. Although the number of participants represented a new high, the number of participating countries declined to thirty-four, with the largest drop affecting states from the South Pacific.[122] Specific factors behind this decrease remain unclear, but costs and organizational difficulties almost certainly played a role. Participation rates from the South Pacific subregion would remain low in future Games as well.

In another important development, several of the Games' sixteen official sports were officially sanctioned by the IPC, a de facto recognition of how far FESPIC had come since its early years. At the same time, there were signs of creeping professionalization at Bangkok that raised questions about FESPIC's larger goals and purpose. The Japanese coach for goalball, for instance, ob-served that his players' experience at the Games was like "using wood in an era of titanium and aluminum." Even though the Japanese team included top-level athletes who had participated in a demanding training camp, they were no match for other teams who had been training intensively for a half-year and were promised financial compensation for victories.[123] Commenting on the impact of the seventh Games, two Thai physicians involved with the classification process applauded the ways in which FESPIC had sparked new interest and developments in disability sports in Thailand, but they also pointed to the possibility that too much emphasis on winning medals might actually detract from the Games' real purpose: "that the society and the government give more attention for the people with disabilities."[124] As FESPIC moved onward, these types of issues would only become more pronounced.

Opening in Busan, South Korea, in October 2002, less than a month after the Asian Games had concluded in the city, the eighth FESPIC Games, like several of their recent predecessors, benefited from their host site's world-class facilities and organizational know-how. Unlike China and Thailand, South Korea had the added advantages not only of a longer history of involvement in disability sports but also of previous experience hosting a large, international sports meet for those with disabilities, namely the 1988 Paralympics. Given that background, it is perhaps not surprising that Busan's organizers took it as their mission to "improve the quality of the Games and provide the new model of mutual development between [the] IPC and FESPIC Federation."[125] One key to achieving that mission was bolstering attendance, and the Busan organizing committee worked closely with the FESPIC Federation to provide as much financial support as possible to maximize participation rates throughout the region.[126] Running from October 26 to November 1, 2002, the eighth Games attracted 2,266 participants from forty countries, including several that joined the Games for the first time. Building on the previous Games, exhibition events in track and field, swimming, and ping-pong were held for athletes with intellectual disabilities, laying the groundwork for similar track-and-field and swimming events at the final FESPIC Games in 2006. Organizers also undertook the painstaking process of securing official IPC sanction for all of the sporting events, ultimately achieving that status for sixteen of the Games' seventeen official sports. In this respect and several others outlined later, Busan's organizers did more than host one of the most successful FESPIC Games to that point[127]: they helped foster the relationships and environments that made possible FESPIC's eventual integration with the IPC.

The ninth FESPIC Games in Kuala Lumpur, Malaysia, opened on November 25, 2006, with the end of FESPIC in sight; the closing ceremony on December 1 would be FESPIC's final event, as the newly established APC assumed the mantle of promoting disability sports in Asia. The Games in Kuala Lumpur reflected this planned change in several respects and ultimately overcame a number of obstacles to end FESPIC's record on a high note.[128] Unlike the recent host sites, Malaysia had never held the Asian Games, and the costs of building new stadiums or a formal athlete's village were obviously prohibitive. In addition, political developments in Malaysia in the years leading up to the Games caused a significant loss of anticipated support from the national level. Faced with such challenges, organizers resorted to a number of measures employed in previous Games: the use of hotels for housing athletes, voluntary contributions from businesses facilitated by governmental tax exemptions, a heavy reliance on volunteers, and various forms of in-kind support, particularly from government ministries. The outcome was far from seamless, as the Japanese delegation's difficulties with transportation and housing revealed, but the ninth Games nonetheless succeeded in attracting a record 3,575 participants from forty-six states. Among those joining FESPIC for the first time were athletes from the Middle East, whose involvement reflected the new geographic boundaries of the APC and offset the noticeable decline in participants from the South Pacific, which was now technically under the purview of the separate Oceania Paralympic Committee.[129]

The Kuala Lumpur Games added sporting events as well, bringing the total to a new high of nineteen official sports. Even as these Games upheld FESPIC's 30 percent novices ideal, their level of competition appears to have continued the upward trajectory apparent in recent Games. Commenting on the monetary rewards that Thailand and Malaysia were offering their medal winners, Japanese team captain Kobayashi Junichi praised these nations' results in the medal tables (second and fourth, respectively) as emblematic of the region's growing commitment to improving disability sports. In an almost ironic twist, Kobayashi observed that if Japan did not want to be left behind in the Asian region (Japan's medal count placed it sixth), it would need to start developing its own long-term plans for strengthening disability sports.[130] On the one hand, Kobayashi's observations revealed how much the standing of disability sports had increased in the region since the first FESPIC Games and that the FESPIC Movement had been instrumental in bringing about this change. On the other hand, the emphasis on medal performance and elite-level competition on display at these final FESPIC Games pointed to a future for disability sports in the region that was going to be driven, for better or worse, by a markedly different set of goals.

Lost in Transition: FESPIC and the IPC

By the time FESPIC dissolved in 2006, disability sports had witnessed dramatic transformations at nearly all levels, changes both exemplified and shaped in particular by the establishment and development of the International Paralympic Committee (IPC). Like much else involving FESPIC, sources addressing its relationship with the IPC are limited. But when examined in combination with the well-documented story of the establishment and development of the IPC, such sources provide a glimpse of the complex and at times contentious interactions that eventually led to FESPIC's replacement by the APC.

As FESPIC's own history demonstrated, disability sports had grown since their early years, involving more countries, more athletes, more disability groups, more sports, and more organizational complexity. It is worth recalling that from its foundation FESPIC aimed to push the boundaries of the Paralympic Movement in both a figurative and literal sense. Its leaders were well aware of the challenges involved in developing and maintaining an international movement, and their work—and demonstrated success—promoting disability sports in Asia and the South Pacific served as a recurring reminder that the still relatively new Paralympic Movement needed to avoid Euro- and American-centrism and give adequate attention and support to athletes from developing nations. The multi-disability approach that FESPIC adopted at the outset also provided concrete proof that it was no longer valid to dismiss such a format as "premature" or a "fundamental mistake."[131] With his focus on the rehabilitative potential of sports, Nakamura had been outspoken on these issues, particularly when addressing Japanese audiences about the need to establish and maintain a set of regional Games.

Naturally, these sorts of developments in and critiques of disability sports were not limited to FESPIC. Faced with both remarkable growth and the ongoing institutional turf wars that resulted from it, in the 1980s leaders in the expanding Paralympic Movement began pushing for greater unification at the international level, a move designed to continue the growth of the movement, streamline the organization of large-scale sporting events, and address the demands of the Olympic Movement and other sports organizations, which found it challenging to coordinate with disparate disability sports groups. After a series of sometimes contentious negotiations, the first step toward international unification came in the form of the International Co-ordinating Committee (ICC), founded in 1982. The ICC was composed of representatives from each of the existing International Organizations of Sports for the Disabled (four in 1982 and six by 1986), with the chairmanship of the committee rotating among these organizations' presidents. For the next several years, the ICC was tasked with organizing multi-disability world Paralympic events, but the committee proved unsatisfactory in the long run, largely for structural reasons. A rotating chairmanship, for instance, was not conducive to long-term stability, and the ICC itself, with its structure based on the IOSDs, did not include any national, regional, or athlete representation.[132]

By 1987, these shortcomings led to demands for a new organization to over-see disability sports at the international level, and after several conflict-ridden meetings, a General Assembly that was convened in Dusseldorf, Germany, on September 21–22, 1989, approved the creation of the IPC. Among the stated missions for the new organization was a commitment "to the integration of athletes with a disability in all major world games besides the Olympic Games. This includes Pan American Games, Commonwealth Games, FESPIC Games, European Games, World Championships and other similar competitions."[133] Because the ICC had already signed contracts for several upcoming Summer and Winter Paralympics, the IPC only assumed sole authority over the Para-lympic Movement in March 1993 when the ICC held its final meeting.

From the perspective of FESPIC, these developments at the international level were unsettling in several respects. Calls for a new organization to unify existing groups working on disability sports understandably sparked concerns that FESPIC might lose its independence and flexibility under such an organ-ization.[134] Those sorts of concerns were not eased—and were perhaps even aggravated—by the fact that the General Assembly in Dusseldorf was sched-uled on days that prevented the attendance of anyone involved with the clos-ing ceremony at the fifth FESPIC Games in Kobe. Indeed, FESPIC president Harry Fang, who was unable to attend the General Assembly, dispatched an official statement of complaint, criticizing the "'dictatorial attitude'" of those who set the meeting schedule. Fang also contended that existing regional organizations like FESPIC should serve as the sole regional representatives in this new organization.[135] The scheduling conflict with the FESPIC Games may help explain why the founding members of the IPC include so few states from East Asia or the South Pacific.[136] Given its role in the Paralympic Movement to that point, Japan's absence from the list is particularly conspicuous, although more understandable considering its obligations as the host country for the 1989 FESPIC Games.

It seems fair to say that FESPIC's earliest experiences with the new IPC did not bode well; however, it would be inaccurate to conclude that the FESPIC Federation's interests were not represented at this first General Assembly or thereafter. Dr. York Y. N. Chow, a member of FESPIC's Executive Commit-tee who had been working with the federation since the 1982 Games in his native Hong Kong, was intimately involved in international meetings leading up to the establishment of the IPC. Chow would continue to play a critical leadership role in the IPC's development well into the 2000s while serving on FESPIC's governing board as well. Another longtime FESPIC supporter, Dr. John Grant, had a similar record of involvement with the ICC, IPC, and

FESPIC, and for much of FESPIC's remaining years, the IPC regional representatives for both East Asia and the South Pacific also sat on FESPIC's governing board.[137] In March 1992, IPC president Dr. Robert Steadward attended
FESPIC's Executive Committee meeting, and in his comments published in
the newsletter *FESPIC*, he praised the federation, expressing his "sincere hope
and desire that the other regions of IPC learn from FESPIC." He continued,
"Although the FESPIC Federation consists of two IPC regions (Asia and South
Pacific), I see no reason why the IPC cannot cooperate and work with FESPIC
for the benefit of both Asia and South Pacific. I foresee FESPIC continuing to
host their regional games with the technical expertise that they have in place,
and the IPC doing its best to assume a role that is, in nature, both supportive
and complimentary [*sic*]."[138] With these reassuring words, Steadward seemed
to suggest that any worries that FESPIC's leaders had were unwarranted.
Time would prove his foresight faulty.

Even though FESPIC had regular connections with the IPC from that
organization's inception, the relationship between the two seems to have been
shaped by ongoing uncertainty about the IPC's structure and mission. At its
founding the IPC structure represented a clear response to criticisms of the
ICC. The General Assembly, for example, had members from National Paralympic Committees, regional organizations, and IOSDs. The IPC Executive
Committee included seven officers and three members at large, all elected by
the General Assembly; six regional representatives elected by their regions;
an athlete representative elected by the athletes; and six members appointed
by the IOSDs. In the original IPC configuration, there was a South Pacific or
Oceania region, and the Asian region was divided into east and west, with a
representative for each. However, the exact nature and purpose of what would
eventually become Regional Committees remained unclear for several years,
breeding uncertainty about FESPIC's role within this new framework.[139] In
March 1993, for instance, the IPC fielded but presumably decided against a
proposal calling for FESPIC to serve as the official representative body for
both the East Asian and South Pacific areas.[140] In 1995, articles in the *FESPIC*
newsletter on the IPC were still grappling with defining its relationship to
the federation, declaring that recent IPC meetings touched on the issue of
"mutual recognition of the IPC and the FESPIC Federation, recognizing
the autonomy of the Federation within our region."[141] More than a decade
after the IPC's founding, FESPIC representatives were still meeting with
the IPC Regional Committees to try to decide how best to classify countries into appropriate regions, a task that proved especially challenging for
several of the former Soviet republics that had joined FESPIC during the
Beijing Games.[142]

As FESPIC continued doing what it had been doing for nearly two decades, its activities fostered a not altogether welcome sense of competition with the IPC. Partly, this situation stemmed from the fact that FESPIC's Games continued to attract new participating states who had yet to join their respective IPC Regional Committee, including some thirteen states active in FESPIC that had not joined the East Asian committee following the 1994 FESPIC Games in Beijing.[143] In 1996, members of the General Assembly voted down a proposal from a special IPC task force that would have eliminated IPC involvement in regional games in order to allow the IPC to focus its attention and resources on holding the Paralympics. At least one critic of the failed proposal cited it as an attempt to give more power to FESPIC and other regional organizations.[144] The failure of the task force proposal meant that FESPIC's Games would continue to fall under the purview of the IPC, though it remained unclear for the next several years exactly what that meant.

As the struggle over regional organizations suggests, the IPC underwent repeated changes to keep pace with the evolving Paralympic Movement. Others have detailed these changes at some length, but two merit particular attention here, because they had direct impacts on FESPIC.[145] For one, the IPC developed a closer relationship with the International Olympic Committee (IOC) beginning in the late 1990s, when IPC president Steadward was asked to join the IOC Commission on Ethics in the wake of the Salt Lake City Olympic bidding scandal. Before that point the relationship between the Olympic and Paralympic Movements had been marked by ebbs and flows: conflicts over terminology and symbols, which had been an issue since the Paralympics' earliest years, continued even after the ICC managed to secure promises of patronage and financial support from the IOC in the 1980s. By the time of the 2000 Sydney Games the IOC–IPC relationship had improved dramatically, culminating in Steadward's election as an IOC member and the signing of a general memorandum of understanding that called for IPC representation on IOC commissions and financial assistance for the Paralympic Movement. In June 2001, the two organizations signed a cooperative agreement, which among other provisions assured the financial viability of the Paralympic Games and guaranteed that host cities and their Olympic Games organizing committees would provide full support for the Paralympics, a development leading to long-awaited joint bidding processes. The original agreement has since been revised or extended, as discussed in chapter 5.

It was in the wake of these developments that Busan hosted the eighth FESPIC Games in 2002. As noted, the organizers of these Games engaged in a concerted effort to foster closer interactions between FESPIC and the IPC. For example, three days before the Games opened, organizers held a FESPIC

Congress that focused on strategies for co-development of the two international organizations. Details about its content remain sparse, but both FESPIC president Hatada and recently elected IPC president Sir Philip Craven joined more than 200 other participants. Over the course of the Games, organizers worked with both FESPIC and the IPC to host nine other meetings, ranging from the FESPIC General Assembly to the IPC Technical Committee Meeting.[146]

One such meeting during the Busan Games led to an important structural change for the IPC, which also had implications for FESPIC. The establishment of the Asian Paralympic Council on October 30, 2002, addressed an earlier IPC General Assembly proposal aimed at clarifying regional partitions. The new council, led by Malaysia's Dato Zainal Abu Zarin, was charged with overseeing disability sports in East, South, and Southeast Asia.[147] More changes for the IPC lay ahead, with the most significant for FESPIC unfolding in 2004, as the IPC revised its regional structure again, shifting from its original six regions to the IOC five-continent model: Asia, Oceania, Africa, Europe, and the Americas. Prompted by its new working relationship with the IOC, in April 2004 the IPC combined the Middle East regional organization with the recently established Asian Paralympic Council. By January 2005 the revamped Asian Paralympic Council had forty member states, including several traditionally outside FESPIC's regional boundaries. The new IPC continental approach also placed renewed emphasis on the creation of a distinct Oceania Paralympic organization that would serve FESPIC's long-standing South Pacific participants.[148] In other words, as the IPC's new IOC-inspired geographical arrangement took shape, the ambiguity of earlier years that had allowed FESPIC to continue its regional activities was fading fast, and it became increasingly clear that FESPIC no longer fit under the IPC umbrella. By May 2004 FESPIC leaders reached a consensus that the future of disability sports in the region would be best served by "complying with the goal of the IPC's reconstruction Movement" and merging with the nascent Asian Paralympic Council.[149]

In 2004, compliance with the IPC's goals was arguably the best, if not the only, option for FESPIC. The two most recent FESPIC Games at that point had both benefited from IPC support, especially in the form of officially sanctioned competitions. The *FESPIC* newsletter made it clear that IPC sanctioning was in fact a pressing concern for the organization, with frequent references to "negotiating with the IPC concerning 'Sanction'" as early as the 1999 Games in Bangkok.[150] Without delving too far into counterfactual scenarios, it is not hard to imagine the possibility that future support would have been less forthcoming if FESPIC's leaders had decided to carry on as if nothing had changed.

Perhaps even more importantly, for FESPIC to continue hosting its Games at the level they had attained in recent years, significant resources, both financial and human, would be essential. Acquiring such resources had long proven one of the greatest challenges for FESPIC, especially considering the fact that the federation itself had virtually no independent funding and relied almost entirely on privately funded volunteers for its staffing.[151] On the human resources side, maintaining the status quo for FESPIC as the new IPC regional organization took shape would mean that increasing numbers of people would be forced to perform double duty, resulting in a new level of organizational redundancy that the region's disability sports community could ill afford. It is also important to note that the Asian Paralympic Council initially had no regional sporting events of its own. Organizers on all sides were surely aware that any attempt to develop a new set of regional games would strain already limited resources in ways that would be detrimental to the promotion of disability sports in the region. Although the new Asian Paralympic Council could have simply adopted the FESPIC Games as is, available sources do not indicate whether that option was even discussed; given both the new regional configurations modeled on the IOC and the IPC's previous unwillingness to recognize FESPIC as an official IPC organization, it seems likely that anything other than Games run for the countries under the purview of the official IPC regional organization would have proven unacceptable. In short, it was increasingly apparent that the best option for continuing to pursue the goals of the FESPIC Movement was to bring FESPIC itself to an end.

That said, the merger promised future benefits as well. If nothing else, when coupled with the ongoing efforts to clarify the IPC's structure and mission, the new agreements with the IOC made integration with the IPC in 2004 look far more appealing and secure than would have been the case even a few years earlier. Proponents of the merger were also optimistic that the IOC–IPC partnership model could be applied to the Olympic Council of Asia (OCA) and the new APC. Their ultimate goal was a joint bidding system for the Asian Games and the new Asian Para Games, a process that promised to raise the profile of disability sports in the region.[152] What was more, in a small but symbolic gesture, the merger agreement indicated that the first games organized by the APC in 2010 would be identified as the tenth regional games as a way of acknowledging their precursors' history, if not their original name.[153] As noted at the beginning of the chapter, the terms of the merger also assured that FESPIC's contribution would be preserved and even highlighted as part of the new organization's constitution. Although FESPIC might be disappearing, its larger mission and legacy, it appeared, were going to live on.

The merger itself was a multistage process formally initiated in May 2004. It involved the establishment of a five-member task force composed of FESPIC and Asian Paralympic Council representatives that was chaired by

Dr. Chang Il Park, who was then serving as vice president for both organizations. Over the next two and a half years, the task force met ten times to plan for the dissolution of both organizations, draft a constitution and bylaws for the new Asian Paralympic Committee, and iron out the procedures and time lines for its establishment. On November 16–17, 2006, Extra-Ordinary General Assemblies for both FESPIC and the Asian Paralympic Council approved the draft constitution and voted to dissolve FESPIC on creation of the APC. Working under IPC regulations, a Provisional General Assembly for the APC held at the same time unanimously adopted the draft constitution, and on November 28, 2006, the first APC General Assembly met in Kuala Lumpur and elected the organization's new officers.[154] With the conclusion of the final FESPIC Games a few days later, the merger was complete, and FESPIC's role came to an end.

By 2018, the APC had already organized three Asian Para Games, with others in various stages of planning or preparation. Remarkably high participation rates and multiple record-setting performances at the first two events in Guangzhou, China, and Incheon, South Korea, gave every indication that by 2014 the merger had already contributed, as promised, to the continued development of sports for those with disabilities in the Asian region. The APC has also expressed a commitment to increasing participation in para-sports for women, as well as athletes from conflict zones or economically developing regions—goals very much in line with FESPIC's founding mission.[155]

At the same time, closer examination reveals that many aspects of the larger FESPIC Movement were lost in the transition. Perhaps the most obvious loss was the partition of the South Pacific region, a logical division from the perspective of alignment with the IOC, but one that made little sense in terms of the history and future development of disability sports in the region. Many participants from this region had been heavily subsidized throughout FESPIC's history, and the obstacles of distance and cost have continued to pose challenges for the Oceania Paralympic Committee.[156] If anything, it seems that the break with FESPIC's Asian countries (including two of the world's top five economies) has meant that would-be para-athletes in the South Pacific region have had to overcome many of the same barriers as in the past, but with even less access to resources.

Another noticeable departure from FESPIC's approach can be seen in the almost exclusive emphasis on elite performance, a development admittedly not limited to the APC, given that FESPIC itself had moved in that direction in its later Games. Yet even as levels of competition rose, FESPIC's longstanding 30 percent novices ideal had helped maintain an ethos of accessibility and broad-based participation that does not appear to have survived the transition to the APC.[157] Recent vision and mission statements for the APC, as well as a recent strategic plan, have all been rooted in the goal of assuring that the organization's Games are "a premier sporting event," one that can produce marketable athletic stars and rivalries, attract spectators, generate media coverage, and attract commercial sponsorship.[158]

On the one hand, the APC has clearly distanced itself from the problematic paternalistic and medicalized approach to disability sports that defined FESPIC, especially in its early years, and the APC is committed to empowering athletes with disabilities, particularly by providing them with the biggest stage possible on which to demonstrate their exceptional talents. On the other hand, the broader commitment to regional outreach and social issues outside of sport that lay at the very heart of FESPIC's mission now appear to have become secondary at best. Where the Games had been a means to an end for FESPIC, for the APC they have become an end—or perhaps more accurately, a "core asset" essential to the continued viability of the APC—in and of themselves.[159] As the 2015–2018 APC strategic plan framed it, "The reality is that the resources of the APC are extremely limited, and the worst thing the organization can do is spread itself too thinly across too many activities. Its overriding priority is clearly the development and delivery of a successful Asian Para Games."[160] Given such clear priorities, it is also not surprising that FESPIC's commitment to research and the sharing of resources and information, particularly as exemplified by its frequent congresses and workshops, has proven less pronounced in the first decade under the APC. This may change given calls for the Asian region to become less dependent on IPC expertise for local management of the Games, but even here, the focus on the Games has been clear.[161]

In terms of the Games, several of the hoped-for results of the merger—namely, closer relationships with the IPC and the OCA, as well as the integration of organizational efforts for the Asian and Asian Para Games—have proven elusive, at least initially.[162] Echoing earlier conflicts between the IOC and the IPC, anecdotal evidence suggests that planning for the respective Games in Asia has been anything but harmonious.[163] The need to host both sets of Games back to back has also created further limitations on the types of places that are willing and able to serve as host. As one of many consequences, the APC, like the IOC and IPC, is finding itself in the position of selling its Games to potential hosts by recommending how they "can derive sufficient legacy benefit to justify the cost involved in hosting."[164] Yet this approach raises a perplexing issue for the APC in its second decade: its track record consists of only three events, two of which were held in economically prosperous societies that already boasted two of the strongest disability sports programs in Asia. Although few would deny the success of these events, they were not exactly "typical" of the Asian region, making them less than ideal examples for demonstrating the amorphous "legacy benefits" being used to convince countries to host despite concerns about costs.

This predicament is one partly of the APC's own making. Despite expectations to the contrary, the region's tenth Games appear to have been called that only for a brief time before being held as the first Asian Para Games in December 2010, and officially the APC as of this writing cites only three regional Games as part of its history, with no mention of FESPIC.[165] The APC's move toward a revised IPC-style constitution that would reflect the "continuous development and professionalism of the Asian Paralympic Committee (APC)" also removed all mention of FESPIC's history from the earlier document.[166] Although a number of people engaged with FESPIC have continued serving with the APC, FESPIC's larger contribution to the promotion of disability sports in the region and the APC's own foundational debt to the FESPIC Movement have remained largely unacknowledged and undervalued. The 2015–2018 strategic plan called for using "best practices and knowhow created through the years by the IPC around the organization of the Paralympic Games" and developing "a knowledge management process so that lessons to be derived from each Games can be translated into the management of future events"; yet evidence suggests that the APC had yet to apply this same approach to the thirty-year history of FESPIC.[167] Like many other aspects of the movement, FESPIC's history, too, had proven a casualty of the merger.

Can You Call It a Legacy if No One Remembers?

In October 2016 and June 2017, I had the opportunity to join small groups of former Kobe FESPIC organizing committee members for dinners and discussions about their activities nearly thirty years earlier. Everyone attending was part of a larger Kobe FESPIC alumni group that has reunited former committee members every year since the 1989 Games. Our conversations those evenings were wide-ranging, and it was readily apparent that those present were proud of their involvement with FESPIC and understandably disappointed that so few people in the city seemed to remember the 1989 Games. Indeed, the forgotten nature of FESPIC proved to be a recurring theme, as committee members also confirmed that they themselves had not known about FESPIC's existence when they were first tasked with bringing to Kobe an international sports event for those with disabilities, despite the fact that the FESPIC secretariat was based in Japan. A similar gap in collective memory also appears to have occurred in Hong Kong, where publicity materials for the city's unsuccessful bid to host the Asian Games in 2006 omitted the 1982 FESPIC Games in declaring that the upcoming 2006 Games would be Hong Kong's first-ever international multi-sport event.[168] It would seem, then, that the situation with the APC represents only the most recent of multiple, repeated forgettings, which raises obvious but important questions: Why has FESPIC been forgotten, and what might this example tell us about the challenges of legacy production for disability sports events more generally?

Given FESPIC's thirty-year history of dealing with a large and diverse region that is home to more than half of the world's population, there were sure to be any number of local, national, organizational, economic, and other factors that contributed to its difficulty in maintaining a presence in collective memory. Three merit particular attention here, because they also point to challenges for disability sports events more broadly. First, FESPIC was a victim of timing, especially in relation to media attention. It emerged in a period when disability sports were still on the fringes of mainstream media and social awareness, and it is worth recalling that the Games were established in part to help generate that kind of awareness in the region. Yet even in societies like Japan that already had a history of engagement with the Paralympics, sports for athletes with disabilities only began to generate wider attention in the late 1990s, an issue examined in greater detail in chapter 4. By the 1990s, the FESPIC Games had come into their own, but were being overshadowed by the more prominent, competitive, and increasingly grandiose Paralympic Games. At best this made FESPIC seem like a regional qualifying event for the "big show," and at worst it made the Games appear sub-par, especially considering FESPIC's continued emphasis on introducing new, non-elite participants to international competition. In either case, FESPIC continued to be at a relative disadvantage in terms of representation.[169]

Second, FESPIC struggled to gain a permanent memory foothold because of the one-time, locally based nature of its events. As noted earlier, this approach had been both instrumental in the successful hosting of individual Games and central to the broader mission of spreading disability sports in the region. However, when coupled with a lack of broader media coverage, the Games had little chance of reaching beyond their local area, especially if that area happened to be overseas. Even if someone developed a genuine interest in FESPIC during the Games, following them in the future would have been extremely difficult for most of FESPIC's history. This lack of follow-up, combined with FESPIC's structure and approach, made it more difficult for FESPIC to foster levels of engagement and interest that would contribute to long-term memories of the events.

FESPIC was premised at least in part on the assumption that even limited exposure to the Games would provide positive benefits, an assumption that remains common for disability sports events today and no less difficult to assess. To be sure, the Games were of enduring significance for many people, as exemplified by the Kobe alumni group's ongoing reunions and the experiences of individual athletes discussed in chapter 5. Yet athletes, organizers, and volunteers had a significantly different FESPIC experience from the vast majority of those encountering the Games as spectators or media consumers. These latter types of experiences did not preclude the possibility of deeper connections, but it seems equally plausible—especially considering the fact that ceremonial elements tended to generate the largest audiences—that most people literally viewed the Games as an interesting spectacle, one that would soon be superseded by an equally interesting, though unrelated, spectacle. Without regular reinforcement of the event and its ideas or at least some way to assure deeper levels of engagement for more people, it is not hard to understand how a one-off FESPIC event, even one that had seemed profound at the time, could easily fade from memory.

And therein lies a third factor: FESPIC lacked the means to perpetuate its legacy. Part of the issue here was resources, as staffing and funding remained tight for FESPIC from beginning to end. Assuring that the individual Games were held proved challenging enough, even without the added burden of tracking what happened in their aftermath. Any effort to maintain the legacy of particular Games was going to have to come from the local site itself, and that, too, was difficult for a variety of reasons. As one example, local elections in Kobe caused significant political turnover following the Games, which dampened enthusiasm for post-Game follow-up. Through no fault of their own (and arguably to their credit), the FESPIC Games in general failed to generate "monumental" products that would keep the movement's name alive in public memory. Even the official monument to the FESPIC Movement is a small sculpture tucked in between buildings at Taiyō no Ie in Beppu. In Kobe, there is no FESPIC equivalent to the Universiade Stadium that hosted FESPIC's opening ceremony. Although linked to the Games, the Village of Happiness complex was already in development years before Kobe decided to host them, and despite their significance for those with disabilities, infrastructural changes like new elevators and curb cuts were hardly the types of projects that generated widespread public recognition once the inconveniences of installation ended. In later years, FESPIC adopted a pattern of following the Asian Games and using many of their venues; as an "add-on" event, however, FESPIC was unlikely to receive any sort of credit for contributing memorable facilities to the host sites. FESPIC's "softer" contributions to hosts such as the oft-mentioned improved social understandings of and approaches to people with disabilities were amorphous and nearly impossible to measure—and if achieved, they were meant to be normalized and taken for granted, a process that would likely render their origins with the Games moot. All these other factors aside, the greatest obstacle to preserving FESPIC's place in public memory was the dissolution of FESPIC itself. In essence, FESPIC handed control of its legacy to another organization that did not have the same vested interest in preserving it. Given that fact and all the other challenges discussed earlier, it should come as no surprise that the memory of the FESPIC Movement's role in the region had begun to fade only a decade after it ended.

Faded though its legacy may be, FESPIC has an undeniable record of contributions to the Paralympic Movement and the disability sports community more broadly. At the very least, FESPIC brought international, multi-disability sporting events to countries and cities where they had never been before. In the process, the Games provided the opportunity for thousands of athletes, coaches, and officials to participate in international competitions, with many doing so for the first time thanks to a combination of outreach, funding, and an emphasis on broad-based participation. Indeed, FESPIC's work in the Asia-Pacific region, much of which was subsidized by voluntary efforts rooted in Japan, could easily serve as an early case study of the benefits and challenges of what is now known as "sports for development." Like the Paralympics, the FESPIC Games also gradually moved away from their rehabilitation-focused roots toward a greater emphasis on athletic ability, a change that has helped athletes in the region achieve ever higher levels of performance. At the same time, FESPIC maintained a commitment to introducing new individuals to disability sports and expanding the category of athlete at the international level. Finally, there can be no denying that, despite differing goals and approaches, FESPIC's thirty years of engagement in the region provided a solid foundation for the APC's ongoing work promoting sports for those with disabilities. Indeed, as the APC seeks to achieve its vision of making "Asia one of the leading regions of the Paralympic Movement in enabling athletes with an impairment to achieve sporting excellence and inspire and excite the world," engaging in efforts to reclaim and preserve FESPIC's rapidly fading legacy would be an important first step. FESPIC had a long-standing history of advocacy, leadership, innovation, and commitment with few equals in the broader disability sports community, a history that the APC could justifiably and proudly call its own. Doing so would not only grant FESPIC long overdue recognition but also bolster the APC's own position within the larger Paralympic Movement. Although FESPIC itself has been lost, its history can still be found.

CHAPTER 3

Japan's "Cradle of Disability Sports"

Ōita and the International Wheelchair Marathon, 1981–

> If I were to go to Tokyo, my efforts would surely be crushed. I have been able to do these types of things because I am in Kyushu.
>
> Nakamura Yutaka, 1988

Every autumn a group of the top athletes from around the world gather in Ōita, a pleasant but peripheral city in southwest Japan generally absent from most people's must-see lists. When it comes to wheelchair marathons, however, Ōita has become a destination on par with Tokyo, London, or New York. At its founding in 1981, the Ōita International Wheelchair Marathon was the first event of its kind—an international, wheelchair-only, long-distance road race—and one of only a handful of long-distance races around the world open to athletes with physical disabilities. Since that time, the number of wheelchair marathons has increased dramatically, with several gaining international prestige, yet the annual event in Ōita has remained the world's largest, featuring both an IPC-sanctioned, multi-division full marathon and a multi-division half-marathon. Together the two races attract 250 or more competitors each year. With the fortieth annual marathon slated for autumn of 2020, Ōita's race boasts an unusually long and rich history. Having already welcomed more than 10,000 racers from more than seventy-five countries, witnessed several world-record performances, and played a prominent role in marathon-related research, Ōita's marathon is, as fourteen-time winner and current world-record holder Heinz Frei put it, "more than a normal marathon."[1] It has become an unparalleled annual celebration of the sport and a highlight of the region's yearly calendar.[2] This chapter explores how Ōita's seemingly anomalous prominence in the world of wheelchair marathons came about and what it has meant to Ōita, its people, and athletes with disabilities.

Even before the Ōita International Wheelchair Marathon began in 1981, Ōita Prefecture had become known as Japan's "cradle of disability sports," a reputation attained in no small part through Dr. Nakamura Yutaka's work with the Paralympics and FESPIC, as discussed in the previous chapters.[3] Nakamura played an equally important role in the establishment of Ōita's marathon; thus, any account of the race's history must once again consider his motivations and methods for launching yet another international sports event for those with disabilities. Much like FESPIC, the marathon was established in response to intersecting international, local, and personal forces, and here, too, Nakamura's factory Taiyō no Ie and its affiliates have proven central to the race and its continued existence.

As an annual event, the marathon has benefited from sustained local government support, making it an ideal site for exploring how and why disability sports have been leveraged for local gains in Ōita. Indeed, as suggested by Nakamura's remarks quoted in the chapter's epigraph—an alleged response to a comment from a member of Japan's imperial family that Nakamura's talents were being wasted in Ōita—it is essential to understand the regional context within which he was pursuing his work. Brief overviews of both Ōita Prefecture's extended history as a hot springs rehabilitation site and the region's connections to military rehabilitation facilities before and during World War II serve as useful reminders that Ōita was not a blank slate when Nakamura began his efforts to promote disability sports in the 1960s. Even if his approach seemed dramatically different, he was building on existing practices and operating in a region that was accustomed to various types of rehabilitation; yet Ōita was still marginal enough to remain open to pushing the boundaries of the status quo. Once Nakamura had proven the value of his approach and helped turn Ōita into "Japan's cradle of disability sports," success beget success, and it became ever easier for him to sell others on his future plans, especially if they might bring additional attention—and money—to the region.

An investigation of Ōita's race over time also points to a number of transformations in sports for those with disabilities. Like other events, the marathon began as a rehabilitation-focused race aiming for broad-based participation. The medically oriented nature of the early years has largely disappeared, but thanks in part to the half-marathon, Ōita's event has remained accessible and appealing for a remarkable range of athletes. At the same time, Ōita's full marathon has trended toward elite-level competition, a development that has raised the potential for growing inequality in Ōita, much as it has elsewhere.

Using the annual marathon to situate such issues in a wider historical context offers a clearer picture not only of how far the race and disability sports have come but also the challenges they face moving forward.

"Japan's Number One *Onsen* Prefecture": Hot Springs Healing

Located on the eastern coast of the island of Kyushu, Ōita Prefecture was established in 1871 as part of the dramatic changes shaping Japan after the fall of the Tokugawa Shogunate (1600–1868) a few years earlier. Before then the area that makes up Ōita today was part of two provinces, Bungo and Bunzen, dominated by the powerful Ōtomo family for centuries. During the intense military struggles occurring in Japan in the late sixteenth century, the Ōtomo family lost its grip on the region, and under the Tokugawa Shogunate, the area was subdivided into multiple, smaller feudal domains. After the collapse of the shogunate in 1868, several of these domains were merged to form Ōita Prefecture, with the new prefectural government based in what would quickly become the prefecture's largest city, Ōita. At present, Ōita Prefecture consists of fourteen cities, three townships, and one village, with a total population of just under 1.2 million people. Like many of Japan's outlying regions, Ōita's last several decades have witnessed significant declines in population and growing income disparity when compared with other prefectures in Japan. Although the prefecture is home to a number of industries and generates a range of specialty products, when people in Japan think of Ōita, they tend to think of *onsen* and for good reason.[4]

Given its location in the "Ring of Fire," Japan has no shortage of *onsen*, or natural hot springs, scattered throughout its many islands. Ōita has been uniquely blessed in this sense. The official 2015 figures from Japan's Ministry of Environment put the total number of hot springs in the prefecture at 4,342, far more than any other prefecture and constituting roughly 16 percent of all such springs in Japan. Ōita also leads the nation in total hot spring output at 279,462 liters of water per minute, and two of Ōita's cities, Beppu and Yufu, regularly rank among Japan's top five *onsen* destinations.[5] The prefecture's *onsen* have long been celebrated for their purported healing powers and for their wide range of temperature and mineral content. In other words, Ōita's current claim to be "Japan's Number One *Onsen* Prefecture" is more than a recent example of boastful tourism rhetoric. For centuries before Ōita became a destination for wheelchair marathoners and even long before the prefecture itself existed, people had been making their way to this region to partake of its plentiful and famous waters.

According to legend, hot springs in present-day Ōita have been used to treat illness since at least the sixth century, and some accounts cite such uses as far back as the age of Japan's founding deities.[6] The earliest written references from the region, which appear in the surviving portions of the eighth-century regional gazetteer *Bungo no Kuni fudoki*, depict a plethora of geothermal activity, including geysers, boiling mud pits, steam vents, malodorous springs, and hot rivers, with at least one site linked to a cure for skin conditions.[7] Later legends describe ailing emperors who sought relief in Beppu's waters during the ninth and eleventh centuries, and they also tell of an itinerant Buddhist preacher from the thirteenth century who used the region's springs to develop sites for healing (and probably converting) the people. Around the same time, Ōtomo Yoriyasu, who controlled the region, is said to have established several facilities for treating soldiers wounded while defending Japan from the Mongol invasions.[8] It is clear that the region developed a local reputation as a hot springs healing site early on.

During the Tokugawa Shogunate, the region's reputation and use as a site for *tōji*—or hot water cure—would continue to grow. Although Tokugawa-era Japan was rightly known for its territorial and status-oriented restrictions on travel and nearly every other aspect of life, the period's peace, stability, urbanization, and improved transportation and communication networks made possible the frequent and often mandatory movement of people, goods, and ideas among Japan's many cities and towns. In this context, places like the coastal town of Beppu, with easy access to sea routes and a marketable "product," gained increased access, exposure, and importance, as demonstrated by the fact that the shogunate, which tended to claim the best resources as its own, eventually assumed direct control over significant portions of the region's hot spring sites.[9] Even though the shogunate carefully regulated the use of their *onsen* for leisure and curative purposes, existing sources suggest that the region, and Beppu in particular, became a popular destination for those seeking to cure their ills. For instance, *Toyonokuni kiko*, a late seventeenth-century travelogue by the Neo-Confucian scholar and botanist Kaibara Ekken included several references to hot spring sites in what is present-day Beppu, making particular note of those frequented by "sick people."[10] A number of other sources indicated that people often spent extended time at the springs for *tōji* treatment, so it is not altogether surprising that by the early 1800s the shogunate had authorized the establishment of eighteen hot spring lodges in Beppu, including three new facilities opened in the first two decades of the nineteenth century.[11] Although Ōita's *onsen* business might not have been booming in the Tokugawa era, it was far from fading away.

Under the rapidly modernizing state that replaced the Tokugawa regime in 1868, *onsen*, like much else in Japan, became subject to dramatic changes. In clear recognition of the earlier medicinal use of hot springs, Japan's new national leaders moved quickly to investigate and regulate *onsen* as part of their broader effort to create a modern public health system in Japan. As historian Nobuko Toyosawa has observed, a key part of this process was a shift in both official and popular discourses on the medical efficacy of hot springs. During earlier periods, the cures produced by *tōji* tended to be explained in terms of the springs' magico-religious qualities. The new approach shifted attention to scientific evaluations of differing mineral content and temperature as keys to understanding and documenting why particular springs would be effective for treating particular ailments. Armed with this new information, popular guides continued marketing hot springs as famous local attractions, but now pointed out that their miraculous healing powers were certified by science and the government's own experts. These experts themselves adopted a different tack, advocating for the establishment of modern, hygienic *onsen* facilities that could provide comprehensive medical treatment for specific conditions.[12]

In Ōita's case, the end of Tokugawa-era restrictions, the development of improved transportation networks, and the combined popular and official attention to *onsen* led to unprecedented growth. The number of lodging facilities in Beppu, for example, increased from 18 in the late Tokugawa era to 140 in the mid-1880s; by 1901 there were 286, with 402 in 1935.[13] Although most of these facilities were intended to accommodate hot springs tourists, the detailed, two-page advertisement for a sanatorium specializing in the treatment of tuberculosis, printed in the 1914 popular guidebook *Beppu onsenshi*, clearly indicates that the region had also become known for several medically oriented facilities, as envisioned by earlier experts. The facility in the ad was linked to one of Beppu's oldest private medical clinics, dating from the late 1890s.[14] A slightly later guide from 1920 dedicated more than 10 of its 144 pages to instructions for those who might be seeking medical treatment in Beppu and included a list of thirty-nine clinics or treatment facilities in the area, many of which were featured in ads as well.[15] Ōita's standing as a leader in modern medical *onsen* treatment received a significant boost in 1931 when Kyushu Imperial University (present-day Kyushu University) opened Japan's first research facility specializing in *onsen* treatment in Beppu. In addition to its multiple laboratories for scientific testing, the research center had medical examination rooms with cutting-edge equipment, spa-like inpatient quarters, and, of course, multiple types of therapeutic baths. It targeted a wide variety of ailments for treatment, including internal disorders, skin diseases, nervous conditions, and unspecified physical impairments. Of particular interest in light of Ōita's later role in disability sports, the new research center also housed a swimming pool, an exercise room, and calisthenics facilities for use by recovering patients, though it remains unclear how these resources were incorporated into treatments.[16] Kyushu University's *Onsen* Treatment Research Center continued to serve as a leading research and treatment site well into the postwar era, eventually becoming the present-day Kyushu University Beppu Hospital.

After an understandable dip in tourism in the late wartime and immediate postwar years, Ōita's growth as an *onsen* destination once again took off. In 1960, just as Nakamura was launching his initial efforts to promote disability sports, Beppu welcomed a record 4.5 million tourists and was home to 964 lodging facilities, including 78 sanatoriums.[17] Among the latter was a brand-new site opened in February 1960 as the nation's first facility specializing in *onsen* treatment for survivors of the atomic bombings in Hiroshima and Nagasaki. Initially established and funded largely through voluntary donations, the Beppu Atomic Bomb Survivor *Onsen* Treatment Center later benefited from significant prefectural support, including an 840,000-yen subsidy provided to upgrade the center in the early 1970s.[18] As the establishment and ongoing support of this new facility suggested, postwar Ōita was continuing a long tradition of pioneering and developing new approaches to and venues for healing, and in this sense, the region would provide fertile ground for those interested in using sports as a rehabilitation technique.

The Military Connection

Considering Ōita's prominence as an area for treating a wide variety of ailments, as well as stories dating from the medieval era about the benefits of *onsen* for recovering warriors, it is almost predictable that the region's hot springs would prove attractive to Japan's modern military. A full examination of the military's involvement in Ōita is well beyond the scope of this chapter, but there is little question that Ōita served as host for several sites used to treat Japan's wounded soldiers and sailors. This history merits closer attention here, because these military facilities were directly linked to the region's postwar emergence as a rehabilitation center for those with disabilities.

Ōita's first military treatment facility had its roots in the Russo-Japanese War (1904–5) when a group of battle-injured soldiers were accommodated in several of Beppu's inns. The reported benefits that trauma patients received from the area's springs sparked the army's interest in establishing a permanent convalescence facility in the region. A temporary army sanatorium was established in 1908 in a local home, followed by another at an inn in 1910. Construction on a permanent site began in 1910, with the new Beppu Branch of the Kokura Army Hospital opening in February 1912 in the Ta no yu neighborhood of Beppu City. Sources indicate that the facility had spacious rooms, great views, and, of course, excellent baths, all ideally suited to the recuperation of army trauma patients.[19] In 1925, the Imperial Japanese Navy followed suit and opened its own hospital in Kamegawa Village, which later became part of Beppu City.[20] Given that there were no naval bases in the immediate area at the time, Ōita's draw was almost certainly its growing reputation as a site for *onsen* treatment and its easy access by sea. As Japan entered into full-scale war with China in 1937 followed by war with the Allied Powers in 1941, the number of ill or wounded increased dramatically, resulting in the need for even more treatment and long-term rehabilitation facilities throughout Japan. With the war escalating, a second Imperial Japanese Army branch hospital was opened at Ishigakihara in Beppu City in 1938.[21] A year later the Welfare Ministry established one of its ten nationwide *onsen* sanatoriums for wounded soldiers in Beppu, and by 1940 Ōita Prefecture had opened a National Tuberculosis Sanatorium and been designated as a regional site for retraining wounded military personnel as elementary school teachers.[22] At some point during the expanding conflict, the naval hospital was also enlarged to provide additional space for the war wounded.[23]

Although it remains difficult to determine specific details on the types of ailments these facilities in Ōita addressed or the forms of treatment they pursued, available sources give some sense of the scale of their efforts. By 1933, several years before Japan's military conflicts escalated to their most devastating levels, the original army branch hospital in Beppu had already accommodated more than 10,000 patients in its first twenty years.[24] As the fighting became more intense, Beppu, according to the Ōita prefectural history, was "completely transformed into a 'medical base.'" Hospital boats arrived in port at least once a month to unload wounded or ill military personnel whose numbers eventually exceeded the space available at the local military facilities, necessitating the use of private inns or clinics as impromptu military hospitals. In response to widespread shortages in supplies, the region produced serums and medical equipment locally, including knives and tweezers made from the area's abundant bamboo.[25]

We know little for sure about the treatments administered, but the region's history makes it safe to assume that *onsen* were central to much of the medical activity in Ōita. Historian Lee Pennington's recent work on wartime rehabilitation practices for disabled veterans at military treatment facilities in Tokyo offers hints about other possible techniques, most notably physical exercise and sports. Imperial Japanese Army physicians in Tokyo emphasized the importance of exercise for war-wounded patients early on, as exemplified by a published essay from October 1938 that appealed to Japan's various sports organizations "to develop 'sports for the sick' . . . sports that physically impaired veterans could participate in after they returned to civilian life."[26] Written by the chief of surgery at Provisional Tokyo Number One Army Hospital, the 1938 essay indicated that exercise was already a key part of the military's treatment regimen that "helped men 'return again to their former bodies.'"[27] Pennington's study documents a wide variety of physical activities used in Tokyo's army hospitals: group and specialized calisthenics, marching, *kenjutsu* (swordsmanship) and other traditional martial arts, and such sports as sumo, swimming, baseball, ping-pong, tennis, and track. All of these activities were expressly linked to specific rehabilitative objectives, but the Tokyo military hospitals also clearly recognized the potential benefits of athletic competition for promoting camaraderie, inspiration, and mental well-being for wounded veterans. Ranging from interhospital baseball games to track-and-field meets, sporting events involving patients were held at several Tokyo hospitals, and a number of such events generated popular notice in wartime media.[28]

The relationship between the Paralympics and efforts to provide rehabilitation for war-wounded veterans in other national contexts has been well documented; indeed, the Imperial Japanese Army's interest in the rehabilitative potential of sports would be far from unique. Yet the connections between the military and postwar disability sports in Japan have remained largely unexplored, in no small part because of the country's complex relationship with war memory. In June 2017, for instance, archivists from the Prince Chichibu Memorial Sports Museum and Library discovered a pamphlet from a sports festival for wounded soldiers held in Tokyo in 1939. Even leading Japanese scholars of disability sports greeted the archival find with surprise and excitement, acknowledging that this aspect of Japan's wartime past was largely unknown.[29] Given such recent discoveries, a fuller study of Japan's wartime engagement with disability sports will likely be forthcoming and prove revealing in several respects, but for the purposes of this chapter, it is necessary to turn attention to what all of this might have meant for Ōita, given its role as a wartime "medical base."

Because most sources describing the origins of disability sports in Japan make no mention of sports at military hospitals, the current lack of information describing similar activities in wartime Ōita is not in itself conclusive. On its surface, the fact that Nakamura's later approach to sports for those with disabilities struck many as revolutionary would suggest that the region lacked exposure to these ideas. But there appear to be other factors at play. Many of the sources from Pennington's work on Tokyo address sports and events for amputees in residence at the military's hospitals during the earlier phase of the war. Nakamura, following Guttmann, was promoting competitive sports especially for those with spinal cord injuries more than two decades later. Considering Japan's struggles to provide adequate food and shelter for its people in the later war years and the immediate postwar period, it is difficult to imagine that Japanese sports organizations made much progress toward the goal of promoting "sports for the sick" outside military hospital settings during the 1940s. In the anti-military environment of Allied-occupied Japan (1945–52), it also seems doubtful that wartime sporting events for disabled veterans would have continued into the postwar period, especially because a civilian-oriented system did not emerge to replace the previous military-based approach. In other words, it is likely that awareness of these past military practices became limited to those who had directly experienced them during the war and who may not have wanted to share their wartime experiences in postwar Japan. Combined with the passage of more than fifteen years without the active promotion of disability sports in postwar Japan, the significant differences in forms of impairment that Nakamura was seeking to address in the early 1960s might explain why he faced an uphill battle in his initial efforts, even if Ōita had previously been home to some form of sports activities for veterans with disabilities. Unfortunately, until further details are uncovered, we can only speculate about the relationship between wartime treatment practices and Ōita's later emergence as a disability sports center. At the very least, military physicians in the region were likely aware of such sport-based techniques, and it is possible—even probable—that some of these approaches were being pursued in Ōita during the war years, which might help explain why the region was among the earliest to embrace similar methods in the postwar era.

If the connection between wartime and postwar treatment practices remains unclear in Ōita, the links between the treatment facilities themselves are readily apparent. As part of the broader demilitarization efforts in Allied-occupied Japan, military medical facilities were rapidly converted to civilian use and placed under the aegis of the Welfare Ministry. For Ōita Prefecture, this transition meant that a region with a population of less than 1.25 million that had previously struggled to keep its prefectural hospital open became home to several national hospitals and sanatoriums almost overnight.[30] As a former "medical base," Beppu hosted a disproportionate share of these "new" national facilities. The city's promise as a potential postwar destination for rehabilitation was clear to the Welfare Ministry, which designated Beppu and three other cities as sites for National Rehabilitation Centers for the Physically Disabled in 1948. Ultimately, only one such center was opened during the occupation years, at the former Provisional Tokyo Number Three Army Hospital.[31]

Even without this formal rehabilitation center, many of Beppu's former military venues emerged as postwar sites specializing in treatment and rehabilitation for those with disabilities. The Army Hospital Branch at Ishigakihara became a national sanatorium in December 1945, and after merging with several other local tuberculosis clinics in 1971, it eventually became the present-day Nishi-Beppu National Hospital, which includes late-stage treatment of severe disabilities among its multiple specializations.[32] The naval hospital became Kamegawa National Hospital in December 1945; in 1950 it merged with Beppu's oldest army hospital at Ta no yu (which had also been converted to a national hospital in December 1945) to become Beppu National Hospital.[33] The National *Onsen* Sanatorium for wounded soldiers established in 1938 was initially converted to a national hospital that was incorporated as a branch of Beppu National Hospital in 1950, but after the end of the Allied occupation, it was once again reconstituted as a national sanatorium, one of only two such centers established in 1952 by the Welfare Ministry to provide institutionalized long-term care for veterans with severe disabilities. In 1954, this facility was made available to nonveterans as well, and only a few months before the Paralympics in 1964, it was transformed into a rehabilitation-oriented site and renamed the Beppu National Center for Persons with Severe Disabilities.[34] Even though we know little about the specifics of their treatment practices, it is not difficult to see how the sheer concentration of military medical facilities in Beppu laid the groundwork for the region to become a center of disability-related treatment in postwar Japan. Working within that context, a newly minted physician with a budding interest in cutting-edge rehabilitation techniques began his formal medical career as chief of orthopedic surgery in 1958 at Beppu National Hospital. Over the next several years Nakamura Yutaka's efforts helped turn Ōita into "Japan's cradle of disability sports," the home of a world-famous marathon, and more.

More than Just the Hobby of a Quirky, Back-Country Doctor

Writing not long after the 2006 dissolution of FESPIC, former president Dr. Hatada Kazuo offered the following observation on the movement's roots in southwest Japan: "Some might wonder why we had the FESPIC Games in Ōita, but there was a simple reason. Dr. Yutaka Nakamura was there."[35] Even given Ōita's long history of involvement with various forms of healing sites and rehabilitative practices, as Hatada pointed out, the region's unlikely emergence as a center for disability sports owed much to Nakamura. Limitations of space preclude a full biographical treatment here, but focused examinations of Nakamura's background and his work in the region offer insights on how he repeatedly managed to mobilize diverse interests to achieve local, national, and even international results, as seen in particular with one of his last endeavors: the establishment of Ōita's Wheelchair Marathon.

Nakamura's initial relationship with both Ōita and medicine were rooted in his family history. Soon after he was born in Beppu in 1927, his father, who had recently completed medical training in the field of urology, opened a private clinic in central Beppu at the site of a former *onsen* lodge. Having spent almost his entire childhood in Beppu or nearby Ōita City where he attended Ōita Prefectural Middle School (comparable to present-day junior and senior high school), young Nakamura had personal experience with Beppu's transformation into a wartime "medical base": his father's clinic was requisitioned for military medical use in the early 1940s. After graduating from middle school in March 1945, Nakamura had hoped to pursue studies in engineering, but acceding to his father's demands, he entered a premedical training school instead and eventually became a scholarship student in Kyushu University's medical program. In 1952, Nakamura decided to specialize in orthopedics.[36]

Nakamura claimed that his initial interest in his field stemmed from his long-standing fascination with machines; orthopedic surgery, as he pointed out, simply used more high-tech equipment than any other medical specialty. Whatever the case may be, Japan's recent wartime needs had brought increased attention to the field, and Nakamura's choice of specialty at Kyushu University meant that he would be training under Dr. Amako Tamikazu, whose already distinguished career included several years at Imperial Japanese Army hospitals in Osaka and later Tokyo; there he became known for treating patients with lower-limb paralysis and for pioneering vocational training programs for wounded veterans.[37] In 1953 Amako urged Nakamura to focus his attention on Euro-American approaches to rehabilitation, a suggestion that would ultimately have far greater impact than anyone could have guessed. Although a number of health-care professionals were traveling to Europe and the United States to observe their practices at the time, contemporary foreign approaches to rehabilitation remained unfamiliar in Japan; Nakamura's work over the next several years would play a key role in changing that.[38]

After completing his medical training in 1957 and assuming his first position at Beppu National Hospital the following year, Nakamura published the first of his several books in January 1960. This study of new rehabilitation techniques, coauthored with his mentor Amako, was a basic instructional text filled with photographs, but given the lack of such resources in Japan at the time, it went through multiple printings and quickly established Nakamura's reputation as an emerging leader in the field. The work was particularly well received by the Health and Welfare Ministry, which encouraged Nakamura to offer lectures at its national treatment facilities throughout Japan.[39] Nakamura's involvement in the preparation and publication of the text helps explain why the Health and Welfare Ministry sent him abroad for six months in early 1960 to continue studying European and American rehabilitation practices. As noted in chapter 1, that trip served as Nakamura's firsthand introduction to Guttmann's approach to rehabilitation through sports, an encounter that would inspire much of Nakamura's future work in Ōita and beyond.

In many respects, Nakamura's initial efforts to promote sports-based rehabilitation in Ōita and his early work with Japan's emerging Paralympic Movement foreshadowed the ways in which he would pursue his goals throughout his career. After pitching an idea and encountering hesitancy or even outright resistance, he would not only persist but would also begin actively campaigning to build support for it. Starting with those linked directly to him—and here it is worth recalling that Japan's first participants at the International Stoke Mandeville Games were his patients from Beppu—he then sought outside allies with overlapping interests, such as Hirata Atsushi, the head of Ōita's Social Welfare Department with roots in the physical education field, and Kashiwa Kameo, a leader in Ōita's local disabled veterans group.[40] Having secured increased backing, Nakamura continued reaching out, visiting schools, talking to PE instructors and medical specialists, and connecting with anyone who might have an interest in his project, actions that led to the establishment of supporting groups and organizations in which he assumed roles that allowed him to lead from behind.[41] Once he managed to achieve a particular goal— the hosting of Japan's first disability sports meet or formal participation in the Stoke Mandeville Games in England, for instance—he shifted his focus and energies to some new project. In doing so, he followed a similar pattern, but with each successive undertaking he benefited from an ever-increasing network of allies and was able to point to his previous against-the-odds successes as one more reason to trust this "quirky, back-country doctor."

Nakamura's establishment of Taiyō no Ie in Ōita offers a case in point.[42] As the Tokyo Paralympics came to a close, Nakamura became convinced of the need for facilities that could help people with disabilities in Japan achieve the degree of self-sufficiency that he had witnessed among foreign athletes at the Games. He launched his first effort to create something along those lines in early 1965. Modeled on Goodwill Industries, Nakamura's so-called Goodwill Factory was envisioned as processing, repairing, and reselling donated goods. He quickly abandoned this approach, however, when the first load of donations proved to be little more than unrepairable, unsellable junk. Despite repeated suggestions that he should stick with what he knew—that is, being a medical doctor—he immediately began formulating a plan to establish a factory that could provide employment for those with disabilities by producing something of its own. With the backing of the well-known writer, Minakami Tsutomu, whose daughter was one of Nakamura's patients, Nakamura worked tirelessly to make this new vision a reality as quickly as possible, securing additional support and funding from many of the same individuals and organizations involved in organizing the recent Paralympic Games.[43] Taiyō no Ie opened in October 1965, providing accommodations and working space for fifteen employees with a variety of physical impairments.

As a hastily organized establishment, the first "factory" was more like a handicraft or cottage-industry workshop, and it faced countless obstacles early on; however, by its first anniversary in October 1966, Taiyō no Ie had already expanded and even welcomed the emperor and empress and the crown prince and princess for tours of its newly constructed facilities. Over the course of the next several years, Taiyō no Ie continued to expand and entered partnerships that allowed the new complex to manufacture products and components for larger companies. Using this approach as a model, the Health and Welfare Ministry officially launched a belated effort in 1971 to create so-called social welfare factories for the disabled at three locations in Japan. For Taiyō no Ie, which was, of course, designated as one of the first potential sites, this process culminated in the establishment of a joint venture with electronics manufacturer Omron in December 1971, a formal partnership that proved to be only the first of many. In 1973, Taiyō no Ie demonstrated its long-term viability by making a profit for the first time, and a year later Japan's Ministry of International Trade and Industry named the company as home for a new model social welfare machining factory. By its tenth anniversary in 1975, Taiyō no Ie could boast that it had become the largest factory in Beppu, with more than 400 employees and a complex of factories, housing, and other accommodations that facilitated independent living and social integration for those with a variety of disabilities. Plans were already in motion to expand to additional cities within and possibly beyond Ōita Prefecture.

Like his earlier and ongoing efforts to promote disability sports in Japan, much of Nakamura's work in relation to Taiyō no Ie was inspired by his observations of practices abroad, as evidenced by his use of Goodwill Industries and later the New York-based manufacturing company, Abilities, Inc., as models for his factory in Ōita. Nakamura's goal was to implement such practices as quickly as possible in Japan, but doing so meant that he could not wait for the national or even local governments to take the lead. He needed to launch these efforts himself close to home, create a network of nongovernmental backers, and establish something that the government could then support or at least sanction. As the company was founded and began to produce results, Nakamura's circle of supporters grew, coming to include national celebrities like Akiyama Chieko, business leaders like Sony cofounder Ibuka Masaru, and Omron founder Tateishi Kazuma, as well as politicians of all stripes. For example, then-secretary general of the majority Liberal Democratic Party, Hashimoto Tomisaburō, first visited Taiyō no Ie in 1971 and later backed fundraising efforts in Tokyo and played a behind-the-scenes role in securing transportation for the first FESPIC Games. In its first decade, Taiyō no Ie also received notable attention from members of the imperial family, including multiple visits by different family members and a donation from the emperor himself in 1971. Nakamura both generated and built on these various connections with his constant promotion of Taiyō no Ie through personal meetings, regular speaking engagements, international conference presentations, and interviews and articles published in a wide range of media outlets.

Given his very deep level of commitment to Taiyō no Ie during its early years, it is all the more impressive that, throughout this period, Nakamura launched several other successful undertakings and remained heavily engaged in the promotion of disability sports locally, nationally, and internationally. In 1966, for example, he founded a new facility, Ōita Nakamura Hospital, only a few blocks from the prefectural offices in Ōita City. Taking full advantage of his political connections at the local and national levels, he also initiated the successful campaign to have Beppu named as a Social Welfare Model City in 1973. Among the first six cities to receive such a designation from the Health and Welfare Ministry, Beppu was the only one with a population below the requisite 200,000 people, a fact that did not prevent Nakamura from pursuing the recognition and the disability-friendly infrastructural developments that it made possible.[44]

In light of Nakamura's early commitment to disability sports, it is not surprising that Taiyō no Ie placed particular emphasis on developing accessible athletic facilities and increasing participation in sports for those with disabilities; from its early years, its facilities and sporting activities were opened to the broader community as a means of fostering access and social inclusion. As noted in previous chapters, Nakamura himself continued his involvement with the Paralympics, especially through repeated service as captain of the Japanese team. His success in founding and developing the FESPIC Movement stemmed in no small part from his reputation in the field of disability sports, but it also owed a great deal to his local standing as a figure who had already repeatedly proven the naysayers wrong, bringing increased attention to his home town and prefecture in the process. In that sense, the first FESPIC Games, Ōita's first-ever international sports event, were simply another such example, and over the next few years, Nakamura's undertakings with FESPIC and Taiyō no Ie would continue to bear fruit.

In 1960 when Nakamura published his book and began his work in the realm of disability sports, he would have been a relatively unknown quantity locally, nationally, and internationally. During the next twenty years, he established a track record that would have been difficult to ignore at any level. Nakamura's efforts had repeatedly proven far more than far-fetched dreams or wishful thinking, so when he arrived at the prefectural governor's office with a plan to launch a wheelchair marathon—something that had never been done before in Japan—local leaders were already primed to take him seriously.

Ōita's First Wheelchair Marathon

The roots of Ōita's wheelchair marathon, like so many of Nakamura's undertakings, lay abroad. Inspired in particular by the formal inclusion of wheelchair racers in the Boston Marathon beginning in the mid-1970s and by expressions of interest from Taiyō no Ie employees, Nakamura was easily convinced that Japan should do something similar. Even though Japan—and most of the world for that matter—had no precedents for incorporating wheelchair participants in existing marathons, Nakamura's enthusiasm was not without merit. In December 1977, Nakamura had organized a 5.4-kilometer wheelchair road race as part of the Eleventh Annual Beppu City Road Race. This shorter competition with its twenty-five participants would be the first of many such 3- or 5-kilometer races that became open to wheelchair participants in local communities throughout Japan over the next several years. Japanese athletes were also beginning to participate in the newly available wheelchair marathons abroad, with four athletes racing for the first time in the Honolulu Marathon in 1977. The initial proposal to host a wheelchair marathon in Ōita came from two Taiyō no Ie employees, Yoshimatsu Tokiyoshi and Kobayashi Junichi. Kobayashi had pointed out that Ōita had its very own well-established road race to work with, the Beppu-Ōita Mainichi Marathon held every February. Bolstered by this growing local interest and promising results abroad, Nakamura saw an opportunity in the making.[45]

Pitching the idea of hosting Japan's first wheelchair marathon as a particularly apt way for Ōita to commemorate the upcoming United Nation's International Year of Disabled Persons, Nakamura approached prefectural governor Hiramatsu Morihiko late in 1980 with a plan for incorporating wheelchair athletes in the next Beppu-Ōita Mainichi Marathon. Hiramatsu was a ready convert. Having been elected as governor only two years earlier and calling for increased regional and local self-reliance, Hiramatsu was an Ōita native who spent several years as a high-ranking Ministry of International Trade and Industry bureaucrat before returning to Ōita to assume a role as vice governor in 1975. He would go on to serve as governor until 2003 and achieve national and international fame as founder of the "One Village, One Product" movement that he pioneered in Ōita. In 1980 the then-new governor and his staff were in the process of planning special events for the 1981 International Year of Disabled Persons when Nakamura allegedly "burst into the Governor's office," eager to share his seemingly simple plan for yet another opportunity to demonstrate Ōita's unique commitment to sports for those with disabilities. Struck by Nakamura's enthusiasm and confidence and no doubt familiar with his track record, Hiramatsu quickly declared his support.[46]

With the governor's blessing secured, Nakamura reached out to the organizations in charge of the annual race, only to be told that the official rules for marathons in Japan required that participants run the race using their legs. Wheelchairs, Nakamura was informed, were like bicycles, so wheelchair racers could not compete alongside nondisabled runners as they were doing in some marathons abroad. Notably, this response in Ōita was similar to the argument against wheelchair participation used by the New York City Marathon for several years. Nevertheless, Nakamura remained undeterred and continued searching for a way to allow wheelchair athletes to compete in Ōita.

The specific timing and details remain vague, but eventually the local track-and-field organizations in Ōita agreed to share their know-how and provide logistic support if a separate, wheelchair-only event were to be established. With continued backing from the governor, a new plan took shape calling for an international marathon in November 1981 that would feature only wheelchair athletes. Yet many in Ōita remained unconvinced. Because most of the Japanese athletes would be competing in their first long-distance race, prefectural bureaucrats expressed concerns about their well-being, pointing in particular to the prefecture's liability if the event were to result in accidents, injuries, illness, or worse. The prefectural police had safety concerns as well and argued that they could not possibly tie up traffic for the three to four hours that would be needed for participants to finish a full marathon. Citing his medical expertise, Nakamura countered with assertions that wheelchair marathons were safe and provided unparalleled rehabilitative benefits for participants. Ultimately the plan to hold the first marathon moved forward, but with a compromise: instead of a full, 42.195-kilometer marathon, Ōita's first race would be a half-marathon, a measure meant to address lingering concerns about health, safety, and traffic.

Organizational work for the first marathon began in March 1981, as soon as the prefecture formally approved the plan to host the event in November of that year. Once again, Nakamura and his fellow organizers found themselves facing a time crunch as they put together an international sporting event from scratch, with few examples to work from. Domestic models, after all, were nonexistent, and even the large marathons in the United States only averaged about twenty wheelchair racers a year, while Ōita was aiming for more than a hundred. To assure that they hit that target, Nakamura mobilized his international connections through Stoke-Mandeville, FESPIC, and various professional organizations to recruit foreign athletes, an effort that resulted in the participation of forty-three wheelchair racers from thirteen foreign countries. Among the foreign competitors were several from FESPIC countries and two recent wheelchair champions from Austria and the United States. Funding details are particularly unclear for the first race, but it appears that many of the international athletes received financial assistance to pay for travel and lodging expenses within Japan, a pattern reminiscent of FESPIC that continued to be the norm for some of the later marathons as well.[47] Beppu City Council member Yoshinaga Eiji assisted with domestic recruitment, often citing his own plans to enter the race when he reached out to acquaintances throughout Japan. Naturally, Ōita was especially well represented with twenty-nine participants, but forty-five athletes from other prefectures in Japan joined the first race as well. In a positive sign for the future, Yoshinaga noted that several more of those he spoke with said they would have participated with more advanced notice of the event. Although the vast majority of the participants were men, the marathon was coed from the beginning, with six women, one of whom was from Japan, competing in 1981.

In what proved to be one of many foundational elements, the staff for organizing and planning the first Marathon appear to have come primarily from the prefectural government itself, including sixteen members of the Disability and Social Welfare Section. In fact, Ōita's first marathon was almost entirely a local operation. Its three official sponsors were the prefectural government, Ōita's Sports Association for the Disabled (headed by Nakamura), and the local *Ōita gōdō shimbun* newspaper, and it was administered by the Ōita Prefecture Athletics Association. As might be expected, Taiyō no Ie staff also played a key role, providing multiple forms of behind-the-scenes support. Although foreign athletes were eventually accommodated at a Beppu hotel known for hosting guests with disabilities, those who arrived early stayed at Taiyō no Ie, which offered its facilities for practice space and for hosting the marathon's opening ceremony. Like Ōita's FESPIC Games, the marathon relied heavily on volunteers, especially for foreign-language support. In addition, volunteers joined more than 200 prefectural police in safeguarding the marathon route on the day of the race. The route itself proved particularly troubling to develop, after worries about safety and traffic tie-ups led organizers to reject the traditional Beppu-Ōita Mainichi Marathon course. Aiming to create a course that would be safe, less disruptive of traffic patterns, easily accessible for large numbers of spectators, and good for racers, organizers eventually settled on a route that began in front of the prefectural office, turned toward the coastline, took multiple passes along the coast, and then finished in the prefectural stadium, a route that has remained largely unchanged to the present.[48]

The sponsoring *Ōita gōdō* newspaper provided extensive press coverage for the first marathon, introducing the event, its organizers, and a number of its racers to local audiences via multiple articles, images, and advertisements. Even the most casual newspaper reader would have had a hard time missing news of the first race or failing to notice that the newspaper itself was a sponsor (nearly every article or ad mentioned that fact). An analysis of the evolution of media coverage for disability sports is provided in chapter 4, but it bears noting that, despite (or perhaps because of) the paper's vested interest, local reporting on the first marathon was vastly superior in almost every respect compared to what was available in national media outlets. *Ōita gōdō*'s early coverage set not only a number of precedents but also remarkably high standards for reporting on future races.

The first Ōita International Wheelchair Marathon itself proved a great success. After an opening ceremony and a mandatory medical evaluation carried out the previous afternoon at Taiyō no Ie, 117 wheelchair athletes competing in six classification categories gathered in front of the prefectural office in Ōita City on Sunday, November 1, 1981, to start their race at exactly 11 a.m. Though some racers dropped out before finishing, organizers' worst fears of crashes or injuries never came to pass. The course turned out to be both fast and spectator friendly. Contrary to the expectations of some, fans provided enthusiastic support, with numbers similar to the annual Beppu-Ōita Mainichi Marathon, and 109 racers finished, including all but 3 of the Japanese athletes. Considering that most of those participating were competing in their everyday wheelchairs instead of the much lighter and more maneuverable racing chairs we are accustomed to seeing today, the high number of finishers was all the more noteworthy.[49]

The most controversial aspect of the marathon ended up being its finish. The top two racers, Georg Freund of Austria and Jim Knaub from the United States, were neck and neck throughout and well ahead of the others. Having reportedly discussed their plan in advance, both men joined hands, raised them into the air, and crossed the finish line together. Since Freund's front wheels had crossed the line slightly ahead of Knaub's, officials declared Freund the winner by less than one-tenth of a second. Arguing that their "Joint Victory of Friendship" should be recognized, Knaub refused to accept his second-place medal, joining Freund in lifting the championship cup instead. The unanticipated outcome posed an immediate dilemma for organizers, especially because the two racers argued that their gesture perfectly symbolized the event's stated goals of promoting equality and camaraderie. As one of the key organizers, Nakamura, a man known for bucking the system, offered a somewhat ironic opinion that many have since come to view as a defining moment for Ōita's marathon. "Wheelchair marathons are competitions, not recreational events," he argued, continuing, "We need to follow the rules, as determined by the race officials."[50] The almost made-for-media controversy sparked press criticisms of organizers as "cold-hearted," but the official decision remained unchanged, leaving no doubt that the Ōita marathon would remain a competition.[51]

The "Joint Victory" controversy did not detract from overall enthusiasm about the event's success. As it concluded, Nakamura told the Ōita gōdō that the race "had more than satisfied the goals for the [first] wheelchair marathon."[52] Foreign athletes praised Ōita's race management, expressing hopes that organizers would hold another marathon the following year.[53] Beppu City councilman Yoshinaga who finished the race in seventy-fourth place, nursing a blister on his left hand, went a step further, saying, "We weren't allowed to participate in the Beppu-Ōita Marathon, but I think this race can help people understand the strength of those with disabilities. Next time, I hope they will make it a full marathon."[54]

Yoshinaga was not alone in his hopes for the future. At a press conference the next day, Governor Hiramatsu praised the event for its unique ability to "capture the hearts and minds of the able-bodied and disabled alike" and expressed his desire to see Ōita host a full-length wheelchair marathon each year.

While acknowledging that there were obstacles to doing so, he said that Ōita would consult with international disability sports organizations to overcome such barriers as planning moved forward.[55] Even though Nakamura had initially pitched the marathon as a special event to mark the International Year of Disabled Persons, his efforts and comments left little doubt that he, too, was intent on seeing the race become an annual event that hosted a true marathon. In fact, on the eve of the first marathon, he had informed *Ōita gōdō* that he hoped "to turn Ōita into an international wheelchair marathon mecca."[56]

Like Hiramatsu, Nakamura was well aware that the organizers would need to overcome a number of barriers to make that happen: the successful completion of Ōita's first race was only the initial step. It was also necessary to convince doubters in Japan and elsewhere about the viability and safety of marathons for those with disabilities, especially given that the international organizations that Hiramatsu spoke of working with were not yet fully behind efforts promoting these types of events. To garner the additional support he would need, Nakamura began by organizing a Marathon Medical Conference at Taiyō no Ie a few days before the first race, which appears to have served as forerunner for a later Wheelchair Marathon Seminar series that preceded Ōita's race for several years. Nakamura also arranged to have several foreign and Japanese racers wear monitors to record their heart rates before and during the race, data he would use to make his case. The following year at the Annual Meeting of the International Medical Society of Paraplegia, he reported the results of his research, which affirmed the rehabilitative benefits of wheelchair marathon racing. That report then served as the basis for his petition to the International Stoke Mandeville Wheelchair Sports Federation in December 1982, requesting that marathons be recognized as one of its officially sanctioned events. After investigating Nakamura's claims, the federation agreed, a result that not only bolstered the case back home for Ōita to host a full marathon but also made it possible for that race in 1983 to become the world's first officially sanctioned wheelchair marathon.[57] Once again, Ōita was breaking new ground in the realm of disability sports and was on its way to becoming the wheelchair marathon mecca that Nakamura had foreseen.

Many Marathons, Multiple Meanings

By the time of Nakamura's untimely death in late July 1984, his efforts at home and abroad had already helped assure that Ōita's young marathon would continue and eventually thrive. The push to turn Ōita's race into a marathon in the truest sense of the word had come to fruition in 1983, when an internationally sanctioned, 42.195-kilometer wheelchair road race was added alongside the existing half-marathon. The growing list of sponsors and supporters had practically guaranteed that Ōita would continue hosting this unique event well into the future. Thanks to that support and the ongoing work of countless organizers and volunteers, Ōita did become, as Nakamura hoped, a premier destination for wheelchair marathon racing in the years following his death. The success of Ōita's marathon and its four decades' worth of history make it a unique vantage point for evaluating changes and continuities in disability sports events and their broader impacts. Unlike most other events, the race in Ōita allows us to see such developments over a significant period of time, at a single site. With that in mind, the following sections offer several observations on the marathon's evolution and what it has meant for a sampling of the many stakeholders who have shaped it.

Over the course of its history, the marathon experienced a number of changes, yet many of its time-tested elements were already apparent in its earliest years. Most significantly, it remained rooted as a local event, even as its national and international reputation grew. Like many of Nakamura's projects, the initial success at the local level generated broader interest. By the second marathon, the event had already drawn the official support of the Japan Sports Association for the Disabled, and as noted below, the race eventually attracted critical backing from a variety of corporate sponsors as well.[58] Yet, for most of its history, the Ōita prefectural government has served as the event's single largest source of both financial support and formal organizational staffing, and Ōita City and the *Ōita gōdō* newspaper have continued to provide significant funding and support.

The reasons behind such local support for the marathon are, of course, manifold, but two merit special notice here.[59] First, the race quickly came to be seen as emblematic of Ōita's distinctive history of and ongoing commitment to creating new opportunities for those with disabilities in the realm of sports and beyond. The linkage stemmed in part from Nakamura's earlier work, as evidenced by repeated local, national, and even international references to the marathon in connection with FESPIC and Taiyō no Ie.[60] Yet it is important to acknowledge that efforts to promote disability-friendly policies and approaches in the prefecture did not end with Nakamura's passing. Throughout the 1980s and 1990s, Ōita was often at the forefront of national campaigns for improving the accessibility of built environments, addressing the needs of Japan's aging society, and promoting social inclusion.[61] A prefectural plan from 2015, for instance, called not only for continuing such efforts but also for achieving the nation's highest rate of employment for those with disabilities.[62] Of course, not all of these developments can be directly linked to the marathon, but as Governor Hiramatsu pointed out, the event served as a de facto annual proving ground for the social welfare or rehabilitation sectors, providing a site for highlighting, evaluating, and even motivating progress toward Ōita's broader social welfare goals.[63] What started as a celebration to mark the International Year of Disabled Persons became a recurring impetus for and symbol of Ōita Prefecture's own achievements.

As his views on the marathon's beneficial roles in social welfare reform suggest, Governor Hiramatsu's commitment to the event was itself a second critical factor that generated ongoing local support, perhaps all the more so because of his lengthy tenure in office. By the time he stepped down, preparations were already underway for the twenty-third annual race, and in the words of his successor, Governor Hirose Katsusada, the marathon had "become one of the most typical sights of late fall in Ōita."[64] Although Hiramatsu was certainly not alone in promoting the event, his early advocacy and continuing support for the race helped assure that the marathon would become and continue be a prefectural "product" even after he left office.

Hiramatsu's commitment to the race must be viewed in relation to his "One Village, One Product" campaign that was just beginning to take shape in Ōita in the early 1980s. Aimed at addressing depopulation, increasing regional productivity, and ending dependence on government subsidies, this campaign sought to mobilize existing resources throughout the region and foster local talent to produce distinctive, yet internationally marketable products.[65] Whether by design or good fortune, Nakamura's proposed international wheelchair marathon aligned perfectly with these ideals, offering the newly elected governor a highly visible annual forum for demonstrating both the validity of his approach and his desire to improve social welfare in the prefecture. The marathon organizers drew on Ōita's expertise in disability sports to craft a one-of-a-kind event that promised to—and eventually did—bring hundreds of foreign and domestic visitors to the prefecture each year. As it turned out, it also generated multiple, highly lauded visits—nine as of 2010—to the prefecture from various members of Japan's imperial family.[66] These potential and ultimately realized benefits help explain why Hiramatsu became an early enthusiastic champion for the marathon at a time when such races were still rare and disability sports in general received minimal attention at home or abroad. Nakamura, it would seem, was not alone in hoping that the wheelchair marathon would turn Ōita into a destination.

The event also fit well with Hiramatsu's larger goals because it could leverage Ōita's existing reputation as Japan's cradle of disability sports to turn the region into a national and even global center for marathon-related research. Nakamura's rehabilitation-related conference and international presentations in connection with the first marathon provided the earliest hints of this possibility. Beginning with the first race, other medical staff from Taiyō no Ie and from several medical schools compiled medical data from participants and presented their findings on the benefits of marathons at medical, rehabilitation, and physical therapy organizations throughout Japan.[67] Similar medically oriented research projects continued well into the 1990s, as evidenced by a variety of papers published in Japanese and international journals.[68] As the marathon, like other disability sports, began moving away from its rehabilitation roots, the research continued, but its focus shifted toward sports science or scientifically based training. For example, Ōkawa Hiroyuki and a group of fellow medical specialists designed and conducted a series of experiments between the eleventh and fifteenth marathons to understand differences in athletes' techniques and how they affected performance. These studies were fueled in part by questions about why multiyear champion Heinz Frei—who participated in the research—was so dominant in the marathon.[69]

Beginning in 1987, the Ōita International Wheelchair Marathon Seminar provided an annual venue for sharing such research. Held on the Saturday evening before the marathon, the seminar was halted after the 1997 race for reasons that remain unclear, but during its ten-year run, it welcomed a wide variety of domestic and international speakers—eventually moving away from medically centered presentations to those featuring coaches and athletes talking about their own experiences with training, nutrition, and equipment.[70] In addition to such marathon-specific research and presentation opportunities, the success and longevity of the marathon also began to attract the attention of those studying event management or sports history, as in the case of this current chapter.[71] More recently, Ōita was once again linked to high-tech research aimed at helping Japanese racers improve their marathon performances at the 2016 Rio Paralympics.[72] With such an impressive record as both a generator of and a destination for research, the marathon more than succeeded in making a name for Ōita at home and abroad, which helps explain its continued prominence on the international website for Hiramatsu's "One Village, One Product" campaign.[73] For the former governor, the marathon came to epitomize his goals—and achievements—in Ōita.

Under Hiramatsu's successor, the marathon changed in character. Arriving in office in 2003 as Japan's national economy was still struggling to recover from the stagnation of the "lost decade" (1991–2010), Governor Hirose (who continues to serve as governor as of this writing) inherited not only the marathon but also a prefecture with a steadily declining population, decreasing tax revenues, and growing income disparity compared with the rest of Japan. As a result, the marathon, like nearly everything else in the prefectural budget, was targeted for cost reductions. By this point, however, the event was established enough at home and abroad that its continuity was nearly assured, and compared with other areas, the proposed cuts were minor. Hirose's initial 2004 fiscal reform plan called primarily for simplification of ceremonial aspects, while leaving support for invited foreign athletes and other elements untouched.[74]

In the end, the 2004 marathon and those after it showed several marked changes from earlier iterations. Most visibly, the opening ceremony was relocated from the prefectural gymnasiums used in the past to the Galleria Takemachi shopping arcade in central Ōita. Following a scaled-down opening ceremony in the arcade's domed square, athletes paraded through the shopping arcade to a local park. The 2004 transition was billed as a way to celebrate the shopping district's one-hundredth anniversary and to allow for greater interaction between athletes and the local population. Without discounting the value of those goals, the shift was almost certainly fueled by the twin desires of reducing costs by using a cheaper venue and drawing visitors to the economically struggling shopping arcade district.[75]

Other celebratory events were also eliminated or simplified to reduce costs. Such measures appear to have proven inadequate to meet cost-cutting targets, because the 2004 Marathon also ended the practice of formally inviting and providing travel support for select participants in the half-marathon, a change that would have been less noticeable to spectators but arguably far more significant for some of the athletes. Although financial support for invited international participants in the full marathon has continued, it, too has been subject to reductions. In the years since he came to office, Hirose's annual remarks celebrating the marathon have left little doubt that he values and supports the event, but the event's financial dependence on the prefecture has led to continued efforts to reduce the local financial burden by trimming costs, increasing contributions from existing donors, acquiring new sponsorships, and adding the first-ever registration fees for participants in 2011.[76]

Complicating matters still further is the fact that overall participation numbers in Ōita's Marathon have been trending downward after peaking in the late 1990s. With the combined full- and half-marathon races, Ōita's event remains the world's largest wheelchair-only marathon and is still one of a handful of full marathons sanctioned by the IPC. Yet it is far from the only marathon available for potential racers, even in Japan. The Tokyo Marathon's elite wheelchair division race was also sanctioned by the IPC in 2016, and in 2017 it was formally added to the Abbott World Marathon Majors Wheelchair Race Series, an elite international point-based competition that notably does not include Ōita's event.[77]

To continue to attract the best racers and thereby maintain Ōita's reputation as a high-level, world-class race in the face of such added competition at home and abroad, in 2010 organizers began offering cash prizes for victories and record-setting times in Ōita's full marathon. After fielding criticism from top-level international athletes that the inadequate prize money in Ōita made their future participation doubtful, organizers more than tripled some of the rewards beginning with the thirty-fifth race in 2015. Although it remains too soon to determine what impact this change will have on participation rates or the future of the marathon in general, it is undeniably clear that the awards will add significantly to the cost of the event. Since it would be out of the question to use Ōita's tax dollars to cover the more than 4.5 million yen slated for the new annual prizes (not counting costs for record-setting-time bonuses), organizers have had to rely even more on the generosity of corporate sponsors that, so far, have proven amenable.[78]

Although this reliance on corporate sponsors for prize money is a relatively new development, sponsorship in various forms has undergirded the event from its earliest years. *Ōita gōdō*, as noted earlier, has been a backer since the beginning, joining a long line of Japanese newspapers that have served as founding sponsors for various sporting events. Details on the marathon's history of sponsorships are relatively sparse, but it seems to have benefited early on from the support of local broadcast media outlets, as well as domestic and international airlines, which presumably provided assistance with participants' travel.[79]

Perhaps understandably, Taiyō no Ie, too, has proven an incredibly important ally, all the more so through its relationships with FESPIC and several larger national corporations. For instance, the official English-language newsletter of the FESPIC Information Center for the Disabled, which was based at Taiyō no Ie, featured prominent advertising for and coverage of the marathon from the earliest planning stages.[80] This sort of promotion and Taiyō no Ie's role in recruitment more generally were essential to the ongoing success of the event. As one recent organizer noted, for many years Taiyō no Ie served as the marathon's "window to the world," because prefectural organizers lacked other means for reaching international athletes.[81]

Taiyō no Ie was linked to more formal sponsorships as well. Its oldest joint-venture partner Omron was among the first companies to become an official sponsor of the marathon, doing so in 1988.[82] Asked about the sponsorship three years later in the business journal *Business Japan*, corporate representatives noted that the company was committing funds to cover roughly one-third of the marathon's budgeted costs, but dismissed suggestions that this was done for advertising purposes. For Omron, sponsoring the marathon was both a natural outgrowth of its relationship with Taiyō no Ie and an obligation stemming from its "nature as a public institution," or what today we might call corporate social responsibility.[83] Based on its placement at the front or top of nearly all recent sponsor-related references, Omron has continued to be a leading sponsor for the marathon and has been joined by other major Japanese companies, including five other top sponsors involved in joint ventures with Taiyō no Ie: Sony, Honda, Mitsubishi Shōji, Denso, and Fujitsu.

Official figures from the 2014 marathon reveal that funds from more than fifteen corporate sponsors, combined with those from Ōita gōdō and other donations, covered nearly half of the event's total costs, a percentage that has likely increased since then, given the need for larger sponsored prizes beginning in 2015.[84] Like Omron's early decision to back the event, some of these sponsors have almost certainly been motivated to contribute out of a sense of social responsibility, a desire that may very well be based on or reinforced by existing ties with the region. At the same time, marketing changes at the event suggest that sponsors might be finding that contributions are also in their corporate interest. In recent years, the marathon has provided increasingly prominent displays of its sponsors, as exemplified by the backdrop used for the opening ceremony and the annual pre-marathon press conference. Links to all of the major sponsors are featured prominently on both the Japanese and English versions of the marathon's website. With the first nationwide live broadcast of the event in 2016, the potential audience for the race and consequently for visual displays of its sponsors expanded dramatically.[85] In addition, many sponsors themselves have begun using their involvement with the marathon for a variety of in-house and external PR efforts, suggesting that distinctions between corporate social responsibility and corporate interest in relation to the marathon may be beginning to blur.[86] Whether this will continue to be the case remains unclear, especially if participation at the race were to decrease in significant ways. Whatever their motivations or future intentions, sponsors have played—and perhaps now more than ever—will continue to play a defining role in Ōita's annual race.

Along with such corporate sponsorships and prefectural support, the third element of what Hiramatsu once described as the marathon's sustaining "trinity" has long been its volunteers.[87] As noted in the first two chapters, a heavy reliance on volunteerism has been a hallmark of Japan's disability sports events since the 1960s, and Ōita's ongoing experience has been no exception. In some years, the number of formal event volunteers assisting with the marathon exceeded 3,000, with numbers in recent years averaging closer to 2,000. A spirit of volunteerism tends to be one of the oft-cited legacies associated with hosting sports mega-events in general, and images of local students greeting foreign marathoners or stories about groups of elderly citizens spontaneously arranging to clear debris from the course before the race seem to suggest that Ōita's marathon bears out such assumptions.[88]

A closer examination, however, reveals a more complex picture. A significant and apparently growing percentage of the volunteers come from outside the prefecture as representatives of companies sponsoring the event. In a recent race, some twenty companies provided more than one-quarter of the total volunteers. Other large groups of volunteers were from prefectural or city offices, the police force, the local Ground Self-Defense Force base, and Ōita's track-and-field association. A number of others were recruited through disability sports or social welfare organizations that have their own vested interests in the race. Can Do, a club founded to provide foreign-language assistance for the first marathon, continues to serve as the source of roughly 200 volunteer interpreters each year.[89]

This organizationally based approach to volunteering has obvious advantages, especially for those planning the marathon each year, a point one of the event organizers emphasized when he met with me in summer 2015. Rather than relying on unpredictable local volunteer recruitment drives, this approach allowed him to work with a set number of representatives from more-or-less predetermined groups and to confirm far in advance exactly how many volunteers he was going to have. From an event management perspective, Ōita's marathon provides an excellent model for the efficient recruitment, training, and mobilization of the volunteers needed to hold the race each year.[90]

Yet the very nature of Ōita's volunteer program also seems to unintentionally limit the potential pool of recruits to those already tied to the event, making it difficult to assess whether the marathon itself has had a positive impact on local volunteerism in Ōita beyond such groups. Given the types of groups involved, it is also difficult to avoid wondering how voluntary some of this volunteering might be. Two organizers told me that another challenge they regularly face is balancing the number and skills of volunteers committed by outside groups with tasks that need to be completed. Failure to get the equation right can mean shortages at key moments or, more commonly, people getting bored, which can result in future recruiting challenges.[91] My own observations of the 2016 marathon seemed to reflect this concern. At many points during the event a significant number of volunteers—whose company jackets made them stand out—seemed to have little to do other than cheer alongside other spectators. Most appeared enthusiastic, but this did not strike me as typical volunteer work.[92]

My point here is not to criticize the approach in Ōita or to imply that the race does not generate meaningful experiences for volunteers, but rather to highlight the importance of looking beyond the numbers and assumptions when exploring volunteerism as a legacy of sports mega-events. Ōita's marathon has undoubtedly benefited from the support of countless volunteers over the years, and many volunteers reportedly enjoy the experience enough to return. But the event also serves as a useful reminder that volunteerism comes in many guises.

The impact of the marathon in Ōita is not, of course, limited to volunteerism. The race is said to attract some 200,000 spectators who line nearly the entire course each year, many with homemade signs encouraging racers in English or Japanese. Although such levels of engagement differ from that required by formal volunteerism, they do suggest that many in Ōita are more than willing to take time out of their weekend to watch the race, much as people in Tokyo, New York, or Boston do for their own local events. The looping nature of the course lends itself particularly well to spectating; it is possible (with a hurried pace) to watch the start, cut to an area near the first checkpoint to see most of the racers, and then head to the stadium in time to catch the fastest half-marathon finishers. The arching Benten Bridge in between the first checkpoint and the stadium is clearly a prime spectating spot. Racers who cross the checkpoint in time go over the bridge twice, reaching high speeds as they descend from either side. During the 2016 race, the sidewalks on both sides of the bridge were packed with people, including several uniformed youth baseball teams, shouting enthusiastically as competitors zipped by, rhythmically thumping away at their wheelchairs' push-rims. Many people remained on the bridge until the last athlete passed. This final racer struggled to make it up the bridge's long ascent. Every push on his rims gained him a few inches, which were marked with new calls of encouragement from the crowd, and as the racer crested the hill, his efforts were rewarded with a speedy descent and a wave of applause and praise.[93]

Over the years, the marathon has provided those following the event in person or via the media with its share of stimulating, exciting, or nerve-wracking sporting moments: photo finishes, maintained or broken winning streaks, world records, and the occasional shocking crash. One of the selling points for the race is the 50 to 60 kilometer/hour downhill speeds that top racers achieve at certain points on the course. Given all the concerns about safety in the early years of the event, the intentional use of these high speeds to market the marathon today reflects how much the sport has changed since 1981.[94] In many respects, the race has become an exciting annual sports spectacle in its own right. But it was always intended to be more than that.

Beyond the Races

From the very earliest discussions about the event as a way to highlight the International Year of Disabled Persons to the most recent race, the marathon has been repeatedly billed as a unique opportunity to help Ōita and its citizens foster positive international relations and create social and physical environments that are welcoming and accessible for those with disabilities. Admirable though they might be, these twin goals, given their amorphous nature, are very difficult to assess in concrete ways. That said, a variety of forms of circumstantial and anecdotal evidence point to the fact that the marathon has had an impact in both respects.[95]

In wheelchair marathon circles, "OITA" is a name that has become known worldwide, having even found its way into a 2012 mystery novel by bestselling American author Craig Johnson.[96] There is no denying that for forty years, the event has succeeded in bringing anywhere from 50 to more than 100 international athletes to Ōita each year, people who might otherwise never have visited the region or even Japan. A fair portion of the foreign athletes are repeat attendees, and their comments characterizing the event as "great" or "the best" reveal that for many the desire to return to Ōita stems as much from the local atmosphere with its enthusiastic spectators and welcoming people as it does from the quality of the race itself.[97]

Despite cost-cutting measures that have resulted in the discontinuation or simplification of several ceremonial events, opportunities for interactions between visiting international athletes and local citizens remain abundant, ranging from welcome receptions at hotels or the airport to visits and talks at local schools and universities.[98] Two of the athletes I spoke with in 2016 said that the opportunities to visit with and answer questions from local youngsters are among their favorite parts of their marathon experiences. One of them noted that he has been coming to Ōita for so many years that he is now meeting the children of youngsters he met years ago.[99] Organizers pointed out to me that these sorts of meet-and-greet or public speaking events served a secondary purpose as well, by providing small honorariums for foreign visitors who had to cover their own expenses of participating in the marathon.[100]

Understandably, the marathon courses and official warm-up venues themselves are closed to everyone except officials and racers, but many of the other events before and after the race are open to the public. At these events, the abundance of volunteer interpreters from Can Do—easily identified by their distinctive jackets—facilitates social interactions for any who want to pursue them. Several of the spectators I spoke with said that they tried to come to the opening ceremony and watch the race each year, though they admitted that they rarely took advantage of the interpreters to talk with the international athletes. Others, including a number of children in wheelchairs at the opening and closing ceremonies, seemed particularly enthusiastic about making connections with Japanese and foreign racers alike, chatting with athletes, shaking hands, and posing for pictures. Several young people even joined in as the group of athletes paraded through the shopping arcade to mark the end of the opening ceremony. We cannot know with any certainty how such informal international exchanges shape people's attitudes and perceptions, but certainly the marathon has increased and regularized opportunities for these sorts of interactions in Ōita.

A similar case can be made for the event's impact on local approaches to those with disabilities. For much of its history, organizers contended that the marathon was a tool for deepening the public's interest in and understanding of disability, often pointing to letters published in the newspaper after races where the writers praised the event for giving them new perspectives.[101] Similar anecdotes about positive or changing social attitudes in Ōita are abundant. Reflecting on their experiences at the marathon over the years, Sakamoto Masato and Sakamoto Ritsuko, a married couple from Osaka, noted that they enjoyed coming to Ōita, because they could go out in the city with their wheelchairs without people staring at them.[102] Writing in 1994 for a weekly social welfare journal, the head of Ōita's Disability and Social Welfare Section linked the marathon to the fact that his office was no longer receiving reports about people in wheelchairs being denied access to taxis.[103] Whether such changes were, in fact, tied to the marathon is difficult to determine, especially given the prefecture's history of extensive exposure to those with disabilities. At the very least, the presence of so many people in wheelchairs, year after year, has made disability ever more visible in Ōita and encouraged the region to become more accommodating.

One example of such trends is the local "barrier-free map" posted for several years on the marathon's Japanese and English websites. Available from at least 2007, the map highlights buildings that offer wheelchair-friendly features such as ramps, elevators, and accessible restrooms. Although a number of the labeled buildings are public facilities, others are hotels or stores—yet the vast majority of establishments in the area, including several hotels, are notably absent from the map. This fact suggests that the map itself could serve as an informal tool for promoting broader awareness of and the development of accessible environments. It clearly demonstrates that Ōita still remains far from barrier-free after forty years hosting the marathon, an instructive point for those seeking to use disability sporting events to promote broader social changes. Ōita's example suggests that the hosting of sporting events might foster change but cannot bring about wholesale change by itself.[104]

Among the more striking, and by many accounts successful, attempts to expand the marathon's desired impact was the "Outreach Workshop" carried out as part of the thirtieth-anniversary celebrations in 2010. In the months leading up to and just after the thirtieth race, local athletes with disabilities visited some sixty elementary and middle schools throughout the prefecture to introduce the marathon, talk more generally about disability and sports, and allow students the chance to try out various adapted sports for themselves. These outreach events in Ōita proved so popular that smaller-scale efforts to promote student and athlete interactions were incorporated as part of the following year's marathon as well.[105] The hundreds of student comments selected for inclusion in the specially produced photo booklet commemorating the program ran the gamut from single-sentence observations on the difficulty of shooting a basketball from a wheelchair to paragraph-long discussions about overcoming adversity through hard work. Diverse as they were, what these comments revealed was that the workshop had inspired many of these children to consider questions of dis-ablement for the first time, one more outcome that speaks to the ways in which the marathon has had an impact on perceptions of disability in Ōita.

Such impacts remain difficult to assess in terms of their broader effect, and it is apparent that not everyone in Ōita welcomes the marathon with open arms. The organizers I met with reported that traffic-related complaints were among the more common issues they have had to address. The latter portion of the full marathon poses particular challenges because athletes with higher needs (T51 in the current classification system) tend to take longer to complete the race, and only a handful of them compete each year. With limited understanding of disability sports and its admittedly complex classification systems, uninformed observers in Ōita see only a single person in a wheelchair seemingly tying up traffic for nearly an hour after many of the other racers have finished. These sorts of impressions then prompt questions about why the marathon does not impose more stringent time limits on participants. Organizers in Ōita expressed regret about the lack of familiarity and empathy inherent in such complaints, but it seems likely that the combination of lower participation rates and extended time frames have led other marathons to cut similarly classified athletes from their races entirely.[106] As just one telling example, the last full marathon at the Paralympics for athletes with T51 classifications occurred in 2004. The very fact that Ōita has resisted such trends in the face of recurring criticism at home is a testament to its organizers' ongoing commitment to assuring that Ōita's marathon remains open to as many participants as possible, one of many elements that continues to make this a one-of-a-kind event.

Balancing Accessibility and Elite Sport

Indeed, Ōita has achieved a reputation among athletes at home and abroad in part because it hosts a well-organized marathon that is highly competitive and extremely accessible—two descriptors that can often seem mutually exclusive in disability sports events today. Both of these features were already apparent in the marathon's earliest years. Like other events Nakamura was involved in organizing, the marathon was rooted in his belief that sports were critical for fostering what its founding statement labeled "physical and mental rehabilitation." In line with trends in disability sports more generally, this explicit reference to rehabilitation was dropped from the event's stated goals in 1995, but language citing the marathon as a source of inspiration and a venue for social engagement for those with disabilities has remained.[107]

Combined with the early lack of models or even regulations for wheelchair marathons, these ideals led organizers to pursue an inclusive approach in Ōita from the beginning: the event has never required qualifying times for either the half- or the full marathon, has offered generous cutoff times at its checkpoints, has encouraged athletes with varying degrees of impairment to participate, and, until 2011, did not require any registration fees. Paradoxically, many of these measures would have been far more difficult to implement if the marathon had been integrated with an existing event as originally planned. All that said, it is also critical to remember that Nakamura sought out the best international athletes to participate beginning with the first race, explicitly rejected the idea of the now famous "Joint Victory" because the race needed to have a clear champion, and aggressively pursued official international sanction for the marathon. In other words, the event that took shape in Ōita was one where elite-level competition and broad-based accessibility were viewed as mutually beneficial or even mutually necessary for the race to achieve its many goals. As Ōita's marathon has evolved since the early 1980s, these two elements have been pursued simultaneously, producing benefits and tensions in the process.

Both elements of the marathon have reflected and been shaped by many of the changes apparent in disability sports more generally. As noted earlier, the growth of wheelchair marathons as nationally and internationally recognized sporting events has proven a mixed blessing for Ōita. Rising interest in the event brought more marathoners to Ōita, but this increased demand eventually translated into the greater availability of other marathons, a development now working against Ōita's interests. The availability of new sports for athletes with disabilities, such as the triathlon, which was first included at the Paralympics in 2016, and hand-cycling, which was added for the Tokyo 2020 Games, will likely have an impact on the race as well.

Because organizers have had to maintain the marathon's official international affiliations, they have also had to negotiate the shifting winds of disability sports organizations; thus, it is not at all surprising that the marathon was endorsed by several different national and international disability sports organizations before securing its current IPC sanction.[108] These different affiliations and the changes that those organizations made in their own regulations led to varying standards for eligibility certifications, classification systems, and wheelchair specifications for Ōita's race over time. As just one example, the marathon now uses the functional classification system used by the IPC for wheelchair racing. Compared with the six morphologically based classes used in 1981, Ōita now has three—T51, T33/52, and T34/53/54—and since 2004, the race has clearly identified male and female winners for each class.[109] Responding to similar international developments, the marathon began enforcing antidoping measures in 2001 and more recently instituted rules banning drafting behind athletes of a different gender or classification.

Improvements in wheelchair technology have revolutionized many sports, and Ōita's race offers a striking case. Changes in wheelchair design at the race are readily apparent in photographs, from the everyday chairs used in the first marathon to the streamlined three-wheeled racers used at present, with many styles in between. Technology's impact on the race has been undeniable, with average race times dropping dramatically as more participants gained access to the constantly improving equipment.[110]

Despite all of these changes—and in part because of them—Ōita's marathon has remained highly accessible. The revised approaches to classification have helped assure that both male and female racers in Ōita are competing against and being evaluated in relation to those with similar abilities, in contrast to other races that do not distinguish between classes or that limit the participation of women or those with higher levels of impairment. In addition, the use of lighter chairs that can be tailored to the size and requirements of individual racers has lessened some of the obstacles for those with higher needs, making it possible for more people at different levels to compete and reach the various checkpoints within the time limits. As organizers themselves proudly report, changes in international trends have also meant that Ōita has become home to "a valuable international competition for T/51 athletes."[111]

If current developments abroad continue in a similar direction, it may become one of the few sites available for both men and women competing in the T33/52 class as well.

International developments aside, long-standing approaches to the event's management have played perhaps an even greater role in maintaining the accessibility of Ōita's marathon. From the beginning, the race imposed minimal restrictions, which has continued to be the case throughout its decades-long history. In particular, the fact that neither race has required qualifying times for entry has allowed them to remain open to nearly anyone willing to race. For many years athletes were required to undergo onsite medical checks before the race, but it appears that nearly all athletes passed these examinations. Pre-race medical exams were eliminated as a requirement in 2005.[112] Even after registration fees were initiated in 2011, at the present rates of 1,000 yen for the half and 5,000 yen for the full marathon, they remain lower than most domestic and international races, reducing some of the potential financial barriers to participation.[113] Initially set at 18, minimum age requirements, too, have dropped over the years. In 2016, the event welcomed racers as young as 14, whereas the oldest competitor was 90. In addition to this remarkable age range, Ōita has become famous for hosting both novice and veteran competitors with a wide variety of skill levels.

As promoters are wont to point out, Ōita's so-called citizen's marathon, or the half-marathon race, has been particularly important to the event's continued inclusiveness, especially as the full marathon has become increasingly competitive. Each year the vast majority of first-time and repeat athletes, as well as the youngest and oldest participants, enter the shorter race.[114] An array of individual accounts reveal that for some, especially young Japanese athletes or those with newly acquired impairments, this event has been a gateway to a new sport or even to a different outlook on life.[115] The half-marathon's continued use of distinct classes, with recognized winners and records in each category, makes it appealing for those seeking competition but not interested in moving to the longer race. Perhaps not surprisingly, a number of those who have moved on to compete in full marathons got their start in the shorter race, whereas others have stuck with the half, entering the annual event for recreational, health, or other personal reasons as diverse as the racers themselves.

The sheer variety of participants who compete in the combined full and half-marathons in Ōita has clearly been part of the event's charm. With its history and distinctive approach, Ōita's marathon has fostered the creation of a distinctive international community of wheelchair racers. This community-building role has stemmed in part from the size and the wheelchair-only nature of the race. As Peter Hawkins, a multiyear marathon participant from the United States, observed, "It's a pretty cool thing to just watch 500 . . . elbows and hear the punching against the wheels. You don't hear that in Boston or New York because those are mostly runners. . . . The sound is completely different with wheelchairs."[116] The combined emphasis on elite competition and accessibility at the race has also meant that even the newest participants find themselves competing alongside some of the world's top racers, a fact that Japanese and foreign participants at multiple levels have referenced as one of Ōita's biggest draws. When Hawkins spoke with me before the 2016 race, he emphasized that Ōita was special because it was the only place where he could compete alongside a recent Paralympic champion, a world-record holder, and a 90-year-old Japanese man who had raced in all but one of Ōita's marathons to that point.[117] For their part, elite competitors enjoy an unmatched degree of renown and adulation in Ōita, as well as the opportunity to share their expertise with a uniquely attentive and appreciative audience. Previous world-record holder Heinrich Köberle of Germany has compared racing in Ōita to the feeling of "returning to my hometown," adding that teaching Japanese athletes with severe spinal cord injuries about his own experiences has been "an honor for me."[118] By promoting these kinds of personal exchanges and social relationships, the marathon has benefited countless individual athletes. It has also shaped the sport of wheelchair marathon racing in Japan and abroad in ways that have extended well beyond race results.

In terms of such results, Ōita's marathon has proven no less central to the sport. The marathon's efforts to promote its elite, competitive side have melded with trends toward increased competitiveness and professionalization in the Paralympic Movement more generally. In Ōita, these developments have been facilitated by the consistency of the race courses, which have remained largely unchanged since the 1980s, fostering their reputation as "technical" courses good for setting personal and international records. As of this writing, Ōita remains home to two world records in the full marathon: the T34/53/54 class, men's record set by Heinz Frei in 1999, and the women's record in the T52 class set in 2008 by Yamaki Tomomi. The race has boasted earlier world records in nearly every other category as well and hosted most of the international and Japanese national record holders at some point in their careers. For the world's best, then, Ōita has long been a destination worth visiting, and their continued participation has become a key part of what makes Ōita's annual race special.

In recent decades, however, it has proven increasingly difficult for Ōita to continue drawing the biggest names in the sport based solely on the marathon's reputation and its distinctiveness as a large wheelchair-only event.

The challenge has stemmed in part from the increased number of wheelchair races. In particular, many of the world's most prestigious marathons have created formal wheelchair divisions that offer significant cash prizes, a trend epitomized by the establishment of the inaugural Abbott World Marathon Majors Wheelchair Race Series in 2016. Several of the top racers themselves have become professional athletes who rely on such high-profile events to maintain and generate interest from sponsors.

In this environment, Ōita has faced several disadvantages. For one, travel to and from Japan comes with significant expense and the potential for jet lag. Compared with marathons in major cities that serve as international transportation hubs, Ōita's race necessitates significant additional travel, which can interfere further with training regimens or competition plans. Since the race also tends to occur just before the annual marathon in New York City, not all top athletes have been willing to make the trip to Ōita to compete in back-to-back races. In terms of publicity, coverage of the event has historically been limited to the local area. The race was not broadcast live nationwide in Japan until 2016, and despite its reputation in wheelchair racing circles, non-Japanese-language media coverage of the race has always been limited. Adding to these challenges have been concerns that declining participation rates from the sport's top athletes might lead to lower levels of competition in Ōita. The understandable fear has been that this change could threaten a downward spiral where the lack of competition drives away other top-level competitors, whose participation in the race has long been seen as essential to the marathon's appeal and thus its continuity.[119]

To offset the challenges of travel to the prefecture, the marathon from its beginning provided various forms of travel funding for "invited athletes." Early on, this category encompassed many of the international participants, including those from developing countries in the Asian-Pacific region. Such support was deemed necessary to assure that the marathon would retain a strong international constituency while also maintaining its ideals of broad accessibility. Today, the marathon continues to cover the costs of travel, lodging, and food for invited athletes—expenses that make up roughly 20 percent of annual costs even after recent cutbacks.[120] However, the category of "invited athlete" itself has become increasingly restricted, limited mostly to those who have already performed at an elite level in the full marathon, a situation that seems to reflect the need to keep these high-level athletes coming to Ōita. To offer additional incentives for such athletes, organizers instituted monetary prizes for the full marathon beginning in 2010. The prizes were initially set up as part of the special celebrations for the thirtieth anniversary, but were maintained at reduced levels for the next several years. As noted earlier, continued concerns about the loss of elite professional competitors prompted dramatic increases in several of the prize categories beginning in 2015. The increased prizes included those for record-setting times, a clear attempt to mobilize the marathon's reputation for speed to lure top-level talent to Ōita.

When the prizes were first established in 2010, they were awarded in equal value to the top male and female competitors in each classification. Changes in the awards since then have resulted in significant differences in relation to both gender and classification. From 2011 to 2014, the top male finishers in most categories received more than their female counterparts, whereas the awards for athletes in the higher-needs T51 class were significantly lower than those for other classification groups. With the increase in prize money beginning in 2015, the gender-based inequalities were eliminated, but those for different classifications were exacerbated: winners in the T34/53/54 class since then receive ten times as much prize money and are eligible for five times as much in time-bonus prizes as those competing in the T51 category.[121]

It is not difficult to find fault with such glaring inequality, but unfortunately, the gap in prize money in Ōita's race is both a reflection of and a problematic response to the present state of elite wheelchair marathon racing. By virtue of qualifying times, if not outright restrictions, the majority of elite marathons, including the Paralympics, are now limited almost exclusively to athletes in the T53/54 category. To offset its inherent challenges compared to these other races and maintain a reputation as one of these elite sporting events, Ōita needed to provide comparable compensation for these athletes; hence, the dramatic jump in prize money for this class of participants. Failure to do so would have made it ever more likely that these racers would simply stop coming to the marathon, a loss deemed potentially detrimental to the event. In contrast, athletes with different classifications find themselves with limited and even decreasing options for competition. This regrettable trend has worked in Ōita's favor, because its marathon can continue to rely on—and even bolster—its reputation as an accessible race to attract the top-level athletes in these categories each year. To put it bluntly, organizers seem to have determined that in the current environment these athletes were likely to come to Ōita, no matter how much they got paid for winning.

By literally devaluing the sporting achievements of female athletes and those with higher levels of impairment, Ōita's prizes render apparent some of the inequities lurking behind the increased emphasis on elite sport at the marathon and in the Paralympic Movement more broadly. Part of the issue, as Paralympic scholar Ian Brittain has observed, is the tendency for this emphasis on elite performance to fall back on a "model that matches societal perceptions and understandings of what sport should look like."[122] For the marathon, this translates to the highest speeds and fastest times, like those generated by top male athletes competing in the T34/53/54 classification. The distinctions in the rewards—as reflected in the outright elimination of certain athletes from other "elite" competitions—reinforce disablist perceptions that the truly "elite" are those who are more functionally able.

Although these outcomes are particularly problematic given Ōita's long-held goal of using the race to improve social perceptions of disability, they are hardly unique to the marathon. The constant reproduction of these types of social biases, combined with a host of other barriers to pursuing disability sports at the elite level, has translated to significantly lower participation rates at the Paralympics for women and for athletes with high support needs. Similar patterns are apparent in the marathon. Although Ōita's races have been open to women from their inception, they continue to face a striking gender imbalance. In its first thirty-six years, the full-marathon race welcomed more than 4,500 participants, but only 231 of them, just over 5 percent, were women. The shifts in classification make exact counts difficult, but in recent years, participation rates for athletes not in the T34/53/54 group have hovered around 10 percent, and most races have no female athletes competing in these categories. Ōita's recent move to significantly increase prize money for women in the T34/53/54 class and to eliminate the differences between men's and women's prizes points to a recognition of the need to promote greater equity, a recognition that may be extended to those competing in different classifications as well. After all, if the goal of increasing the prize money is to lure more of the best to Ōita, equalization of the prizes should theoretically increase participation across the board and bolster the marathon's reputation as a site that truly values both competition and accessibility. Whether such changes or any of the theoretical benefits of increased prize money will be achieved remains to be seen.

Moving forward, maintaining Ōita's twin emphasis on competition and accessibility is going to face continued challenges. The newer, high-profile wheelchair races in Japan and abroad are here to stay, along with the geographic barriers Ōita faces. With increasing cash awards to offset these disadvantages, the event appears likely to become more dependent on its sponsors, whose own support for the event is likely far more contingent than any would like to admit. Despite the prizes, participation numbers in almost all categories have continued to drop, and the prohibitive costs of equipment, training, and travel are threatening to create a whole new set of inequalities in the marathon, much as in disability sports more generally. Indeed, the millions of yen being spent on prize money and travel support for elite athletes are emblematic of the disparities in disability sports between the Global North and South.[123]

As the marathon moves forward, searching for ways to address these and other challenges, it may end up becoming a very different event. Yet this does not need to be a negative development. Ōita, it is worth remembering, has a history of bucking trends and breaking new ground. By drawing from local models like FESPIC and its own distinctive community and ethos, Ōita has the opportunity once again to do something different or perhaps new. In the process, it can offer unique insights for other disability sports events struggling with similar challenges. Whatever shape Ōita's race eventually assumes, the marathon has clearly had a profound impact on the region, its people, and the world of wheelchair marathon racing. Thanks in no small part to its history, local roots, and global reputation, the event seems likely to continue bringing athletes—new and returning, foreign and domestic, young and old—together in Ōita each autumn for the foreseeable future.

CHAPTER 4

A Turning Point

The 1998 Winter Paralympics in Nagano

> The Paralympics to this point have received limited
> newspaper and television coverage. This time was
> different. Our newspaper company dispatched some
> 40 journalists to Nagano and provided extensive daily
> coverage on the front pages, the society pages, and the
> sports pages. Television coverage was considerable,
> too, and it was increased further in response to viewer
> requests.
>
> Kotani Naomichi, 1998

With the 1998 Nagano Winter Paralympic
Games, Japan achieved a status unique among Paralympic hosts. Only a handful
of countries had hosted more than one Paralympics, and Japan became the
first to hold both the Summer and Winter Paralympic Games. Nagano's
Paralympics were also the first Winter Games held outside of Europe since
they were initiated in 1976, and they set a new and long-standing record for
the number of athletes competing.[1] Thus, the 1998 Nagano Paralympics were
only the latest example of Japan's ongoing—and often groundbreaking—
contributions to the international Paralympic Movement. Nagano's Games
arguably had an even more significant impact at home. Tokyo's 1964 Paralympics, described in chapter 1, had proven foundational in many respects, but
by 1998 much had changed in Japan and in the Paralympic Movement. This
chapter explores key differences between Tokyo and Nagano that explain why
the 1998 Games came to be seen as a turning point, fostering what some have
dubbed the "normalization" of disability sports in Japan.[2]

To understand the differences apparent in Nagano and their consequent
impacts, it is necessary to situate the Games in their larger sociohistorical context. The 1998 Winter Paralympics were organized and held against a backdrop of increased attention to disability-related issues. In the years leading up
to them, Japan was deeply engaged in several international disability awareness and rights programs linked to the United Nations, and the 1990s were

marked in particular by significant changes in national activism, policies, and approaches related to disability. Such changes also reflected growing domestic concern about Japan's rapidly aging population. The Nagano Games were able to capitalize on these developments, and many of the measures pursued in connection with the Winter Paralympics reflected broader national and international concerns. Although these background factors tend to be overlooked in accounts of the 1998 Games and their impact, I emphasize them here in part to check the common tendency to portray the Paralympics themselves as *the* driving forces for changes. Nagano's Games generated disability-related improvements in Japan, but they did so—or sometimes failed to do so—in no small part because of the sociohistorical environment in which they were held.

Along those same lines, the environment for disability sports in 1998 was different in almost every respect from that of the Tokyo Games thirty-four years earlier. At the international level, the Paralympics had continued to develop and expand, formally welcoming athletes with a wider variety of impairments and developing closer connections with both the Summer and Winter Olympic Games. By the early 1990s, Olympic hosts, like Nagano, were more or less expected to hold the Paralympics, even though the bidding processes remained separate. As disability sports took root and flourished in countries around the world, the Paralympics moved away from their rehabilitation-oriented origins toward an emphasis on elite-level performance. Many of these changes in the Games were tied to organizational reforms discussed in chapter 2 that eventually culminated in the establishment of the International Paralympic Committee (IPC) in 1989. From the very beginning, then, Nagano's Games were embedded in an international sports scene with little resemblance to that of 1964.

The situation within Japan had also undergone a dramatic transformation since Tokyo's earlier Games. Although not yet part of "mainstream" awareness, Japan's involvement with disability sports had become much deeper and more frequent. As the examples of FESPIC and the Ōita International Wheelchair Marathon from earlier chapters indicate, Japan had become a leader in the realm of disability sports well before 1998. Japanese athletes were regularly engaging in a wide range of events at home and abroad and, just as importantly, were increasingly competitive at the international level. Fueled by rising international and domestic expectations, the years leading up to Nagano were marked by significant changes in support for and views of Japanese Paralympians. In terms of representational practices, these changes often translated into official approaches that sought to portray participants as elite athletes like their Olympic counterparts, yet this transition proved far from seamless, as older rehabilitation-focused understandings lingered. Outlining the evolution of both the international and the domestic disability sports scene around the time of the 1998 Paralympics brings these unique characteristics into high relief and clarifies how and why these Games became a turning point for disability sports in Japan.

As Kotani Naomichi, an editor for the *Yomiuri* newspaper, observed in the statement quoted in the epigraph, Nagano's Games were especially noteworthy because of the increased media attention they generated. Studies of media coverage since 1998 have verified Kotani's assertions, demonstrating that this period was, in fact, very different. The Nagano Paralympics proved to be a watershed in both the amount of coverage given to disability sports and the ways in which Japanese media outlets presented Paralympic sports and athletes. To highlight these important changes, the chapter devotes particular attention to examinations of media coverage over time. These comparisons of media treatments of earlier and later disability sports events also reveal continuities in representational trends that persisted up to and even after the Nagano Games, underscoring the need for a more nuanced understanding of the relationship between the Paralympics and the media. Because Nagano's Games were one of the first Paralympics to make extensive use of the Internet, I conclude the chapter with an exploration of the potential benefits and pitfalls associated with the growing use of new media forms since the 1998 Games.

Different Times, Different Games

Official accounts date the inception of the Nagano Paralympics to 1990, nearly a year before Nagano won the right to host the 1998 Winter Olympics. Even at this early point, potential organizers had already begun exploring the possibility of holding the Paralympics, because they were aware of increasing pressure on Olympic venues to host these Games as well. The first formal indication of Nagano's intent to hold the Winter Paralympics came during the September 15, 1990, press conference for the International Olympic Committee (IOC) meeting in Tokyo. As part of his presentation, prefectural governor and head of Nagano's Olympic bid committee Yoshimura Gorō declared, "We also want to hold the Winter Paralympic Games and share the pleasure of winter sports with more people, including those with disabilities."[3] After this public pronouncement, informal organizational efforts related to the Paralympics continued, gaining new momentum after the city was selected as the Olympic host in June 1991. In November 1991, the IPC dispatched its official letter requesting that Nagano uphold the "efforts to establish a tradition" by "hosting the 1998 Paralympics Winter Games at the same site and venues of the 1998 Olympic Winter Games."[4] More planning, committee work, and formal declarations of support from Japanese national and local governments followed, culminating in Nagano's official bid for the 1998 Winter Paralympics. During its general meeting in Berlin, the IPC formally named Nagano as the Paralympic host site on September 10, 1993. The Nagano Paralympic Organizing Committee, commonly dubbed NAPOC, was established on November 16, 1993. Just over four years later in March 1998, NAPOC would succeed in hosting an event that the IPC praised as "the best Paralympics of the Summer and Winter Games held so far."[5]

The reasons behind the success of Nagano's Paralympics were, of course, multifaceted, but there is no denying that, compared to the 1964 Tokyo Paralympics, those in Nagano benefited in particular from both time and timing. The Games in 1964 had been an afterthought. In contrast, discussions about hosting the 1998 Paralympics were initiated before organizers were even certain that Nagano would be holding the Olympics. Quite simply, this meant that organizers in Nagano had much longer to prepare for their event. This extra time translated into a range of other benefits, including more extensive PR and fundraising campaigns, increased opportunities for volunteer and spectator recruitment, and greater attention to issues of accessibility. In the case of accessibility, the timing for Nagano's Games was also especially fortuitous. During the years surrounding the Games, international and domestic attention to disability-related issues was notably greater than had been the case three decades earlier, thanks in part to a series of international and national campaigns focusing on disability, as well as growing concern about Japan's rapidly changing demographics. Combined with the extended time frame, these background factors help explain changes in NAPOC's approach to promoting the Games and especially organizers' greater interest in using the Paralympics to foster barrier-free environments in Nagano and elsewhere in Japan.

Well aware that many in Japan were still unfamiliar with the Paralympics or disability sports, organizers in Nagano were driven from the beginning to expose as many people as possible to the Paralympics and its athletes. To achieve this end, NAPOC launched an intensive, wide-ranging, and well-supported publicity campaign almost immediately after its formation. Preliminary budgets for the Games earmarked more than 10 percent of expenditures for publicity-related expenses alone, and their final costs amounted to nearly triple the original estimates.[6] With extra time and resources, organizers engaged in marketing efforts in Nagano that had simply not been feasible for Tokyo's earlier Games. In fact, publicity efforts in Nagano were much more similar to those pursued for the recently held FESPIC Games in Kobe, reflecting the increased time and funding, and perhaps the fact that the chairman of NAPOC's publicity subcommittee had also helped organize Kobe's event.[7]

As in FESPIC's PR efforts, Nagano's promoters used a series of public contests to decide on mascots, slogans, and songs that would represent the upcoming Paralympics. The earliest of these national competitions was launched in December 1993, only a month after NAPOC was established.[8] Nagano's Games also relied on print-based outreach campaigns, producing a variety of regularly updated pamphlets, posters, and leaflets that were distributed throughout Japan and abroad. Between September 1994 and February 1998 NAPOC published nineteen editions of *Paralympic News,* an eight-page newsletter featuring details on organizational activities and introductions to Paralympic sports and Japanese athletes. With print runs of nearly 8,000 copies, *Paralympic News* was distributed widely, especially among schools and groups in the Nagano area. On the eve of the Games, NAPOC produced and sold an official ninety-six-page, pocket-sized guidebook; a separate directory of Japanese participants was also prepared for the Games.[9] Naturally, organizers employed traditional advertising, too, including newspaper ads, radio and TV spots, and fliers on Japan Railways trains.[10] At the same time, NAPOC turned to some of the newest outreach tools available, setting up an official webpage a year before the Games, a development that is explored later in the chapter. Expanding on NAPOC's promotional efforts, monthly publications from the Ministry of Health and Welfare, the Japan National Council of Social Welfare, and the Japanese Society for the Rehabilitation of Persons with Disabilities ran regular article series introducing the Winter Paralympics, their sports, and their athletes to readers.[11]

NAPOC took advantage of the longer planning time frame to organize a series of "warm-up" ceremonial events designed to raise interest in the Games, again adopting an approach similar to that of FESPIC in Kobe. The first of these events was a ceremony and parade held in March 1994 in central Nagano to mark the arrival of the Paralympic flag from Lillehammer, Norway, the previous Winter Games host. As the Paralympics approached, NAPOC celebrated key milestones—3 years, 1,000 days, 2 years, 500 days, 1 year, 300 days, 200 days, and 100 days to go—with increasingly elaborate events in Nagano. The earlier occasions often featured announcements of slogan and mascot contest outcomes, whereas those occurring closer to the Games were used for local outreach and peddling Paralympic-related products and tickets. By the time the Paralympics arrived, organizers were selling more than sixty Paralympic-branded products. Many of these goods bore images of Parabbit, the official symbol for the Games represented by various rabbit characters derived from a stylized combination of the recently adopted Paralympic symbol of the tricolor *taegeuk* spirals and the Chinese character for "naga" from Nagano. Throughout this pre-Games period, NAPOC representatives and their larger-than-life costumed mascot traveled to a number of disability sports events outside Nagano, setting up information booths with photo displays, PR videos, Paralympic merchandise, and sporting equipment to try out. From October 1996 to January 1997, NAPOC also joined the organizing committee for the Nagano Olympics in a nationwide "caravan" designed to ensure that enthusiasm for both events was not limited to the host region.[12] These sorts of events illustrate Paralympic organizers' proactive approaches to raising awareness about their Games.

As the sale of Paralympic merchandise suggests, publicity campaigns in Nagano often went hand in hand with fundraising efforts. Given the depressed state of Japan's post-bubble economy in the 1990s and the pressure on Japanese companies to support the Olympic Games, NAPOC was mindful that financing the Paralympics was going to be challenging, especially if potential corporate sponsors remained unconvinced of broader public support for the event. From the beginning, the prefectural and local governments hosting the Paralympic events were planning to cover the bulk of costs (nearly 75%) with limited support from the national government. At the same time, organizers were counting on other income streams. As with Tokyo's earlier Games, NAPOC sought out donations from groups like Japan's Rotary and Lions Clubs, organizations linked to sports gambling, and social welfare or medical associations. Financial contributions came from a variety of other sources as well, including a donation link on the official website. PR campaigns themselves often performed double duty as fundraisers, as exemplified by the Paralympic poster displays and accompanying donation boxes set up at JUSCO department stores in the Nagano region and eventually other areas of Japan.[13]

In contrast to Tokyo, NAPOC successfully cultivated multiple corporate sponsorships, with some thirty-six companies offering formal support for the Games. Originally, organizers had planned to sell advertising rights to official sponsors, but initial inquiries fell flat in part because of corporations' concerns about the potential for confusing overlap with Olympic advertising in a fiscally tight market. Fortunately, NAPOC had enough time to change course. Rather than requesting that would-be sponsors pay for rights, organizers began asking them to support the Paralympics in whatever way they could as part of their "social contribution activities."[14] In exchange, sponsors' names and logos would feature prominently in Paralympic-related materials, with the specific nature of such displays dependent on the type and level of contributions. As the Games approached and the long-running PR campaigns began to reap dividends in the form of rising public attention to the Paralympics, businesses proved increasingly willing to sign on. Ultimately, they offered more goods, services, and financial contributions than organizers had anticipated. Corporate contributions were more than three times greater than original estimates, with the final tally accounting for well over 10 percent of all revenues. In this sense, Nagano's Games demonstrated that, with time and the right approach, the Paralympics could be highly marketable, even in a less-than-ideal economic environment.[15]

Ticket sales served as further evidence of the Paralympics' broadened appeal in Nagano. Although both the Lillehammer and Atlanta Paralympic Games had charged for tickets, no disability sports event in Japan had ever charged any sort of admission fee for spectators. Pointing to the increasingly elite level of Paralympic sport and the pride of Paralympians, NAPOC decided to follow the model of recent Games and sell tickets for all of the Paralympic events. Organizers worked with a variety of travel companies and other existing ticket sellers to market tickets at some three thousand locations in Japan and abroad. At less than $10 in most cases, the price points for tickets were relatively low, and significant discounts were available for groups, students, and those with disabilities. Presales began in May 1997 as part of the celebration marking the 300-day countdown to the Games and ended in February 1998. NAPOC originally planned to sell same-day tickets as well, but before the presale period ended, all of the tickets had been sold. By the close of the Nagano Paralympics, more than 151,000 people had attended events as paying spectators, definitively marking a turning point for disability sports in Japan.[16]

The revenue from ticket sales contributed a relatively small amount to the Games' overall budget, because making money on admission fees had always been secondary to organizers' desire to foster broad exposure to the Paralympics. In fact, nearly one-third of the tickets were sold to school groups from the Nagano region at sharply reduced rates. Many schools attended Paralympic events as part of their involvement in Nagano's pioneering "One School, One Country" campaign. Through this Olympic and Paralympic education program, students at local schools learned about specific countries and then met and supported athletes from those countries during both sets of Games. A variety of anecdotal comments from students and educators suggest that attending Paralympic events, the tickets for which often proved cheaper and more available than Olympic events, played an important role in broadening students' understanding of and interest in what they had been learning in school about the Games and their athletes.[17]

Nagano's torch relay represented another striking example of NAPOC's efforts to promote direct, mass involvement with the Games, particularly for local residents with disabilities. Highlighting Japan's history of involvement with the Paralympics, the relay began on February 25, 1998, with a torch-lighting ceremony at the site of Tokyo's 1964 Paralympics. The nine-day event culminated in the lighting of the Paralympic Flame during the opening ceremony, thereby establishing a direct link between Nagano's Games and all of the relay's 754 formal participants and more than 180,000 spectators. The relay itself consisted of two main elements: a prefectural relay that featured the bulk of participants and passed through 149 of Nagano Prefecture's neighborhoods, and a final relay in Nagano City that delivered the torch to the opening ceremony on March 5. Some 351 local teams applied to participate in the relay, of which 120 teams were selected; 80 of these five-person teams included at least one local resident with a disability, with 21 composed entirely of those with disabilities. For the final leg of the relay through Nagano City, organizers received 295 applications from throughout Japan and abroad and selected 20 teams, the majority of which also included members with disabilities.[18]

Rich in symbolism, spectacle, and PR potential as it was, the torch relay proved particularly attractive to corporate sponsors and media outlets. Both Coca Cola and NTT Communications provided financial support.[19] Japan's three major daily newspapers featured the torch-lighting ceremony on their front pages, and their regional affiliates offered coverage of various parts of the relay up through the final day. Perhaps understandably, the most extensive press attention came from Nagano's local newspapers, which provided maps of the relay route, multiple daily reports and photos, and regular quotes from relay participants and spectators. The local *Shinano mainichi* newspaper, for instance, featured relay runner Miura Jirō, a 64-year-old from the village of Miyata. Miura, who had a form of muscular dystrophy, had spent the last fifteen years campaigning to improve accessibility throughout his home town. Mirroring organizers' intended outcome, Miura pointed to local spectators' enthusiastic response to the relay as a sign of improved awareness of disability in the region.[20] There was no denying that the torch relay had provided a wide swath of Nagano's population, disabled and nondisabled alike, with a direct encounter with the Paralympics.

As another means of expanding the influence of the Games, organizers held hundreds of cultural and social events linked to the Games. Ranging from musical concerts to folk craft exhibits, many of the events held before and during the Paralympics were meant to serve as forms of publicity, raising awareness of the Games among those who might not otherwise be attracted to or be aware of disability sports events. Other activities, especially those hosted for international athletes during the Games, provided opportunities for promoting intercultural exchange and introducing aspects of local history and culture.

Perhaps the most prominent and influential cultural event associated with the Games was Art Paralympics Nagano 1998. Proposed and organized by a group of volunteers, Art Paralympics was a multi-week, multi-site festival of visual and performing arts meant to complement the sporting events by giving artists with disabilities forums to display their talents. At its conclusion, the festival had engaged more than one thousand artists and performers and attracted tens of thousands of attendees. Paralympic researcher Kazuo Ogura has argued that the Art Paralympics not only brought attention to the previously overlooked work of artists with disabilities but also unsettled stereotypes by challenging the notion that disability was something that needed to be overcome. Thus the festival fit well with the broader goals of the Paralympics and epitomized organizers' desire to assure that the impacts of holding these Games in Nagano extended well beyond athletic venues.[21]

One key to that expanded impact was the work of volunteers, as exemplified by their role in the Art Paralympics. NAPOC, like organizers for earlier disability sports events, realized that reliance on volunteerism was both a necessity and an important means of fostering local citizens' engagement with the Paralympics. Initial recruitment drives, launched in June 1994, proved quite effective, with nearly seven thousand people applying to assist with the Games in some way. The majority of applicants were interested in helping out with cultural events, but 3,195 people ended up serving as official volunteers. These individuals participated in multiple training sessions and assisted with specialized aspects of event management, ranging from transportation and interpretation to ID checks and trash pickup. With the luxury of extra time for recruitment and training, NAPOC was able to identify and address particular areas, such as information technology, where they needed more volunteers. Organizers also tried to match work sites and tasks to applicants' abilities and interests, resulting in the more efficient use of—and ideally better experiences for—volunteers.[22]

Volunteers in Nagano did not simply wait for organizers to tell them what to do; in many cases they assumed the lead, with impressive results. The Nagano Para Bora no Kai (NPBK), a particularly active group of volunteers based in Nagano City, offers a case in point: it was members of this group who proposed and organized the Art Paralympics. Formed in November 1994, NPBK brought together existing volunteer groups, local organizations interested in social welfare, and individual volunteers, including many with some form of impairment. With support from Nagano City and its own members, NPBK held monthly meetings and published a seasonal newsletter. In support of NAPOC, group members often helped organize countdown events and regularly assisted with merchandise sales and other promotional activities. During the Games, NPBK set up a special booth at Nagano's central train station to assist attendees and encourage passersby to support the Paralympics in any way possible.[23]

Yet NPBK was more than a cheerleader for NAPOC, as an overview of one of the group's newsletters attests. The fall 1996 edition, for instance, included details on upcoming NPBK events, calls for more volunteers, and requests for suggested outreach activities for the upcoming Games. Large portions were devoted to information and photos from the recent Atlanta Summer Paralympics, with particular attention to Japanese athletes and their experiences at the Games. Another story reported on a local middle-school PE teacher who had become interested in wheelchair basketball after working with a Nagano-based club; inspired by this experience, he was planning to teach the sport during an upcoming service trip to Syria. Other stories in the newsletter mentioned NPBK's recent inspection tours of Nagano's sports venues to assure that they would be truly accessible. Several articles addressed the group's outreach presentations at local middle schools, including details that were shared with students about a study tour to the United States where some members met pioneering disability rights activist, Ed Roberts. The newsletter published a mix of student responses as well, with several noting students' increased interest in Paralympic sporting events after hearing the presentations. One particularly telling comment highlighted a student's realization that Japan needed to do a better job of making sure that its streets were safe and accessible for everyone. While NPBK members were certainly promoting Nagano's upcoming Paralympics, their newsletter showed that they were actively seeking to use the Games to promote other ends as well.[24]

Human-Friendly Games

Indeed, many of NPBK's activities before and during the Paralympics centered on issues of accessibility and creating more disability-friendly communities in Nagano. In addition to the visits to Paralympic venues mentioned in the newsletter, in the lead-up to the Games NPBK members joined with several other local and national groups to carry out multiple inspections in Nagano City with an eye toward accessibility. During the Paralympics, NPBK assumed primary responsibility for using a variety of adapted vehicles to transport spectators who needed extra assistance because of physical impairments. Volunteers from the group were also instrumental in helping NAPOC develop and use a special snow wheelchair that would allow spectators to reach the outdoor venues.[25]

NPBK was certainly not alone in linking the Paralympics to the promotion of accessibility at the Games; NAPOC itself emphasized the need to reduce or eliminate barriers for both athletes and spectators. Unlike Tokyo's Paralympics, those in Nagano were planned alongside the preceding Olympics from the early stages, which meant that organizers had not only more time but also more opportunities for input. Such differences were particularly apparent in the Athletes' Village. From the beginning, both individual rooms and public spaces were designed with accessibility in mind: wide doorways, ramps, low counters, large bathrooms equipped with handrails, braille signage, and a range of other modifications were quite literally built into these spaces. Athletic venues, too, were set up to assure that appropriate parking, walkways, elevators, seating, and restroom facilities would be available to accommodate the needs of athletes and spectators. The extra time also allowed NAPOC to identify and sometimes address potential problems, particularly given that they had hosted a series of pre-Paralympic athletic events at the same venues. For example, one such event held in 1997 revealed poor visibility from some of the wheelchair seating sections, which prompted plans to expand and elevate the viewing area during the Paralympics.[26]

Facing the added challenges of dealing with cold temperatures, ice, and snow, especially at outdoor venues, NAPOC embraced diverse strategies to help athletes and spectators reach and enjoy the events. Their transportation approach mixed tried-and-true technologies like lift-equipped buses and vans with locally developed devices such as the snow wheelchair and other powered snow vehicles modified to carry one or more wheelchairs. During the events themselves, NAPOC provided accessible warming tents, as well as specially designed blankets and heaters for wheelchairs. Volunteer sign-language interpreters were available throughout the Games to assist those with hearing impairments, and at indoor venues, special real-time FM broadcasts and freely available radios were provided to allow anyone with a visual impairment to follow the events. Both before and during the Games, NAPOC also printed braille versions of many of its publications, including the official guidebook for the Games. As these various measures suggest, organizers sought to ensure that accessibility would be more than just a buzzword at Nagano's Paralympics.[27]

In addition to NAPOC's efforts at Paralympic sites, a range of local governments and other organizations used the Games as opportunities to pursue their own "barrier-free" agendas. For instance, a 1995 story from the *Shinano mainichi* newspaper reported that officials from the village of Hakuba, the Paralympic venue for cross-country skiing, had participated in a program where they used wheelchairs or eye masks to experience for themselves the lack of accessibility. Participants also received instruction on the proper procedures for carrying people in wheelchairs up and down stairways—a necessity because many sites in the village, including train stations, lacked elevators or accessible ramps.[28] Similar sessions were undertaken at other venues, reflecting elements of "human-friendly community development projects" that were intended to help local areas identify and address accessibility issues before the Paralympics, thereby moving their communities closer to a barrier-free ideal.

Perhaps the most intensive campaign occurred in Nagano City. Nagano's own "human-friendly" project had been launched in 1993. To evaluate the effectiveness of earlier campaigns while identifying and ideally addressing problems before the Games were held, city officials, volunteer groups like NPBK, the local chambers of commerce, transportation providers, and a host of other stakeholders joined forces in August 1997 to spend several days inspecting downtown roads, shops, hotels, and public transportation networks to assess their accessibility. Thanks in part to widespread participation from local citizens with disabilities, the inspections revealed a number of shortcomings, ranging from bicycles blocking the tactile pavement used by the visually impaired to a lack of accessible restrooms in some large stores, banks, and hotels. Some of these issues were more easily addressed than others, but at the very least, these types of campaigns made it far more difficult for local officials and others to claim ignorance when it came to questions of accessibility in the Nagano region.[29]

In the years leading up to the Games, greater attention to barrier-free ideals was also increasingly apparent in local policies and funding decisions. In 1992, even before it was officially named as the Paralympic host, Nagano City updated a preexisting long-term accessibility plan and launched an immediate implementation of improvements by building ramps, adding sidewalk curb cuts, and refurbishing existing accessible restrooms. These and similar projects were pursued over the following years at locations throughout the area, many of which had little direct connection with the Paralympics themselves. In 1996, Nagano City also revised a set of social welfare guidelines dating from 1982, pursuing a new approach that emphasized "minimizing barriers as much as possible" and fostering a "normalization mindset" toward accessibility issues.[30]

The city's revised guidelines coincided with and came partly in response to the implementation of Nagano Prefecture's new Social Welfare Community Development Ordinance, enacted in March 1995. The prefectural ordinance aimed to "promote comprehensive social welfare community development by setting appropriate standards that will allow for the safe and easy use of facilities by individuals with disabilities and other needs."[31] It included a lengthy list of regulations spelling out accessibility expectations for facilities or services that welcomed the public. Beginning in 1996, nearly all

new construction or renovation of such facilities was expected to align with
the specified standards, and existing facilities were encouraged to find ways
to comply as well. For those looking (or needing) to pursue barrier-free modifications, financial support was available in the form of special government
subsidies or loans from the local Small and Medium Enterprise Promotion
Fund. One such subsidy helped private bus companies in the region purchase
lift-equipped buses before the Games.[32]

A World beyond the 1998 Games

Given these sorts of policy changes, the financial outlays that they entailed,
and the various human-friendly campaigns just described, it is understandable
that many people at the time and since have credited Nagano's Paralympics
with advancing barrier-free principles in the region and in Japan more broadly.[33]
At the very least, it would seem that these Games—much like the FESPIC
Games in Kobe—served as a fresh and pressing incentive for enacting preexisting plans and measures designed to support those with disabilities. Yet
therein lies a key point, one that can be easily overlooked when focusing on
the legacies of these sorts of events: neither Nagano nor Japan was a blank
slate, waiting for the Paralympics to leave their marks. To understand why
and how the 1998 Paralympics had the impact that they did, it is also necessary to take into account a number of factors beyond the Games themselves.

For one, the response to the Paralympics in Nagano was grounded in the
region's significantly longer history of engagement with progressive disability-
related approaches. As early as 1975 (predating the first Winter Paralympic
Games), the Ministry of Health and Welfare designated Nagano City as one
of its Social Welfare Model Cities. The city's initial long-term plan for promoting accessibility dated from the early 1980s and was explicitly linked with, if
not directly inspired by, the UN International Year of Disabled Persons. The
guidelines that the city later revised in the lead-up to the Games had already
been on the books for more than a decade. The initial tagline for these older
guidelines, "Developing a community where everyone can live well," reflected a clear commitment to fostering greater accessibility, even if the
guidelines themselves lacked the legal heft that the later prefectural ordinance provided.[34]

These earlier policies serve as reminders that many people in the region
had been working to improve accessibility well before the Paralympics. Miura
Jirō, the Paralympic torch runner from Miyata Village who had been active
locally for some fifteen years, was a case in point. In addition, support for hosting the Games in Nagano emerged early on at both the governmental and

volunteer levels in no small part because organizers were not starting from scratch. A volunteer group like NPBK might have been formed specifically in response to the Paralympics, but many of its members were already engaged in various forms of disability-related advocacy. As just one example, Ikeda Jun, a vice chair of NPBK, had been a long-time prefectural case worker who had become involved with the Independent Living Movement as it was beginning to gain support in Japan during the late 1980s and early 1990s. A key participant in NPBK's school outreach programs, Ikeda was instrumental in launching the group's study tour to the United States. In the months immediately following the Paralympics, he helped establish Human Net Nagano, an NGO dedicated to promoting and supporting opportunities for people with disabilities to live independently in their home communities. Although Human Net Nagano might be considered a legacy of the 1998 Games, it also exemplifies the debt that such legacies owed to people like Ikeda, who had already laid the groundwork for the Paralympics to deliver results at the local level.[35]

A second major factor behind the impact of Nagano's Games was the significant shift in policy and law occurring in Japan as a whole in the years leading up to the Paralympics. A survey of key laws related to disability in Japan shows that the national government passed or revised six such laws between 1993 and 1998, with several other new or amended measures put in place within a few years of the Games.[36] As an example, the new 1994 law known as the "Heartful Building Law" called for improving the accessibility of public buildings, and it clearly served as the impetus and legal backbone for the similar Nagano prefectural ordinance and the revised Nagano City guidelines discussed earlier. Among its provisions, the national law established the subsidies that could be used to implement approved barrier-free construction or remodeling plans at the local level. Following up on a significant 1993 revision of the Fundamental Law for Disabled Persons, which originally dated from 1970, the prime minister's office also issued the Government Action Plan for Persons with Disabilities in 1995. This seven-year plan was "based on the philosophy of rehabilitation (which aims at fulfilling human rights at all stages of the life cycle) and normalization, which aims to create a society in which persons with disabilities are equal to those without disabilities with respect to daily life and activities."[37] With references to many of the new or forthcoming legal changes, the plan targeted seven areas, including various efforts to improve accessibility and promote independent living. It cited sports specifically and characterized the upcoming Nagano Paralympic Games as an example of Japan's promotion of sporting opportunities for those with disabilities.

On its surface, this cluster of legal and policy changes in the years surrounding the Nagano Paralympics seem to offer further evidence of the Games' impact on Japan. A closer look, however, reveals that many of these changes stemmed from a unique confluence of domestic and international pressures, with the Paralympics assuming a relatively minor role in the mix when it came to disability policies. Domestically, Japan's disability rights movement was entering its fourth decade in the 1990s. A full examination of the movement (which like most movements was complex and multifaceted) is beyond the scope of the present chapter, but generally speaking, in the 1980s the movement began to move away from its protest-centered, welfare-oriented roots. As legal scholar Katharina Heyer has observed, activists' approaches in the 1980s onward tended to focus on lobbying local and national governments to gain financial and logistical support for a "broad list of issues that affect people's daily lives: the right to live in the community, to be educated along nondisabled peers, to have access to employment, and to navigate the public sphere."[38] Many elements of Nagano's human-friendly campaigns, the volunteer activities linked to the Games, and Japan's policy changes reflected such aspects of the disability rights movements' broader goals and approaches. Much of this sort of activism in Japan had little direct connection with the Paralympics, though the Games almost certainly offered advocates an opportunity to gain additional leverage as they pursued their goals, especially on the ground in Nagano.

Japanese policymakers at nearly all levels were also responding to concerns about changing demographics. As noted in chapter 3 in relation to Ōita, rural depopulation presented problems for many regions in Japan throughout the postwar period. The situation was further complicated by the fact that younger people tended to be the ones relocating to the cities, leaving rural areas with shrinking and increasingly older populations. By the 1980s, government reports were sounding the alarm about the rapid aging of Japan's populace nationwide, a result of declining birthrates and increased longevity. According to estimates at the time, by 2020 more than 20 percent of Japan's population were expected to be older than age 65.[39]

This "graying of Japan" posed challenges for many sectors, but its impact was definitely felt in the disability-related measures implemented in the 1990s, as exemplified by the 1995 Government Action Plan for Persons with Disabilities cited earlier that described rehabilitation in relation to "all stages of the life cycle." Heyer's study of Japanese government reforms suggests that concerns about the elderly often served as a more pressing driver for change than an increased commitment to disability rights.[40] It is not surprising then that many of the policies and campaigns from this period explicitly referenced the elderly or aging. The less-used official name of the 1994 "Heartful Building Law," for instance, was the Law for Buildings Accessible to and Usable by the

Elderly and Physically Disabled Persons. Ordinances and guidelines in Nagano, too, cited the region's aging population as a major justification for the need to implement changes. Descriptions of the "human-friendly" campaigns almost invariably linked them to fostering greater accessibility for both the elderly and those with disabilities, usually with little recognition that accessibility needs for people in those groups might differ dramatically. Supporters often cited statistics to highlight the necessity for all these local efforts, figures that perhaps unintentionally seemed to underscore the greater urgency of meeting the needs of the elderly: as of October 1996, 16.31 percent of Nagano City's population was over the age of 65, in contrast to 2.91 percent who had a documented disability.[41] Obviously, concerns about Japan's aging population had little to do with the Paralympics themselves, but it is easy to see how the 1998 Games benefited from growing attention to issues of accessibility in this context. Here again, it also appears that those interested in pursuing change, particularly in Nagano, latched onto the Paralympics—and especially the additional publicity and pressure they brought—as a tool to help them address these sorts of long-standing challenges in Japanese society.

In addition to these domestic factors, changes in Japanese policy and law were being influenced by developments at the international level. As planning for the Paralympics began in the early 1990s, the UN Decade of Disabled Persons (1983–92) was nearing its end, but the succeeding Asian and Pacific Decade of Disabled Persons (1993–2002) continued to pursue and expand on the UN campaign's goals. These extended development programs were too complex to explore in detail here, but overviews of both offer insights on how they influenced Japanese policies at the time. Both campaigns laid out ambitious agendas that aimed "to improve the situation and status of persons with disabilities," particularly by encouraging national governments to implement measures for improvement in targeted areas over the course of the decade.[42] Although UN-affiliated groups or committees took a leading role in both campaigns, they were supported, and often compelled to act, by a variety of international experts, global advocacy organizations, and national stakeholders. During each of the decades, key individuals tied to the programs met at regular intervals to assess progress being made toward the outlined goals, establishing a degree of accountability for participating countries. These international or regional meetings not only served to highlight achievements or shortfalls but also provided opportunities to revise goals and targets.

By the end of the UN Decade, the agenda had been modified from an initial focus on prevention, rehabilitation, full participation, and equality to one that gave greater attention to "equalization of opportunities for disabled persons."[43] Reflecting, in part, the ongoing international growth of the Independent Living Movement and other similar forms of disability-related activism, this changing agenda emphasized disability rights, independence, integration, and greater involvement of people with disabilities themselves in these efforts. In late 1992, the United Nations Economic and Social Commission of Asia and the Pacific picked up these revised priorities when it launched the Asian and Pacific Decade, a development program motivated by the region's booming economy, diversity, unique challenges, and high percentages of both aging populations and individuals with disabilities. The original agenda for this follow-up decade campaign emphasized the national implementation of legislation and policies that would help the region achieve "full participation and equality of persons with disabilities."[44] As the campaign neared its end, efforts were increasingly oriented toward a rights-based, barrier-free approach. This first Asian and Pacific Decade has since been followed by two others in the region, with the most recent aiming to "Make the Right Real" by 2022.[45]

Naturally, responses to these UN development programs differed dramatically, and recent work in the field of disability studies offers critical reminders that such attempts to impose purportedly universal definitions and values across such a diverse set of places and people were inherently complicated and problematic.[46] In Japan's case, many of the measures related to disability enacted in the 1980s and 1990s were directly tied to these international campaigns. As Heyer's study of the UN Decade's impact on Japan points out, the UN campaigns and mandates not only helped inspire the shifts in the Japanese disability rights movement discussed earlier but also pushed the government to adopt international "normalization" ideals as guidelines for revising its disability policies.[47]

These new commitments and forms of activism continued, and arguably deepened, with the Asian and Pacific Decade. The seven-year time frame for the 1995 Government Action Plan for Persons with Disabilities, for instance, was clearly meant to coincide with the endpoint of the Asian and Pacific Decade. Japan's official report prepared for the meeting that concluded the decade campaign in 2002 explicitly linked policy changes during the previous two decades to UN-related efforts. Giving minimal attention to any earlier measures or activism, the end-of-decade report begins with the 1980 establishment of the national government's Headquarters for Promoting the UN International Year for Disabled Persons. Additional details about successive long- and short-term programs, plans, and legal changes—all of which overlapped with the international campaigns in terms of both timing and goals—highlighted the ways in which Japan had been largely successful in meeting expectations associated with these international development projects.[48] Based on this report, Japan could now claim to be a leader on these issues in the region.

Japan's engagement with these long-running UN-affiliated development programs and the impacts of that engagement were certainly not contingent on the hosting of the Paralympics. Taking these international pressures and their concomitant domestic elements into account, however, does provide a clearer picture of how Nagano's Games occurred at a particularly opportune moment, one that left Japan, and more specifically Nagano, primed for the Paralympics. The UN agendas and the Japanese domestic measures they inspired made specific, if limited, reference to sports as a form of culture that needed to be accessible for those with disabilities. It is thus possible to see the enthusiastic embrace of the Games during this period as both consequence and evidence of Japan's international commitments.

At the same time, the Paralympics served as an amplifier for broadcasting the ideals of the UN movements within Japanese society. This role was exemplified by NAPOC's rhetoric about the Games' broader purpose and goals. Official materials produced for Nagano's Paralympics gave little more than passing attention to the UN or Asian and Pacific Decades themselves, yet the language used in these materials was strikingly different from that of Tokyo's organizers more than three decades earlier. In the materials prepared for Nagano, the references to rehabilitation so prominent in reports and writings in the 1960s and throughout the early years of FESPIC were largely absent. In their place were frequent allusions to awareness, accessibility, opportunity, independence, and the UN mantra of "full participation and equality."[49] In part, the move away from rehabilitation reflected developments in the Paralympic Movement's approach to sports, which are discussed in the next section, but the telling use of UN terminology also speaks to the extent to which these international ideals had permeated the Paralympics in Nagano. It also brings us back to an important question: What role did the 1998 Games actually play in realizing these abstract international goals of accessibility, equality, and participation in Japan?

As outlined in the preceding pages, crediting the Paralympics alone for the changes occurring in Japan and Nagano would be overly simplistic, because so many other factors were involved. Yet there are several ways in which the 1998 Games seem to merit their reputation as a turning point, even beyond the realm of disability sports. Unlike the earlier Games in Tokyo, Nagano's Paralympics offered far more opportunities for people with disabilities—especially nonathletes—to engage with and even shape the event. This difference reflected both broader changes occurring in Japan at the time and new approaches on the part of Nagano's organizers. The work of NPBK, the human-friendly campaigns, and other such efforts also indicate that disability advocates were able to tap into the official and popular publicity associated

with the Games to present their ideas to a new and dramatically expanded audience. It seems fair to say, then, that the Paralympics played a role in raising
awareness about disability and accessibility issues, particularly in the Nagano
region. Yet it is also important to acknowledge how challenging it can be to
evaluate such changes in awareness or participation. The available evidence—
much of it anecdotal—tends to focus on the times, places, and people most
associated with the Games, making it difficult to determine broader, long-term
impacts.

Accessibility would appear to offer a more concrete (literally in some cases)
example of the impact from Nagano's Paralympics. Although concerns about
creating a "barrier-free" society were hardly unique to Nagano during this period, the Paralympics provided both an opportunity and a deadline to demonstrate Japan's and the region's accessibility bona fides.[50] With the world
turning its gaze to the region, Nagano did not have the luxury of waiting until
the end of the Asian and Pacific Decade to act: accessibility had to become
more than lip service in Nagano, and changes had to happen immediately. The
urgency created by the upcoming Paralympics combined with the other domestic and international factors to generate the flurry of accessibility-related
policies, campaigns, and actions pursued in Nagano before and during the
Games. In marked contrast with Tokyo 1964, several of the accessibility measures associated with the Paralympics also outlived the event itself, because
they were encoded in policy or incorporated into the built environment or
transportation networks. As just one example, Nagano's barrier-free Athletes'
Village was converted into apartments, housing that served as a first-time independent apartment for one of the members from Human Net Nagano beginning in late 1998.[51] Although it is not clear how many other people with
disabilities were able to take advantage of these facilities, it is no stretch to say
that their very availability—along with the presence of countless new curb
cuts, elevators, and accessible restrooms—was inextricably linked to the 1998
Paralympics.

Unfortunately, Nagano's Games also exhibited shortcomings in terms of
accessibility. By many accounts, the various human-friendly campaigns in the
region provided a remarkably effective means for raising awareness about the
barriers that individuals with disabilities faced on a daily basis in their communities. But awareness (and new guidelines) did not always translate into
barrier-free environments, as seen in particular with the persistence of accessibility problems in Nagano that were documented in the August 1997 campaign only six months before the Paralympics. Infrastructural or building
changes required time, money, and motivation, and for whatever reason the
proper combination was not always there for Nagano's Games.[52] These

lingering barriers might help explain reports from the time indicating that people with disabilities were not very visible outside the athletic venues or Paralympic Village. In other cases, the "barrier-free" fixes—such as the temporary structures built in some area hotels to overcome the customary step into the bathroom—generated their own new barriers while failing to address the problems for the long term. Even the sports venues, which were generally lauded for their attention to accessibility, faced criticism for usability issues: they had less-than-ideal and often segregated seating, small elevators, limited accessible restrooms, and long distances between seating, elevators, and restrooms.[53] From the perspective of some critics, these problems apparent in Nagano were not unique to these Games but rather exemplified broader patterns in Japanese society. In an effort to become barrier-free, Japan was starting to make progress on the "hard side," with the widespread recognition that barriers existed and with new facilities being built to code. On the "soft side"—motivation, understanding, acceptance, appreciation, and general approaches to disability that went beyond the letter of the law—there was still a long way to go.[54] Nagano's Games did not (and ultimately could not) make Japan or even Nagano barrier-free, but the changes in and discussions about accessibility that they helped spark demonstrated the power of the Paralympics as a tool for pushing a barrier-free agenda at home. In so doing, they not only marked a dramatic shift from Japan's first Paralympics in 1964 but also set the stage for the ongoing campaigns connected with the 2020 Paralympics that are addressed in chapter 5.

"None Other than Competitive Sport": The Evolving Disability Sports Scene

Among the many differences between Tokyo's Paralympics in 1964 and those in Nagano, the shift in focus away from rehabilitation was particularly striking. As noted in chapter 1, organizers for the 1964 Games tended to downplay the importance of competition to focus attention on the medical and social benefits of the Games. Three decades later, the focus for Nagano had swung nearly 180 degrees, with organizers repeatedly emphasizing that the Paralympics were, first and foremost, a competitive sporting event involving some of the world's most elite athletes. Although this marked shift certainly reflected the broader developments in approaches to disability discussed earlier, the driving forces behind the changed emphasis came from the realm of disability sports. With its intentional efforts to forge closer connections with the Olympic Movement, the still relatively new IPC set the tone for Nagano's

Games from the earliest planning stages. The IPC's goals and approaches were reinforced by trends and developments in Japan's disability sports scene that helped make the 1998 Paralympics remarkably different from those held in Tokyo more than thirty years earlier. This combination of factors also positioned Nagano's Games to have a profound impact on disability sports at multiple levels—from bolstering the status of the IPC to reshaping how athletes with disabilities were represented.

The origins and early organizational history of the IPC are well documented in other works and were presented in chapter 2 in relation to FESPIC. In connection with Nagano's Winter Games, three overlapping aspects of the early IPC merit brief consideration here. First, the IPC was still a relatively young organization when Nagano began planning for its Games. Established in 1989, the IPC only assumed organizational control over Paralympic events after the conclusion of the 1992 Winter and Summer Paralympic Games; in other words, the 1998 Paralympics were only the third Games held under the direction of the IPC.[55] The IPC had a vested interest in seeing that these Games happened in Nagano and that they suited the image of the Paralympics that the committee was working to cultivate.

By design then, Nagano's Paralympics were going to be operating with a very different set of guidelines than had been the case in 1964, and official materials make it very clear that NAPOC coordinated closely with the IPC from the beginning. For instance, scattered throughout the official report on the 1998 Games are references to activities or approaches carried out in line with *The Paralympic Handbook for Organisers of Paralympic Games*, which was enclosed with the first official correspondence from the IPC requesting that Nagano host the Games.[56] Taking advantage of the lengthy planning phase, NAPOC provided regular updates on planning at IPC meetings, hosted IPC officials for multiple onsite inspections, organized several "pre-Paralympic" international disability sporting events to test the region's readiness, and dispatched study groups abroad to observe and report back on various IPC events, including both the Lillehammer and Atlanta Paralympics.

IPC influence was especially apparent in relation to the sporting competitions themselves. Venue design, officiating, antidoping measures, and the classification of athletes all bore direct signs of substantial IPC engagement from beginning to end.[57] NAPOC's approach to the classification of athletes, in particular, revealed and reinforced the IPC's still-emerging position as the international authority on disability sports. When Nagano received the official invitation to host the Games, no medical specialists in Japan held IPC certification for classifying winter sport athletes, something that is hardly surprising since the IPC itself was only a few years old, with its first Winter Paralympics still to come. But almost immediately, NAPOC began dispatching several Japanese specialists to IPC-affiliated sports events abroad so that they could acquire the necessary training and have IPC certifications in hand before Nagano's Games.[58] As this example demonstrates, NAPOC proved to be a reliable and even beneficial partner for the IPC as it charted its new leadership of the Paralympic Movement.

The situation in Nagano also reflected a second feature of the early IPC, notably its relationship with the Olympic Movement and with the International Olympic Committee (IOC) in particular. The IPC was established, in part, to facilitate better interactions with the IOC, but the relationship between the two in the 1990s was still in the formative phase. As noted, the bidding processes for the Olympics and Paralympics during this period were still separate, and Olympic hosts were not obligated to hold the Paralympics. This point is reflected in the language in the IPC's first official letter to Nagano's would-be Paralympic organizers on November 8, 1991: Nagano was asked "to consider the possibility of hosting" as part of the IPC's continuing "efforts to establish a tradition" of Paralympic Games being held in the Olympic host cities.[59] The case for this tradition was bolstered by a (relatively short) list of recent and upcoming cities that had agreed to host both events. In addition to such calls to participate in a clear invention of tradition, the letter pitched joint hosting as ways to cut costs for the Games and build on the logistical knowhow of Olympic organizers, a pitch that seemed to overlook the fact that the easiest way to keep costs down and avoid organizational hassles was not to host the Paralympics, as many Olympic cities had chosen to do after Tokyo's 1964 Games.

Of course, when the IPC dispatched its letter, it already had a strong indication that Nagano was going to accept, given previous formal expressions of interest in the Paralympics during the Olympic bidding process. The first public statement came from Nagano's governor during the IOC meeting in September 1990. In January 1991, Nagano's written response to the IOC inspection committee's questionnaire also confirmed that "if Nagano were named the 1998 Winter Olympic host city, it was prepared to accept the Winter Paralympic Games."[60] The timing of such official statements raises an interesting question: Were early expressions of willingness to host the Paralympics seen as a way to bolster Nagano's case for its Olympic bid?[61] The scandals that later plagued the IOC in connection with the bids for the Olympics in Nagano and Salt Lake City suggest that Olympic promoters at potential host sites had been seeking any sort of advantage possible, and they would almost certainly have been aware of the newly emerging relationship between the IOC and IPC. In that context, Olympic organizers in Nagano had little to lose by offering to host the Paralympics, and they could point to Japan's track record in disability sports to demonstrate that this was more than an empty commitment. Whatever the specific motives behind the decision to pursue both Games, there is little question that Nagano's Olympics and Paralympics were linked from early on, in no small part because of developments unfolding within international sports institutions.

The changes at the top were replicated—and reinforced—on the ground in Nagano in various forms of coordination between NAPOC and the Nagano Olympic Organizing Committee (dubbed NAOC). From shared office spaces to joint publicity tours, both committees worked together far more closely than had been the case with Tokyo's events in 1964. Cooperative efforts throughout the process contributed to the improved accessibility of venues and the Athletes' Village. The committees carried out several joint training sessions for volunteers, and a number of staff were directly involved in planning and holding both events. NAOC also helped NAPOC cut its costs by sharing resources and supplies acquired in connection with the Olympics.[62] In this sense, Nagano's experience lived up to, and perhaps even exceeded, the IPC's promised benefits of hosting joint Games.

Yet the relationship was not all smooth sailing. NAOC resisted calls for holding exhibitions of Paralympic sports during the Olympics, pointing to organizational challenges and the fact that they had already "invested a great deal in the Paralympics."[63] A controversy over national team uniforms less than a year before the event sparked widespread attention and criticism as well. The Japanese Olympic Committee (JOC) initially denied requests to allow Japanese Paralympians to wear the same uniforms as the Olympic team and only relented under pressure from the prime minister and the Ministry of Education.[64] The uniform controversy highlighted the lingering tensions between the Olympic and Paralympic Games, and the negative publicity it generated and the ultimate reversal from the JOC indicated that the relationship between the two sets of Games was then still in flux.

The uniform controversy also exemplified a third aspect of the young IPC's approach: the promotion of the Paralympics as an international, elite sporting event on par with the Olympics. As noted in chapter 2, the Paralympics and disability sports in general had been gravitating toward an emphasis on elite, competitive sports for several years before this, a shift in focus that became even more pronounced with the formation of the IPC. In part, this shift reflected the IPC's explicit goal of establishing stronger ties with the Olympics, with many insisting that being parallel to the Olympics meant "that the Paralympic Games must be serious and that they must be only for elite athletes—distant from any notion of recreational sport."[65]

The emphasis on elite competition was also part and parcel of how the still evolving IPC was seeking to define itself and its mission. As the initial correspondence with Nagano put it, "The mandate of IPC . . . is to organize Paralympic Games and World Championships for ALL [sic] categories of disabilities. One of the important aims of IPC is to integrate events for disabled athletes into competitions for able-bodied and to give top-level sportsmen and women the exciting thrill of being part of the elite sportsmovement [sic] in the world."[66] At the time, the IPC's "mandate" and aims of integration were far less clear-cut (and far more controversial) than this letter implied, but the letter left little doubt that elite sport was at the center of IPC concerns. In an article published in a Japanese sports medicine journal just before Nagano's Paralympics were held, IPC president Robert Steadward employed a bit of historical oversimplification to reinforce this connection, citing 1989—the year of the IPC's establishment—as the turning point in the disability sports movement when emphasis shifted from rehabilitation to "competitive sports focusing on sporting excellence, and high-level performance."[67] For the IPC, the ability to deliver elite-level sports competition was clearly integral to its leadership claims in the realm of disability sports.

Given this broader context, it is hardly surprising that NAPOC's official report described the Paralympics as "an event for the disabled that gathers the world's highest-level athletes" and outlined an official "Hosting Philosophy" that listed "giving the disabled an opportunity to participate in high-level competition" first among NAPOC's goals.[68] Official materials in general are littered with references to competition and elite athletes, with many echoing Steadward's idea that an emphasis on rehabilitation in connection with the Paralympics was (or should be) a thing of the past. A NAPOC pamphlet targeted would-be volunteers with this reminder: "When hearing about the Paralympics, there is a tendency to think of it in terms of medical care or assistance, but the Paralympics are competitive sporting events involving highly trained athletes."[69] A number of Paralympians used their "Word of Greeting" space in the official directory of Japanese athletes to comment on the highly competitive nature of these Games. One alpine skier claimed that in his mind the "Paralympics and Olympics are the same," and several other Paralympians reminded spectators to view them as athletes, rather than disabled people.[70] It is worth recalling here, too, that the decision to charge for tickets at the 1998 Paralympics was framed in terms of the elite-level competition at the event. With their record number of "elite" athletes and sold-out competitions, Nagano's Paralympics broke new ground and in the process offered a strong case that the IPC was on the right track.

Disability Sports in Japan

If some involved with Nagano's Games were only beginning to realize that the Paralympics were "none other than competitive sport," for others more intimately engaged with disability sports in Japan, the rising level of international *and domestic* competition would have been far from surprising.[71] In the decades since Japan first hosted the Paralympics, the disability sports scene at home had changed on multiple fronts, with several significant developments unfolding largely in response to the upcoming Games in Nagano. Fujita Motoaki, a leading scholar of disability sports in Japan, subdivides the years leading up to 1998 into three periods, each building on the preceding one. His framework is useful for understanding the domestic context for Nagano's Paralympics and why they marked a moment of transition.

For Fujita, the years up to 1975 were a foundational period, marked by the institution building and international engagement detailed in previous chapters.[72] The establishment of the Japan Sports Association for the Disabled (JSAD) after the 1964 Games was obviously critical during these years, but so too was the launching of annual national sports meets in 1965. Over the years, official reports demonstrate that these meets provided increasing numbers of men and women with venues for developing and displaying their athletic skills. Japan's national meets were also significant because they embraced a multi-disability format from the beginning. In addition, because these events customarily followed the annual Kokutai or National Sports Meets, they moved to a different prefecture each year, generating the potential for increased local awareness of and access to disability sports well beyond the Tokyo region or other rehabilitation-related sites.[73] Another key domestic development during this foundational period was the opening of the Osaka Municipal Disability Sports Center in 1974, the first such venue in Japan dedicated to sports for those with disabilities.[74] Together with rehabilitation-oriented sites like those in Ōita, the Osaka Center provided a valuable model for future sites in terms of both facilities and staffing.

The period from 1976 to 1990 was defined by the continued expansion of disability sports throughout Japan.[75] The number of facilities available for athletes with disabilities jumped dramatically during these years, going from a mere handful to ninety-one by 1990. Domestic sporting events and organizations also proliferated, with many groups and competitions focusing on the promotion of particular sports, including several winter sports that were only beginning to attract international attention. Another milestone for disability sports came in 1985 when JSAD launched a formal system for training and certifying disability sports specialists. The new system helped standardize event officiating in particular but also laid the groundwork for future developments in the training of new disability sports instructors and coaches throughout Japan. All of these factors and the ongoing opportunities for competing at home and abroad were beginning to have an impact on athletic performances as well, even though the most dramatic improvements for Japanese athletes were still to come. Despite these positive developments, Fujita points out that throughout this period disability sports remained more or less segregated from nondisabled sports and largely invisible to the broader public.

Fujita's third period, from 1991 until Nagano's Games in 1998, witnessed a particularly dramatic increase in visibility, thanks in large part to significant changes in Japanese media coverage of disability sports, an issue explored in the following pages.[76] The establishment of sport-specific organizations and sports facilities continued, and the development of certification programs at universities and technical schools beginning in 1993 resulted in a significant increase in the number of qualified disability sports specialists. Reflecting international developments, it was also during these years that sports for athletes with intellectual impairments began to gain national recognition in Japan. Although some local areas had offered competitions for individuals with intellectual disabilities earlier, a recurring national event was not organized until 1992. These Games were soon followed by formal affiliation with the Special Olympics in 1994.

The increasing emphasis on high-level, elite performance at the international level during the years immediately preceding Nagano's Games understandably sparked a desire to help Japanese athletes remain competitive. Recruitment and training received greater attention in Japan, and qualifying events and ranking systems were put in place to ensure more selectivity and improved performance of athletes. The best example of such changes was the establishment of the Japan Paralympics in 1991, which focused initially on swimming and track and field. Japan Paralympic events for skiing and sledge hockey were launched soon after in 1993 and 1994, respectively.[77] As Nagano's Games drew closer, "athlete strengthening" took on even more prominence as athletes and promoters alike sought to use the upcoming Games to demonstrate that Japan, too, was an elite-level competitor at the Paralympics. Behind the scenes, domestic research and design efforts also sought to assure that Japanese athletes had access to the most up-to-date adapted sports equipment. Beginning in 1995, many of these overlapping measures benefited from increased financial support from the central government.[78]

These national developments and their results were on prominent display as Nagano prepared for and hosted Japan's first Paralympics in more than thirty years. Nagano itself was no stranger to disability sports by that point. In 1958 Nagano Prefecture was among the first places in Japan to host a local sporting event for individuals with disabilities. In the intervening years, the Nagano area also established a reputation as a wheelchair basketball powerhouse, and the Hokushin district in Nagano began hosting local sports tournaments for physically and intellectually disabled athletes during the late 1980s.[79] Taking advantage of its natural environment, its reputation as a winter sports mecca, and the upcoming Games, Nagano Prefecture launched its own "athlete strengthening" movement aiming to increase the number of participants and medal winners from the prefecture in the still relatively new field of winter disability sports. From 1993 onward, the prefecture's Disability Winter Sports Promotion Project sought to recruit and train local athletes, ultimately producing impressive results: of Japan's seventy athletes, twenty-one had some connection to the prefecture, and six of them won medals at the Games.[80] Because they included high-level international competitors, the various "Pre-Paralympic" events hosted in Nagano also served as a key element of the broader athlete strengthening program, allowing Japan's athletes to hone their skills and identify targets for improvement in advance of the Winter Games themselves.[81]

The cumulative outcomes of Fujita's three periods of development were behind many of the "groundbreaking" sporting elements associated with Nagano's Paralympics. The first formal inclusion of medal events for athletes with intellectual impairments at these Games reflected trends at both the international and domestic levels, but it is worth noting that this important Winter Paralympic "first" was never a given. The possibility of incorporating these medal events generated much debate among NAPOC, the IPC, and the international organization overseeing sports for intellectually disabled athletes—often centering on questions of classification and Japan's relative lack of experience with these sports, which were just beginning to gain national attention. Eventually, NAPOC overcame its initial concerns, agreeing in early 1997 to include competitions in cross-country skiing for athletes with intellectual impairments at these Games.[82]

As the host country, Japan might be expected to field a large team for Nagano's Paralympics, but both the size and success of the national delegation seemed to indicate that the intense recruiting and strengthening efforts leading up to the Games had significantly enhanced normal home-team advantages. The team itself was more than double the size of the largest Japanese delegation ever dispatched to the Winter Games and nearly as big as the Japanese team at the Summer Paralympic Games in Atlanta in 1996. Japan has yet to come close to the size of the seventy-athlete team for any Winter Games since Nagano.[83]

The oft-referenced "medal rush" at the Nagano Paralympics, too, reflected the dividends of Japanese investment in winter sports for those with disabilities. With forty-one total medals—twelve gold, sixteen silver, and thirteen bronze—the overall medal count for Japanese athletes at Nagano remains by far the highest for Winter Paralympics and ranks among Japan's top five medal counts for all Paralympic Games.[84] As some at the time (and many since) have pointed out, these impressive numbers can be somewhat deceiving.[85] Japanese athletes won a disproportionate number of their medals (17 total) in the women's ice sledge speed races. Because of the difficulties of classification and the small number of eligible athletes, most of these races featured fewer than five athletes, with several having only three; Japan fielded two or three competitors in each race, virtually assuring one or two medals in each competition.

Nevertheless, Japan's ability to field multiple athletes when most other countries could not spoke to the impact of the aggressive recruiting and training efforts leading up to the Games. It is also worth observing that several medal winners in Nagano continued to be successful at later Paralympics. Even after sledge speed racing was dropped as a Paralympic sport after Nagano, some athletes continued to find success in other sports. For example, Tsuchida Wakako, who won two golds and two silvers in women's sledge racing in Nagano, went on to become a top international competitor in wheelchair racing, with a career that has included multiple Paralympic medals and a world record set at Ōita's Marathon in 2013.[86] In other words, the years-long push to assure that Japanese athletes with disabilities could compete at an elite level on the global stage reaped results for and beyond Nagano, representing yet another reason these Games have been hailed as a turning point.

Toward the Normalization of Disability Sports

As the ongoing successes of Japanese Paralympians after Nagano suggest, the Winter Games, like the earlier Paralympics in Tokyo, exerted their most direct impacts on the continued development of disability sports in Japan and beyond. Internationally, Nagano's Games made several significant contributions to the Paralympic Movement. In addition to being the first Winter Games held outside Europe, the 1998 Paralympics attracted new participating countries and a record number of athletes, bolstering the prestige and reach of the movement. As a relatively new organization, the IPC realized multiple benefits from these Games, ranging from enhanced ties with the Olympic Movement to the reinforcement of IPC ideals and governance. In particular, Nagano's Games and the responses to them confirmed the notion that the Paralympics could be marketable, especially if the focus remained on elite performance. Even some of the challenges associated with the 1998 Games—apparent gaps in the *Handbook for Organisers*, lingering tensions with the Olympics, questions about how to incorporate athletes with intellectual impairments, and ongoing concerns about classification, safety, and fairness—benefited the IPC by drawing attention to areas for future improvement.

In the immediate aftermath of Nagano's Games, Japan's disability sports scene also underwent a number of key changes that built on preceding developments. Just a month after the Winter Paralympics ended, the Ministry of Health, Labor, and Welfare convened a nongovernmental group of Paralympians, sports organizers, academics, media figures, and other stakeholders to outline suggestions for the future of disability sports in Japan. The resulting report from this "Roundtable on Disability Sport" cited the recent Games, praising many of the positive developments mentioned earlier. Yet the report was looking forward, not back, and in the views of participants, much work remained to be done. Generally, the report called for adopting a "normalization" approach toward disability sports. Although roundtable participants acknowledged that sports still had an important role to play in rehabilitation efforts and in increasing social awareness of disability, they argued that Japan needed to move beyond that: the country needed to foster opportunities for more people with disabilities to pursue sports both in their daily lives and at the elite level. In other words, disability sports had to be viewed and treated more like nondisabled sports. To achieve these abstract goals, the report drew attention to several specific measures, ranging from increased financial support to active promotion of sports for those with intellectual disabilities. Group members also noted that normalization and improvements necessitated much closer interaction between disability sports organizations and the Ministry of Education, the Japanese Olympic Committee, and the Japan Sport Association, all of which oversaw various elements of nondisabled sports.[87] Many of the initiatives and measures mentioned in the report were already beginning to be implemented in the lead-up to Nagano's Games, and the roundtable participants were pushing for them to continue and expand. To be sure, none of these suggestions were binding, but the ministerial decision to convene the group and publish its report pointed to a higher level of government receptiveness sparked in part by Nagano's Paralympics.

Given the emphasis in this report, it is perhaps not surprising that the next few years witnessed several organizational changes in Japan that exemplified the broader goals of normalization, greater opportunities for participation, and improved competitiveness. In 1999, JSAD expanded its purview to include athletes with intellectual disabilities, and in 2003 it expanded again to include athletes with mental illnesses. The Japan Paralympic Committee was founded in 1999 and tasked with recruiting and training elite-level athletes. Taking a step toward integration, JSAD established an official affiliation with the Japan Sport Association in 2000, and that same year disability sports were formally addressed in national plans for promoting sports more generally.[88] Although Nagano's Games were certainly not the only factor driving these sorts of changes, many of which were years in the making, the 1998 Paralympics provided advocates with strong evidence to support their case that disability sports merited more attention and support at the national level. It is equally important, however, to acknowledge what several critics pointed out after the Games ended: much of the funding for promoting disability sports in connection with Nagano's Paralympics plummeted thereafter.[89] In this sense, Nagano's Games not only laid the groundwork for later developments that are discussed in chapter 5 in relation to Tokyo's 2020 Paralympics but also served as a cautionary tale for those seeking to continue the promotion of disability sports after the conclusion of the 2020 Games.

As a host, Nagano understandably saw several specific impacts from the Paralympics in terms of disability sports, including the establishment of Sun Apple, a prefectural social welfare center that featured multiple sports facilities and programs for those with disabilities. Planning for the center began in 1992, and with funding provided by the prefectural government, the facility opened a month after the Games in April 1998. Together with its four regional satellite facilities that opened in later years, Sun Apple served more than 2.6 million people in its first twenty years.[90] In addition to the local athlete strengthening programs and various regional sports events discussed earlier, the 1998 Paralympics sparked the founding of the prefectural adapted sports organization in 1994, as well as Nagano City's disability sports association in 1997. Since the Winter Games, both organizations have remained actively involved in promoting a wide variety of sports in the region and beyond.[91]

It is also more than happenstance that Nagano was selected to host the first Special Olympics World Games held in Asia. These 2005 Winter World Games merit a full study in their own right, but even an overview of official materials reveals the close connection with Nagano's earlier Games. When Special Olympics International approached the Japanese national organization about the possibility of hosting the Winter Games, Nagano was the go-to choice thanks to its successful track record with large-scale winter sporting events and early commitment to promoting sports for those with intellectual impairments. Using organizational and promotional approaches similar to those for the Paralympics, the Winter World Games eventually welcomed nearly two thousand athletes from eighty-four countries for competitions in sixty-two events. With nearly 10,000 volunteers, more than 90,000 spectators, and dramatically increased media coverage, the 2005 Special Olympics marked another success for Nagano, earning high praise from Special Olympics chairman Timothy Shriver, who dubbed them "unequivocally the best Special Olympic World Winter Games in history."[92] With these Games in the books, Nagano had not only achieved another first but also bolstered and renewed the region's earlier commitments to the promotion of a barrier-free society.

"Support Me as an Individual Competitor, Not a Disabled Person"

The repeated emphasis on elite-level sports and performance associated with Nagano's Paralympics had a profound influence on the ways in which Japan's athletes were represented before, during, and after the Games. Athletes associated with Nagano's Paralympics received significantly more attention as a group and as individuals than had been the case with those participating in Tokyo's Games in 1964. This increased attention came in many forms, ranging from the expanded mass media coverage addressed in the following section to the greater prominence of athletes in official documents. Like those for Tokyo, the official reports and promotional materials for Nagano still regularly featured organizers and their commentaries, but thanks to developments in disability sports in Japan and the formal emphasis placed on hosting an event appropriate to the "highest-level athletes," Japanese Paralympians were clearly featured more in the marketing campaign for Nagano.[93] For instance, one set of posters used during the Games depicted five different Japanese athletes, each of whom was fully outfitted in his or her sports equipment.[94] In the months leading up to the Games, periodicals connected to government ministries and rehabilitation-oriented organizations published a range of articles on the Paralympics. Although many of the early pieces described developments in the organizational process or explained particular Paralympic sports, articles appearing closer in time to the Games featured detailed interviews with Japanese athletes who had been named to the national team. After the Paralympics, many of these same journals ran interviews with medal winners as well.[95] Perhaps the most concrete example of increased recognition of athletes in connection with Nagano was the official directory of Japanese Paralympians published by JSAD on the eve of the Games. The directory not only featured photos and basic information about the sports, classifications, and home prefectures of every single Japanese competitor but also included multiple comments from each of them, addressing topics from training regimens to their broader hopes for the Nagano Paralympics.[96]

The official directory exemplified another impact that became apparent in Nagano: the changing nature of these representations. Japanese athletes linked to Nagano's Paralympics not only received more attention but were also much more likely to be treated like athletes, rather than individuals seeking medical or social rehabilitation. While the official directory provided information on athletes' impairments, their comments were overwhelmingly focused on preparations for or expectations about the upcoming competitions. Similarly, the promotional posters depicting athletes were each labeled with the individual's sport, with no specific references to disabilities. Published interviews from specialty journals both before and after the Games also concentrated on practice routines, expectations, competitors, and challenges. The Ministry of Health and Welfare's April 1998 interview with alpine skier Obinata Kuniko offered a case in point. Obinata, who won three medals in Nagano—gold (Japan's first in any Winter Paralympics), silver, and bronze—started with a brief account of how she took up alpine skiing, but both the interviewer's questions and her responses then focused on more general sports concerns, such as training, comparisons with foreign rivals, the challenges of balancing employment and a busy athletic schedule, and the need for additional support for disability sports if Japan wanted to build on its recent successes. As a Paralympian at the very top of her sport, Obinata did not ignore the fact that sports played a role in rehabilitation and recreation, but that was not her story. She was a competitor, and from her perspective, the Nagano Games had done much to show Japanese society that the Paralympics were "not rehabilitation, but competitive sport."[97] Yet even as she offered this positive evaluation of the recent Games, Obinata expressed some skepticism about the extent to which perceptions of Paralympians in Japan had actually changed.

Indeed, it is critically important to note that the connection between disability sports and rehabilitation did not disappear with Nagano's Games. The persistence of older understandings of disability sports was particularly apparent in materials from organizations that did not deal with these sports on a regular basis. For instance, an article from the National Land Planning Association's monthly magazine used decades-old language to describe the role of the Paralympics in providing "bright hope" and promoting friendships, with hardly any mention of athletic competition.[98] Similarly, a February 1998 article from the Ministry of Education's monthly journal shared basic details about the upcoming Paralympics and their sports but somehow neglected mention of elite-level competition. Its description of the Games also hewed remarkably close to those from thirty years earlier, emphasizing the role of the Paralympics in promoting hope, courage, and international goodwill.[99] Other education-oriented publications seemed to follow a similar logic. In discussing the educational significance of the Paralympics, a January 1998 article in the journal *School Sports (Gakkō taiiku)* by longtime disability sports advocate Nakagawa Kazuhiko focused almost exclusively on rehabilitation.[100] Another 1998 article from a journal targeting elementary school teachers noted that Paralympic athletes had acquired "high-level competitive skills through intense practice," but this detail was nearly buried amidst far more numerous references to the "inspiration" (*kandō*) that the Games provided, particularly for "able-bodied" (*kenjōsha*) spectators.[101] Based on these sorts of articles appearing so close to the Games, it would seem that promoters in Nagano were not entirely effective in selling a new view of the Paralympics and their athletes.

In part, this lack of effectiveness stemmed from muddled messaging. Many of these articles directly referenced the Nagano Paralympic theme, "Connection and Inspiration" (*fureai to kandō*), often echoing the official language used to explain it.[102] Thus the official materials themselves harkened back to older language, even as they simultaneously proclaimed a new purpose for the Paralympics: elite competition. Connection, inspiration, and high-level performance were not mutually exclusive—one need only consider how similar language could easily be applied to the Olympics. But given the challenges inherent in shifting perceptions of the Paralympics, organizers were not really doing themselves favors with these baggage-laden phrases, and their use pointed to lingering tendencies to view the Paralympics as something other than an elite sporting event, even among organizers. As Saitō Yoshihiko, an athlete with disabilities himself noted in a critical essay published after the Games, organizer's use of slogans like "The joy of living" for an event that was supposed to be for the world's best athletes exemplified a significant disconnect between rhetoric and approach. He also questioned the use of insensitive language on a promotional poster pulled from distribution because of widespread opposition to its content. The poster allegedly read, "We are human whether or not we have both hands. We are human whether or not we have both legs. We only need mental strength to overcome handicaps."[103] To Saitō's examples of organizational disconnects, we might add the decision to use "Hope" as the theme for the opening ceremony in Nagano. As Saitō observed, the issue was not that organizers should refrain from using disability sports events to foster inspiration or hope, but rather that the real focus in Nagano still seemed to be centered on overcoming disability rather than the competitive sports that the rhetoric cited.[104]

I would suggest that what Saitō was describing in the case of Nagano reflected more than just problems with NAPOC or Japanese attitudes toward disability: it was a manifestation of what disability sports scholars have called the "Paralympic paradox."[105] In Nagano, promoters were trying to expand the reach of the Paralympics by using elite athletes to appeal to and inspire a largely nondisabled audience. To a certain extent, this meant downplaying disability while emphasizing performance and achievement. At the same time, the Paralympics were supposed to inspire and benefit those with disabilities, necessitating ongoing attention to the impairments of the athletes, even as the Games moved away from their earlier emphasis on sports as a form of rehabilitation. Nagano's Games came at a point of transition in the international and national Paralympic Movement. They also predated efforts on the part of the IPC to articulate a clear ideology or set of written goals, a process that did not occur until 2003 and even at that point resulted in what some have described as a "rather vague and empty" motto: "Spirit in Motion."[106] In many respects then, it is hardly surprising that Nagano served as center stage for a perhaps unresolvable clash of competing discourses about the purposes and goals of Paralympic sports more broadly.

At the heart of this clash in Nagano were the Japanese athletes, which might explain why some spoke about sports' role in helping them overcome disabilities, whereas others felt compelled to insist that they were elite athletes seeking to win. Yet even those whose comments focused more on rehabilitative aspects would likely agree with alpine skier Maruyama Naoya's request that fans support him "as an individual competitor, not a disabled person."[107] Unlike in Tokyo, even the newest athletes in Nagano were there to compete. For all of Japan's athletes, the Paralympics had become the pinnacle, not the gateway to recovery. By the end of the Nagano Games, the idea that Paralympians were elite competitors was clearly gaining ground, thanks in no small part to extensive media coverage and a number of Japanese victories. At the same time, implicit questions about the ultimate purpose of the Paralympics remained largely unaddressed. In this sense and others, the Nagano Games revealed continuities and differences with the 1964 Games, highlighting some of the ongoing dilemmas faced by the Paralympic Movement as it looked toward Tokyo in 2020.

Mass Mediated Games: Nagano in Perspective

In addition to their many other ground-breaking elements, the 1998 Nagano Paralympics have often been cited as a moment of transition in mass media coverage of disability sports in Japan, and for good reason. The 1998 Games not only generated a remarkable number of print and broadcast media reports but also pioneered new means for sharing information about the event via the Internet. The shifting representations of Paralympic athletes and these Games also owed much to changes in media approaches, as reporters sought to align their coverage with the focus on competition coming from Nagano's organizers and participants. All that said, it is critical to remember that Paralympic supporters in Japan had long been actively pursuing and cultivating media attention. Closer examinations of the resulting coverage reveal that, as much as the Nagano Games' media coverage differed from earlier years, it also reflected a number of similarities.

To shed light on both changes and continuities up through and beyond the 1998 Paralympics, the remainder of this chapter focuses on four aspects of mass media coverage. Changes in the quantity of coverage are the most obvious development since the 1960s. On their surface the increased numbers of articles and reports suggest a tale of remarkable progress, with Nagano marking a major turning point. Yet more thorough analyses raise important questions, indicating the need to look beyond the amount of coverage when assessing the media and its impact. Examinations of regional press coverage offer insights on the critical role that these less prominent news outlets have played in promoting disability sports in Japan and highlight meaningful differences between local and national coverage. Qualitative explorations of media representations of athletes over time also draw attention to connections between older rehabilitation-oriented approaches and the ongoing reliance on inspirational discourses in Japanese coverage, although recent developments do point to a greater awareness of problematic representational practices. I conclude with an interrogation of new media forms that have their roots in Nagano's Games but seem poised to play a pivotal, if still indeterminate, role in 2020 and beyond. A comprehensive analysis of each of these aspects or trends could easily provide enough material for four stand-alone chapters, so the goal here is to provide a sense of how key elements of media coverage evolved in the more than five decades since Japan began its engagement with the Paralympic Movement.

In recent years, Paralympic media coverage has received increased academic attention, although most of this research has focused on European or American contexts. Linguistic barriers have largely prevented scholars outside Japan from accessing the rich archive of Japanese source materials, as well as several recent studies that Japanese scholars have produced using these media-related resources. In the hopes of breaking down some of these barriers, I describe several of these Japanese-language studies here alongside data from my own studies of Japanese press coverage of FESPIC events and the Ōita Marathon. Much of the scholarship coming out of Japan has focused on newspapers, a reflection of the availability of full-text, searchable databases for three of Japan's major dailies: the *Asahi*, *Yomiuri*, and *Mainichi* newspapers. These databases have allowed researchers to document even passing references to the Paralympics or disability sports with remarkable precision. Broadcast coverage, in contrast, has proven far more difficult to study, especially for the earlier years when coverage was dominated by NHK, which has long been stingy about access to its archives. In this area, however, recent Japanese studies and survey results have begun to improve our understandings of how the Paralympics and its athletes have been portrayed in Japanese television programming. Thanks to Japan's long history of engagement with the Paralympic Movement at multiple sites, an examination of the evolution of Japanese print and broadcast coverage promises unique insights on the past and present role of the media for the Paralympics in Japan and elsewhere.

Media Bubbles

Long before Tokyo's Paralympic Games in 1964, sports in Japan were completely intertwined with the media.[108] Therefore, it is hardly surprising that mass media would come to play an important role in disability sports. Given how difficult it has been for the Paralympics to attract attention in other countries, however, the degree of media attention that the Paralympics and disability sports have generated in Japan is striking, resulting in far more extensive coverage than one might expect. Reporting before 1960 was more or less nonexistent, but attention to the 1964 Games was remarkable for the time and included multiple articles in the major urban dailies and a mix of live and recorded broadcasts on the NHK public television network. The various FESPIC Games and the wheelchair marathons in Ōita also received significant media attention, especially at the local levels. Nagano's Games were understandably famous for the media's response, and if the extensive pre-Games reporting is any indication, Tokyo 2020 could end up being the best-documented Paralympics to date.

As noted at several points in this book, such coverage has been no accident. Organizers for all of these disability sports events in Japan were well aware of the benefits of media coverage and incorporated media outreach as central components of their planning from the beginning. Official materials also make it very clear that organizers frequently sought to make it as easy as possible for media outlets to cover and promote these events. In many instances, media companies had established official sponsorship roles, helping assure increased coverage in both print and broadcast forms.

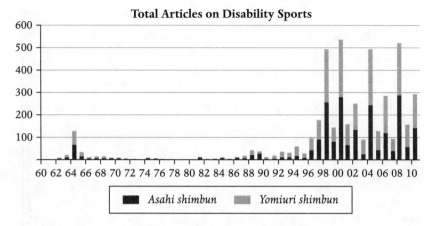

FIGURE 4.1. Yearly references to disability sports from 1960 to 2010 in the *Asahi* and *Yomiuri* newspapers (Fujita 2013: 54). Courtesy of Dr. Fujita Motoaki and Mr. Kamon Yoshio of Sōbun kikaku.

Fujita Motoaki, a leading scholar on disability sports in Japan, has published several analyses that offer insights on long-term trends in Japanese newspaper coverage. Figure 4.1 summarizes his analysis of articles on disability sports published in the *Asahi* and *Yomiuri* dailies from 1960–2010.[109] Fujita's searches produced zero articles for the years between 1900 and 1960, as well as the year 1973, but the spike connected to the 1964 Games accounted for 127 articles from the two newspapers. After 1964, coverage dropped significantly with the number of articles only exceeding 100 again in the lead-up to Nagano's Games, a detail that makes it clear why the 1998 Paralympics have been characterized as a turning point for Japanese media coverage.

Figure 4.2 updates Fujita's research with more recent coverage and additional information from searches of the *Mainichi* newspaper.[110] In particular, it documents the remarkable change in coverage after 2013 when Tokyo was named as host for the 2020 Games. The jump for Nagano still stands out, with total articles for 1998 topping out at a then-record high of 630; however, the number of articles in these three national dailies nearly doubled between 2013 and 2014 and has continued to climb.

Fujita's findings were also borne out in the experiences of Yamaguchi Ichirō, a reporter for the *Mainichi* newspaper who has been writing on disability sports for more than twenty years. Yamaguchi noted minimal interest during his early years of reporting, followed by a significant increase in media attention during the 1998 Games and truly dramatic jumps in coverage since 2013.[111]

As important as these dramatic shifts in recent years have been, we should not let them obscure two other points: the less abundant, though still important,

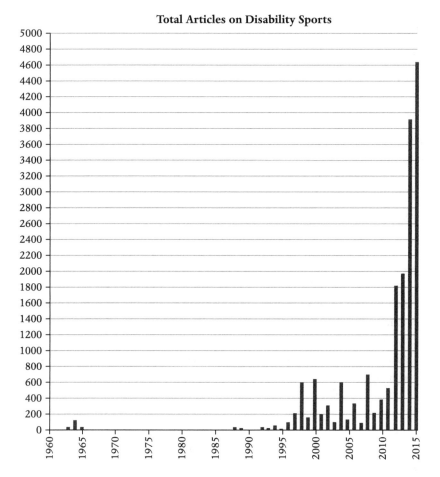

FIGURE 4.2. Yearly references to disability sports from 1960 to 2015 in the *Asahi*, *Mainichi*, and *Yomiuri* newspapers. Composed using data compiled and shared by Dr. Fujita Motoaki.

earlier coverage and the lack of sustained media interest in disability sports after these mega-events have ended. Before 1961, coverage of disability sports was largely absent in Japan, which means that the jump to nearly 130 articles in 1964 represented a manifold increase that is arguably even more numerically significant than more recent changes. It is also important to remember that Fujita's findings only account for a portion (substantial though it is) of Japan's print media outlets. In my own research, in addition to finding front-page coverage in the major dailies, I encountered articles on the 1964 Paralympics in mainstream magazines, several sports newspapers, and in local newspapers, such as those from Ōita. It is difficult to know how many readers at the time saw these reports, but considering the fact that media options were far more limited than they are today, the coverage in 1964 might have been more conspicuous than the numbers alone suggest.

It is equally noteworthy that, over the next several decades after the 1964 Games, coverage dropped drastically. This drop appears all the more telling when one recalls that Japan hosted national disability sports events every year since 1965 and that Japanese athletes were regularly engaged in international competition from 1962 onward, including regular participation in the Paralympics and two FESPIC Games hosted by Japan in 1975 and 1989. Fujita's results revealed that it was not until 1996, a Summer Paralympic year leading up to Nagano, that the number of articles again topped 100, after which point coverage has tended to remain higher. Although less dramatic than the drop after 1964, similar "bubbles" of media coverage have been documented in connection with other disability sports events after Nagano. The various peaks after 1998 on Fujita's graph in Figure 4.1 corresponded to Paralympic years. In general, Summer Games have attracted more attention than the Winter Games, and off-years have witnessed sometimes significant declines in coverage.[112] Another example of media bubbles can be seen in the establishment and then dissolution of two specialty magazines for disability sports in connection with the Nagano Paralympics. Both were established around 1995, but ceased publication soon after the Games.[113] Perhaps it goes without saying, but what these various bubbles suggest is that disability sports media coverage has been—and continues to be—event dependent, with bigger and more prestigious events attracting more attention. As the events end, so too, does the attention, a trend that casts doubt on assumptions about the long-term awareness-raising potential of disability sporting events.

Another press study by disability sports scholar Araragi Kazuma provides a more nuanced view of media coverage between Tokyo's 1964 Games and those in Nagano. Focusing on coverage in the *Asahi* newspaper between 1945 and 1999, Araragi used a method that measured not just the number of articles but also their relative length, the size of their headlines, and their use or lack of images. In general, Araragi's results paralleled those in Fujita's study, though the more focused approach drew attention to additional, smaller examples of media bubbles occurring in connection with international events. The *Asahi* published only slightly more content in 1975 and 1989, years that corresponded, respectively, with the FESPIC Games in Ōita and in Kobe.[114] Given Japan's pioneering role in these events, the relative lack of media attention they received is all the more striking and speaks to perceptions of prestige and perhaps location—neither was held in or near Tokyo—as additional factors shaping print coverage of disability sports events.

In terms of broadcast media, sports historian Sakita Yoshihiro recently gained special access to NHK's archives to examine coverage of the 1964 Paralympics. His study of television broadcasts leading up to and during the 1964 Games documented forty-two distinct news stories and nineteen other programs aired between July 1962 and November 1964. These broadcasts included live coverage of both the opening ceremony and one of the Japanese team's wheelchair basketball games. Of course, such programming was less extensive than that provided for the preceding Olympics or for disability sports events today, but the amount of NHK's coverage in the early 1960s demonstrates that the Paralympics were certainly not ignored during their earliest years in Japan.[115] Given the state of broadcasting at the time and especially NHK's dominant market share, it is arguable that even this limited coverage might be on par with the coverage we find available today. People simply have more options now and are unlikely to watch something just because it is on television. In fact, a survey by NHK indicated that, despite record amounts of broadcast coverage for the Rio de Janeiro Summer Paralympics, less than 30 percent of those surveyed had watched coverage more than once during the Games, and roughly 29 percent reported that they did not watch it at all.[116]

Academic studies of later broadcasts in Japan remain limited, though official reports, commentaries, and survey results from Nagano and later Games offer some insights on how this aspect of media coverage has continued to evolve. For one thing, it is widely acknowledged that Nagano's Games received "unprecedented" attention from broadcast outlets, even though it is important to note that such references generally lack details situating Nagano in a broader historical context.[117] Based on accounts from the time, television reporting for Nagano does seem to have differed markedly from what had preceded it in recent memory. Live coverage of the opening ceremony was available on several local and national networks, and NHK eventually opted to offer live broadcasts of the closing ceremony in response to popular demand. Kondō Fumito, a chief producer for NHK, noted a few months after the Games that Nagano marked "the first time that NHK had provided full-scale broadcasting of the Paralympics," including nightly "Paralympic Hour" shows, special programs, the live broadcasts of ceremonies, and regular stories during news broadcasts. For Kondō, another key aspect of his network's efforts in Nagano was the need to draw on the expertise of both those who specialized in sports and those who worked with social welfare coverage.[118] In this sense, NHK's coverage seemed to reflect some aspects of the tensions described earlier.

In the years since Nagano, there is clear evidence that broadcast programming on the Paralympics and disability sports in Japan has been increasing. A disability sports research group affiliated with the Yamaha Motor Foundation for Sports examined Japanese television coverage for the Summer Games in Beijing, London, and Rio de Janeiro. With more than 234 hours of total coverage, the 2016 Paralympics received nearly three times as much airtime as the London Paralympic Games in 2012. Notably, NHK maintained a dominant role in Paralympic coverage over the course of these three Games, benefiting from the fact that it offers programming on both its general and education channels and has exclusive broadcast rights to the Paralympics themselves. The survey results indicate that other television networks in Japan only began to turn their attention to the Paralympics since 2013 when Tokyo was awarded the 2020 Games. Their coverage levels have remained well below that of NHK, but this new attention from other networks clearly fueled the dramatic jump in hours of programming for the Rio de Janeiro Paralympics in Japan.[119]

As Japan prepared to host the 2020 Games in Tokyo, upward trends in broadcast coverage continued, taking on a variety of forms. For anyone following disability sports on Japanese television, it is now much easier to find live reporting for major international events, including the Ōita International Wheelchair Marathon.[120] Several major networks set up regular Paralympic-related programming as well, ranging from a well-advertised biopic series on Paralympians airing on the pay-per-view network WOWOW to the child-friendly animated series on disability sports running on NHK.[121] Athletes with various impairments were also featured with increased regularity as guests on Japan's numerous talk shows, and even the number of television advertisements featuring Paralympic athletes increased.[122] All of these developments marked positive trends in terms of both print and broadcast media even before the Games themselves began.

At the same time, it appears that like much else associated with the Paralympics, media coverage is now experiencing one of its periodic bubbles. The question of how coverage of disability sports can be sustained after the Games is among the many issues included in what many have dubbed the "2021 problem" for disability sports in Japan. Determining the impact of this increased coverage also remains difficult, because survey results continue to suggest that overall viewing rates remain low and that even the most successful Japanese Paralympians continue to be little known in Japan.[123] It is also critical to remember that the dramatic increases in coverage—important though they may be—are only part of the story: the nature and type of such coverage also need to be taken into account.

Of Dogs and Old Men: Regional versus National Coverage

Like any major event, the opening ceremony for the first FESPIC Games in Ōita was planned to the smallest detail. Yet even the best-laid plans can go awry, as evidenced in this case by a stray, barking dog that unexpectedly joined the opening procession. For perhaps obvious reasons, the dog did not make an appearance in official accounts, nor was it featured in the relatively limited reporting on these Games in national newspapers. The only reason anyone knows about this dog's "participation" in the first FESPIC Games at all is because of local media coverage. Alongside its far more extensive coverage of the Games and their athletes, the *Ōita gōdō* newspaper included a short account and photo of the dog strutting beside the parading participants.[124]

The story of this dog is obviously not central to understanding the broader history of the Paralympics in Japan, but it does draw attention to the fact that local media outlets offer a unique perspective on disability sports events and their participants. In contrast to other areas around the world, the local mediascape in Japan remains remarkably diverse. A number of cities or prefectures support one or more local newspapers or broadcast networks, and the national broadcast or print conglomerates often rely on local affiliates or publish regional pages to speak to the interests and needs of local consumers. Perhaps because such coverage is inherently limited in its reach and more challenging to access, it is largely overlooked in the recent Japanese scholarship on disability sports and media. This lack of scholarship belies the fact that local coverage of disability sports has long been prolific in many regions. Local reporting needs and practices have also resulted in surprisingly detailed and nuanced stories about Paralympic athletes and disability sports more generally. Therefore, giving attention to coverage at the local level promises to enrich our understandings of how disability sports are perceived on the ground. By looking at specific examples from the FESPIC Games and the Ōita Wheelchair Marathon we can also see important differences from—and potential problems in—the national media.

Figure 4.3 details the yearly breakdown of the 266 total articles related to the FESPIC Games that appeared from 1972 through 2017 in all editions currently included in the databases for Japan's three major dailies: the *Asahi*, *Mainichi*, and *Yomiuri* newspapers.[125] This chart is noticeably different from Figures 4.1 and 4.2 that portrayed coverage of disability sports more generally. Here, too the bubbles related to events are noticeable, with the "peaks" all reflecting coverage of specific FESPIC Games (1975, 1977, 1982, 1986, 1989, 1994, 1999, 2002, 2006). Because the FESPIC Games were last held in 2006,

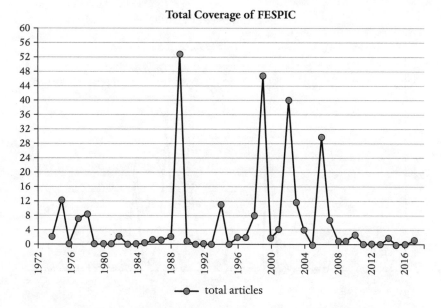

FIGURE 4.3.   Total yearly newspaper articles related to the FESPIC Games from 1972 to 2017 in all editions of the *Asahi*, *Mainichi*, and *Yomiuri* newspapers.

coverage understandably tapered off after then, with later articles appearing in connection to FESPIC's role as predecessor of the Asian Para Games. The Kobe FESPIC Games in 1989 stood out as a defining moment for media coverage, suggesting once again the impact that hosting such events can have on media attention. The rapid jump from 1994–99 paralleled results elsewhere, pointing to a "Nagano effect" in coverage of FESPIC as well. That said, it is also clear that overall reporting on FESPIC saw a general decline from 1989 onward, rather than the upward trend apparent in the earlier figures based on Fujita's analyses. This decline seems all the more striking given that this same time period witnessed FESPIC's growing integration with the IPC and increasing emphasis on elite competition, as discussed in chapter 2. At the very least, these details raise questions about common assumptions that link improved media attention to the focus on elite performance.

Incorporating information about local newspaper coverage of FESPIC sheds additional light on this downward trend. Figure 4.4 overlays the totals in Figure 4.3 with yearly numbers of local or regional reports, articles that accounted for 162 of the 266 articles on FESPIC between 1972 and 2017. Several elements distinguish local from national coverage. First, by its very nature, local coverage reaches a more limited audience, but the size of that audience can vary dramatically. An article from a regional paper published

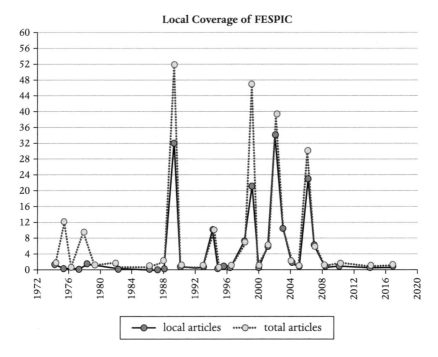

FIGURE 4.4. Total yearly number of articles related to FESPIC and a separate count of local articles published in various editions of the *Asahi*, *Mainichi*, and *Yomiuri* newspapers from 1972 to 2017.

for the Kansai district (which includes the cities of Osaka, Kyoto, and Kobe—Japan's second-largest urban area) is addressing a significantly larger population than an article published on the Ehime prefectural page of the daily *Mainichi*. What all this coverage shares in common—and the reason I group it together—is its limited reach: traditionally only someone in the specific region or locale would be able to access these "local" articles, which makes them different from those published in the national editions. Second, the local articles represented on the chart all appeared in an edition of one of the three major dailies, but the database archives for these newspapers remain incomplete for areas beyond the major cities, particularly in years before 1995. As these searchable databases incorporate more local news outlets, our picture of early coverage of events such as FESPIC is likely to change. Finally, Figure 4.4 does not reflect articles about FESPIC that were published in truly local newspapers, such as the *Ōita gōdō shimbun* or the *Kōbe shimbun*, both of which played sponsoring roles in the Games hosted in their respective communities. The lack of searchable indexes or databases for these local newspapers prevented accurate quantification of their articles. However, surveys of microfilm copies revealed that each of these papers offered reporting before the FESPIC Games, with extensive daily coverage during the event itself. Incorporating reports from these sorts of media outlets into the chart would drive the number of local articles and the overall totals even higher. In Kobe's case, the paper's coverage in 1989 would likely push the total number of articles above 100.[126]

Even without including articles published in Ōita's or Kobe's newspapers, Figure 4.4 shows that, from 1989 onward, local accounts from various regions made up a disproportionate share of articles on FESPIC in the three major dailies. Indeed, without local reports, coverage of the last two FESPIC Games—which were among the largest and most competitive to that point—would have dropped below that provided for the first Games in 1975. The precipitous drop in national-level coverage helps explain the downward trend in overall attention to FESPIC and serves as a striking example of the bursting national media bubble in the years that also occurred after Nagano's Paralympics. At the same time, the consistent coverage at the local level points to ongoing, though perhaps scattered, interest in disability sports, a trend that merits closer attention than it has received to date.

In contrast to one-time events such as the Paralympics and FESPIC, Ōita's International Wheelchair Marathon has been held every year at the same venue for decades, which makes it a unique case for examining trends in media coverage at both the national and local levels. Figure 4.5 depicts the yearly results for the 561 total articles related to Ōita's marathon from all available editions of the *Asahi*, *Mainichi*, and *Yomiuri* newspapers published between 1981 and 2016.[127]

Before turning to an analysis of local coverage of the wheelchair marathons, several points of comparison with other studies merit notice. Although there is a steady increase in coverage over time, with a marked jump beginning around 1998, most of the peaks and valleys apparent elsewhere do not line up with the marathon, a reflection of its being an annual event. For instance, the spike in relation to the 2008 Paralympics reported in Fujita's studies appears here as part of a decline, and the increase in 2006 for coverage on the marathon stems from the fact that it was the first time a Japanese male finished first in the race. Most notably, unlike the dramatic upward trend in connection with Tokyo's 2020 bid, we see a move in the opposite direction for marathon coverage. In other words, the increases in media attention occurring as a result of Tokyo's 2020 Games have not necessarily been universal.

Figure 4.6 juxtaposes the total coverage with details on the articles published in the local Ōita editions of the three major newspapers. Here again, these are articles that only someone reading the paper in Ōita would have

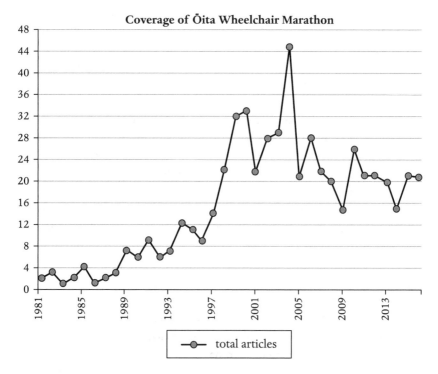

Coverage of Ōita Wheelchair Marathon

FIGURE 4.5. Total yearly newspaper articles related to the Ōita International Wheelchair Marathon from 1981 to 2016 in all editions of the *Asahi*, *Mainichi*, and *Yomiuri* newspapers.

access to. And like the case of FESPIC, the database archive remains spotty for local coverage before 1995, which may skew the results low in early years. Neither the number of total articles nor those for local coverage account for articles published in the local *Ōita gōdō shimbun* newspaper, which has been an official sponsor of the race since the beginning. Reviews of microfilmed copies revealed that *Ōita gōdō* provided fifteen to twenty stories on the marathon in an average year. Content on the marathon has been featured on the front page of the paper since the beginning, and full-page ads and notes from other sponsors for the race have been common throughout. In several instances coverage was even more extensive. The *Ōita gōdō* newspaper marked the thirtieth anniversary of the race in 2010 by adding a thirty-part series of feature stories to its normal coverage. Including such coverage from this local newspaper would dramatically change the way this chart looks and highlight even more the prominence of local reporting.[128]

But even without incorporating details from *Ōita gōdō*, it is apparent that in most years after 1996, articles from the Ōita editions of these major news-

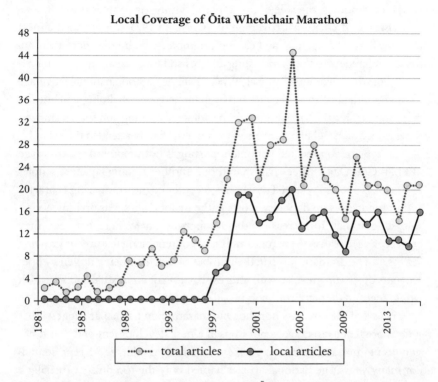

FIGURE 4.6. Yearly total number of articles related to the Ōita International Wheelchair Marathon and a separate count of local articles published in various editions of the *Asahi*, *Mainichi*, and *Yomiuri* newspapers from 1981 to 2016.

papers account for the majority of articles on the race. For a number of re-cent years, coverage of the marathon in editions outside Ōita dropped significantly, approaching levels similar to the race's early years, despite re-markably high levels of competition at the race. This slide in coverage chal-lenges narratives on rising media interest in disability sports, but ironically, it may stem, at least in part, from positive developments in wheelchair mara-thon racing. Ōita is not the only show in Japan anymore: these races are far more common today than when the event launched in the 1980s. Though it is harder to document, I would suggest that location and perceptions of pres-tige may be beginning to play a role as well, especially since the Tokyo Mara-thon now includes an elite wheelchair racing division of its own.

Numbers aside, there are several other noteworthy differences between the national editions and the local coverage of FESPIC and the Ōita marathon. Until recently, nonlocal stories—by which I mean those in the national editions of the newspaper—tended to focus on more spectacular elements, such as torch relays, ceremonies, the role of the imperial family, or competition winners. For instance, the national coverage of FESPIC in 1975 concentrated almost exclusively on the opening and closing ceremonies, with little more than numerical references to the participating athletes and minimal attention to the results. For the Ōita International Wheelchair Marathon, national coverage throughout the history of the race has been limited overwhelmingly to brief articles announcing the top finishers, with additional coverage on special anniversaries or occasions when members of the imperial family attended the event.[129]

This type of abbreviated national reporting is not unique to the coverage of FESPIC or Ōita's wheelchair marathon. Another leading Japanese scholar of disability sports, Watari Tadashi has recently begun comparing character counts for articles on disability sports in the major dailies. His preliminary results suggest that the increase in the numbers of articles in recent years may be deceptive, because the actual amount of content being featured is growing far less.[130] The dramatic jump in the number of articles is being driven by brief accounts of sporting results, with little explanation or contextualization, which would seem to detract from their broader impact.

Analysis of the coverage for the Ōita marathon in particular suggests that such abbreviated coverage is not in itself a new development and that it has significant implications in how such events and their athletes are represented. For many years, the national articles named only the top finisher (usually a foreign male) and the top Japanese finisher (who was also a male). They gave minimal attention to the women who have participated in the race since it began in 1981. Eventually, the top female athletes were given attention in national coverage as well, especially in years where Japanese women dominated the race. Yet even in more recent years, the national coverage only reported results for the group of athletes competing under classifications with the lowest level of physical impairments. What this means is that anyone reading the brief national accounts would not necessarily realize that Ōita's marathon is one of the few competitive races worldwide that remains open to marathoners with higher levels of impairments.

In contrast, local articles on the race can be two to three times as long as those in the national editions and tend to offer far more detailed breakdowns of results. They give attention to the top finishers in *all categories*, as well as lists of non-elite local athletes who competed in the race. Although I would not go so far as to suggest that the national press outlets are deliberately hiding the presence of these other racers, the coverage they are providing serves to reinforce ableist perceptions that the truly elite athletes worthy of attention are those who are more functionally able. By simply ignoring other classes of athletes—even when they win—such coverage completely fails to educate potential readers on this often challenging feature of disability sports. After all, one cannot begin to understand differences in classification if it is not even apparent that they exist.

In addition to providing more nuanced reporting on results, local coverage has proven far more effective at giving voice to athletes. For the wheelchair marathon, these differences stem in part from more detailed coverage of the event, with the frequent use of quotations from athletes about their expectations or observations of their performance. Yet this deeper coverage is itself rooted in the needs of local newspapers or the "local desks" associated with larger media conglomerates, and in that sense the situation is hardly unique to Ōita. In his reporting for *Mainichi*, for instance, Yamaguchi Ichirō noted that many of his early articles ran on various local pages, because he realized that the local desks were always looking for content.[131] My examinations of stories on FESPIC and the Ōita marathon suggest that many other reporters found themselves in similar situations, as a significant portion of the local articles depicted in figures in this chapter were feature stories about "hometown" athletes competing in events.

These sorts of feature stories in local coverage often focus on victorious athletes, but they do so with far more nuance than an article noting a list of medal winners. They often include information on how these athletes came to disability sports, as well as details on their training, past achievements, and future goals. In other instances, local feature stories provide accounts of nonelites who would rarely merit national press attention. Here we might recall the story of Miura Jirō, the participant in Nagano's Paralympic torch relay who was featured in the local *Shinano mainichi* newspaper. Perhaps because of its annual need for multiple stories, *Ōita gōdō*'s reporting on the marathon has been particularly rich, with stories on both elite competitors and those like 90-year-old Kudō Kanejirō, who as of 2016 had participated in all but one of Ōita's thirty-six races without winning any sort of prize.[132] This sort of local coverage has offered diverse representations of athletes with disabilities, demonstrating that people are pursing sports for an equally diverse set of reasons. To put it another way, this local coverage makes it clear that not everyone participating is in it, to win it.

In an essay published in December 2016, media researcher Yamada Kiyoshi suggested that one of the ways to improve overall participation in disability sports in Japan is to use television coverage to craft media sports hero narratives for athletes with disabilities. In his view doing so would create a new set of stars, who would presumably inspire others to develop an interest in disability sports.[133] A variety of anecdotal evidence suggests that exposure to Ōita's marathon has been instrumental in bringing more people into the sport, but as noted in chapter 3, Ōita has proven successful in part by emphasizing both the elite side and the accessible side of its event.

Although I am certainly not against giving elite athletes with disabilities their due—and there has been no shortage of impressive athletes in Japan to draw from—studies about the negative impacts on perceptions of disability associated with the London Paralympic Games should give us pause about the emphasis on elite-level athletes that seems to drive most recent media coverage. Not all of those with disabilities can or want to pursue sports, and among those who do, only a select few will ever perform at a Paralympic level. But if the overwhelming representation of disability in the media is that of the elite Paralympic hero, this image may have little resonance with the vast majority of those living with some sort of impairment, even as a means of inspiration. Some of the evidence from the London Games also suggests that this type of coverage might foster false societal expectations that those with disabilities must necessarily be aiming for Paralympic glory.[134] By regularly sharing stories that do not focus solely on the elite or those aiming to be elite, local coverage in places like Ōita plays a critical role in representations of disability sports by offering alternative views on the variety of roles that disability sports play in people's lives.

The diversity of coverage at the local level is also a reminder that analysis of media has to take into account the diversity of Japan itself. Even if their geographic impact might be limited, there are a number of areas like Ōita where these types of alternative narratives have long been part of the mediascape. As dominant as Tokyo's voice tends to be in Japan's media, it is not—and should not be—the only one speaking about disability sports. Further research is necessary to give these local materials and the athletes they portray the attention they deserve and to document the ways in which local media are continuing to shape understandings of the Paralympic Movement in Japan.[135]

From Rehabilitation to "Inspiration Porn"?

Local media coverage has played a critical role in Japan, but it is not without its flaws. For both national and local coverage, a third trend is the surprising persistence of the rehabilitation-related focus from the earlier years. Even as the Paralympics have become increasingly elite at all levels and in all regions, many media outlets continue to rely on patterns that link sports to some sort of recovery. Here again, Nagano reflected a moment of transition, but one where competing approaches remained apparent. The explicit focus on rehabilitation in the media faded, but in its place there was an increased emphasis on inspirational discourses that maintained a focus on overcoming disability. Echoing patterns seen elsewhere, Japanese coverage has maintained this emphasis on the inspirational role of disability sports and their athletes. Recent developments, however, suggest that the nature of coverage for 2020 might have begun to shift in several respects. Qualitative analyses of trends in the media's representational practices since 1964 offer insights on these changes and what might have driven them in Japan.

As media coverage of the Paralympics and disability sports took shape in Japan in the 1960s, media narratives tended to echo those being used by organizers. This development was not surprising, given organizers' careful efforts to promote media attention that aligned with their goals. For instance, Sakita's study of NHK coverage for the 1964 Games highlights the prominence of rehabilitation themes. His research reveals that organizers also significantly outnumbered athletes in terms of representation in much of NHK's programming.[136]

For print coverage, the tendency to view disability sports as a form of rehabilitation in the earliest years was reflected in the placement of most newspaper coverage of disability sports events on the society pages, rather than the sports pages. Fujita Motoaki's work demonstrates that this pattern remained dominant well into 1990s.[137] Yamaguchi, the reporter for the *Mainichi* newspaper whom I spoke with, pointed out that for many years those in charge of the sports pages were adamant in their view that disability sports were not sports, suggesting how entrenched this pattern became after the introduction of disability sports in the 1960s.[138]

Print coverage of the 1964 Games also tended to rely heavily on representations of Japanese athletes as patients who were using the Paralympics for their own recovery. As just one example, the magazine, *Weekly Yomiuri* (*Shūkan yomiuri*) ran an article soon after the Games ended under the headline "A Battle between Patients and Members of Society: What the Paralympics Taught the Japanese." The five-page article provided an overview of the 1964 Games that included details on the ceremonies, three photographs, comments from organizers, and brief accounts of several competitions. Echoing the official approaches discussed in chapter 1, the overall theme of this article was the shortcomings of Japan's approaches to rehabilitation, as exemplified by comparisons between foreign and Japanese participants.[139]

Similar references to superior foreign athletes were not uncommon in press coverage of the 1964 Games, and Watari Tadashi observed that many of the newspaper photographs featuring athletes were of foreigners, a pattern that also hewed close to official representations.[140] Evoking the sociologist Erving Goffman, Watari characterized media coverage of the Tokyo Paralympics as a form of "ritual inattention." Reporting on the Tokyo Games rendered those with disabilities in Japan more visible in nondisabled society than before, but did so in ways that would not disrupt social expectations, especially because the time frame for such coverage was limited to the liminal period surrounding the Games.[141]

Turning to coverage of Nagano in 1998, it was widely acknowledged both at the time and later that media coverage again followed the lead of organizers, this time by treating the Paralympics as an elite sporting event. Kodama Kazuhiko, an early scholar of disability sports coverage, suggested that the high-level performances, especially Japan's "medal rush," helped sell media producers on the "news value" of the Paralympics and the need to cover Japanese athletes. In his 1998 survey of editorials from various regional and national newspapers, Kodama demonstrated that print media outlets were quite explicit about the need to focus on the competitive aspect of the event, often citing parallels between the Olympics and Paralympics.[142]

As noticeable as this sportification of media coverage for Nagano's Games was, it was not entirely different from earlier reporting. In his 1998 critique of the Games, Saitō Yoshihiko observed that, in contrast to the Nagano Olympics, media coverage for Paralympic events tended to evoke stories of hardship and difficulty and relied heavily on adjectives like "inspiring" in describing the actions of athletes. For Saitō, despite increased recognition of Paralympic athletes, such coverage, which focused on athletes overcoming disability, remained largely "disability focused."[143] Similarly, Fujita's analysis indicated that most articles on the Nagano Paralympics were still appearing on the society pages, though the number on the sports pages had increased dramatically throughout the decade.[144] Along those same lines NHK producer Kondō Fumito explicitly noted that his broadcast team for Nagano included those specializing in both sports and social welfare stories.[145] In terms of media coverage then, disability sports in Nagano were being treated not only as "sports" but also as something else, a situation that paralleled the competing representations at the official level.

In the years since Nagano, the nature of media coverage has continued to evolve. Beginning with the 2000 Summer Paralympics, for instance, the number of Paralympic-related articles on the sports pages finally exceeded those published elsewhere in the newspapers, with the years since seeing a general upward continuation of this trend.[146] Nevertheless, many of these articles on the sports pages provided little more than basic details on wins and losses, and it is still not unusual to find more detailed coverage of disability sports and their athletes on the society or local pages.[147] During a 2011 interview, wheelchair basketball star Kyōya Kazuyuki recognized that media attention to disability sports had increased over the course of his career, but lamented the fact that most newspapers still did not really seem to view them as sports, because stories for most events and athletes still appeared outside the sports pages.[148] Up through the 2012 London Paralympics, broadcast media, too, seemed slow to change, with the overwhelming majority of coverage appearing on NHK's education network. Researchers interpreted this pattern as a sign of an ongoing reliance on rehabilitation-oriented views of disability sports.[149] In another example, it was only in 2015 that those evaluating the annual televised broadcast of Ōita's marathon footage in the Kyushu region suggested that future years downplay the rehabilitative aspect.[150]

All of these findings point to both significant change and the remarkable persistence of patterns of media representation that were established decades ago in Japan. Of particular note is the continued reliance on narratives connecting sports and recovery. Japanese coverage is hardly alone in this respect, given that one of the most frequent criticisms of present-day media coverage of disabled athletes is the reliance on "medicalized stereotypes of disabled people as 'super-crips' who courageously overcome their disability and the issues that come with it to achieve and to be 'normal.'"[151] To be sure, such coverage is often influenced by the stories that athletes tell about themselves, a topic explored further in chapter 5.

Yet the ongoing prominence of "overcoming" narratives in media coverage raises important questions about the role of inspirational discourses that have often been tied to disability sports in Japan and beyond. We might ponder whether the inspirational qualities of these events are really all that different from those associated with nondisabled sports. Who exactly is supposed to be inspired by disability sports and how? Do these inspirational discourses have a real, sustained impact, or do they simply make people feel good without really having to do anything to improve the lived experiences of those with disabilities?

Such questions were at the heart of Saitō's 1998 critique of the Nagano Paralympics, and given that the Paralympic Movement has taken to citing inspiration as part of its explicit goals, they seem even more worth asking today. A number of scholars examining media coverage outside Japan suggest that many of the representational practices employed in the media have resulted in a form of "inspiration porn," or the tendency for nondisabled society to treat people with disabilities as objects for inspiration.[152] Here, too, Japan has historically seemed to exemplify rather than buck the broader trend, as evidenced by heavy reliance on the language of overcoming, inspiration, and courageousness to characterize the performances of athletes with disabilities.

There is evidence, however, that Japan's coverage is heading in a different direction, especially in the years since Japan's successful bid to host the 2020 Games. As media interest has increased and greater attention has been given to questions of disability-related language in Japanese society in general, more reporters have become aware of the potential for their work to rely on stereotypes or potentially problematic inspirational discourses. For example, research by Fujita and others showed that earlier coverage in Japan tended to fit international media patterns, such as the framing of images to hide disabilities or the focus on emotion instead of action.[153] In contrast, examinations of newspapers in connection with the 2016 Rio de Janeiro Paralympics pointed to more nuanced analyses of the Games and their athletes.[154] Television broadcasts associated with the Rio Games also reflected a shift, with decreasing coverage on NHK's educational network and increasing coverage nearly everywhere else—an indication, perhaps, of a new (or arguably renewed) emphasis on the Paralympics as an athletic event rather than a form of social welfare.[155]

It is also apparent that Japanese scholars, journalists, and athletes are actively tackling the thorny issues of media representations and their broader impacts, as exemplified by a workshop held in July 2018 that explored the relationship between the Paralympics and ableism.[156] In my 2017 interview with Yamaguchi Ichirō, who currently serves as a senior member of the Olympics/Paralympics Promotion Office for the *Mainichi* newspaper, he readily acknowledged the tendency of earlier Japanese coverage to rely on a sort of inspiration porn (*kandō poruno*), noting that phrases related to overcoming and inspiration were almost epithets for disability sports in Japan. He was optimistic that more extensive and nuanced reporting—combined with more familiarity with disability sports on the part of reporters, editors, and potential readers—would help media coverage avoid these issues in the future.[157] Concerns about inspiration porn were also raised at several other workshops and presentations I attended while conducting research in Japan during 2017, suggesting fairly widespread familiarity with the problem, if not a straightforward solution. Whether these promising developments will continue remains to be seen, but Tokyo's 2020 Paralympics, like those more than fifty years earlier, are certain to have a profound impact on how disability sports will be reported for the foreseeable future. In that sense, it behooves us to give careful attention to ongoing representational practices in the media.

For Better or Worse? The Rise of New Media

One final media trend merits attention because it, too, has links with Nagano and has already proven pivotal for Tokyo 2020: the emergence of "new media." At present, scholarship on the role of new media in disability sports is still relatively limited, with little focus on its historical background.[158] Yet, with a constantly growing body of source materials, new media represent a potentially rich, if not overwhelming, field for ongoing research. This may be especially true in the case of disability sports, because several athletes and organizations, including the IPC, have embraced blogs, websites, live streaming, and an ever-growing list of social media platforms to connect with audiences. The goal here is to provide historical context and consider some of the implications of the growing reliance on new media outlets in Japan.

The turn to new media in the Japanese context has been both a reflection of broader technological and social developments and a response to frustrations with mainstream media that have historically offered limited coverage of even major international events. Although this aspect of the Games has been almost entirely overlooked, Nagano's Paralympics were at the forefront of some new media developments. As part of its general promotional efforts, NAPOC opted to take advantage of new technology, working closely with IBM's Japan affiliate to launch a website a year in advance of the Games. The site was designed from the beginning with accessibility in mind. Data were presented in ways that would be compatible with screen-reading software, and the layout employed large-size icons with colors and backgrounds that would be easy to see. Much of the content was available in both Japanese and English, and it included information on the events and venues, as well as links to purchase Paralympic merchandise and tickets. A messaging system allowed people to share comments with participants. As the Games approached, organizers coordinated with participating National Paralympic Committees to gather and post descriptions of athletes. During the Paralympics themselves, results were posted within an hour of each competition. Such information on events and athletes proved especially useful for mainstream media reporters, as well as the many schoolteachers and children participating in the One School, One Country educational programs in the Nagano region.[159]

By November 1997, the website was already registering about 10,000 hits a day, and results naturally spiked during the Games themselves, with more than seven million hits over ten days, bringing the total number of hits for the website to more than thirteen million. Although these numbers paled in comparison with the record-setting 600 million hits on the Nagano Olympic site, they were unprecedented for a Paralympic Games, opening up a new forum for people to engage with the event. The messaging system alone received more than five thousand messages, most of which were words of encouragement or praise directed to athletes.[160]

Nagano's website also stands out in the history of new media for the first-time use of live streaming for the Paralympics. In response to the general lack of live TV coverage for most events, organizers took advantage of improving technologies and the support of IBM and numerous volunteers to stream nearly eighty-two hours of live coverage that captured an estimated 80 percent of the Games' competitions and ceremonies. The live-streaming teams included recording crews, announcers, and support staff, all of whom were provided with official media credentials. The resulting access improved their coverage, which was accessed more than 21,000 times, a striking figure given the still relatively low levels of international Internet availability in 1998. As commentators at the time noted, Internet broadcasting still had a long way to go before it would rival traditional media, but Nagano's Paralympics were a successful test case.[161] The embrace of this pioneering approach in Nagano seems all the more remarkable considering that the IPC did not launch its own live-streaming network until several years later, in connection with the 2006 Winter Games in Turin.[162]

In more ways than one, Nagano was just the beginning when it came to innovative uses of technology to generate improved access to and visibility for disability sports in Japan. A case in point would be the nonprofit organization STAND, founded by Itō Kazuko in 2005, well before Tokyo won its bid to host the 2020 Games.[163] Inspired by her own lack of exposure to disability sports before a chance encounter with wheelchair track and field, Itō began her work in 2003 by launching efforts to provide Internet broadcasts of several high-level disability sports events that were almost completely ignored in the mainstream media. After its founding, STAND served as a de facto marketing service for a variety of sports and athletes. It organized promotional and fundraising events, sought out partnerships with companies like Japan's IT giant NEC to explore new approaches for broadcasting competitions, and established a clearinghouse website that both produced and shared original footage of athletes and events beyond the Paralympics.[164] In 2010, STAND joined forces with well-known sports journalist Ninomiya Seijun to establish the *Challengers TV* website. Although it is now one of several similar sites available, the founding goals of *Challengers TV* were to provide a venue for highlighting disability sports events and athletes and to promote disability sports in Japan as sports rather than a form of rehabilitation.[165] The website regularly features news stories, interviews, photos, and videos and hosts a large collection of links to athletes' private blogs.

As Tokyo prepared to host the Paralympics for a second time, there was no shortage of media content. Many affiliated organizations boasted attractive and regularly updated websites complete with their own collections of video clips, athlete interviews, and other resources. Most also shared content regularly on multiple social media platforms, including Facebook, Twitter, Instagram, and YouTube. One of the most prolific sharers of content was the Paralympic Support Center, which clearly benefited from its affiliation with the Nippon Foundation, but even smaller-scale organizations like the disability sports association for Nagano City relied on a variety of new media forums to share information.[166]

Japanese athletes, too, embraced new media, but from a variety of approaches. For instance, professional wheelchair tennis star Kunieda Shingo maintains a personal website, as well as an official Facebook page that had more than 17,000 followers, but as of this writing he has only a minimal presence on Twitter and Instagram.[167] In contrast, track-and-field Paralympic medalist Ashida Hajimu has a webpage with a blog, a Facebook page with 1,600-plus "Friends," a Twitter feed with more than 1,200 followers, and a much smaller Instagram following.[168] These two athletes were hardly unique in making use of multiple new media outlets as they sought to bring greater attention to themselves and their sports, which raises an important question: What does the presence of all this content on new media mean for disability sports in Japan?

On the one hand, it is not hard to see these developments as positive. New media have freed athletes and supporters from relying on previously uncooperative mass media networks. These various platforms provide widespread access to a range of information on athletes and sports that would have been unimaginable only a few decades earlier. It is now far easier for fans and potential fans to engage with these sports and athletes directly. New media also give athletes and organizations a degree of agency over what they say and how they say it. In addition, proponents of new media argue that the increased availability of new content will lead to increased awareness and interest, which will in turn eventually promote improved coverage from traditional media. At the very least would-be reporters now seem to have easy access to a wide variety of information, making it harder to claim ignorance as a reason for a lack of quality coverage.

On the other hand, new media are not without problems and challenges, not least of which are concerns about privacy that continue to plague many social media platforms. Improved technology and software—particularly in the form of smartphones, tablets, and new applications—have made these new media outlets accessible to an ever-growing number of people, including those from less developed regions and those with various impairments, but this process remains far from complete. Therefore, heavy reliance on new media may exacerbate already existing gaps in access to information on disability sports.

Moreover, the rapid proliferation of media platforms can present its own problems. Picking an outmoded app could easily limit the size of an audience, no matter how interesting the content might be. This means that athletes and organizations are faced with the challenge of maintaining an ongoing presence in multiple forums simultaneously. Opting for this approach, however, places a not insignificant burden on the athletes themselves. It shifts responsibility for giving attention to disability sports away from the mainstream media and society in general and back to the individual athlete.

Another concern is that the increasing reliance on new media could take the pressure off mainstream media networks to step up and provide coverage, and it might even risk further marginalization. The link between social media and the potential for social fragmentation is no secret. Without the larger media presence to generate broader initial awareness, it is not hard to imagine that most consumers for new-media-based disability sports content will be those who are already familiar with the sports and athletes or those who have actively sought out the content.[169] How many people are going to look for something if they do not even know it exists?

Perhaps then, the best that can be hoped looking forward is a continued concomitant growth of both new and traditional media coverage, with each complementing the other. Whatever role new media ultimately take, its growing prominence is one more example of how disability sports coverage in Japan today has experienced significant change since Tokyo's first Paralympics. Here again, Nagano proved to be a turning point, breaking new ground in Japan's mediascape and leaving Tokyo better placed to reap results in 2020.

CHAPTER 5

Athletes First

Preparing for the 2020 Tokyo Summer Paralympic Games

> I am Mami Sato. And I am here because I was saved by sport. It taught me the values that matter in life. The values that Tokyo 2020 is determined to promote worldwide.
>
> Satō Mami, 2014

On September 7, 2013, Tokyo's delegation delivered its final forty-five-minute pitch for the 2020 Olympic and Paralympic Games during the 125th International Olympic Committee Session in Buenos Aires, Argentina. Leading off for Japan was Satō Mami, a 31-year-old Paralympian who had only learned of her starring role ten days earlier. Opening with her dramatic declaration that she "was saved by sport," Satō's speech focused on how sports helped her overcome the loss of her leg to cancer at the age of 19 and how sports later served as a source of inspiration for her and countless others when her hometown was struck by the devastating tsunami on March 11, 2011. Satō's performance garnered high praise at home and abroad, and her emotionally charged speech was frequently credited with setting the tone that helped Tokyo win its bid.[1]

At the time, Satō's opening role took many—including Satō herself—by surprise. Her prominence in the bid presentation certainly differed from the experiences of earlier athletes. As detailed in previous chapters, Japanese athletes in the 1964 Tokyo Games had minimal roles in the organizational processes, and even in Nagano, the controversies over the use of shared national uniforms suggested a less-than-wholehearted embrace of Paralympians. In many respects then, Satō's experience in 2013 pointed to important changes in how Japan was approaching the 2020 Paralympics. This chapter focuses on Japan's preparations for the 2020 Games, shedding light on what changed and did not change after 1998 and why. In doing so, it also explores key questions about the role Tokyo's second Paralympics were envisioned to play in 2020 and beyond.

Some of the biggest developments for Tokyo 2020 stemmed from institutional changes at the international and national levels. Brief examinations of Japan's three most recent Olympic bids, for instance, offer striking evidence of ongoing, significant changes in the bidding process for the Paralympics. In addition, recent years in Japan witnessed a combination of increased funding for disability sports, new forms of organizational support, efforts to integrate nondisabled and disability sports under a single government ministry, and legal changes related to both sports and disability. These types of changes reshaped the environment for disability sports in Japan, even before the Paralympic opening ceremony in August 2020.

Like Nagano's Games, the Paralympics in Tokyo continued to be explicitly linked to broader efforts to improve accessibility in Japanese society. Given the ongoing and in some ways intensifying international, national, and demographic pressures that Japan has faced since 1998, it is not entirely surprising to see such continuities. Yet the centrality of accessibility-related issues in bid materials, organizational plans, and promotional efforts for the 2020 Paralympics differed markedly from earlier Games, raising several questions explored later in the chapter. The 2020 Games do appear to have had significant impacts on accessibility, but it remains necessary to assess those impacts in ways that do not obscure sociohistorical contexts or ignore inherent challenges.

Drawing from a variety of marketing materials and firsthand observations, this chapter also details several multifaceted efforts to promote the Paralympics in Tokyo. Frequent activities ranging from school-based educational programs and academic conferences to participatory exhibitions and museum displays made the Paralympics difficult to ignore as Tokyo prepared to become the first city in the world to host the Summer Games for a second time. These efforts clearly built on Japan's years of engagement with the Paralympic Movement and took full advantage of the increasing media attention discussed in chapter 4. Understandably, many of these promotional activities were tied to the Tokyo government as the official host city, but corporate and other nongovernmental supporters assumed a conspicuous role as well. The Nippon Foundation, a private nonprofit philanthropic organization, was especially instrumental in promoting the 2020 Paralympics. Explorations of such promotional efforts offer insights on both continuities and significant changes from earlier Games.

Reflecting Tokyo's "Athletes First" catchphrase, promotion of the 2020 Games relied heavily on Paralympians from its inception, as exemplified by

Satō's bid speech. To understand this development within a broader context, the chapter concludes with biographical sketches of five athletes, each of whom competed in at least one of the international sporting events discussed in this book. These sketches show how these athletes were drawn to disability sports, how they have characterized the role of sports in their lives, and how their stories have been shared. To be sure, these accounts are not comprehensive life stories, nor can they fully represent the diverse experiences of the countless individuals with disabilities in Japan who have engaged in sports since the 1960s. Taken together, however, they provide a general sense of how the experiences of athletes have evolved in Japan. Documenting the stories of this handful of athletes also highlights the need for continued studies that move beyond simplistic, feel-good "overcoming" narratives. Although the Paralympic Movement indeed has had a significant impact on the lives of many in Japan and beyond, the sampling of lived experiences in these sketches also serves as a reminder that many questions and challenges still need to be addressed.

Integration or Cooptation? The Changing Environment for Disability Sports

If Nagano's 1998 Paralympics already bore the marks of the emerging partnership between the Olympics and Paralympics as explored in the previous chapter, it should come as no surprise that ongoing developments in this relationship continued to shape Japan's approach to the Paralympics leading up to Tokyo 2020. In the years after Nagano, the International Olympic Committee (IOC) and the International Paralympic Committee (IPC) negotiated a series of agreements clarifying their relationship and organizational approaches to the Olympic and Paralympic Games. Although the specific details of many of these agreements tend to be cloaked in secrecy, the broader contours and impacts (for better or worse) on the Paralympics have been well documented by several scholars.[2] In addition to offering financial support from the IOC for the Paralympics beginning in the early 2000s, the agreements also provided a guarantee that the Paralympics would be held soon after the Olympics at the same sites. In other words, hosting the Paralympics was no longer a voluntary, add-on event.

In addition to simply mandating the need to host both events, the initial Games Co-operation Agreement signed in June 2001 called for a common organizing committee for both Games, integration of the Paralympics into the Olympic Games budgets, and the assignment of marketing and broadcasting rights and responsibilities for upcoming Paralympic Games to the host site organizing committees in exchange for undisclosed fees to the IPC. The first Games officially bound to these terms were those slated for 2008, which were in the final stages of the bidding process as the agreement was signed. Later IOC–IPC agreements modified several details, but under the revised terms, Olympic host cities are obligated to host and jointly organize the Paralympics up through the 2032 Games. For Tokyo's 2020 Games, the 2012 agreement is of particular importance, because it solidified the practice of joint bidding, significantly increased funding for the IPC, and opened the door for the IPC to participate more actively on IOC committees, including the IOC Athletes Commission.[3]

These evolutions in the IOC–IPC relationship are clearly reflected in Japan's recent Olympic bids. The oft-overlooked 2008 bid from Osaka, for instance, is telling for a lack of attention to the Paralympics. The official 2001 report on the city's failed candidature directly referenced changes in expectations about hosting the Paralympics, noting that many of them were unfolding as Osaka was preparing its materials for submission. While asserting that organizers had been thinking about the Paralympics from the earliest stages, the report itself offered minimal support for that claim. The subcommittee focusing on the Paralympics was established only in November 1998, several months after Nagano's well-publicized Games and more than a year after the Japanese Olympic Committee (JOC) had selected Osaka as Japan's candidate.[4] Notably, Osaka's domestic rival, Yokohama, had explicitly outlined plans for the Paralympics in its 1997 proposal, including calls for joint organization from the earliest planning stages.[5] To be sure, the JOC's selection of Osaka resulted from many factors, but failure to integrate Paralympic planning into a proposal was obviously not yet a deal breaker.

Other aspects of Osaka's official report suggested that the Paralympics remained an afterthought throughout much of the bid period. The brief sections related to the Paralympics (roughly 4 total pages out of more than 300) focused less on actual plans than on the challenges raised by the need to incorporate the event into the bid process. The post-bid report also admitted that the official candidature file failed to address the status of Paralympic delegations, and it documented no references to the Paralympics or to the involvement of Paralympians when Osaka's final presentation was delivered in Moscow on July 13, 2001.[6]

In stark contrast to Osaka, Tokyo's unsuccessful bid to host the 2016 Summer Games exemplified the still emerging "one bid, one city" approach, which required potential hosts to outline plans for both sets of Games. Even the titles of committees and publications for 2016 highlighted this shift. Where the two events had previously stood alone, materials for the "2016

Olympic·Paralympic Games" were now being produced by the "Tokyo Olympic·Paralympic Bid Committee." Tokyo's candidature file had a separate section on the Paralympic Games that included not only information on Paralympic events and venues but also a detailed budget, legacy goals, and plans for guaranteeing accessible lodging and transportation.[7] The official 2010 post-bid report referenced several promotional efforts involving Paralympians and cited increased attention and support for disability sports as one of the successful outcomes of the bid experience.[8] Tokyo's bid for 2016 also broke new ground by integrating Paralympians themselves into the final pitch presentation in Copenhagen on October 2, 2009. About midway through the presentation, Paralympic shooter Taguchi Aki introduced Paralympic swimmer Kawai Junichi, who outlined the Paralympic plans by explaining, "All of us at Tokyo 2016 believe the Olympic and Paralympic Games to be a single, unified celebration of sport and culture."[9] Although Tokyo's 2016 bid failed to win over the IOC, it marked a significant shift in Japan's approaches to the Paralympics.

It has been widely acknowledged that Tokyo's approach to 2020 drew heavily from its recent unsuccessful bid, something particularly apparent in relation to the Paralympics.[10] Throughout the bid and ongoing preparations, the joint organizational efforts continued to be on prominent display. The "Tokyo Olympic·Paralympic" paired phrasing became so standard in references to these Games that it was occasionally applied retroactively (and inaccurately) to descriptions of the 1964 Games—a striking example of reinterpreting the past in light of present-day understandings. As required, the 2020 candidature file again included a section dedicated to the Paralympics. Much of its content and even wording paralleled the 2016 materials, with similar levels of detail on the events, venues, accessibility concerns, and legacy projects. Accounting for inflation, budgets were also comparable. Perhaps the most notable change was the nearly threefold increase in funding for operational costs related to sports venues and the Olympic/Paralympic village. These added costs were seemingly offset by additional government subsidies.[11] As noted earlier, the 2020 bid presentation also expanded on the earlier integration of Paralympians by having Satō initiate the program, speaking even before the prime minister, the governor of Tokyo, and other high-powered delegation members.

In the years since 2013, organizational efforts only reinforced the connections between the Olympics and Paralympics. Anyone seeking information on the Paralympics needed only to click on the organizing committee's sleek, joint website or a host of other joint pages on different social media platforms.[12] After a false start because of concerns about plagiarism, the current, coordinated logos for both Games were unveiled simultaneously in April 2016 and could be found side by side with near ubiquity in pre-Games Tokyo.[13] A national design competition and then an unprecedented vote exclusively by children from nearly 17,000 Japanese elementary schools led to the announcement of coordinated mascots in February 2018.[14] Building on promotional efforts in 2016, campaigns for 2020 included both Paralympic- specific activities, discussed later in this chapter, and multiple joint events that featured Olympians and Paralympians, including various countdown celebrations.[15] Several Japanese Paralympians were also actively involved in the 2020 Athletes Commission from its inaugural meeting in early 2015, a clear manifestation of the ongoing institutional integration of the Olympics and Paralympics at the international levels.[16]

The critical changes stemming from the IOC–IPC partnership were complemented on the ground by several domestic developments since Japan's last Paralympics in 1998. On the Japanese legal front, changes to a number of laws had a direct impact on organizational efforts for the 2020 Games. For example, Japan's Basic Act for Persons with Disabilities was amended in 2004 and then revised in 2011, and an antidiscrimination law was passed in 2013: both included provisions requiring "necessary and reasonable accommodation" to address social barriers. A number of other laws and policies related to employment and accessibility were also implemented in the decade leading up to Japan's successful 2013 bid. Although many of these measures were referenced in the candidature materials in relation to the Paralympics, their implementation had less to do with the upcoming Games than with efforts to align existing domestic approaches with international standards. In particular, Japan was seeking to ratify the United Nations Convention on the Rights of Persons with Disabilities, which the government had initially signed in 2007. After years of policy revision and creation, ratification was finally achieved in January 2014, with most new legal measures scheduled to go into full effect by 2016.[17] These reforms marked another step toward Japan's national shift from a welfare-based approach to one centered on rights. For the Paralympics, these legal changes meant that the 2020 Games were going to be bound by a different set of formal regulations than were any of the previous events held in Japan.

Legal changes also had a direct impact on disability sports in Japan. The 2011 revisions of the Sports Basic Act included several references to and provisions for disability sports. This simple change had dramatic and immediate effects. The 2012 National Sports Plan, for instance, outlined several efforts to promote and strengthen disability sports. Since the 1960s, oversight of sports in the Japanese government had been divided between two different ministries, but in 2014, efforts began to integrate nondisabled and disability sports under a single ministry, a process that culminated in the establishment of the Japan Sports Agency (Supōtsu chō) in 2015 to oversee all sports.[18] For Paralympic athletes, one consequence of these institutional realignments has been greater access to national training facilities, which are currently focused on improving the international competitiveness of all of Japan's athletes. Here again, these changes overlapped with the bid processes and the early planning phase for the upcoming Games, but it is important to recall that many had roots in the years immediately following Nagano's Paralympics.

In addition to legislative changes, institutional support for disability sports increased in several other respects. The 1999 establishment of the Japan Paralympic Committee in the aftermath of Nagano's Games was followed in 2003 by the creation of the Paralympians Association of Japan (PAJ), which gained legal corporate status in 2010. PAJ is made up of and led by athletes who have represented Japan at the Paralympics, and it seeks to connect and support Japan's Paralympians, promote interest in disability sports more generally, and foster "Sports for Everyone." The association's activities, particularly in the lead-up to Tokyo's Games, ranged from participation in promotional events to the establishment of a scholarship program for potential Paralympians. PAJ also ran regular workshops for athletes and offered training in the English language for international competitors. In the summer of 2018, PAJ members carried out a survey of the accessibility in the area around Tokyo's high-performance training facilities and then released a detailed report on accessible routes and potential barriers or hazards.[19] As a group of athletes for athletes, PAJ played a key role in increasing the prominence and visibility of Paralympians in connection with Japan's organizational efforts.

In 2015, the Japan Sports Association for the Disabled (JSAD)—now known in English as the Japan Para-Sports Association (JPSA)—celebrated its fiftieth anniversary by unveiling a new emblem based on the "motif of the wings of a firebird . . . to convey the attractions of para-sports with a sense of lively motion."[20] Even before this point, changes for JSAD had involved more than names and symbols, with important implications for the 2020 Games. In 2011, it acquired the status of a public interest incorporated foundation, and in 2014 the association began seeking corporate partners that would contribute at least 10 million yen annually. By January 2019, the campaign had resulted in official partnerships with more than thirty corporations representing a variety of major industries. These partnerships were part of a larger strategy not only to support JPSA's activities but also to assure that, by 2020, 80 percent of Japan's Paralympians would be fully supported by the private business sector.[21]

Private sector funds, particularly from the Nippon Foundation, also allowed for the establishment of the Paralympic Support Center in November 2015.

The Center provided office space, funding for staff, as well as logistical, legal, and accounting services for more than twenty disability sports organizations, many of which lacked even basic resources and staffing. In 2017, the Nippon Foundation launched its Para Athlete Scholarship Program that aimed to support fifty potential para-athletes by 2020 with scholarships for selected colleges or high schools.[22] The Paralympic Support Center and Nippon Foundation were also instrumental in the construction of the new Nippon Foundation Para Arena, a gymnasium and training facility designed for and dedicated to para sports that opened in the summer of 2018.[23] An unrelated facility that opened in Tokyo in 2017 has since become world famous for offering a prosthetic "blade library." Established by Xiborg, a Japanese company that designed prosthetic limbs for runners, the crowdfunded blade library allowed people to try out, for a small fee, different running blades on an indoor track under the guidance of professional, amputee coaches.[24] These types of facilities and forms of support—often tied to voluntary, private contributions—created new opportunities for athletes with disabilities, even before the Paralympics.

As significant and perhaps laudatory as this apparent embrace of the Paralympics and their athletes in Japan might be, it also raises important questions. For instance, what will happen to all of this private support after the Paralympics? This is a question that many in Japan are grappling with, a point addressed in the coda to this book. It is also worth noting that the need for specialized and privately funded facilities like the blade library and the Para Arena stem from an ongoing lack of access to equipment and facilities for those with impairments because of costs, inaccessibility, or in some cases unwillingness to allow these athletes to use existing sports venues. These new opportunities are exciting, but it also seems reasonable to consider the root causes behind the lack of access and to acknowledge that addressing them is going to take more than building new facilities in the Tokyo region. Although many connected to the Games have posed these questions, doing so cannot in itself change the situation.

For Paralympians, the recent trend of increased government support and greater access to Olympic facilities undoubtedly was a welcome development, but the accompanying emphasis on medal counts, as exemplified by JPSA's 2014 public declaration of medal targets for 2020, was not without concern.[25] In particular, announcements in early 2019 that the Japan Sports Agency would focus its funding on events most likely to produce medals sparked worries about drastic budget cuts from domestic sports federations on the Olympic side. Given the new shared oversight, there was every reason to believe that those Paralympic sports where Japan generally fares poorly would experience budgetary pain as well.[26] This sort of "merit-based" approach might win more medals, but it was also a blatant example of government-sponsored favoritism that might very well perpetuate existing inequalities and make it harder for less "successful" programs to succeed or even recruit athletes in the future.

On a more philosophical level, the attention to medal counts suggested that Japan's recognition of and support for the Paralympics resulted in no small part from links to nationalism. Indeed, Watari Tadashi's preliminary examinations of Japanese media coverage in recent years point to growing usage of terminology related to nationalism or national identity in representations of disability sport. On the one hand, this tendency seemed to reflect the ongoing integration of nondisabled and disability sports, so that Paralympians are increasingly likely to be seen and portrayed as representatives of Japan like their Olympic counterparts. On the other hand, as Watari's work points out, these linkages between Paralympians and nation seemed to be premised on understandings of "sport" that are limited in scope. They not only often failed to account for the diversity of disability sports but also focused attention overwhelmingly on a relatively small pool of exceptional, elite individuals.[27] Beyond 2020, it remains to be seen whether funneling support and funding to build elite sport for the sake of national prestige will have an impact on the lives of those with disabilities or on societal understandings of disability other than some abstract sense of inspiration.

And even at the inspirational level there are lingering questions. It is not a stretch, for instance, to interpret Satō's inspiring bid-opening account of overcoming through sports as a sort of national allegory: using sports to overcome adversity was at the heart of the larger message that Tokyo was trying to convey with its bid for the 2020 Olympics and Paralympics in the aftermath of the 2011 "triple disaster." But is the goal of the Paralympics today really about recovery? In his study of potential legacies of the 2020 Games, Kazuo Ogura noted that members of the bid committee and sports associations in Japan started emphasizing the Paralympics as a potential counter to criticisms about spending so much on the Games at a time when many felt that the reconstruction of areas affected by various disasters should be given priority.[28] Although the focus of such arguments (and of Satō's speech) was on the inspirational potential of both Games, the link to older rehabilitation-oriented discourses—the very ones that the Paralympics were seeking to relegate to the past with their emphasis on elite performance—remains clear.

Along the same lines, I would suggest that the repeated emphases on Paralympic-related improvements in accessibility discussed in the following section served as a sort of "moral cover" for the well-documented, exorbitant costs of the 2020 Games, even though most of those costs had little to do with accessibility projects. As pessimistic as this appraisal of co-optation might sound, such an approach would hardly be unique to Japan; many have observed that the IOC's own increasing support for the IPC came in the wake of widespread negative publicity generated by bidding scandals.[29] My point here is not to question organizers' commitments to accessibility or to the Paralympics, but to highlight the ways in which a focus on integration might overshadow other aspects of the relationship between the Olympics and Paralympics. If runaway Olympic costs were to become linked in popular consciousness with largely unrelated efforts to promote accessibility, this would hardly be a positive development. The controversies surrounding the potential cancellation of the Paralympic Games in Rio de Janeiro because of Olympic cost overruns have already generated debate about imbalances in the IOC–IPC relationship.[30] Perhaps ongoing attention to Tokyo's Games can spark further discussions about the risks of co-optation for the Paralympics in the future.

Accessibility: Realization of a Long-Awaited Paralympic Dream?

Whether it actually provided moral cover for high costs, there is no denying that improved accessibility was a central theme from the earliest stages of the organizational efforts for Tokyo's 2020 Games. Such a focus was not a new development, as demonstrated by the previous examples of Kobe's FESPIC Games and even more so the Nagano Paralympics. Creating barrier-free environments was also among the four guiding principles for the Paralympics in Yokohama's unsuccessful domestic 2008 bid. Tokyo's 2016 candidature materials, too were replete with references to accessibility. Clearly then, the connection between disability sports and the promotion of improved accessibility did not begin in Japan with plans for 2020. Tokyo's more recent approach built on these earlier efforts, reflecting both continuities and differences from earlier Games. Despite many promising developments, recent reports and observations from Tokyo also show how difficult it continues to be to realize accessibility goals even when the Paralympics are coming to town.

The focus on accessibility for Tokyo 2020 was already apparent in the official bid proposal, which included details on fostering social inclusiveness and plans for guaranteeing the accessibility of venues, transportation, housing, and communications.[31] Comparisons with earlier materials reveal that many of these same details and phrasings were used for the 2016 proposals and even echoed earlier language. That said, the 2020 bid made several additions that subtly shifted attention to a broader social agenda for these Games. For example, the section in the candidature file outlining plans for the Paralympics began with a new statement: "The overall philosophy of the Tokyo 2020 proposal is to deliver a Paralympic Games which will show how social inclusion and non-discrimination, and full consideration of the needs and interests of people with a disability, can create a better world and provide a brighter future for the entire community." A few paragraphs later the file added a new phrase highlighting Tokyo's status as "one of the most accessible cities in the world in regard to public transport and public facilities." The additional phrases emphasized how hosting the Games in Tokyo would "demonstrate to the world how, across the entire community, a city can use new technologies and architectural innovations to ensure such access" while sparking "a further improvement in these capacities, contributing to even greater social inclusiveness" for Tokyo itself.[32] By foregrounding accessibility and social inclusion, the 2020 bid not only built on previous efforts in Japan but also aligned its language with broader international trends, as exemplified by the UN Convention on the Rights of Persons with Disabilities, which Japan was preparing to ratify as the bid was unfolding.

As in the case of Nagano some twenty years earlier, Tokyo's successful bid was followed by a series of other reforms and initiatives related to improving accessibility. Among the prime differences, of course, were the scope and potential impact of Tokyo's efforts, given the city's size and its political, economic, and media prominence in Japan. The organizing committee for 2020 also benefitted from the fact that the IPC itself began giving greater attention to accessibility issues in the mid-2000s, a process that eventually led to the creation of its *Accessibility Guide* in 2009.[33] In March 2017, Tokyo's organizers unveiled their own *Tokyo 2020 Accessibility Guidelines*, which complemented those prepared by the IPC. Although not legally binding, the committee's guidelines were developed to help "all affiliated organizations, administrations, and operators understand the accessibility needs for the Games": this extension of the same standards to all participating groups was envisioned as ideally avoiding some of the confusion and shortcomings apparent in Nagano.[34] As noted earlier, implementation of such measures for 2020 benefited as well from legal changes mandating reasonable accommodations in Japan.

A variety of governmental initiatives bolstered the organizing committee's accessibility efforts. As host, the Tokyo metropolitan government worked closely with organizers to compile a guide to accessible spectator routes for all venues and to assure increased availability of barrier-free restrooms throughout the greater Tokyo area.[35] Issued in December 2016, the metropolitan government's all-encompassing 2020 action plan, "New Tokyo. New Tomorrow," called for barrier-free access to all of the Games' sites. Beyond the venues themselves, the plan set the goal of assuring no-step access to train and subway stations throughout Tokyo by 2020. Many references in the plan cited criteria from the *Tokyo 2020 Accessibility Guidelines,* which were not formally released until several months later, a fact that highlights the degree of coordination between Games organizers and city planners from early on.[36] In 2018, Tokyo announced plans for revising its barrier-free building bylaws, including new specifications for wheelchair-accessible hotel rooms, measures that sparked a degree of controversy, as noted later.

At the national level, the government of Japan established the Universal Design 2020 Action Plan in February 2017. Comparing the upcoming Paralympics with those in 1964, this national plan echoed earlier bid materials, citing the 2020 Games as an "opportunity to show the world the progressive approaches of a mature society" and a chance for "our country to take a major step towards becoming an inclusive society (*kyōsei shakai*)."[37] In addition to a number of abstract goals, the plan also called for concrete measures aimed at addressing social, physical, and communication barriers in Japan; many such measures were again explicitly linked to those outlined in the *Tokyo 2020 Accessibility Guidelines.* A number of proposed improvements fell under the bailiwick of the Ministry of Land, Infrastructure, Transport, and Tourism. Not surprisingly, this ministry began revising a range of national standards and policies in the lead-up to the Games. As just one example, new standards set for implementation in 2019 required all lodging facilities with more than fifty rooms to have at least 1 percent of rooms accessible to wheelchair users.[38]

As exemplified by the 2018 accessibility survey carried out by the Paralympians Association of Japan, barrier-free campaigns connected to Tokyo's Games also benefited from various forms of support on the ground. The Ministry of Land, Infrastructure, Transport, and Tourism consulted regularly with several private sector groups and individuals as part of its efforts.[39] Several Japanese companies also became involved in promoting accessibility in Tokyo and beyond. For instance, the Japanese government commissioned Hitachi, Ltd. and Navitime Japan Co. to develop a new accessible navigation app for the city of Tokyo. Based on the specific accommodation needs indicated by an individual (such as wheelchair use or visual impairments), the app prepares optimal accessible routes between a starting point and destination. The final, beta-tested version was slated for release in advance of the 2020 Games.[40] The drive for greater accessibility in transportation also had an impact on the automobile industry, as evidenced by Toyota's 2017 "universal design" JPN Taxis that can accommodate wheelchairs without needing to dismantle or fold them up to place in the trunk.[41] Toyota's new taxis represent a more traditional aspect of the company's broader "Mobility for All" campaign, which was launched in July 2018. The campaign's multilingual website provides details about several futuristic prototypes designed to address a wide variety of mobility needs in Japan and beyond.[42]

Crowdsourced websites and apps like *Accessible Japan,* WheeLog! and Bmaps are other examples of private efforts to tackle accessibility-related concerns that have already proven beneficial before the Games even began. Developed and maintained by longtime Japan resident Josh Grisdale, *Accessible Japan* is a website that provides up-to-date English-language reviews on the accessibility of tourist sites and a searchable database of barrier-free hotels in Tokyo and several other Japanese destinations. Because this sort of information can be difficult to find even for those with Japanese-language skills, Grisdale's site is meant to address a significant information gap for the greatly increased number of individuals with various impairments who have been coming to Tokyo in recent years.[43] Both Bmaps and WheeLog! are free smartphone apps designed to collect and share information about accessible routes and facilities with others. Initially developed in Japan in 2016 and 2017, respectively, both apps are available in English and can be used anywhere in the world, though their most detailed content remains focused on Japan.[44]

Given this combination of ongoing official, private, and even popular efforts to improve accessibility, it is understandable why the IPC cited Tokyo 2020 as an exemplary case for demonstrating how the Paralympics can have a positive social effect on host countries.[45] Within Japan too, politicians and organizers alike characterized the Paralympics as a moment ripe with promise and potential for change. For both Prime Minister Abe Shinzo and Tokyo governor Koike Yuriko the Paralympics represented "an opportunity" to transform Japanese society to make it more inclusive and accessible for all.[46] As Japan Paralympic Committee president Yamawaki Yasushi emphatically put it in 2014,

> The Tokyo 2020 Paralympics will change a social perception and remove a barrier in people's mind towards impairment. I strongly believe that the Paralympics have the power to change and create a more equitable and inclusive society. We need an inclusive society. Inclusive means equal opportunities and participation not only for people with impairments, but also for every member of society. The Tokyo 2020 Paralympics will be a kind of gateway to the future—a golden opportunity to leave a legacy, which connects to an equitable, comfortable and inclusive society.[47]

At the surface level, it seems almost pointless to question these stakeholder references about the impact of the Paralympics in achieving accessibility goals.

The Games certainly provided a unique opportunity for Japan to implement much-needed reforms, and many of the examples explored in this section demonstrated how the Paralympics and the IPC have directly sparked changes in Tokyo and beyond. Yet it is imperative to move below the surface, because the situation in Japan (and everywhere else) is at once more complex and more challenging than it might appear.

For one, whatever successes Japan ultimately achieves in accessibility or inclusiveness in connection with the 2020 Games will have been the cumulative result of years of work on the part of many people throughout Japan, not just a group of Tokyo-based bureaucrats, Games organizers, or IPC officials active for seven years. Japan's history of engagement with these issues is largely absent from references to the impacts of Tokyo's 2020 Games. This longer history raises a second point worth considering: relying on one-off sporting events to promote social change is a fraught proposition. Japan had already hosted two previous Paralympics, two FESPIC Games, and countless other international disability sports events, many of which aimed for social outcomes similar to those for Tokyo 2020. With that history in mind, we might even wonder why Japan had not already become more inclusive and accessible than it is. Although the 2020 Games have presented an opportunity to spark change, that opportunity needed to be seized, and even then, the window for action was more limited than Paralympic promoters would probably like to admit. For example, evidence emerging from the 2012 London Paralympic Games, which were widely viewed as the most successful ever, suggests that the political will for change tends to dissipate soon after the publicity from the Games fades.[48] Moreover, it is particularly important to note that changes in Japan have been driven by much more than interest in a disability sporting event. Even without delving into complex counterfactual arguments, it is not hard to imagine that Japan's approach to these Games might have been different were the nation not facing its current demographic dilemma of a rapidly aging and shrinking population. Even though Japan's approach to the Paralympics might have been exemplary, that approach is a product of particular sociohistorical contexts that are easily overlooked in surface-level evaluations.

Focusing on the Paralympics as the driving force for change can also obscure challenges to those changes. After all, if the event and policies they spark are the focus, minor shortfalls can seem insignificant, even though they often point to more substantial issues. The accessibility of venues offers a good example. As other scholars have noted, the impacts of the Paralympics are most apparent in areas directly linked to the Games—the venues, the Athletes' Village, and the public spaces around them—but it also bears acknowledging that Paralympic guidelines are nonbinding and make allowances for temporary or human-resource-based fixes "when it proves difficult to implement the permanent environmental development."[49] In Tokyo, a survey conducted by the *Mainichi* newspaper in April 2017 revealed that 80 percent of existing Olympic venues were failing to meet barrier-free targets for wheelchair seating.[50] In another example that same year, the *new* permanent venue, Musashino Forest Sport Plaza, also fell short when actual users with disabilities tested the facility in the months before it was slated to open.[51] In September 2019, less than a year before the Paralympics, the *Mainichi* ran an editorial critiquing organizers' failure and seeming unwillingness to provide braille materials or audio guides explaining the (extremely convoluted) process for acquiring tickets. Calling into question the organizing committee's commitment to the stated goals of "diversity and harmony," the editorial pointed out that relying solely on text-to-speech software might be inadequate and seemed to ignore the committee's own explicit guidelines about the need to make public documents available in multiple formats.[52] Despite widespread acknowledgements that these sorts of shortcomings should be addressed, even organizing committee members admitted that there were no guarantees that this would be the case. At the very least these failures to broaden accessibility suggested a lack of attention to official accessibility goals that did not bode well for areas beyond the direct purview of Games' organizers.

The approach to improving access to Tokyo's rail network is a case in point. Station accessibility in Tokyo's action plan is defined as a single, step-free route from station entrance to platform, an admirable goal that would certainly make Tokyo's trains and subways more accessible than those in many other cities around the world. Closer attention to the fine print and experiences on the ground, however, reveal some limitations in the plan. It explicitly excludes stations where it is "difficult" to maintain elevators for structural reasons and does not address train stations that serve less than three thousand people daily.[53] Moreover, in cases where a single, step-free route is in place, a number of factors can complicate its accessibility. Some stations, for example, do not have elevators, but rather chair lifts or specially designed escalators. Although these mechanisms allow for stair-free access, they necessitate the assistance of a station attendant, thereby limiting independence, as well as causing significant delays and perhaps unwanted public attention. In other instances, the route may include an elevator, but because there is only a single route, individuals unfamiliar with the station can be easily turned around or have to travel to a point far from where they boarded or exited the train. Signage has improved in recent years, but it has remained far from simple or intuitive. In large stations such as Shinjuku or Shibuya that are notoriously difficult to navigate for everyone, an easily missed sign can leave someone with a disability facing a barrier at seemingly every turn. The point here is not to scorn Tokyo's efforts at promoting accessible transportation, but to highlight the inherent difficulties in doing so. If even a concerted effort in an already remarkably accessible area is facing challenges to becoming barrier-free, then those challenges should not be overlooked, no matter how exciting an action plan sounds on paper.

In other instances, some accessibility measures in Tokyo seemed to have been implemented without adequate input from those they aimed to benefit. Not long after their release, Toyota's JPN Taxi's sparked complaints from wheelchairs users about the complicated and time-consuming boarding process and the resulting reluctance of drivers to pick them up. To their credit, the company responded in February 2019 by announcing plans to revamp and, in some cases, retrofit the vehicles to reduce boarding times from ten minutes to just three or four.[54] The Tokyo metropolitan government's barrier-free bylaw revisions for hotel rooms came under similar fire for "decisions made strictly on paper without carrying out actual testing."[55] Groups for those with disabilities conducted their own tests, revealing that Tokyo's proposed specifications would prevent the use of many "barrier-free" hotel rooms by anyone in larger-than-average wheelchairs or especially electric wheelchairs. As reports of these critiques first emerged, government officials cited the "intense negotiations" that had already gone into the draft bylaws; they were ultimately approved and went into effect in September 2019 without addressing the concerns raised by disability advocates.[56] Both of these cases not only point to breakdowns in usability testing but also highlight the importance of engaging with all potential stakeholders when developing barrier-free measures. Therein lies another challenge to achieving universal design goals. Different impairments require different accommodations, and negotiating such accommodations requires time, money, and a willingness to implement them—all of which seemed to be running short for Tokyo as the Games approached.

And what of Tokyo's larger goal for 2020 of making Japan more inclusive by fostering new attitudes and approaches toward disability? For reasons that had little to do with the Paralympics, in recent years the country dealt with several scandals, controversies, and crimes linked to issues of disability. The horrific murders of nineteen people at a care facility for the disabled in 2016 and the ongoing exposure of stories recounting forced sterilizations of individuals with disabilities under Japan's eugenics law that was on the books until 1996 are among the most well-known and disturbing events occurring since Japan won the right to host the Games.[57] In summer 2018, news also broke that government offices and ministries all over Japan had been padding their numbers for several years to make it look like they were fulfilling legal hiring quotas for those with disabilities when this had not been the case.[58] Initial government attempts to address several of these issues met with criticism for rushing to enact quick, inadequate fixes without addressing underlying issues. Additionally, in October 2018, a promotional poster associated with the Tokyo metropolitan government was removed after complaints that it was sending mixed and insensitive messages with its (out-of-context) quotation from a Paralympian declaring, "Disability is nothing but an excuse. If I lose in a game, it only means I'm weak."[59] At the very least, these various occurrences raised questions about the broader commitment to "barrier-free hearts and minds (*kokoro no baria furī*)" that was so often referenced in official materials. Can the increased exposure to disability-related issues generated by the Paralympics help tackle these sorts of problems, especially because awareness of the Paralympics seems to be approaching an all-time high in Japan? It is, quite honestly, difficult to say, and previous Paralympics in Japan and elsewhere do not provide much in the way of assurances either. Part of the answer will likely hinge on whether the current debates and discussions in Japanese society about these situations continue or whether they get overshadowed by the spectacle of the Games themselves.[60] For like any spectacle, Tokyo's 2020 Paralympics only require watching; commitment to something more—accessibility, inclusivity, equality, nondiscrimination—has to come from those doing the watching.

NO LIMITS, TEAM BEYOND, and *I'mPOSSIBLE*: Promoting the 2020 Games

Thanks in no small part to the increasing media coverage discussed in chapter 4 and Tokyo's prominence in Japan's mediascape, the 2020 Paralympics achieved a remarkable degree of visibility well before their planned opening in August 2020. Such attention was purposefully generated. As with earlier Games and events hosted in Japan, organizers and a wide variety of affiliated promoters pursued an aggressive marketing campaign from the outset. Bid materials for the Paralympics outlined a broad-based outreach strategy to tap any potential means of sharing information or otherwise promoting the Games—from traditional and social media platforms to promotional programs and work with sponsors. Tokyo's Paralympics earmarked a smaller percentage for promotion—4 percent of the proposed budget—than was the case in Nagano, but even this seeming shortcoming was made up in other ways.[61] Additional promotional support, both direct and indirect, came from sponsors like Toyota and especially from the Nippon Foundation. Examples of such contributions are described in this section alongside examinations of several promotional programs developed by Tokyo as the host city. Although most of these campaigns continued into 2020, many of the firsthand observations here date from 2017, when I was based in Tokyo for research.

Naturally, the joint Olympic-Paralympic organizing committee was a driving force for marketing the Games in Tokyo. The official website and social media feeds were filled with information on events for both Games. This committee's promotion campaign for the Paralympics included such tried-and-true approaches as countdown events, torch-relay applications, and mascot contests, several of which were carried out in close cooperation with the Olympics, as noted earlier. Because of their official status, these events invariably generated notice from a variety of media outlets, providing regular nationwide reminders (in case anyone could miss it) that the Games were coming to Tokyo.[62]

Some of the more elaborate and interesting promotional efforts connected to Tokyo 2020 were put on by affiliates of the organizing committee. In many of these cases, marketing took earlier ideas—educational campaigns, exhibition events, and volunteer recruitment—and dramatically expanded their scale and scope, a perhaps logical outcome given the immensity of both Tokyo and the contemporary Summer Paralympics. The Paralympic educational program is a good example, in which Nagano's lauded "One School, One Country" approach was taken to an entirely new level for Tokyo. In addition to recruiting more than 280 "host towns" throughout Japan, campaigns for 2020 included the development of a joint Olympic–Paralympic educational program, complete with teaching modules and resources for primary through secondary school students.[63] The teaching resources included not only classroom-based content about Paralympic values and the Games themselves but also hands-on units for students enabling them to experience various Paralympic sports. What is more, the program targeted not only Tokyo but also all of Japan. Technically, the educational program was sponsored by the joint organizing committee, but in another example of Japan's ongoing contributions to the Paralympic Movement, the Paralympic-related resources being used were a version of the IPC-approved, English-language *I'mPOSSIBLE* materials, developed by the Agitos Foundation, the IPC's development arm "in close collaboration with the Japanese Paralympic Committee," and with financial support from the Nippon Foundation's Paralympic Support Center.[64] Thanks in no small part to the generosity of the Nippon Foundation, by August 2018 Japanese versions of *I'mPOSSIBLE* texts had already been distributed free of charge to some 36,000 schools in Japan, and many of the materials were available for download online. Although actual usage remains difficult to document, the sheer reach of this program was unprecedented.[65]

The Tokyo metropolitan government was another key player in promotional efforts, offering several expansive campaigns. Launched in 2015, the city's NO LIMITS CHALLENGE program focused on providing direct exposure to Paralympic sports to people throughout greater Tokyo. NO LIMITS CHALLENGE events were held nearly every weekend at different locations around Tokyo. Many were set up to coincide with preexisting festivals or sports activities, and they varied in their approach and size. Although some of the campaign's events featured more passive elements like temporary photo exhibits, a significant portion included Paralympic athletes demonstrating their skills, and most sought to engage participants—and especially young people—directly in some form of disability sports. Events were advertised on the campaign's website and social media outlets, but they seemed specifically tailored to grabbing the attention of people who did not seek them out intentionally.[66]

Beginning in 2016, the end of Japan's famed "Golden Week" (a string of national holidays from late April to early May) each year was marked by elaborate NO LIMITS SPECIAL events hosted at high-traffic areas in Tokyo, including the Ginza and Marunouchi districts. After seeing advertisements on Facebook and at several train stations, my family and I attended the 2017 NO LIMITS SPECIAL held in Ueno Park, right next to the entrance of the Ueno Zoo. The free event was a festival in its own right, complete with crowds, a temporary basketball stadium, food trucks, displays, hands-on activities, and contests. Musical and other performances added to the festival atmosphere. In keeping with the goals of providing direct exposure, participants were able to try out wheelchair racing, weight lifting, boccia, wheelchair basketball, and several other sports. Over the course of two days, celebrity emcees also introduced the crowd to several of Japan's top Paralympians, who showed off their skills and then often followed up with interviews or Q&A sessions. Perhaps not surprisingly, reporters were also scattered throughout the site. A few days later, a conversation with a new Japanese acquaintance about my research topic elicited an unprompted reference to a TV news clip he had seen about this very event, suggesting that NO LIMITS CHALLENGE was doing just what it was meant to: raising awareness of the Paralympics.

One of the many booths set up at the NO LIMITS SPECIAL event in Ueno was dedicated to another of the Tokyo metropolitan government's promotional programs, TEAM BEYOND. Initiated in 2016, this campaign sought to spark greater interest in the Paralympics from potential fans in Tokyo and elsewhere. With signup sites available at many events and online, the program employed a traditional bandwagon approach, highlighting the involvement of both celebrities and everyday individuals to encourage everyone to join the TEAM and support Paralympic sports and athletes. By the end of January 2018 TEAM BEYOND announced that it had already recruited more than one million members. In contrast to the formal—and generally successful—volunteer drives associated with both the organizing committee and the metropolitan government, TEAM BEYOND offered potential members a low-stakes means for engaging with the Paralympics, because members were not necessarily obligated to participate in activities. Instead, TEAM BEYOND served as a sort of educational clearinghouse for information on athletes and sports, as well as Paralympic-related events and television programming. Members could opt to receive regular newsletters, visit the official website, or follow the campaign's social media feeds for updates, and they were also eligible to enter various contests and drawings for commemorative products. These information conduits were clearly designed to encourage members to attend and engage with the Games when they arrived in Tokyo in summer 2020. Another of the campaign's activities, the BEYOND AWARD, solicited artworks and performance pieces related to the Paralympics from throughout Japan and published award winners in various age divisions on the TEAM BEYOND website.[67]

As part of its outreach activities, TEAM BEYOND organized its own events as well, which often included musical and celebrity guest performances, explanations of various disability sports, exhibition matches, and opportunities to try out adaptive equipment. The largest of these events was the BEYOND FES (short for BEYOND FESTIVAL) held over several days in October 2018 in the busy Marunouchi district outside Tokyo Station. In addition to guest performances and multiple display or experiential booths, BEYOND FES offered sports demonstrations and athlete "talk shows" and served as the venue for announcing the BEYOND AWARD winners. BEYOND FES also included a weekday conference to share information about the benefits of supporting the Paralympics for potential corporate and organizational sponsors. In fact, TEAM BEYOND had welcomed corporate or group members since its inception, and as of early 2019 listed 140 such members on its official site. Most TEAM BEYOND events listed several of these companies or groups as supporters. Because many of these corporations or organizations were smaller in scale than the average Olympic and Paralympic sponsors, TEAM BEYOND's approach opened the door for new groups to develop a vested interest in supporting the Paralympics for 2020 and possibly beyond.[68]

In terms of providing both financial and institutional support for promoting the 2020 Games, the Nippon Foundation played an outsized role. An international nonprofit philanthropic organization, the Nippon Foundation has a complex and in some ways controversial history that is beyond the scope of this chapter. Although it was involved with activities related to disability and inclusiveness well before these Games, direct engagement with the Paralympics and Tokyo's Games in particular date to 2014 with the establishment of the Nippon Foundation Paralympic Research Group. The Research Group aimed to conduct academic research on the Paralympics in Japan and elsewhere "to study a range of issues related to what shape the Paralympics should take."[69] Since its establishment, it hosted several dozen workshops, supported countless symposia and talks, published multiple volumes of a research journal, and conducted several research studies and surveys, many of which incorporated both Japanese and international specialists. In short, the Research Group has proven a boon to Paralympic studies in Japan while playing a key role in integrating ongoing domestic discussions with broader international academic study of the Paralympics. Having participated in or attended several Nippon Foundation affiliated events and benefited from the resulting research and contacts, I can testify firsthand to the positive shift in the field that has resulted from the Nippon Foundation's support.

To the great benefit of the 2020 Paralympics, the Nippon Foundation did not limit its focus to academia. In 2015, it announced the establishment of the Paralympic Support Center, which would provide 10 billion yen through 2021 to support Paralympic sports and athletes in preparation for the 2020 Games.[70] A quick comparison shows how generous this financial support truly was: the original budget for the Paralympics called for roughly USD 80 million of governmental support, which would cover 50 percent of costs. The funds pledged by the Nippon Foundation in 2015 amounted to roughly USD 81 million of *extra* support, funds that had not been included in the original budget estimates. Given such figures, it is understandable why the Nippon Foundation name or logo appeared so frequently in connection with many of the promotional efforts and other forms of support for the 2020 Paralympics, including the *I'mPOSSIBLE* educational campaigns and the construction of new facilities.

The Paralympic Support Center also actively engaged in multiple promotion efforts of its own. Like many of the other promotional campaigns, it maintained a catchy website that was also designed to be very accessible, with buttons to easily change font sizes and colors. The site featured information on Paralympic athletes and events, but with both Japanese and English versions, it dramatically expanded its potential reach.[71] The Paralympic Support Center's art photo magazine *GO Journal* featuring Japanese athletes also offered content in both languages.[72] For domestic audiences, the center maintained an active social media presence and launched a youth-oriented newspaper that included information on many of the other promotional campaigns discussed here, highlighting how many of these programs were both complementary and intentionally redundant.[73] Other Paralympic Support Center activities included Paralympic Sports Days, which rotated to different areas around Japan in an effort to assure that enthusiasm for the Games reached beyond Tokyo, as well as an annual Para Ekiden race in Tokyo, where teams from all over Japan made up of individuals with different types of impairments competed in an extended relay race. The Ekiden event I observed with my family on a chilly spring day in 2017 was well attended, with an enthusiastic crowd and large numbers of volunteers. The Paralympic Support Center also organized annual Parafes (short for Para-festival) events, which followed the pattern of many other promotional activities, combining live celebrity performances with athletic exhibitions and opportunities to try out sports. The third Parafes held in November 2018 attracted a new record crowd of 6,000.[74] Given these sorts of events and all of the other forms of support flowing from the Nippon Foundation, it is not hard to imagine that the situation in Tokyo would have been quite different without such backing. Yet in this sense, the Tokyo 2020 Paralympics were more similar to previous Games than they might at first have appeared; although much had changed, they continued to be heavily reliant on forms of voluntary support. Fortunately for the 2020 Games, that support proved to be quite generous.

In addition to formal campaigns, the 2020 Paralympics also benefited from what might be thought of as indirect or perhaps passive forms of promotion. The side-by-side use of Olympic and Paralympic logos was a case in point; they were everywhere in 2017, from the doors at my sons' public schools to fences on construction sites. It also was not unusual to encounter advertisements that had little to do with the Games themselves depicting athletes with some form of impairment. In many cases these ads were associated with companies sponsoring the Games, the JPSA, or one of the other promotional campaigns. Based on the shared outfits of cheering sections at several different disability sports events I observed, it appeared that companies like Mitsubishi, Toyota, Suntory, and others were actively encouraging employees to attend such events.[75] During visits to sites connected with Toyota, which has been a worldwide partner of both the Olympics and Paralympics since 2015, I stumbled across displays featuring Paralympic athletes at Toyota's high-tech Mega Web entertainment site in the Odaiba district and found an exhibit of advertising posters from previous Olympic and Paralympic Games in the lobby of their

Tokyo office building. I learned that Toyota later converted a portion of this Tokyo building lobby into a boccia court.[76]

The Paralympics were featured at unaffiliated sites in Tokyo, too. The National Shōwa Memorial Museum (Shōwakan) mounted an entire exhibit on the graphic designer who created the posters for the 1964 Paralympics, including the now-famous poster of wheelchair archery as part of its advertisement. The Edo-Tokyo Museum incorporated details of the 1964 Paralympics into its exhibits, and the single-room museum at Haneda airport gave passing attention to the 1964 and 2020 Paralympics in its featured Olympic/Paralympic display in June 2017. Admittedly, my research interests made me particularly attuned to such examples, but even three years before the Paralympics were scheduled to begin, all of these sorts of passive and active promotional efforts were already making the 2020 Games hard to miss. As one Tokyo taxi driver aptly noted after asking what I was studying at Waseda University, "Yeah, they've been working hard on the Paralympics."

From Patients to Pros: The Athlete's Experience

As should be clear from the descriptions of various promotional activities for the 2020 Games, athletes were central to these efforts and many other aspects of organizing for Tokyo 2020. In many respects, this development was not surprising, because Tokyo's 2013 candidature materials explicitly stated that the "design of the Tokyo 2020 Paralympic Games will truly have the interests of the athletes in mind" and that a "key feature of the promotional activities will be the athletes, as spokespersons, educators and inspirational heroes and role models."[77] Tokyo's commitment to an "athletes-first" approach proved to be much more than a savvy sales pitch to the host selection committee. At the same time, it is useful to realize just how different this approach was from the experiences of earlier Japanese athletes, because even candidature materials for Tokyo's unsuccessful 2016 bid were less clear than the 2020 bid on the involvement of athletes. To offer additional perspective on the 2020 Games and provide a sense of the differing experiences of individuals engaged in disability sports over time, I close the chapter with brief stories from five athletes, each of whom had a connection to at least one of the events examined in this book. Although these brief sketches cannot hope to offer a complete picture of the disability sports scene in Japan since the 1960s, taken together they point to patterns and themes that merit acknowledgment and will, I hope, lay the groundwork for future inquiries.

Suzaki Katsumi

Suzaki Katsumi's introduction to disability sports was part and parcel of his rehabilitation.[78] After a motorbike accident left him with severe injuries resulting in paralysis from the waist down, Suzaki transferred to the Beppu National Hospital specifically to take advantage of the new approaches to rehabilitation that Dr. Nakamura Yutaka was promoting. His engagement in sports and other exercises began immediately after his transfer, which was around the same time as Nakamura and others began actively recruiting participants for the 1964 Paralympics. Initially, Suzaki was largely unaware of the Paralympics and was surprised when he was selected to participate, especially because he had been at the hospital for a shorter time than most of the other patients. During our interview in 2017, he explained that his preparations for the Games were extremely limited not only because of time but also because both facilities and coaches were lacking. His practice for the freestyle swim, for instance, consisted almost exclusively of using the rehabilitative hot springs bath at the hospital. Without accessible on-site facilities or someone to help him get to and use a local pool, he only managed to swim in a standard-sized pool once or twice before the Paralympics.

At the 1964 Tokyo Games themselves, Suzaki competed in six different events, including swimming, basketball, track-and-field competitions, and ping-pong. The open structure of the Games at the time allowed for such diverse involvement, but as Suzaki pointed out, he did not necessarily choose his own events, having been instructed by medical staff (and probably Nakamura) to enter certain competitions in part for their potential health benefits. Looking back on the Games, Suzaki described the challenges of competing against others with far more training. Several memories he recounted were of the performance gaps between foreign and Japanese athletes and of his poor competition results stemming from his inexperience. For example, he recalled borrowing a much lighter foreign wheelchair for a race, but having his time be exactly the same as when he raced with his regular chair, because he did not know how to use the new-style chair to best effect. Despite what he characterized as memorable "failures" (*shippai*), he observed that having the opportunity to compete was a positive experience for himself and others. Although he noted that the Paralympics helped shift some people's perspectives on disability to an extent, he also noted that such progress was tempered by the persistence of ideas that disability was something that should be hidden. Some people, he indicated, still viewed the Paralympics as more akin to an embarrassing freak show than a sporting event.

On a personal level, Suzaki's involvement with the 1964 Games seemed to help him address fears that he would become a burden to his family or be forced to live the rest of his days laid up in a hospital. As excited as he was to share his stories about the Paralympics, Suzaki acknowledged that the most important thing for him after 1964 was not his participation in the event or his continued involvement in sports, but rather the fact that he found a job after leaving the hospital that allowed him to earn an independent living. Work, as he explained, was always his primary goal and focus, and he continued working until just a few years before our interview.

Yet he still found time to engage in sports, and as a longtime Ōita Prefecture resident, he had ample opportunities to do so. Over the years, he participated in several of Taiyō no Ie's athletic programs, including basketball in his younger years and sports like boccia more recently. Although he could not recall any of the events he participated in except for basketball, Suzaki joined many other Ōita residents in competing in the first FESPIC Games, which were held in the prefecture in 1975. He also raced in three of the early Ōita wheelchair marathons. At the time of our conversation he was 75 and still extraordinarily active. When weather permitted, he raced his wheelchair at a nearby park, averaging about 100 kilometers a month, though he admitted that he had to be careful not to overdo it; some months he raced fewer kilometers. Suzaki's experiences in the early 1960s seemed to inspire a lifelong interest in sports, and living in Ōita has provided access to facilities, teams, and events that has allowed him to continue pursuing and adapting that interest to his changing lifestyle.

Because so few Japanese participants from 1964 remain in good health today, Suzaki's firsthand accounts of Japan's first Paralympics received renewed attention as Tokyo prepared to host its second Games. I first heard his story in the summer of 2017 while viewing a television talk show focusing on the Paralympics. The television interview with him was one of several others, including a brief piece put out in English by the IPC.[79] When I reached out to an acquaintance at Taiyō no Ie to ask for a meeting with Suzaki, she mentioned that he had been quite busy interacting with the media in recent years. Although not surprising, such interest merits notice in part, because it differed from the situation at the time of Tokyo's first Games. To be sure, Suzaki does appear in some of the photographs and other official materials from the 1964 Paralympics, but his story and those of most other Japanese Paralympians did not receive widespread attention at the time. Accounts of the earlier Games from athletes' perspective are exceptionally limited in both length and number. Fortunately, Tokyo's current focus on athletes is having an effect retroactively, prompting new explorations of athletes' experiences in the past.[80] Although our understanding of the Paralympics in Japan is better for having had the chance to hear stories like Suzaki's, it also seems clear that other stories from this early period of Japan's engagement with the Paralympics have already been silenced.

Gamō Akemi

Gamō Akemi's first exposure to sports came through her school, when her PE teacher at her junior high school for visually impaired students encouraged her to enter a regional track-and-field competition.[81] Her victory in the 100 meter dash at that competition would become the first of many sporting accomplishments for Gamō. As a junior and senior high school student, she set several records at track-and-field and swimming competitions throughout Japan. Gamō's experiences not only reflected the important role that schools for the visually or hearing impaired long played in the promotion of disability sports in Japan, as noted briefly in chapter 1, but they also showed how opportunities had expanded for those looking to do more. During her summer break in 1986, Gamō climbed Mount Fuji, and in 1987 she achieved nationwide press coverage after completing the full marathon race in Honolulu. According to the *Asahi* newspaper, 20-year old Gamō finished the race amidst rain and strong winds in five hours and forty-three minutes alongside her guide runner, her younger sister, "the two of them connected at the wrist by a rope."[82] In 1988, Gamō represented Japan at the Seoul Paralympics, competing in four swimming events, with her best finish placing her fifth.[83]

Given her already impressive record of sporting achievements it is perhaps understandable why Gamō was one of two local Kobe athletes chosen to deliver the Athletes' Oath at the opening ceremony of the fifth FESPIC Games in 1989.[84] On September 16, Gamō became the first Japanese athlete to win a gold medal at these Games, and she would go on to win three more gold medals in swimming over the next several days. Describing swimming as "life work," she continued swimming well after her success at FESPIC.[85] Although she did not accomplish her goal of swimming at the Paralympics again, Gamō continued to achieve success in local and national swimming competitions over the next several years. She also took on a leadership role with Kōbe Rakuei club, the local swimming organization for athletes with disabilities where she carried out her own training.[86]

Gamō's athletic feats received broader attention at the time than did those of Suzaki. While in high school, she entered and won a national speech contest sponsored by the *Braille Mainichi* newspaper in 1986. In her winning speech she talked about her athletic experiences and goals, including her plans to compete as both a marathon runner and a swimmer. The feature article in the *Mainichi* national edition discussing the speech contest win marked an early account of her experiences with sports.[87] Gamō's marathon run the following year generated wide interest and even inspired the production of a special television drama.[88] Reflecting the general lack of media attention to the Paralympics at the time, her participation in Seoul's Games went largely unacknowledged in 1988, and her gold medal at FESPIC drew only a brief mention in national media outlets. By far the most extensive coverage Gamō ever received came from the local *Kōbe shimbun* newspaper, which ran a series of articles on local athletes competing at Kobe's FESPIC Games. The local paper greeted her first gold medal victory with reminders of her earlier speech contest, noting that she had now fulfilled both of her expressed goals.[89] Gamō was also among a handful of athletes featured in the short official documentary produced for the 1989 FESPIC Games.[90]

Although she received a good deal of notice at the time, the nature of it was fleeting. By the time of Kobe's FESPIC Games, sports were already an important part of her life and they continued to be so afterward. Yet her continued pursuit of the "life work" of swimming was only documented on the homepage of her local swimming club's website, which provides a far more detailed accounting of its history than many other similar organizations at the grassroots level.[91] As with Suzaki, much of her later engagement with sports did not attract notice beyond a limited circle, a necessary reminder of how important it is to go beyond the national headlines when seeking to understand disability sports' impact on the lives of even relatively recognized athletes.

The media attention Gamō received also retained older patterns of problematic representation. Although acknowledging her athleticism and her accomplishments, the language of her coverage relied heavily on references to her overcoming or "not losing out to" her visual impairment, something that she had been living with since birth.[92] The *Mainichi* article about her speech contest win ended not with her athletic accomplishments, but by noting that she was also pursuing "bridal training" such as tea ceremony and flower arranging.[93] Perhaps most dramatically, the 1990 television drama inspired by her run at the Honolulu Marathon transformed her years of experience and training as a visually impaired athlete into the story of a nondisabled woman who suddenly lost her sight after a traffic accident but managed to "overcome her suffering through the marathon."[94] As impressive as Gamō's athletic career was by 1990, for some it was apparently not quite inspirational enough.

Hiromichi Jun

In the very first pages of his 2004 autobiography, Hiromichi Jun offered read-ers a clear indication that he was more than an average athlete. After sharing personal details about his hometown, birth date, and height, he described his occupation as "professional wheelchair athlete," noting a few pages later that he had long devoted his life to wheelchair racing in particular and had recently decided to go pro. As he put it, "Racing is my job."[95]

Of course, Hiromichi was not always a professional wheelchair athlete. As a boy growing up in Osaka, he had reportedly always been good at sports, but his introduction to wheelchair sports came after a motorbike accident left him with permanent spinal cord injuries at the age of 15. Hiromichi quickly mas-tered the basics of wheelchair usage, leading his physical therapist to introduce him to sports not at the hospital but at the Osaka Municipal Disability Sports Center, which happened to be one of the most well-established disability sports centers in Japan. He claimed to be immediately hooked, visiting the center daily as soon as he checked out of the hospital.

Taken in particular with the high speeds achieved in racing, Hiromichi entered his first wheelchair race, a half-marathon in Osaka in 1991, and later that same year he made his debut at the Ōita International Wheelchair Mara-thon. He has continued racing right up to this writing, competing at home and abroad at different distances. Among his many accomplishments was a second-place finish at the 1996 full marathon in Ōita, the highest finish to that point by a Japanese male athlete, and for many years he reigned as Japan's top male finisher in marathons at home and abroad. He has competed in four Paralympic Games—Sydney, Athens, Beijing, and London—entering multiple events at each and win-ning both silver (Sydney) and bronze (Athens) medals in the 800 meter race. In recent years, he has traveled to twenty or more competitions annually, often entering in multiple events and continuing to post impressive results.[96]

Even in the early years of his racing career, Hiromichi demonstrated an al-most single-minded dedication to sports. In 1995, he traveled to the United States to train with Jim Knaub, one of the world's top wheelchair racers at the time, and just a few years later Hiromichi would seek out regular training in Switzerland with another wheelchair marathon great, Heinz Frei. In 1999, Hi-romichi moved from his native Osaka to Ōita and took a job with a Honda affiliate of Taiyō no Ie, which allowed him more flexibility for training and travel for competition. After gathering support from several sponsors, in early 2004, he left Honda to become an independent professional athlete. By 2019, he was racing as an affiliate of Puma Japan with roughly twenty sponsors or contractual partners.[97]

While racing itself is clearly Hiromichi's job, he has also embraced multiple opportunities to share his experiences with others and to foster the development of disability sports. Beginning in 2006 he was central to efforts aimed at establishing and continuing to organize an IPC sanctioned track-and-field event in his adopted home of Ōita. The resulting meet became one of the largest annual track events in Japan.[98] Hiromichi also took on leadership positions in the Paralympians Association of Japan and has served as executive director of Sports of Heart, an organization launched in 2012 in connection with Itō Kazuko's nonprofit organization STAND, discussed in the previous chapter.[99] Sports of Heart holds large-scale annual festivals aimed at generating awareness of sports and arts programs for those with disabilities. The 2019 festival was held at two venues: Tokyo and Ōita.

Hiromichi became a regular on the lecture circuit even before he went professional. According to his personal website he averages about twenty lectures a year for schools, businesses, and other organizations. The titles of his lectures—"Towards Tomorrow," "Towards a Dream," and "If I'm Going to Live . . ."—indicate that he is as much a motivational or inspirational speaker as an ambassador of disability sports.[100] In 2017, when the principal at my son's public middle school in Tokyo heard about my research project as we were completing enrollment paperwork, he excitedly informed me that the school had recently hosted a speaker who shared how a bike accident and resulting disability transformed his life for the better, allowing him to become a professional athlete and to do things he never would have done otherwise. He was talking about Hiromichi, whose story of overcoming obstacles and striving for goals the principal found ideally suited to his middle-school charges.

As a professional athlete, Hiromichi has clearly achieved a much higher profile than either Suzaki or Gamō. Clearly, he has benefited from the fact that his career overlapped with a period of growing media and popular attention to the Paralympics in Japan. Both the local and national press, for instance, have been regularly documenting his racing achievements since the late 1990s. But as his frequent lectures and published autobiography suggest, he has also assumed an active role in self-promotion. Hiromichi has been the subject of countless interviews, especially those associated with the new media and publication outlets discussed in chapter 4, and he has been very active on social media platforms as well. In Ōita, he has his own radio show on one of the local stations and appears regularly as a local TV commentator.[101] To an extent, Hiromichi's situation reflects his unique status as a professional reliant on such publicity and the sponsorships it can help generate. Yet his experience also points to a significant increase in receptivity to and interest in athletes with disabilities in Japan, something also apparent in the stories of the following two athletes.

Tsuchida Wakako

Like Hiromichi, Tsuchida Wakako began her athletic career as a teenager and has gone on to become a professional wheelchair racer.[102] After a 1992 traffic accident during her second year of high school left her with permanent spinal cord injuries, she was introduced to disability sports while recovering. On leaving the hospital, she was able to explore a variety of sports, including basketball and track, at the Tama Disability Sports Center in Tokyo, a well-known facility not far from her home. In 1993, she participated in an ice sledge racing exhibition event that she learned about through the sports center, an experience that led to her competing in the Lillehammer Paralympics a few months later. Despite intense training leading up to the Games, her first Paralympics produced disappointing results, but her next Paralympics, the 1998 Games in Nagano, were a different story. As one of the key athletes in Japan's "medal rush" in 1998, Tsuchida won four Paralympic medals in ice sledge racing, two gold and two silver, and she set a world record in the 1,500 meter race. As exemplified by the widespread media coverage they received in Japan, Tsuchida's achievements in Nagano played an important role in generating greater awareness of the Games and their athletes. In the years ahead, Tsuchida not only continued competing and attracting media notice but also became well known as an advocate for disability sports in Japan.

Nagano's Games marked an important competitive turning point for Tsuchida as well. As noted in chapter 4, decreasing numbers of competitors in ice sledge races led to this competition's elimination from the Winter Paralympics after 1998. Tsuchida then focused her efforts on track and field, where she had already had some success, having finished first in the women's division of the 1996 half-marathon in Ōita. Over the next several years she accumulated a remarkable set of sporting accomplishments, too lengthy to detail here. Among the highlights were multiple marathon victories in races all over the world, as well as two different world records in the marathon. Tsuchida has competed at several different distances in five Summer Paralympic Games—Sydney, Athens, Beijing, London, and Rio de Janeiro—winning multiple medals. Her gold medal win in the 5,000 meter race in the 2004 Athens Games made her the first Japanese athlete to win gold in both a Winter and Summer Paralympics. In 2017 Tsuchida began competing in international paratriathlon events and quickly emerged as a top medal contender for the 2020 Games being hosted by her home city.[103]

Tsuchida's turn to professional racing came in 2001, though she has continued working with different companies as well, most recently, Yachiyo Industries. Yachiyo is an automotive parts company that has been working with Honda R&D Taiyō (one of several Honda affiliates of Taiyō no Ie) to design and develop high-tech racing wheelchairs. Tsuchida was featured prominently on Yachiyo's corporate website in 2019. In fact, the section dedicated to her race results appears to have been updated more regularly than her own website.[104]

At various points in her career, Tsuchida has been outspoken about the unique challenges that athletes with disabilities face as they seek to compete at the elite level. In addition to the struggles of finding time and money to train, travel, and compete—challenges faced by any elite competitor—Tsuchida has pointed out that the adapted equipment necessary for her and others can be prohibitively expensive and requires frequent repair or replacement, situations that can make it difficult to compete without some sort of sponsorship.[105] Such observations reflected Tsuchida's particular experiences, but they also exemplified her broader commitment to improving familiarity with and support for disability sports in Japan. Like Hiromichi, Tsuchida has made herself available for talks and seminars, yet perhaps the best example of her efforts was her book published in 2010 in the lead-up to the London Paralympics. *The Complete Guide to Sports for the Physically Disabled* (Shintai shōgaisha supōtsu kanzen gaido) includes her own story, as well as her interviews with several other top-level Japanese Paralympians.[106] With easy-to-understand explanations of various sports, information on disability sports centers and competitions all over Japan, and an entire chapter dedicated to examples of volunteer and corporate support, Tsuchida's *Complete Guide* is clearly intended to serve as an educational and outreach tool for both potential athletes and potential supporters. Her advocacy and records of athletic achievement were no doubt behind her selection as captain of the Japanese team for the London Paralympic Games in 2012, another groundbreaking moment for Tsuchida, as she became Japan's first female Paralympic team captain.[107] Tsuchida also played a leading role in Tokyo's efforts to bring the Games back to Japan, figuring prominently as a bid ambassador, serving as a member of the 2020 Athletes Commission since its formation in 2015, and continuing to support various promotional campaigns.[108]

The sheer variety of Tsuchida's achievements have meant that her story has been told and retold in many different venues and formats, from interviews in semi-official publications to her own personal blog. Tsuchida was among six athletes included in a 2004 collection of biographies on Paralympians published with the support of the JPC on the eve of the Athens Games, and she was also among the featured athletes in a work on the Ōita marathon produced that same year.[109]

Tsuchida's firsthand accounts include an autobiography published just before the 2012 London Paralympics.[110] Throughout the work, Tsuchida weaves together details from her personal history with examples from her athletic experiences, frequently sprinkling her account with critical commentaries on the status of disability sports in Japan at the time. Echoing early promoters of disability sports in Japan, she frames many of her critiques in terms of Japan's shortcomings in relation to other—often unspecified—countries.[111] Tsuchida's autobiography, like her earlier *Complete Guide*, is clearly oriented toward fostering improvements for athletes and people with disabilities more generally. At the same time, the work is explicitly framed and marketed along inspirational lines. The foreword links Tsuchida's personal stories and her approaches to life and competition with the 2011 triple disaster in Japan, which would still have been quite fresh in the minds and lives of many readers.[112] But as the promotional blurb on the jacket informs readers, this is a book about "how to produce a maximally positive mindset," and the recurring use of the verb for transcending or overcoming (*koeru*) in the book title and each of the chapter titles leaves little doubt about its intended tone. As much as Tsuchida's autobiography aims to challenge people to think about disability sports in different ways, it is also—as the subtitle itself indicates—meant to inspire by offering her unique version of "words to move forward."

Tani (née Satō) Mami

Having begun this chapter with Satō Mami's role in bringing the 2020 Games to Tokyo, it seems only appropriate to offer some information about her past and ongoing engagement with disability sports, details that also help explain how she became a key spokesperson in 2013.[113] As Satō noted in her bid-opening speech, she came to disability sports after losing her leg below the knee because of an aggressive case of bone cancer. At the time of her initial diagnosis she was in her second year of college at Japan's prestigious Waseda University, where she was a member of the school's cheerleading squad. In fall 2002, Satō returned to school after her surgeries and treatment, and as she struggled to readjust, she decided to look into sports, having enjoyed being a runner and swimmer throughout her childhood. An internet search led her to the Tokyo Metropolitan Sports Center for the Disabled, where she took up swimming and later was introduced to track and field. Her near-daily visits to the sports center led to her soon becoming interested in testing her skills in competition, eventually setting her sights on making it to the Paralympics in Athens or Beijing. Despite earlier success at the national level, she failed to qualify for the 2004 Paralympics in swimming. Her coach convinced her that she had nothing to lose in trying to make the Japanese national team in track and field, even though she had just taken up the sport and had less than four months to prepare for the last qualifying event. In the end, she earned a spot to compete in the long jump at the Athens Games, becoming Japan's first woman to compete at the Paralympics with a prosthetic leg.[114] After Athens, Satō would qualify for the long jump at the Beijing and London Paralympics as well, with her best results being a sixth-place finish in Beijing. More recently, she has turned her athletic focus to the paratriathlon, where she has won several international races under her married name, Tani Mami. Like Tsuchida, Tani was eager to make the Japanese team in the paratriathlon at the 2020 Paralympics in Tokyo.

Even before she competed in the 2004 Games in Athens, Satō's experiences were already garnering significant attention within Japan. She was featured on an NHK television sports program in early 2004 and was starting to receive invitations to give talks on overcoming adversity. When she graduated from Waseda in March 2004, she received one of the university's highest honors, the Ono Azusa Memorial Award, which was given in recognition of her having "overcome obstacles, giving courage and hope to those around her."[115] In the time between her graduation and the Paralympics, Satō took a position working for the Japanese beverage and food company Suntory in its recently established Sports Fellowship Promotion division. She has remained with Suntory ever since and is currently working in its Corporate Social Responsibility (CSR) division promoting a variety of sports events and activities. In 2019 Suntory featured Tani on the CSR section of its website noting the "activity support" that the company provided for her as part of its Suntory Challenged Sports Project.[116]

Much like Hiromichi and Tsuchida, Satō has had multiple opportunities to share her story through media coverage, regular presentations, interviews, and published works. Yet this attention differs from that received by the other athletes profiled here in that it not only has been more extensive but also began before she had established a record of athletic achievements. For instance, Satō's biography was one of those included in the same JPC-affiliated volume with Tsuchida Wakako that came out just before the 2004 Athens Games. Satō was the only athlete pictured on the book jacket—with full-page photos covering both the front and back—and her account was featured first.[117] Even though she had only just qualified for her first Games, Satō was clearly being promoted as a face of the Paralympics in Japan.

Satō's first autobiographical account, *Lucky Girl* (Rakkī gāru), came out just before the 2004 Athens Paralympics as well. The autobiography was reissued in October 2013 with a special book jacket highlighting her recent bid presentation, and another edition was published in 2014, including the English and Japanese texts of her then-famous speech in Argentina.[118] Satō has written two other autobiographies, one published on the eve of the 2008 Beijing Paralympics that went through at least three printings and another targeting a young adult audience that was published in 2012 after the London Games.[119] This most recent youth-oriented book is a more comprehensive account of the story about Satō that was included in some middle-school Japanese language arts textbooks. The 2012 autobiography also incorporated details about how the earthquake and tsunami in March 2011 destroyed her childhood home and prevented contact with her family for a nerve-wracking week.[120]

Given the remarkable prominence Satō had achieved and her well-known personal connection to the 2011 disaster, her selection as a leading spokesperson for Tokyo's candidacy in 2013 made all the more sense, and it is clear that her role in Argentina made her even more recognizable as Japan's face of the 2020 Games. She herself noted jokingly in an interview a year later that she continued to be "noticed by 'middle-aged ladies' in the streets."[121] At the same time, Satō's story and her recognition in Japan offer a reminder that the narratives associated with athletes—and especially athletes who achieve a level of celebrity—are never just about their athletic achievements. In Satō's case, her affiliation with one of Japan's elite educational institutions, her career with a major transnational Japanese company, and her connections in Tokyo are all key elements of her story and its marketability. As with many of the other athletes discussed here, inspiration is also central to Satō's stories and their social resonance. Indeed, perhaps because she was only just beginning her Paralympic career, her earliest accounts are focused almost solely on how she—portrayed as wearing a near-constant smile—beat cancer, overcame obstacles, and continued to pursue athletic glory, not unlike the inspirational cancer-comeback stories of Mario Lemieux or Lance Armstrong.

With her continued engagement in disability sports over the years, Satō went on to join many other athletes in seeking to foster greater awareness of and interest in the Paralympics and disability sports more generally, as demonstrated in particular through her promotional work for Tokyo's Games. Even before that point, Satō returned to school to pursue a master's degree in sports business, focusing on the environment for disability sports in Japan and abroad.[122] Several of Satō's later works and comments are also more explicit about challenges that disabled athletes face and the need to change social perceptions of disability in Japan. In her role as an advocate, Satō has benefited from the changed environment around disability sports and the very nature of her job at Suntory. The company supports her ongoing athletic career, and her CSR work centers on promoting sports for those with disabilities and, more recently, for those in disaster-affected regions of Japan like her hometown. As she explained in 2018 when asked how she manages all of these seemingly competing undertakings, "So I don't think in terms of work–life balance. For me, work and life aren't two separate things; they flow together seamlessly. You might call it 'work–life integration.'"[123]

In the last several years, Satō has returned to the media spotlight under her married name Tani Mami. Much of this coverage has centered on her efforts to earn a spot competing in the paratriathlon at the Tokyo Games. While I was dining out in Tokyo in 2017, for example, the restaurant's television happened to be tuned to a program about Tani that documented her training regimen and racing experience and showed her husband and young son anxiously awaiting her arrival at the finish of a paratriathlon race. At the time, Tani's multiple international victories were sparking hopes of medal opportunities for 2020. A series of reports beginning in summer 2018 cast a shadow on this potential feel-good ending. Because of the limited number of competitors, organizers announced in August that several paratriathlon races were being eliminated from the 2020 Paralympics, including those for female athletes classified in the same category as Tani (PTS4). Fortunately for Tani and others in her situation, the international governing organization for triathlons agreed in late November 2018 to allow mixed-classification races, opening the door for Tani to compete in Tokyo, but making it significantly harder for her to win there.[124] Whether or not Tani ultimately wins her first Paralympic medal, it is likely that many in Japan will be following her story.[125]

Patterns, Problems, Potential

As Tokyo made final preparations for the Games in 2020, Japan also reached the sixty-year anniversary of its initial encounters with the Paralympics. Given that history, the five sketches provided here can only begin to convey the complexity of athletes' experiences with disability sports in Japan. These accounts do, however, provide a sense of how much those experiences changed between Tokyo's first and second Paralympic Games. They also draw attention to a number of patterns, issues, and matters ripe for future inquiry— some unique to Japan and some relevant beyond that country.

For one, these five stories all point to the importance of access to facilities and to expertise in fostering interest in and opportunities for pursuing disability sports. The initial exposure to sports came via the hospital or rehabilitation center for athletes who acquired their impairments or via an informed and proactive teacher for Gamō. But that initial exposure was only part of the story. All of the athletes discussed here benefited from regular, nearby access to specialized facilities and programs. The resources that they were able to tap into were mostly situated in urban regions with histories of involvement with disability sports, a situation hardly unique to Japan. This concentration of programs in certain places raises important questions: How much access do people outside of particular, urban regions have to facilities, coaches, and informed educators, and how do people find them to begin with? Since facilities specializing in disability sports serve both as gateways for future athletes and spaces for continued personal engagement with sports at a recreational or fitness level, it is perhaps not surprising that many in Japan have been asking these same sorts of questions. Although the access-related gaps are not in themselves new, the 2020 Games managed to bring greater attention to them and helped inspire a new push for increasing the number of trained instructors throughout Japan to facilitate the spread of sports even in locations without full-fledged disability sports centers.[126]

Looking at these athletes' stories side by side also highlights the heavy reliance on inspirational discourses, a phenomenon that has been well documented in other national contexts as well. On the one hand, such an emphasis seems almost natural, because sporting performances on the whole have a remarkable power to move people emotionally, and anyone competing at an international level is going to be an extraordinary individual. On the other hand, scholars such as Danielle Peers have argued convincingly that the feel-good inspirational narratives of overcoming so often linked to athletes with disabilities are far less innocent than they appear on their surface. They are not only deeply embedded in historical systems of oppression, power, and control, but they also serve to reconstruct the idea of overcoming as the norm or the social expectation. In this sense, any failure to overcome—or, perhaps more accurately, achieve—stems not from social barriers or lack of opportunities, but from individual weaknesses or personal failings.[127] Viewed from this standpoint, seemingly inspirational phrases like "God will not give you trials that you cannot bear" or "If you have a goal, everything can be overcome" take on a different connotation.[128] My point here is not to imply that the Japanese athletes discussed here were intentionally trying to impose a potentially oppressive viewpoint on others with disabilities, but rather to question the taken-for-granted, positive nature of these inspirational discourses. The examples provided also suggest that representations of athletes with disabilities are being produced and consumed in relation to a particular form of what I described elsewhere as a "sports star paradigm."[129] Further studies of the emerging cluster of disability sports stars in Japan may help us better understand how their representations differ from those of other sports celebrities, and why inspirational discourses remain so rooted in their stories.

Finally, comparisons of these athletes' experiences over time indicate that broader interest in and support for the Paralympics have changed dramatically since 1964. At the same time, these stories also suggest gaps in awareness of the Paralympics that raise interesting questions, especially given the aggressive marketing push surrounding the 2020 Games. The stories here clearly reveal that a number of athletes in Japan were able to take advantage of the changing environment around disability and sports to assume roles in promoting these sports and the Paralympics that would have been unimaginable for many in 1964. Of course, the impact these increased roles will have in the long term remains to be seen. On another note, the multiple biographical and autobiographical works available for the three stars active in the years since Nagano provide further support for claims that the 1998 Games marked an important turning point for disability sports in Japan. It also bears stating that the works mentioned here are a small handful of the books written about or by athletes with disabilities that have become available since the early 2000s. For anyone looking, there is no shortage of material on the Paralympics in Japan today. But therein lies a key question: How much do people look for that sort of information? How likely are people to simply know about these Games? Although the sample set is small, it is telling that none of the athletes here mentions the Paralympics as a motivation for their turn to disability sports. What does figure much more prominently in their initial exposure to sports (with the exception of Suzaki's clearly exceptional case) are events much closer to home—events at the local, regional, or national level. Although the Paralympics represent a sort of pinnacle drawing all eyes to the leader board on the international stage, the stories here suggest that the future of disability sports in Japan might be better served by focusing less on medal counts and more on the grassroots beyond the capital. But then again, perhaps the impact of Tokyo's 2020 Games will ultimately prove different.

Coda
The 2021 Problem

There are a lot of people who wonder if this isn't just a
bubble, so there is uncertainty about where to go from
here.

Asō Manabu, 2017

As I sat in the office conference room of the Japa-
nese Para-Sports Association (JPSA) in April 2017 interviewing Asō Manabu
about his work with the FESPIC Movement, his comment on the concerns
about a potential "bubble" for disability sports reminded me of my own first
visit to the office of the organization tasked with overseeing these sports in
Japan. It was June 2011, and much of Japan was still coming to terms with the
all-too recent (and in some ways ongoing) 3–11 triple disaster. Power shortages were causing offices, train stations, and public facilities throughout the
country to dim lights and turn down or shut off air conditioning. Every place
in Tokyo seemed dark and hot.

At that time, the Japan Sports Association for the Disabled (JSAD) was still
using the older version of its English-language name, and the organization's
office was located in a different, much older building on the back streets of
Tokyo. Despite following the directions on the website, I got turned around
on the way there and ended up asking a nearby taxi driver taking his break
if he recognized the address. It was only after we both puzzled over a detailed map of the neighborhood for several minutes that we realized I had
walked by the building multiple times without knowing it because of inadequate signage.

I had written in advance about my visit and my research project, so when
I arrived and knocked on the open JSAD office door, I was immediately in-

vited into a small office, packed with desks, paperwork, and people. After brief introductions, a few of us gathered in a corner of the office with a small table and some chairs that seemed to have been set aside for welcoming visitors like myself. As I spoke with the staff about my search for resources on the Paralympics, they were exceptionally helpful, providing me with countless materials, including a copy of a documentary film on the 1964 Paralympics that I never would have found otherwise. They also allowed me to borrow several official reports for a couple of days to read and copy the sections I needed for my research. I vividly remember feeling like I had stumbled into a scholar's treasure trove. I also recall asking staff members about the rumors circulating at the time that Japan was going to bid again for the Olympics and Paralympics despite the recent disasters. They predicted that Tokyo would be bidding again in 2013 and somewhat presciently noted that, given recent events, the bid would probably be framed around the idea of recovery.

Six years later, with the 2020 Games only three years away, I traveled to the offices of the JPSA for my prearranged interview with Asō. At the new office, located in a much nicer building on the main road, I arrived in a decorated entryway with a countdown clock, closed doors, and a phone for announcing my arrival. After a call and a brief wait, Asō emerged from the office and escorted me to the large conference room where we sat at a table using a couple of the room's many chairs and spoke for the next hour about his long-standing involvement with disability sports in Japan and the Asian region. After his comment about the bubble near the end of the interview, I could not help but glance around the room and realize that the space—empty but for the two of us—was only slightly smaller than the entire JSAD office had been six years before this. Although I was well aware that a lot had changed since 2011, at that moment the concerns about the current situation being a bubble seemed not at all far-fetched. And I, too, wondered what the future of disability sports was going to look like when the 2020 Games ended.

This coda explores that question, looking in particular at how some in Japan have begun grappling with what has been dubbed the "2021 problem" (2021 *mondai*). Introducing ideas from Japanese scholarship to a broader, English-speaking audience, and sharing my own observations, of course, does not give me the ability to predict the future. What I hope to offer instead are additional insights on the challenges and opportunities ahead for Japan and perhaps other countries, as people in these societies seek to assure that the impact of the Games proves as lasting and significant as possible.

One of the things that makes the current situation for disability sports in Japan all the more remarkable (bubble or not) is the fact that almost none of it existed sixty years ago. The preceding chapters have shown how Japan experienced a dramatic transformation in the realm of disability sports, all in less than a single lifetime, a point I was reminded of when speaking with 1964 Paralympian Suzaki Katsumi. After the introduction of the Paralympic Movement to Japan in 1960, the decision to host the 1964 Paralympics sparked the establishment of institutions, organizations, competitions, and patterns that laid foundations for the continued development and promotion of Japan's domestic disability sports scene. Although critically important to what we see in Japan today, these early developments were not uniformly positive, as exemplified by some of the problematic representational patterns that also took root in this period. Thanks to Tokyo's 2020 Games, Japan's embrace of the Paralympics at a relatively early stage in the movement has become a more familiar part of the broader history of the Games, but lack of access to source materials and language barriers have tended to prevent closer analyses of these early years before now.

These same challenges also hid some of Japan's significant contributions to the international movement in the years since 1964. The now defunct FESPIC Games may have largely disappeared from popular and even institutional memory, but their roots in Ōita, their more than thirty-year history, and their impact on the development of disability sports in the region and the international Paralympic Movement more generally are too important to continue to overlook. The same could be said of Ōita's famous wheelchair marathon, which for almost forty years played pivotal roles at the individual, local, national, and international levels, yet remained largely unfamiliar to those outside the sport or the city. Even within Japan, people were constantly surprised when I mentioned how long the annual race had been going on. All of this is to say that Japan's contribution to the international disability sports scene has been longer running and more significant than most people realize. While Paralympic advocates have often used Japan's perceived backwardness as a rhetorical device to promote needed change, it is worth recalling that Japan has been a leader in the movement as well.

Since they represented a turning point in multiple respects, Nagano's 1998 Winter Paralympics Games stand out as another defining moment in Japan's engagement with the Paralympic Movement at home and abroad. They not only contributed to the institutional strength of the nascent IPC but also helped reshape how the Games were organized, conceptualized, and shared within Japan, particularly in relation to changes in media coverage of the event and its athletes. Indeed, the debt that Tokyo 2020 owed to the many changes stemming from Nagano often goes unstated. Tokyo 2020 promoters clearly built on Japan's track record of contributions to the larger Paralympic Movement, as seen most clearly through the organizing committee's close involvement with international Paralympic educational activities. Organizers for Tokyo's second Paralympics also capitalized on more than fifty years' worth of trends, changes, and improvements, combining all of that with an influx of new institutional, promotional, and economic support to prepare for a Summer Paralympic Games that would be unlike any before.

All that said, it is equally important to consider the impact of Japan's historical engagement with the Paralympics beyond the realm of sports or successful sporting events. In this area, the story is less triumphant and necessarily equivocal. At several points, this study has observed how assessing the impacts of one-time or even annual events of any sort is a fraught prospect given the limitations of available resources beyond the anecdotal level. Nevertheless, it is possible to see several ways in which the Paralympics and sports for those with disabilities were integral elements of shifting approaches to or understandings of disability in Japan since the 1960s. Early on, the Games were inextricably linked to the promotion of new rehabilitation techniques and methods, and the rehabilitative benefits of sports continued to be seen as primary well into the 1990s, even as the views of athletes and some event organizers began to reorient toward competition before that time. As problematic as this rehabilitative emphasis is now seen to be—for multiple, understandable reasons—it is also important to acknowledge how events like the FESPIC Games and the Ōita International Wheelchair Marathon coupled that approach with the goal of promoting broad-based accessibility to sports. These events intentionally opened the door to a wide range of individuals who might not otherwise have had the opportunity to participate in sports at all.

This earlier approach to broader accessibility stands in marked contrast to the emphasis in later years, particularly in Nagano's Games. Influenced by the push toward elite competition coming from the IPC and domestic athletes alike, the focus on rehabilitation was dropped; the discourses surrounding the 1998 Paralympics centered on notions of equality and accessibility in keeping with international campaigns and domestic shifts in Japan that were pushing the country toward a rights-based understanding of disability. Here I would note that in contrast to FESPIC, the Paralympics were trending toward exclusivity rather than open access. In the process, they were also becoming ever more reliant on inspirational potential as the means to promote greater interest in and opportunities for people with disabilities to pursue sports. Accessibility in Nagano was increasingly linked with the creation of barrier-free environments, generating significant discussion—if not always satisfactory outcomes—about how Japan might better meet the needs of its aging population, as well as those with impairments. Many of the social-impact elements in Nagano were even more evident in the organizational efforts for Tokyo

2020, in no small part because they were built into the process from the earliest phases. Even if limitations and shortcomings were already apparent before the Games, the increased urgency of Japan's demographic situation and the outsized influence of Tokyo as the national capital, major media hub, and largest metropolitan area in Japan all promised an impact in terms of accessibility and social awareness well beyond anything Nagano could have achieved.

Taking into account this history of changes and developments, it is more than fair to say that the Paralympic Movement has had an important impact—uneven though it may be—on Japanese society beyond the realm of sports. I would, however, add a caveat. In popular parlance, it is not unusual to encounter references to the Paralympics "transforming" people, cities, or even societies, and to some extent, this notion makes sense—with countless stories and even my own work seemingly lending support to the idea. At the same time, such phrasings seem to obscure a key element necessary to understanding how and why the Paralympics have the influence they do: the people. To put it another way, the Paralympics in and of themselves do not transform or change anything; rather, people use the Paralympics to pursue and implement change. The impacts that have resulted from Japan's sixty-year history of engagement with the Paralympics have been brought about not through some mystical transformative power inherent to the Games, but because people like Nakamura Yutaka refused to believe that "no" was the only answer when he proposed a new approach. Transformation has come from athletes discovering a passion and turning it into their lifework. It has come from volunteer translators and racers returning year after year to make Ōita's marathon feel like a home course, or from organizational leaders who worked with skeletal, often volunteer, staffing and inadequate offices for most of the past sixty years, while still managing to hold regular competitions or even launch new ones. Changes have come from athletes and coaches pushing for equal access to facilities and resources or from volunteers and activists carrying out usability or accessibility checks and publicizing their results. Important developments have come from journalists questioning their own approach to covering athletes with disabilities and sometimes even from politicians and government bureaucrats who use such events to push forward reforms or projects. In short, the Paralympics and disability sports have had an impact in Japan because people in Japan have made them matter. This was as much the case in 1960 as it is today, a point that brings us back to the future and the challenge of making the 2020 Games matter in the long run, too.

In recent years, legacy has become a critical question for both the Olympics and Paralympics, and Japan's 2020 Games were no exception.[1] Thanks to his historical research, ongoing survey work, and a nonacademic writing style, leading disability sports scholar Fujita Motoaki has laid out a particularly clear and astute articulation of the 2021 problem in his recent book, *How to Enjoy the Paralympics* (Pararinpikku no tanoshimikata). In line with Asō's concerns shared at the beginning of this coda, Fujita cites economic factors as one of the largest hurdles ahead for the disability sports environment in Japan. After outlining the dramatic increases in governmental funding for disability sports since 2014 (which amounted to a 100 percent increase from 2014 to 2016 when his book was published), Fujita explains that much of this funding will simply disappear after 2020. He is certainly well aware that comparatively high levels of government spending in connection with Nagano's Games were more or less zeroed out afterward, a precedent that does not bode well for Tokyo 2020. Fujita also highlights the significant additional support currently being provided by the Nippon Foundation, as manifested through its establishment of the Paralympic Support Center. This financial support, too, he explains, is officially slated to end in 2021.[2] According to Kazuo Ogura, another scholar and head of the Paralympic Support Center who has written on the question of legacy for 2020, the lost revenue is projected to be offset by increased private sector sponsorship, but at this point it seems unclear why private sector businesses will be motivated to continue contributing after the Games have concluded.[3]

From Fujita's perspective, the likely loss of significant governmental funds and of the Nippon Foundation's support will create two additional challenges: maintaining institutional structures and facilitating the recruitment and training of athletes. In the lead-up to the Games, the Paralympic Support Center provided several national, sports-specific organizations with office space and institutional support that were previously unavailable. Without Nippon Foundation funds, that arrangement will become untenable, potentially forcing these organizations to revert to earlier, essentially volunteer-based patterns. Although Fujita is hopeful that it will be possible to maintain the Center beyond 2020, he acknowledges that this may not be possible. In that case, he contends that these organizations will have to streamline their efforts and reduce costs as much as possible, while also seeking out additional support from the private sector. The goal in the long term—with such efforts supposedly already underway—is for each sports organization to become self-sustaining.[4] The problem here, of course, is that each of these organizations will be competing against each other for an increasingly smaller slice of the metaphorical pie. In other words, the future situation here is far from ideal if the Paralympic Support Center closes as planned.

Additionally, much of the present governmental funding and significant portions of the support coming from the Nippon Foundation were dedicated to the recruitment and training of potential athletes for the 2020 Games. As Fujita observes, the loss of these funds will make it impossible to continue with approaches that relied on cost-intensive, large-scale events used to raise awareness, find new athletes, and then get them into training as quickly as possible. Fujita's worry is that failure to come up with new approaches will lead Japan down the same path as other former hosts that saw declining sports participation rates after their Games.[5]

To continue recruiting new talent, Fujita proposes a solution very much in keeping with his role as an educator. Looking forward, he sees the key to success as reaching potential athletes early on at the grassroots levels, particularly through schools or rehabilitation facilities. He argues for incorporating more training on disability sports into required curriculums for school PE instructors, nurses, doctors, and physical or occupational therapists. Such training would provide these people with greater familiarity with these sports and make them aware of the opportunities available to people with a variety of impairments with whom they might interact. Perhaps more importantly, this approach would address a current gap in exposure and access to sports for individuals with disabilities who do not attend specialized schools or do not have access to more specialized rehabilitation centers. With additional training, a teacher or therapist encountering students or individuals with some form of impairment would not only feel more comfortable integrating them into athletic activities on the spot but would also be able to connect them to local and national sports organizations to pursue their interests further and continue developing their skills.[6] With calls for 30,000 trained disability sports specialists (who in most cases are volunteers) nationwide by 2020, the JPSA is clearly thinking along similar lines, but the comprehensiveness and ambitious scope of Fujita's proposal make it unique.[7] Those same factors potentially make it more difficult to achieve, because it would require several programs at all levels of the training process to rework standards and incorporate new materials and instructors. As Fujita notes, in perhaps a bit of an understatement, "Efforts to change such a situation will be necessary."[8] Although I generally agree with Fujita about the importance of pursuing this grassroots approach, it needs to be paired with efforts to assure access to both equipment and existing sports facilities throughout Japan. If sports wheelchairs are not available or not allowed in some local gyms—as widely reported when the Nippon Foundation Para Arena opened in Tokyo in 2018—then even having a conscientious and well-informed gym teacher or physical therapist might not be enough.[9]

In discussing legacies of the 2020 Paralympics beyond the realm of sports, Fujita points to barrier-free urban environments and changing attitudes as potential long-term benefits. He notes that increasing media coverage and awareness-raising programs in schools and communities all over Japan are likely to have a positive effect on people's perception of disability sports and those with disabilities more generally.[10] Given his own focus on the disability sports themselves, it is understandable that Fujita does not offer more thorough discussions on the need to assure that barrier-free campaigns and changed attitudes do not end with the Paralympics. But these issues, too, are a key piece of the 2021 problem. The history outlined in the preceding chapters provides plenty of warnings about the risks of assuming that these legacies are somehow natural or permanent outcomes of hosting the Games. Media bubbles pop, funds dry up, popular enthusiasms wane, and even entire movements can fade from memory. Although it is clear that many in Japan are seizing the opportunity of Tokyo's second Paralympics to push for change, making those changes happen and making them stick beyond 2020 are both going to take a lot of work. But Japan's history of engagement with the Paralympic Movement also shows us that people in Japan are up for the challenge.

NOTES

Introduction

1. See for instance, the IPC Media Centre page, "Tokyo Governor: Paralympics the Priority for 2020" Media Centre for Official Website of the Paralympic Movement, August 7, 2017, https://www.paralympic.org/news/tokyo-governor-paralympics-priority-2020.

2. *Kyodo News*, "Koike Says 2020 Paralympics Will Determine Aging Tokyo's Fate," August 3, 2017, https://english.kyodonews.net/news/2017/08/de9f7f426aba-koike-says-2020-paralympics-will-determine-aging-tokyos-fate.html.

3. For English-language overviews of this period and the long-term impacts of these beliefs, see Karen Nakamura 2006, 31–36; and Stevens 2013, 26–28.

4. On medieval and early modern periods, see Karen Nakamura 2006, 36–38; on blind musicians in Tokugawa, see Tan 2019. Tan has a forthcoming book on the history of blindness in Japan.

5. Karen Nakamura 2006, 39–40.

6. On *misemono*, see Markus 1985.

7. On early schools for deaf and blind children, see Karen Nakamura 2006, 40–43; on other schools and their PE programs, see Fujita 2013, 28–34.

8. On pre–World War II approaches to disability, especially in relation to veterans, see Pennington 2015, 20–54.

9. Pennington 2015, especially 93–194.

10. For overviews of postwar changes in relation to wounded veterans, see Pennington 2015, 195–223. Mark Bookman has a forthcoming dissertation that will address this period with particular attention to accessibility and inclusivity in Japan; see also Bookman 2018.

11. For an English-language overview on disability rights activism in Japan, see Stevens 2013, 31–36; for more on early movements, see Hayashi and Okuhira 2001.

12. On activism through the late 1990s, see Hayashi and Okuhira 2001, 863–68. On disability law, activism, and intersections with international movements in Japan, see Heyer 2015, 123–66 and 188–202; for an English summary of Japan's legal changes in the last decade, see Shirasawa Mayumi, "The Long Road to Disability Rights in Japan," *Nippon.com*, October 2, 2014, https://www.nippon.com/en/currents/d00133/the-long-road-to-disability-rights-in-japan.html.

13. On these demographic trends, see Matanle 2017.

14. In addition to the English-language works cited earlier, see Karen Nakamura 2013 and Kayama and Haight 2014. For examples on sports in Japan, see Guttmann and Thompson 2001; Frost 2010; Kietlinski 2011; Miller 2013; and Kelly 2019.

15. In addition to official reports, English-language materials include Chiang 2010a, which has limited availability. Kazuo Ogura has written several articles in English, but most are in a specialized Japanese journal that is little known outside Japan; see Ogura 2015a, 2015b, 2018.

16. Fujita Motoaki's work cited earlier offers the most comprehensive sociological study of disability sports in Japanese. On wheelchair marathons, see Nakamura and Ogata 2004; on wheelchair basketball, see Watari 2012; for works targeting a more general audience, see Fujita 2016; Itō 2012; Nakamura Tarō 2002; Takahashi Akira 2004; and Tsuchida 2010.

17. Scholarship on sports mega-events is abundant, although much of this literature overlooks the Paralympics; see, for example, Andranovich, Burbank, and Heying 2001; and Dickson, Benson, and Blackman 2011. Two edited volumes on the Paralympics include essays on their legacies and impacts; many are cited in the following chapters. See Darcy, Frawley, and Adair 2017; and Brittain and Beacom 2018.

18. Misener 2015.

19. Peers 2015.

20. Purdue and Howe 2012. My work complements and has also been informed by Braye, Dixon, and Gibbons 2013; Gilbert and Schantz 2008; and Howe 2008. My analyses of representations of athletes have drawn insights from Bundon and Clarke 2015; Jackson, Hodges, Molesworth, and Scullion 2015; Howe and Parker 2012; Le Clair 2011.

21. Much of the scholarship on disability sports addresses contemporary events and athletes. Studies of Paralympic history in English are limited to works that did not have access to Japanese-language source materials. See Bailey 2008 and Brittain 2010, 2014.

1. Tokyo's Other Games

1. NYD 1988, 66.

2. The Tokyo Games are officially counted as the second Paralympics after those in Rome, but Japan was the third country to host the International Stoke Mandeville Games.

3. When I began research for this project in 2009, studies of the Paralympics in Japan, even in Japanese, were extremely limited. The situation has changed dramatically: there are now several academic and popular works in Japanese addressing the Games' history. For example, Japan's national television network NHK aired a historical drama during the summer of 2018 that focused on the life of Nakamura Yutaka, whose work promoting the Paralympic Movement in Japan is detailed in several chapters.

4. Before the publication of my articles that are incorporated into this chapter, the most detailed account in English was Bailey 2008, 26–30. More recent English works include Brittain 2012, 65–81; and the English translation of Ogura Kazuo's Japanese-language work (2015a).

5. Among the earliest academic studies on the history of the 1964 Games in Japanese is Araragi 2002b. More recent works include Ogoura 2015. Fujita Motoaki, a leading scholar on disability sports in Japan, has published scholarly and popular works that focus mostly on contemporary issues but provide historical context (2013, 2016).

6. NHK Kōsei Bunka Jigyōdan 1965.

7. Thomas and Smith 2009; Tynedal and Wolbring 2013.

8. Bruce 2014; Hargreaves and Hardin 2009; and Thomas and Smith 2009, 135–52.

9. "The Thirteenth International Stoke Mandeville Games" 1964.

10. The reference was linked to the "father" of the modern Olympics, Pierre De Coubertin. See Bailey 2008, 24.

11. Bailey 2008, 15–18.

12. Bailey 2008, 18–20; see also Brittain 2010, 8–11.

13. Bailey 2008, 18.

14. Bailey 2008, 25.

15. The website is regularly updated and standardized; see earlier description on the archived IPC website: International Paralympic Committee 2012, "Tokyo 1964," archived, official website of the Paralympic Movement, January 19, 2012, https://web .archive.org/web/20120119094314/http://www.paralympic.org/Paralympic _Games/Past_Games/Tokyo_1964/index.html.

16. Bailey 2008, 27.

17. International Paralympic Committee, 2012, "Tokyo 1964."

18. On Watanabe's background, see NSSSK 1985, 11; see also KSSSTUI 1965a, 26.

19. Bailey 2008, 27. For Watanabe's account of her interaction with Guttmann, see Watanabe Hanako 1965, 4.

20. Nakamura Yutaka 1975, 11; Watanabe Hanako 1965, 4.

21. Fujita 2013, 34–35; 2016, 12–13.

22. NSSSK 1985, 12; NYD 1988, 81.

23. NSSSK 1985, 18; on interactions with these specialists, see Masuda 1965, 8.

24. NSSSK 1985, 28; see also Masuda 1965, 9. To date, I have found no references to this event in English. A German-language account of the Games appears to exist, but with limited availability: *Festschrift: Internationales Versehrten-Sportfest Linz 1963* 1963.

25. Brittain 2014, 74.

26. NSSSK 1985, 22. Many of the following details are also reported in KSSSTUI 1965a.

27. NSSSK 1985, 12.

28. NSSSK 1985, 22.

29. NSSSK 1985, 22. For a similar account of this meeting that also mentions Dazai's statement, see Nihon Shōi Gunjinkai 1967, 320.

30. NSSSK 1985, 22.

31. Nihon Shōi Gunjinkai 1967, 320.

32. NSSSK 1985, 22.

33. NSSSK 1985, 22–23 and 443.

34. NSSSK 1985, 23; for names of the founding members of the committee, see KSSSTUI 1965a, 26–27.

35. On Ujiie's role, see Masuda 1965, 8. Terada refers to the impact of his personal interactions with Nakamura in NSSSK 1985, 26.

36. Formed in 1917 by several business clubs in the United States, the Lions Clubs became an international organization in 1920, with the first Japanese club formed in 1952. Lions Clubs International focuses on humanitarian service projects with special commitments to youth programs and addressing visual impairment. In 1928, the Osaka Asahi Shimbun Newspaper Company established the Asahi Shimbun Social Welfare Organization to address the ongoing needs of victims of the 1923 Kantō earthquake. The organization provides disaster relief, as well as various forms of assistance for the

disabled, the elderly, and children. Formed in 1960 by the national radio and television network NHK to mark the thirty-fifth anniversary of NHK's first broadcast, the NHK Public Welfare Organization adopted a similar mission emphasizing direct relief and social welfare programs targeting the disabled and children. Leaders of the NHK Public Welfare Organization may have seen the Tokyo Paralympics as a way to establish a public role for this relatively new organization.

37. NYD 1988, 81–82.

38. *Yomiuri shimbun*, "Shintai Shōgaisha no kokusai kyōgi: Pararinpikku," July 21, 1961, p. 9. The author is unclear, but the article uses photos and quotations from Watanabe Hanako.

39. On Kasai's postwar role, see Pennington 2015, 200; and Takemae 2003, 418.

40. NSSSK 1985, 12; Kasai 1964c, 17.

41. NSSSK 1985,12–13.

42. For one example in the press, see *Mainichi shimbun*, "Kōtaishi gofusai to te awase," August 9, 1962, evening edition, p. 7.

43. NSSSK 1985, 13.

44. Araragi 2002b, 16 and 18.

45. NSSSK 1985, 26.

46. Tagsold 2009.

47. NSSSK 1985, 13–16. For a photograph of the Ministry's authorization document, see Tōkyō-to Edo Tōkyō Hakubutsukan 2014, 170.

48. NSSSK 1985, 27–28.

49. NSSSK 1985, 29–31.

50. NSSSK 1985, 27.

51. KSSSTUI 1965a, 42 and 65–66.

52. NSSSK 1985, 27 and 30. For a picture of one of the donation boxes, see Tōkyō-to Edo Tōkyō Hakubutsukan 2014, 170. Specific figures vary for the total amount donated.

53. Bailey 2008, 27.

54. NSSSK 1985, 28.

55. NSSSK 1985, 445.

56. NSSSK 1985, 16–20 and 444.

57. NSSSK 1985, 29.

58. NSSSK 1985, 36–42.

59. NSSSK 1985, 446.

60. NSSSK 1985, 42–43.

61. NSSSK 1985, 32.

62. NSSSK 1985, 43.

63. KSSSTUI 1965a, 26–27.

64. NYD 1988, 455–56.

65. NYD 1988, 47.

66. NYD 1988, 49.

67. NYD 1988, 52; see also Nakamura Yutaka 1975, 12–18.

68. NYD 1988, 66; see also Nakamura Yutaka 1975, 18–19.

69. NYD 1988, 66.

70. NYD 1988, 66.

71. Nakamura Yutaka 1975, 19.

72. Nakamura Yutaka 1975, 19.

73. Terada Muneyoshi's recollections of this interaction are discussed in NSSSK 1985, 26.

74. NSSSK 1985, 26. Like much else associated with these Games, the specific timing of this interaction with Nakamura is unclear. Terada indicated that it occurred "around May 1962." Nakamura's biography simply quotes Terada's recollections, providing no clarification.

75. NYD 1988, 70–71.

76. NYD 1988, 71–72.

77. NYD 1988, 83.

78. NYD 1988, 84.

79. KSSSTUI 1965a, 80–84. Sources vary on the number of participants. Numbers here reflect those from the official report.

80. KSSSTUI 1965a, 84–87.

81. KSSSTUI 1965a, 87.

82. KSSSTUI 1965a, 128.

83. On decisions of later potential hosts, see Brittain 2010, 12.

84. NSSSK 1985, 29–30. On references to original plans to host a unified event, see Kasai 1964b, 7.

85. Brittain 2010, 12.

86. KSSSTUI 1965a, 89.

87. NSSSK 1985, 66–68.

88. For more on Taiyō no Ie and Nakamura's role in promoting disability sports see the following two chapters.

89. These observations are based on my analyses of Paralympic coverage in several national newspapers, including *Asahi shimbun*, *Mainichi shimbun*, *Yomiuri shimbun*, and *Nihon keizai shimbun*, as well as several national and regional sports papers: *Hōchi shimbun*, *Nikkan supōtsu*, *Chūnichi supōtsu* (Tokyo), *Sankei supōtsu* (Osaka), and *Chūnichi supōtsu* (Osaka). For an in-depth analysis of mass media see chapter 4.

90. See Kasai's welcome to participants in "The Thirteenth International Stoke Mandeville Games" 1964. For another example, see NHK Kōsei Bunka Jigyōdan 1965.

91. Thomas and Smith 2009, 135–52.

92. KSSSTUI 1965a, 169–73.

93. KSSSTUI 1965a, 169.

94. KSSSTUI 1963, 5.

95. KSSSTUI 1963, 11.

96. Kōhō Bukai 1964, 13–14.

97. Kōhō Bukai 1964, 12.

98. Kōhō Bukai 1964, 12.

99. KSSSTUI 1964, leaflet, no pages.

100. KSSSTUI 1964.

101. For examples of such critiques, see Brittain 2010, 92–96.

102. KSSSTUI 1965b.

103. KSSSTUI 1965b, 53.

104. KSSSTUI 1965a, 204–10.

105. KSSSTUI 1965a, 27.

106. KSSSTUI 1965a, 40–41.

107. Kōhō Bukai 1964, 11–14.

108. NHK Kōsei Bunka Jigyōdan 1965.

109. "The Thirteenth International Stoke Mandeville Games" 1964.

110. KSSSTUI 1965a, 73–79.

111. The English-language program includes official comments from Guttmann and Kasai; slightly different Japanese versions of these speeches are provided in the official report: "The Thirteenth International Stoke Mandeville Games" 1964; and KSSSTUI 1965a, 81–83.

112. KSSSTUI 1965a, 83–84.

113. Kasai 1964c, 17.

114. Kasai 1964a, 35.

115. KSSSTUI 1965a, 10–11.

116. KSSSTUI 1965a, 28–37.

117. Watanabe Hanako 1964a, 4.

118. Kōhō Bukai 1964, preface.

119. Kōhō Bukai 1964, 16.

120. Nakamura published widely on various aspects of rehabilitation and sports, including two articles specifically related to the Paralympics that were published in specialized medical journals: Nakamura Yutaka 1964, 1965.

121. NHK Kōsei Bunka Jigyōdan 1965. According to official reports, there were several documentaries that were produced in connection with the 1964 Paralympics. Despite my best efforts to locate the others during my research, I was able to access only this NHK-affiliated film; the others were presumed lost. However, in 2019, one of these films originally produced in 1965 by the now defunct Daiei Film Company was rediscovered and re-released by Kadokawa Pictures, which acquired Daiei's assets in the early 2000s. Due to the late and limited re-release, I was unable to view the film in time to incorporate an analysis in this book. The documentary is titled *Tokyo Paralympics: Festival of Love and Glory* (*Tōkyō Pararinpikku: ai to eikō no saiten*); see Watanabe Kimio 1965.

122. NHK Kōsei Bunka Jigyōdan 1965.

123. Nakamura Yutaka 1975, 19.

124. The specific Japanese word is *akarui*, which appears in several different forms. The word itself is polysemic and has a complex history of usage tied to both wartime and postwar Japan. It also has connotations of cheerful and clean. In the sources referenced here, the word is often explicitly juxtaposed with *kurai*, which can mean dark, dull, gloomy, sorrowful, or bitter. Despite all of these potential variations, I translated *akarui* consistently as "bright" to highlight its repeated usage across a variety of texts.

125. Nakamura Yutaka 1975, 24.

126. Watanabe Hanako 1964a, 4. Watanabe raised similar concerns in one of her earliest essays on the Paralympics, a *Yomiuri* newspaper article published in summer 1961: Watanabe Hanako, "Toki no me: Pararinpikku," *Yomiuri shimbun*, July 8, 1961, p. 7.

127. Watanabe Hanako 1964b, 173–74.

128. KSSSTUI 1965a, 204–207.

129. Kasai 1964a, 34.

130. Kasai 1964c, 18.

131. Kasai 1964c, 18–19.

132. KSSSTUI 1965a, 79. Details about this meeting and the crown prince's comments are at the end of the section denoting the imperial family's involvement.

133. NHK Kōsei Bunka Jigyōdan 1965.

134. Frost 2010.

135. Nakamura Yutaka 1965, 436.

136. See Terada 1965, 36–38.

137. "Kokusai Shintai Shōgaisha Supōtsu Taikai no kaisai ni tsuite" 1964.

138. For Guttmann's comments, see Bailey 2008, 27; for Ikeda's use of the phrase, see NSSSK 1985, 26.

139. Tagsold 2009.

140. In his *Weekly Asahi* interview, Kasai (1964a, 36) explicitly references the Japanese flag flying at the Paralympics.

141. For one example, see Kasai's official welcome in KSSSTUI 1965a, 81–82. The leaflet distributed during the Games (KSSSTUI 1964) also reflects this idea.

2. Lost Games

1. Park 2010, 126.

2. On plans to digitize by 2009, see Asō 2010, 20. Few archives or libraries maintain copies of materials related to FESPIC; the best collection is in a storage closet at the Taiyō no Ie offices in Beppu, Ōita, Japan, but they are uncataloged. Even people working in those offices did not know what was in this collection.

3. Much of the writing on the FESPIC Movement is in the form of retrospectives after its dissolution; in English, this includes the difficult-to-find work, Chiang 2010a. A recent English-language volume on the Paralympics (Brittain and Beacom 2018) includes no references to FESPIC, even though several essays address countries where the FESPIC Games were held. In Japanese, see the special issue of the JSAD monthly magazine commemorating the end of FESPIC (JSAD 2006). For a brief overview in Japanese prepared for a broader audience, see Nakamura Tarō 2002, 174–80. Other academic work is limited mostly to brief Japanese articles on specific Games, often written by individuals connected to the events. Most of these works are cited later in the chapter.

4. APC 2019, Asian Paralympic Committee, 2019, http://www.asianparalympic .org/. One of the only non-Games-related search results was the APC's response to the passing of former FESPIC president Hatada Kazuo, but it, too, offered no explanation of FESPIC's relationship with the APC.

5. For the revised constitution, see APC 2018, "Constitution," Asian Paralympic Committee, November 2018, http://www.asianparalympic.org/constitution. For the previous constitution, see archived version: APC 2011, "APC Handbook," Asian Paralympic Committee, June 2011, http://web.archive.org/web/20110725021911 /http://www.asianparalympic.org/apc/apc/apc_handbook.asp.

6. APC 2019, "Our History," Asian Paralympic Committee, 2019, http://www .asianparalympic.org/history. Earlier archived versions of the website included more references to FESPIC and the merger, but all such references appear to have been excised from later versions; see APC 2009, "About APC," Asian Paralympic Committee, August 2009, http://web.archive.org/web/20090824185004/http://www .asianparalympic.org/apc/apc/apc_aboutapc.asp

7. Nakamura Yutaka 1975, 196–97.

8. D1KK 1975, 15.

9. Nakagawa 1975, 51.

10. Nakamura Yutaka 1975, 197. Nakamura cites Kasai's hesitance in D1KK 1975, 15.

11. Kasai quoted in NYD 1988, 271.

12. Nakamura Yutaka 1975, 196.

13. See Nakamura's letter to Ludwig Guttmann, reproduced in Chiang 2010a, 184–85. For more on Beppu's recognition by the ministry, see chapter 3.

14. Nakamura Yutaka 1975, 198. Such claims overlook the fact that technically the Olympics and Paralympics are not national but are city based. Eventually the FESPIC Games became "national" events in several respects, particularly outside Japan.

15. Specific dates for these early planning stages are unclear, and sources occasionally conflict; details here reflect my best efforts to reconstruct timelines with the available materials. On efforts to reach out to Australia, see Nakamura Yutaka 1975, 197; for Nakamura's letter, see Chiang 2010a, 184–85.

16. Guttmann's response is reproduced in Chiang 2010a, 186–87.

17. Details from this early period come from Nakamura Yutaka 1975, 196–202; D1KK 1975, 15–16 and 24–26; and NYD 1988, 270–75 and 281–90. On FESPIC being Ōita's first international event, see Nakamura Yutaka 1975, 201.

18. On invitees, see D1KK 1975, 34.

19. Nakamura Yutaka 1975, 199.

20. Nakamura Yutaka 1975, 200–201.

21. See his comments on deciding to push for these Games in Nakamura Yutaka 1975, 196–98.

22. For a copy of the FESPIC constitution see D1KK 1975, 29–32; it is also reproduced in Chiang 2010a, 178–83.

23. Nakamura Yutaka 1975, 200.

24. Ujiie 1975, 21. It seems likely that Ujiie was referring to original plans developed during the early meetings with Nakamura; on the final structure being in place by the time the constitution was approved in October 1974, see Hatada 2010a, 9.

25. Nakamura Yutaka 1975, 197; and D1KK 1975, 15.

26. Nakamura Yutaka 1975, 206.

27. Hatada 2010a, 9; Grant 2010, 26.

28. NYD 1988, 294. This became one of his most famous quotes, though it is worth noting that the beach reference here conveys not luxury, but simplicity and perhaps poverty.

29. Fujiwara 2006, 10. Fujiwara was commenting in particular on the second Games, but many of his comments and critiques were applicable to the first four FESPIC Games.

30. Grant 2006, 9.

31. NYD 1988, 289; Nakamura mentions this incident briefly in D1KK 1975, 15–16.

32. D1KK 1975, 15–16.

33. Nakamura Yutaka 1975, 199.

34. D1KK 1975, 16; Nakamura's biography offers a slightly different version of the story, noting that Burmese athletes were waiting at the airport but had not been granted permission to travel: NYD 1988, 295. There is also confusion about which country delegation was delayed.

35. D1KK 1975, 16.

36. Details on the delegations, including which athletes might have been first-time participants, are sparse. These details are from D1KK 1975, 7; for verification of some numbers, see also Ujiie 1975, 17.

37. NYD 1988, 291.

38. On the opening ceremony see NYD 1988, 290–91; and Ujiie 1975, 19–20.

39. Nakamura Yutaka 1975, 10.

40. Yoshinaga was one of several athletes featured in the Official Report: see D1KK 1975, 17–19. Yoshinaga (2006, 13) is also featured in the special JSAD magazine on FES-PIC. On the presence of the crown prince, see D1KK 1975, 13–14; Grant 2010, 26.

41. Hatada 2010b, 37–38.

42. Takahashi Hiroshi 2006, 14.

43. Fujiwara Shinichirō had recently taken a job at the Osaka Sports Center for the Disabled, and he described the performance level of sports in these early Games as "*hidoi*," or terrible; see Fujiwara 2006, 10.

44. Nakamura Yutaka (1975, 207) described her as "mascot-like." Other observations are based on my analysis of local press coverage of the event.

45. On results, see D1KK 1975, 12; for Nakamura's response to the basketball game and a full list of the national medal tables, see Nakamura Yutaka 1975, 206–09.

46. Hatada 2010b, 38.

47. Nakamura Yutaka 1975, 210. I have not found the English-language version of the comment.

48. Details here are from NYD 1988, 279, 295, and 302. Unfortunately, soon after his arrival Mr. Slamat became ill, was hospitalized, and later died.

49. My surveys of *FESPIC*, the movement's newsletter produced out of Taiyō no Ie from 1975 to 2006, reveal that this newsletter was distributed widely throughout the region and tended to feature regular stories on the company and its activities for those with disabilities. It frequently printed letters from abroad with questions or praise.

50. Reports only provide overviews of costs and income: D1KK 1975, 58.

51. D1KK 1975, 52–53.

52. On room rates, see Nakamura Yutaka 1975, 201. On modifications, see Hatada 2010b, 36. It is unclear whether the expenses of modifications were paid by the hotel, but based on an article in the local paper *Ōita gōdō shimbun*, it appears that the hotel did cover significant portions of the costs: *Ōita gōdō shimbun*, "Fesupikku e no shōtai: chū," May 25, 1975, p. 9.

53. D1KK 1975, 52.

54. *Ōita gōdō shimbun*, "FESUPIKKU senshu dan no 'ashi,'" May 21, 1975, p. 11.

55. *Ōita gōdō shimbun*, "FESUPIKKU he no zen'i no rin," May 27, 1975, p. 11.

56. See D1KK 1975, 55–57; specific goods or services are not described.

57. D1KK 1975, 58.

58. NYD 1988, 288; Nakamura Yutaka 1975, 199–201. Setagaya Boroichi is several hundred years old and has been designated as one of Tokyo's cultural assets. Sources are unclear and sometimes conflict on fundraising and other figures. See also D1KK 1975, 58. Details on the forty-five Ōita businesses contributing to the group appear in *Ōita gōdō shimbun*, "FESUPIKKU ni kikin," May 30, 1975, p. 4.

59. NYD 1988, 302; see also Hatada 2010b, 41–42.

60. On changes in the fund, see in particular, "FRF to be Enlarged" 1978, 1.

61. I was unable to gain access to an official report from the second Games. Details here drawn primarily from Dunstan 2010. Additional information was available in Nakagawa 1978, 2006; Nakamura Yutaka 1978; and "2nd FESPIC Games Ended in Success" 1978. Figures and information on sports from Chiang 2010a, 144 and 146–47; and "2nd Parramatta" 2006.

62. Like the second Games, records for Hong Kong are lacking. Details here are drawn primarily from Chiang 2010b. Additional information is available in Hatada 2010b, 42–43; "Third FESPIC Games in Hong Kong" 1983; and Yamazaki 2006. Figures and information on sports from Chiang 2010a, 144 and 146–47; and "3rd Hong Kong" 2006.

63. Without better records, it is difficult to determine the exact date when Fang took over.

64. Chiang 2010b, 62.

65. The records for these Games, too are limited. General information is drawn from Bourke 2010; Hatada 2010b, 43–45. For information on plans, see Manurung 1985, 1986. Figures and information on sports are from Chiang 2010a, 144 and 146–47; and "4th Surakarta" 2006.

66. Hatada 2010b, 43–45. For a summary of these tours soon after they were held, one that was clearly trying to put a positive spin on a bad situation, see Nojiri 1985, 4.

67. Bourke 2010, 82. Several of these difficulties were detailed in Japanese accounts of the Games, see Ibusuki 1987; Takano 1986; and Anzai 2006. The *FESPIC* newsletter gathered and published several critiques of the fourth Games in its 1987 issue; see "Impressions of the 4th FESPIC" 1987. An editorial, apparently speaking for the FESPIC Executive Committee, served as a gentle rebuttal to such comments, reminding everyone of the goals of FESPIC: "Editorial" 1987.

68. Announcements about Kobe's plan to host were included in the same 1987 issue of *FESPIC* that also had all the critiques of the fourth Games, and the Kobe Games received extensive coverage in the next four issues as well. Yotsutani Natsuko—who as of this writing is a manager with Taiyō no Ie, had served as Nakamura's assistant and was involved in organizational efforts for Kobe's FESPIC Games—told me that Kobe's desire to host saved or rescued FESPIC, especially after Surakarta (in discussion with author, Taiyō no Ie, Beppu, Japan. July 14, 2017).

69. 1989NFKT 1990, 21–22.

70. 1989NFKT 1990, 23–24.

71. For background information on the Village of Happiness, see its English-language website, Kōbe Shimin Fukushi Shinkō Kyōkai 2009, Village of Happiness KOBE, 2009, http://www.shiawasenomura.org/english/village_of_appiness_kobe .html.

72. 1989NFKT 1990, 125.

73. 1989NFKT 1990, 33 and 125.

74. 1989NFKT 1990, 17.

75. On the variety of events, see 1989NFKT 1990, 347–54. For the new budget line, see 1989NFKT 1990, 345.

76. 1989NFKT 1990, 17 and 31.

77. For preparations for all official sports, see 1989NFKT 1990, 30 and 78–92. On the addition of soccer in Japan, see 1989NFKT 1990, 86; and Kondō Kazuo 2006, 22.

78. On demonstration sports, see 1989NFKT 1990, 294–95. On twin basketball, see "About Twin basketball" Japan Wheelchair Twin Basketball Federation, March 15, 2019, http://www.twinbasket.com/whatis/.

79. For numeric overviews and breakdown of participants by country, see 1989NFKT 1990, 16–18.

80. The following details on recruitment of participants are drawn from 1989NFKT 1990, 38–42.

81. On funding-related issues, see 1989NFKT 1990, 33–34, 125–28, and 345–46.

82. 1989NFKT 1990, 43–45.

83. For comparisons of sports at the different events, see Chiang 2010a, 146–47.

84. On volunteers, see 1989NFKT 1990, 160–67 and 312–14. On nongovernmental support, see 1989NFKT 1990, 126–28 and 345–46; sponsor and donor lists are in 1989NFKT 1990, 445–50.

85. On lodging arrangements, see 1989NFKT 1990, 93–98 and 315–21; see also an article by one of the organizers in a city planning journal: Matsuo 1989, 136–37.

86. 1989NFKT 1990, 112–15 and 336–40; and Matsuo 1989, 137.

87. 1989NFKT 1990, 125–26.

88. 1989NFKT 1990, 345–46.

89. 1989NFKT 1990, 32.

90. On the various promotional contests and materials, see 1989NFKT 1990, 129–37.

91. Ōkura 1976.

92. On these marketing aspects, see especially 1989NFKT 1990, 126–28.

93. On the organizing committee itself, 1989NFKT 1990, 25–27; lists of committees, assignments, and members are in 1989NFKT 1990, 431–42; for other figures, see 1989NFKT 1990, 16–18.

94. 1989NFKT 1990, 488.

95. 1989NFKT 1990, 29–30. These international groups included the ISOD, IBSA, CPISRA, ISMGF, and International Federations for badminton and soccer. On these organizations, see Brittain 2010, 37–38.

96. Brittain 2010, 39–40.

97. 1989NFKT 1990, 28–31 and 78–92.

98. For assessments of the event especially in comparison, see Fujiwara 2010; and nearly the entire January 1990 issue of FESPIC's newsletter: *FESPIC* 1990, 1–7.

99. On FINS and support for media in general, see 1989NFKT 1990, 330–35.

100. 1989NFKT 1990, 142–43.

101. 1989NFKT 1990, 120–21 and 144.

102. 1989NFKT 1990, 333.

103. For preliminary budget numbers, see 1989NFKT 1990, 125.

104. See the special section devoted to his participation: 1989NFKT 1990, 179–80.

105. 1989NFKT 1990, 137–41; see also Matsuo 1989, 137–38.

106. 1989NFKT 1990, 151–59.

107. 1989NFKT 1990, 347–54; Matsuo 1989, 138–39.

108. 1989NFKT 1990, 171.

109. The section of the report on the ceremonies includes multiple photos: 1989NFKT 1990, 192–209.

110. 1989NFKT 1990, 296–303.

111. For overall statistics related to the Games, see 1989NFKT 1990, 16–18.

112. A documentary film about the event includes clips from ceremonies and several other events at the Games; see 1989NFKT 1989.

113. Fujiwara 2006, 10.

114. On China's involvement with disability sports, see Yong 2010, 91–92; for an overview of disability sports in China that makes no mention of FESPIC, see Mao and Sun 2018. On disability rights organizations in China during this period, see Kohrman 2005.

115. The official report for these Games was available in the archives at Taiyō no Ie in Beppu. It is in Chinese with translations in English: Organizing Committee 1994. Many of the details in the report are summarized in Yong 2010. Participation figures are also available in "6ᵗʰ Beijing" 2006.

116. Kohrman 2005, 113–14.

117. Yong 2010, 99.

118. Yong 2010, 97–98. See references to issues with housing and food for these Games in Elgin and Moloney 2015; and on problems with food and water, see Yamashita 2006, 24.

119. Hatada 2010b, 48.

120. Taiyō no Ie holds what appears to be an abbreviated English-language translation of the official report from these Games: Secretariat of the FESPIC Bangkok '99 1999. Many of the details that follow are drawn from other accounts.

121. Hatada 2010b, 49–50. On Thailand's disability sports programs at the time, see Takamine 2010, 104–08.

122. For numbers and sports, see "7ᵗʰ Bangkok" 2006. For participating countries in comparative perspective, Chiang 2010a, 144–45.

123. Ikeda Taka 2006.

124. Tongsiri and Taweesangsuksakul 1999.

125. Han 2010, 110. An English-language version of the official report for these Games was available at Taiyō no Ie: Busan FESPIC Games Organizing Committee 2003. Key points are summarized in Han's account.

126. Han 2010, 112.

127. For figures on participation and details on sports, see "8ᵗʰ Busan" 2006. For details on IPC certification and the efforts to achieve it, see Busan FESPIC Games Organizing Committee 2003, 97–107.

128. I was unable to access the official report for these Games. Details are drawn primarily from Zarin 2010; and Hatada 2010b, 51–52.

129. On participant numbers, see "9ᵗʰ Kuala Lumpul [sic]" 2006; and Chiang 2010a, 144–47.

130. Kobayashi 2006. For these final Games, the Japan Paralympic Committee produced a report focused on the Japanese national team's preparations and experiences as part of the committee's "athlete strengthening" activities: Nihon Pararinpikku Iinkai 2007.

131. See earlier references to Guttmann's stance on multi-disability events.

132. For the most comprehensive examination of this period in the Paralympic Movement, see Bailey 2008, especially 43–137; for an abbreviated overview, see Brittain 2010, 37–43.

133. Bailey 2008, 107.

134. Hatada 2010b, 47; this concern would become a recurring theme in the *FES-PIC* newsletter.

135. Bailey 2008, 102. For a more veiled criticism, see "From the Secretariat" 1990.

136. For a list of founding states, see Brittain 2010, 40.

137. On Chow's involvement, see Bailey 2008, 100 and 102. From January 1990 onward, the *FESPIC* newsletter regularly included information on FESPIC leaders who were involved with the IPC. For a list of FESPIC leaders, see Chiang 2010a, 148–162.

138. Steadward 1992.

139. On the early structure, see Bailey 2008, 92–137.

140. Bailey 2008, 141; notably the failure of this proposal does *not* appear to be mentioned in the September 1993 issue of the *FESPIC* newsletter.

141. Dunstan 1995.

142. Bailey 2008, 213. The *FESPIC* newsletter provided a detailed overview of these meetings, see "President Report, 1999–2001" 2001. For a timeline of these and other FESPIC-related events, see Chiang 2010a, 132–43.

143. Bailey 2008, 161–62. Multiple *FESPIC* newsletters include references to the importance of national organizations joining the IPC.

144. Bailey 2008, 186. I was unable to gain access to full issues of the *FESPIC* newsletter for significant portions of this period.

145. See Brittain 2010, 23–33; Bailey 2008, 140–224.

146. Han 2010, 112.

147. On the history of the APC, without the details of the merger, see the APC website: APC 2019, "Our History," Asian Paralympic Committee, http://www.asian paralympic.org/history.

148. On regional realignments during this period, see Bailey 2008, 226–63.

149. Park 2010, 125. An overview of the plan for the merger and the final decision to merge were reported on in the *FESPIC* newsletter, beginning with the August 2004 issue. I was unable to access the issue from 2005.

150. "From the Secretariat" 1998.

151. Longtime FESPIC organizer, Asō Manabu cited such concerns as a driving force behind the merger when I spoke with him (interview with author, JPSA office, Tokyo, April 12, 2017).

152. Park 2010, 125; Zarin 2010, 122; also referenced in the *FESPIC* newsletter: "Background and Point of Consideration on Merger between FESPIC and APC" 2004.

153. Park 2010, 126. These same details were also provided in the *FESPIC* newsletter: "FESPIC and APC Agreed to Form a Task Force for the Purpose of Merge" 2004.

154. Park 2010, 127–29.

155. For such goals, see APC 2019, "Vision & Mission," Asian Paralympic Committee, http://www.asianparalympic.org/vision-and-mission.

156. On contemporary challenges of disability sports in Oceania, including references to FESPIC, see Maharaj 2011.

157. For observations on differences in emphasis that were apparent well before the merger, see Hatada 1998. Notably this article was preceded in the journal by a Japanese translation of an essay written by Steadward (1998) that discussed the emphasis on competition at the Paralympics. See also Nakamura Tarō (2002, 220–21), who suggested that both approaches were equally important to the promotion of disability sports.

158. This phrase is listed first in describing the role of the APC; see APC 2019, "Vision & Mission. See also the official strategic plan in APC 2015, 6.

159. APC 2015, 6.

160. APC 2015, 6.

161. APC 2015, 11.

162. APC 2015, 7.

163. This observation is based on informal comments offered during a symposium I attended in 2017 in reference to organizational efforts for the 2014 Asian Para Games in South Korea: "Linkage of the Olympics and Paralympics," Conference at Waseda University, Tokyo, March 5, 2017.

164. APC 2015, 11.

165. See APC 2019, "Games," Asian Paralympic Committee, http://www.asianparalympic.org/. This name change can be tracked on archived English versions of related websites. Between March 14, 2010, and May 14, 2010, the label "10th Asian Para Games" near the top of the site was modified to "Guangzhou 2010 Asian Para Games," duplicating the title above it. Compare the two sites: "Guangzhou 2010: Asian Para Games: The 10th Asian Para Games," archived, March 14, 2010, https://web.archive.org/web/20100314055630/http://www.gzapg2010.cn:80/en/; and "Guangzhou 2010: Asian Para Games" archived, May 14, 2010, https://web.archive.org/web/20100514035622/http://www.gzapg2010.cn:80/en/.

166. For this introduction to the revised constitution, see APC 2018, "Constitution," Asian Paralympic Committee, November 2018, http://www.asianparalympic.org/constitution.

167. APC 2015, 7.

168. Chiang 2010b, 68.

169. For more on media coverage of FESPIC see chapter 4.

3. Japan's "Cradle of Disability Sports"

1. Heinz Frei quoted in ŌKKMTJ, 2010, 126.

2. Tsūrizumu Ōita 2019, "Ibento jōhō," Ōita-ken kankō jōhō kōshiki saito, 2019, https://www.visit-oita.jp/events/index.

3. For one example of the frequent references to Ōita as the cradle or birthplace of disability sports, see Hiramatsu 1984, 2.

4. For a brief overview of Ōita past and present, see Ōita-ken 2018. Like many places in Japan, Ōita's prefectural boundaries were in flux until 1876. For a more detailed description of the establishment of Ōita Prefecture, see Ōita-ken Sōmubu Sōmuka 1984, 113–22.

5. Figures for all *onsen* in Japan are available at Kankyōshō n.d., "Onsen ni kan suru dēta," Kankyōshō, accessed August 6, 2019, https://www.env.go.jp/nature/onsen/data/index.html. There are a variety of sites that rank *onsen*; for one example, see H. I. S. gurupu 2019, "Ninki onsenchi: onsen rankingu," Tabi puro presented by H. I. S., 2019, https://www.his-vacation.com/onsen/ranking/.

6. Hori 1966, 2. For a brief history of *onsen* in the Beppu area, see Beppu-shi Kyōiku Iinkai 2012, 69–92.

7. For an English translation of extant sections of *Bungo no Kuni fudoki*, see Aoki 1997, 233–47.

8. Hori 1966, 6, 7, and 10.

9. Ōita-ken Sōmubu Sōmuka 1989, 393.

10. A copy of the relevant section is provided in Beppu-shi Kyōikukai 1933, 552–53.

11. For overviews on the Tokugawa period, see Beppu-shi Kyōiku Iinkai 2012, 69–83; and Ōita-ken Sōmubu Sōmuka 1989, 393.

12. Toyosawa 2008, 74–130.

13. Ōita-ken Sōmubu Sōmuka 1989, 394 and 407–408.

14. Hagiwara 1914, front matter. The guide's author claims to have been drawn to Beppu in search of a cure. Most of his descriptions of springs include details about the water's chemical makeup and lists of specific ailments that each spring is suited for treating. On the history of the advertised clinic, see Beppu-shi Kyōikukai 1933, 429.

15. Ueno Kazuya 1920, 28–38 and front and back matter.

16. Ōita-ken Sōmubu Sōmuka 1989, 410–11; for additional details including lists of twelve different categories of conditions treated at the center, see Beppu-shi Kyōikukai 1933, 373–75.

17. Ōita-ken Sōmubu Sōmuka 1989, 394 and 407–408.

18. Hori 1966, 101. Details on prefectural support are found in Ōita-ken Sōmubu Sōmuka 1991, 202. For an example of an early study on outcomes, see Hatta 1964.

19. Beppu-shi Kyōikukai 1933, 399–400. Kokura Army Hospital itself was located in a prefecture to the north and dated to the late 1800s.

20. Hori 1966, 52–53.

21. Hori 1966, 67.

22. During the war, the Japanese government underwent frequent reorganizations; at any given point, a facility might end up under the purview of different offices within the bureaucracy. On onsen sites for soldiers and Ōita's role in training programs, see Kōseishō Gojūnenshi Henshū Iinkai 1988, 221 and 487–88. For more details on these wartime training programs for wounded veterans, see Hemmi 1982. On the sanatorium, which opened in 1938, see Ōita-ken Sōmubu Sōmuka 1988, 349.

23. Ōita-ken Sōmubu Sōmuka 1988, 15 and 354. The history provides few specifics.

24. Beppu-shi Kyōikukai 1933, 400.

25. Ōita-ken Sōmubu Sōmuka 1988, 354. Ōita remains famous for bamboo crafts.

26. Pennington 2015, 107–108.

27. Pennington 2015, 108.

28. Pennington 2015, 106–14. On popular interest, see Pennington 2015, 182–86.

29. The Chūnichi newspaper featured an article about the discovery of the pamphlet on its front page. Several scholars were quoted, including Fujita Motoaki. Chūnichi shimbun, "Kyū Nihongun, shōbyōhei ni supōtsu kokunai hatsu taikai no panfu hakken," August 7, 2017, p. 1. The original article and images were reproduced online at a rehabilitation news website: gene 2019, "Riha NEWS: dai 1-kai: Nitchūsensō-ka, shōbyō-hei ni kyū Nihongun ga kokunai hatsu supōtsu taikai kaisai panfu hakken," Riha no me, 2019, https://gene.themedia.jp/posts/2807513.

30. On the history of the prefectural hospital, see Beppu-shi Kyōikukai 1933, 429; and Ōita-ken Sōmubu Sōmuka 1986, 377–81. On the transition from military to civilian administration in general, see Kōseishō Gojūnenshi Henshū Iinkai 1988, 592–93.

31. On the planned establishment of these centers, see Ueda 2013.

32. For an overview of the hospital's history, see Kokuritsu Byōin Kikō Nishi Beppu Byōin 2019, "Enkaku," Kokuritsu Byōin Kikō Nishi Beppu Byōin, 2019, https://nishibeppu.hosp.go.jp/about/cnt1_00027.html.

33. For Beppu National Hospital's history, see Kokuritsu Byōin Kikō Beppu Iryō Sentā 2019, "Enkaku," Kokuritsu Byōin Kikō Beppu Iryō Sentā, 2019, https://beppu.hosp.go.jp/goannai/enkaku/index.html.

34. For the history of the Beppu National Center, see Beppu Judo Shōgaisha Sentā 2019, "Sentā no gaiyō," Kokuritsu Shōgaisha Rihabiritēshon Sentā Jiritsu Shien Kyoku Beppu Judo Shōgaisha Sentā, 2019, http://www.rehab.go.jp/beppu/guide/history.html. On the Welfare Ministry's role, see Kōseishō Gojūnenshi Henshū Iinkai 1988, 777. On dates for establishment of the veterans' facility, see Hori 1966, 87.

35. Hatada 2010b, 31–32.

36. Much of this paragraph and those following reference sections of Nakamura's biography: NYD 1988, 2, 12–14, 22, 25, 27 and 455–57. A history of Beppu from 1933 lists Nakamura Byōin, presumably his father's clinic, as one of several private facilities in the area; see Beppu-shi Kyōikukai 1933, 430.

37. On Nakamura's choice, see NYD 1988, 33. On Amako, see NYD 1988, 36. For more on Amako's background and wartime role, see Ueda 2016; see also an informational pamphlet produced about rehabilitation in Kyūshū for the Forty-Ninth Annual Meeting of the Japanese Association of Rehabilitation Medicine: Dai 49 kai Nihon Rihabiritēshon Igakkai Gakujutsu Shūkai 2012, 3–4.

38. NYD 1988, 36.

39. On the book and its reception, see NYD 1988, 44–47.

40. On Kashiwa's involvement, see Nihon Shōi Gunjinkai 1967, 320.

41. This "leading-from-behind" approach would not be unusual in Japanese groups, where leadership positions are often held by those with the most prestige.

42. Details from the following paragraphs on the founding and early history of Taiyō no Ie are drawn from a variety of sources; see in particular NYD 1988, 119–252; Nakamura Yutaka 1975, 28–195; and the official history of the company produced in 1975: Taiyō no Ie Shintai Shōgaisha Shokunō Kaihatsu Sentā Kaihatsuka 1975.

43. Minakami is also known as Mizukami Tsutomu.

44. On Nakamura's role in the application process, see NYD 1988, 259.

45. On early wheelchair marathons and Japanese participation, see Nihon Kurumaisu Supōtsu Kenkyūkai 1991, 2. On the early road race, see NYD 1988, 322. A reproduced article from *Ōita gōdō shimbun* offers details on Nakamura polling people for ideas; see "Mae e: dai 30 kai Ōita Kokusai Kurumaisu Marason: dai 2 bu: ishizue 2" 2010. On Yoshimatsu's role, see Nakamura and Ogata 2004, 95. An update to the official marathon website in late 2019 removed several sections, including one with information on the event's history. As of this writing the history section has not been restored. See the archived version, with most extensive details in the Japanese version: ŌKKMTJ 2018, "Hisutorī," archived, Ōita Kokusai Kurumaisu Marason Taikai, October 16, 2018, https://web.archive.org/web/20181016064005/http://www.kurumaisu-marathon.com/contents/history/history.html.

46. There are timeline discrepancies in existing sources. Nakamura's biography does not mention early interactions with Hiramatsu, and Hiramatsu himself does not mention the initial plan to pursue a joint marathon. Other sources indicate that he was involved from the earliest stages. On efforts to launch the marathon, see in particular,

Nihon Kurumaisu Supōtsu Kenkyūkai 1991, 2; NYD 1988, 378–83; Nakamura and Ogata 2004, 4–5. For additional information on Hiramatsu and especially his "One Village One Product" movement, see International OVOP Exchange Committee 2017, Kokusai Isson Ippin Kōryū Kyōkai, 2017, http://www.ovop.jp/jp/.

47. Sources on financial data for the early races are scarce, but Yotsutani Natsuko—who as of this writing is a manager with Taiyō no Ie and had served as Nakamura's assistant during the early years of the marathon—confirmed that invitees were offered financial support for travel (in discussion with author, Taiyō no Ie, Beppu, Japan. July 14, 2017).

48. Details on sponsors and course are from *Ōita gōdō shimbun*, "Daiikkai kokusai kurumaisu marason taikai," October 30, 1981, p. 1. On accommodation for athletes and the role of Taiyō no Ie, see *Ōita gōdō shimbun*, "Rokka kuni no senshu ken iri," October 28, 1981, p. 15. On the recruitment of athletes, staffing, and the route, see *Ōita gōdō shimbun*, "Kurumaisu marason hatsu no kokusai taikai: ge," October 31, 1981, p. 15. See also *Ōita gōdō shimbun*, "Kurumaisu marason hatsu no kokusai taikai: jō," October 29, 1981, p. 15. For additional information on the route, police involvement, and volunteers, see two *Ōita gōdō shimbun* articles reproduced in OKKMTJ 2010, 106. Details on resistance to the event from prefectural officials are found in Nakamura and Ogata 2004, 4. On interactions with local track association, see NYD 1988, 378–79; and Nihon Kurumaisu Supōtsu Kenkyūkai 1991, 2–3. Archived versions of the official website include results and digital versions of the official commemorative books from the first marathon onward; see OKKMTJ 2019, "Shashinshū," archived, Ōita Kokusai Kurumaisu Marason Taikai, March 2, 2019, https://web.archive.org/web/20190302171943 /http://www.kurumaisu-marathon.com:80/contents/photo/photo.html.

49. For details on the first race, see NYD 1988, 379–80; and the official commemorative booklet, Ōita-ken 1982, 31–37.

50. NYD 1988, 380; a similar statement is quoted in Hiramatsu's recollections of the event in Nakamura and Ogata 2004, 6.

51. Hiramatsu commented on media criticism in Nakamura and Ogata 2004, 6–7. Though generally not reflected in *Ōita gōdō*'s articles, such critiques were apparent in the otherwise limited national newspaper coverage of the event; see *Mainichi shimbun*, "'Yujō to byōdō' ni, naze jun'i," November 2, 1981, p. 23.

52. *Ōita gōdō shimbun*, "Chikara no kagiri . . . kandō no dorama," November 2, 1981, p. 15.

53. Nihon Kurumaisu Supōtsu Kenkyūkai 1991, 3.

54. *Ōita gōdō shimbun*, "Chikara no kagiri . . ."

55. *Ōita gōdō shimbun*, "Kurumaisu marason furu kōsu de mainen: Hiramatsu chiji ga kisha kaiken," November 3, 1981, p. 5.

56. *Ōita gōdō shimbun*, "Kurumaisu marason hatsu no kokusai taikai: jō," October 29, 1981, p. 15.

57. Details on Nakamura's research and his pursuit of official sanction for the event are from NYD 1988, 380–82.

58. JSAD and the Health and Welfare Ministry are only listed as supporters in materials from the first race; see Ōita-ken 1982, 38. JSAD would be listed as an official sponsor in later years.

59. The local approach to the marathon is an excellent example of Laura Misener's (2015) "para-sport leveraging framework."

60. For one example, see Hiramatsu 1984. FESPIC's own newsletter, *FESPIC*, covered the marathon yearly from 1981 until FESPIC's dissolution in 2006. The marathon was frequently highlighted in Health and Welfare publications; for one example, see "Shōgaisha shakai sanka ibento hanazakari" 1994.

61. Hiramatsu offers examples in Nakamura and Ogata 2004, 24–27.

62. Details of the 2015 plan are in Ōita-ken 2018, 10–12.

63. Hiramatsu's claims are from Nakamura and Ogata 2004, 23–24.

64. OKKMTJ 2003, 1.

65. On the "One Village, One Product" campaign, see the Japanese or English version of the official website: International OVOP Exchange Committee 2017, Kokusai Isson Ippin Kōryū Kyōkai, 2017, http://www.ovop.jp/jp/.

66. OKKMTJ 2015d, 3. This was an informational pamphlet prepared for the thirty-fifth marathon organizational meeting that organizers shared with me when I met with them soon thereafter.

67. Nihon Kurumaisu Supōtsu Kenkyūkai 1991, 5.

68. For two examples of this marathon-related medical research, see Nakamura Tarō et al. 1995; in English see Ide et al. 1994. An entire chapter in Nakamura and Ogata's (2004, 97–130) edited book on the marathon is devoted to its medical benefits.

69. Nakamura and Ogata 2004, 209–34.

70. A detailed write-up on the first of these events was provided in "Technical Seminar," 1987 *FESPIC* 13 (December), 2. Other issues of the *FESPIC* newsletter provide lists of presentation titles. Information on seminar presentations is provided in the commemorative marathon booklets from 1987 to 1997. A similar one-time event was hosted in connection with the thirtieth-anniversary celebrations and is described in that commemorative booklet.

71. On the marathon in studies of event management, see Namikoshi and Tomita 1999, 160–64; Matsumoto 2008.

72. Takemi Nakagawa, "Some Rio Wheelchair Marathoners Will Be Racing in Hondas," *Nikkei: Asian Review*, September 12, 2016, https://asia.nikkei.com/Business/Some-Rio-wheelchair-marathoners-will-be-racing-in-Hondas.

73. International OVOP Exchange Committee 2017, Kokusai Isson Ippin Kōryū Kyōkai, 2017, http://www.ovop.jp/jp/.

74. For details on Ōita's difficulties during this period, see Ōita-ken 2018. For Hirose's fiscal reform plan in relation to the marathon, see Ōita-ken Kinkyū Gyōzaisei Kaikaku Honbu 2004, 18, 39 and 49.

75. On the relocation, see Hirose's opening comments in OKKMTJ 2004, 1. Additional details on changes appeared in a detailed timeline prepared for the thirty-fifth marathon organizational meeting that organizers shared with me: OKKMTJ 2015c, 3–6. During my repeat visits to Ōita, it was hard to miss the disparity between the arcade area, which often had several vacant store fronts, and the newer, vibrant shopping, dining, and entertainment complex several blocks away at the train station. A similar pattern is apparent at many arcade districts in Japan.

76. OKKMTJ 2015c, 3–6.

77. On Tokyo's race, see Tokyo Marathon Foundation 2019, "Tokyo Marathon 2020 Race Information," August 2019, https://www.marathon.tokyo/en/about/outline/. On the Abbott competitions, see World Marathon Majors LLC 2019, August 2019, https://www.worldmarathonmajors.com/.

78. For explanations of the need and motivation for the change, see OKKMTJ 2015d, 13–14.

79. Very general information on supporters is provided in Ōita-ken 1982.

80. The newsletter was usually produced annually, with the first article on the marathon appearing in April 1981.

81. Kudo Norifumi and Gotoh Keiko, in discussion with author, Ōita prefectural offices, Ōita, July 14, 2017.

82. Omron appears as a formal sponsor beginning with the eighth race: OKKMTJ 1988.

83. "Kigyō no 'kanmuri' senryaku nau dai 1 kai: Shinshōsha ni supōtsu no rin o: Ōita Kokusai Kurumaisu Marason—Omuron" 1991.

84. This financial information is from OKKMTJ 2015b. Presumably this single-sided document was prepared for the thirty-fifth organizational meeting; it was shared with me in June 2015.

85. Details on benefits for potential sponsors are available on the official website, which also includes several files regarding sponsorship: OKKMTJ 2019, "Kyōsan kigyō boshū," Ōita Kokusai Kurumaisu Marason Taikai, 2019, https://kurumaisu-marathon.com/.

86. For examples, see Omron and Mitsubishi's internationally oriented PR sites featuring the marathon and other activities: Omron Corporation 2019, "Social Welfare," https://www.omron.com/about/social/welfare/; Mitsubishi Corporation 2019, "Project Activities," Dream as One, https://www.mitsubishicorp.com/jp/en/dreamasone/report/. For additional information on sponsorships, see Matsumoto 2008, 89–90.

87. For Hiramatsu's description, see Nakamura and Ogata 2004, 10–14.

88. Matsumoto 2008, 95; see also the section on volunteers in Ōita-ken Fukushi Hokenbu Shōgai Fukushika 2000, 44.

89. For details on volunteers in earlier marathons and information on Can Do, see Matsumoto 2008, 94–95. Figures for volunteers from a recent race, presumably in 2014, were part of a printed presentation that organizers shared with me in June 2015: OKKMTJ 2015a, slide 6.

90. Katayama Takaki and Chino Eto, in discussion with author, Ōita prefectural offices, Ōita, June 24, 2015. For additional emphasis on the benefits of this approach, see Matsumoto 2008, 95.

91. This point came up during both my meetings with organizers. Katayama and Chino, in discussion with author, 2015; and Kudo and Gotoh, in discussion with author, 2017.

92. Having visited the city and met with organizers on previous occasions. I came to Ōita during the autumn of 2016 specifically to observe the thirty-sixth marathon. I arrived in Ōita a few days before the race was held on October 30, 2016, and departed the following day for other research sites. During my stay, I gathered promotional materials; followed local media; attended the opening and closing ceremonies; spoke with several participants, spectators, and local citizens; and observed different portions of the race.

93. Photos of the bridge from previous years suggest that the baseball teams are regulars.

94. The full-color leaflet distributed for the thirty-sixth marathon includes times, details on the course, lists of competitors, and a number of points introducing the

unique elements of wheelchair marathons, such as speed. The leaflet highlights Ōita's special standing because of its large number of racers, history, inclusiveness, and popularity with foreign athletes: OKKMTJ 2016a.

95. To the best of my knowledge, data on pre- and post-event changes in local attitudes have not been collected or maintained.

96. There are several references to this fact in Japanese, see for instance, Kanō 2000, 57; and Yamaguchi 1993, 65. Similar comments appear in OKKMTJ 2010, 119. One of the characters in Johnson's (2012, 90) novel had raced in the marathon.

97. A sampling of such comments from a variety of racers, both foreign and domestic are included in the thirtieth marathon commemorative book: OKKMTJ 2010, 118–21.

98. Many of these encounters are documented on the marathon's official website.

99. Peter Hawkins and Matthew Davis, in discussion with author, opening ceremony of Ōita International Wheelchair Marathon, Ōita, October 29, 2016. Hawkins referenced his generational encounters in Ōita.

100. Kudo and Gotoh, in discussion with author, 2017.

101. These goals are still explicit in the commemorative book for the thirty-sixth race; OKKMTJ 2016b, 2 and 42. References to such letters are in Hiramatsu 1984, 12; see also Koga 1985, 38.

102. Their story is reported in an *Ōita gōdō* article reproduced in "Mae e: dai 30 kai Ōita Kokusai Kurumaisu Marason: bangai hen 5" 2010.

103. These stories are related in Komori 1998, 57.

104. An update of the website in late 2019 removed the map and other sections; as of this writing the barrier-free map had not been restored. For an older version see the archived site: OKKMTJ 2018, "Barrier-Free Map," archived, Oita International Wheelchair Marathon, August 23, 2018. https://web.archive.org/web/20180823144039 /http:/wheelchair-marathon.com/contents/barriar/barriar.html. At various points, local editions of Japan's national newspapers have featured critiques of Ōita's lack of accessibility, despite the prominence of the marathon. For two examples, see *Asahi shimbun*, "Ōita Kokusai Kurumaisu Marason, kyō sutāto (saguru)/ Ōita," November 12, 2000, local page, Ōita 1; and *Mainichi shimbun*, "Kisha nikki: chansu/ Ōita," November 8, 2007, local edition, Ōita 21.

105. On the workshops, including extensive photos and multiple reflections, see Dai 30 kai kinen Ōita Kokusai Kurumaisu Marason Taikai kinen jigyō 2010. On events the following year, see OKKMTJ 2015c, 6. During February 2017, I had an informal conversation with a middle-school principal at Nishiwaseda in Tokyo who commented on the positive impact of hosting a similar event for his students featuring wheelchair marathoner Hiromichi Jun.

106. Katayama and Chino, in discussion with author, 2015.

107. Each of the marathon commemorative books includes a section listing the goals; the difference in phrasing is notable when comparing the language from earlier books with those from 1995 onward.

108. Summaries of these various transitions are listed on the marathon timeline: OKKMTJ 2015c.

109. OKKMTJ 2015c. For classifications in the first race see Ōita-ken 1982, 39. For details on changes in classification during the first ten years, see Nihon Kurumaisu Supōtsu Kenkyūkai 1991, 6.

110. On improved performance during the early races, see Nihon Kurumaisu Supōtsu Kenkyūkai 1991, 8–11; the differences are even clearer in later races; see Fujita 2013, 51.

111. Details about the T/51 athletes and the absence of other races are included in OKKMTJ 2015a, slide 5.

112. OKKMTJ 2015c, 4.

113. On the rationale for fees and comparisons with other races, see OKKMTJ 2015d, 15.

114. On the importance of the half-marathon in particular, see OKKMTJ 2015a, slide 5; and Nakamura and Ogata 2004, 241–46.

115. For an example of the impact on young people with disabilities, see "Ōita Kokusai Kurumaisu Marason Taikai" 1996, 35; for additional examples of the marathon's impact on Japanese competitors, see Nakamura and Ogata 2004, 71–72 and 95–96.

116. Hawkins quoted in Heather Doyle, "Malverne's 'Wacky' Wheelchair Athlete Wins over Youth," *Malverne Patch*, January 21, 2011, https://patch.com/new-york/malverne-lynbrook/malvernes-wacky-wheelchair-athlete-wins-over-youth.

117. Hawkins, in discussion with author, 2016.

118. Köberle quoted in Nakamura and Ogata 2004, 182.

119. On these concerns and the rationales for increasing the amount of prize money, see OKKMTJ 2015d, 13–14.

120. This financial information is based on information from the 2014 race: OKKMTJ 2015b. In 2007, these expenses represented 25% of costs as noted in Matsumoto 2008, 92.

121. Award amounts for the thirty-fifth Marathon and comparison with other races are in OKKMTJ 2015d, 8 and 13; details on annual prizes have been included on the official website as well, and as of this writing, award amounts were unchanged.

122. Brittain 2010, 152. For additional insights on these problematic developments in the Paralympic Movement, see Howe 2008, especially chapters 6 and 8.

123. The inequities in disability sport have not gone unnoticed in Japan; see for instance, Nakamura and Ogata 2004, 238–40. Fujita Motoaki (2016, 168–72) has also raised these concerns.

4. A Turning Point

1. Nagano's record of 561 athletes was only broken in 2018 when Pyeongchang, South Korea, hosted 567.

2. Nakamura Tarō 2002, 168–70; see also Watari 2012, 108 and 129–32.

3. NPTKTSI 1998, 20.

4. A copy of the letter is provided in NPTKTSI 1998, 21.

5. On the years preceding the Games, see NPTKTSI 1998, 20–23 and 373–75. Quote on the IPC view is from NPTKTSI 1998, 7.

6. NPTKTSI 1998, 271 and 277.

7. Official reports make no direct reference to Kobe's FESPIC Games, but the head of NAPOC's publicity subcommittee was Ite Seiichirō, a JSAD staff member who had also been involved in organizing the Games in Kobe. For list of committee members, see NPTKTSI 1998, 321.

8. NPTKTSI 1998, 32–33 and 373.

9. NPTKTSI 1998, 39; for a directory of athletes produced by JSAD, see NSSSK 1998.

10. NPTKTSI 1998, 43.

11. See for example, issues of *Kōsei*, *Gekkan fukushi*, and *Nōmaraizēshon* in the months before the Games.

12. On Parabbit, see NPTKTSI 1998, 33; on events, see NPTKTSI 1998, 40–42.

13. On finances and donations, see NPTKTSI 1998, 271–78.

14. NPTKTSI 1998, 222.

15. For projected and actual contributions, see NPTKTSI 1998, 271 and 277, respectively; for the list of specific contributions, see NPTKTSI 1998, 332–33. For details on approaches to corporate sponsors, see NPTKTSI 1998, 222–27.

16. On ticket sales, see NPTKTSI 1998, 163–67. On the reasoning behind the sales of tickets and details on prices and availability dating from the pre-sale period, see "Nagano Pararinpikku kaisai ni mukete: nyūjō-ken ga hanbai saremasu" 1997.

17. On student ticket sales, see NPTKTSI 1998, 167; and Ogura 2015b, 47–49. The official record of the "One School, One Country" campaign includes several pages on the Paralympics, many of which feature images of and comments from students: see Nagano-shi Kōchō Kai 1999, 194–95 and 222–29. For discussions on differences in access to Olympic and Paralympic tickets, see Yamada Yukihiko 1999, 62–63; Yamada's article is one of several by local educators about the impact of the Olympics and Paralympics on their schools that are featured in a special issue of *Shinano kyōiku*; for others that reference the Paralympics, see *Shinano kyōiku* 1999, 12–19, 20–24, 25–27, 28–34 and 44–51. Comments from students about the Paralympics are also included in a collection of writings from volunteers: Wārudo yū Kawanakajima-chō yūsen hōsō 2001, 121–23 and 137–39.

18. Details on the torch relay and ceremonies are in NPTKTSI 1998, 79–88. For information used as part of team recruitment, see: "Nagano Pararinpikku kaisai ni mukete: Nagano Pararinpikku seika rirē no rirē chīmu boshū ni tsuite" 1997. Additional details on the relay, with special attention to the role of school groups in the event, are provided in Nagano-shi Kōchō Kai 1999, 222–23.

19. On corporate sponsors' interest, see NPTKTSI 1998, 83 and 332.

20. Details on coverage reflect my examination of *Shinano mainichi* articles from February 25 to March 6. On Miura, see *Shinano mainichi shimbun*, "Pararinpikku seika rirē: nanbyō to tatakau otto sasaeru tsuma ninin sankyaku Miyata de seien," March 1, 1998, p. 30.

21. On cultural events, including a full list, see NPTKTSI 1998, 195–205. For an explanation of the goal of these events, see "Nagano Pararinpikku kaisai ni mukete: 'Bunka Puroguramu' tte nani?" 1997, 60–61. On the Art Paralympics specifically, see NPTKTSI 1998, 263–67. For reports from individuals directly involved with the Art Paralympics, see Maruta 1998; and Koike 1998. For detailed examinations of the event and its significance in English, see Ogura 2015b, 59–64.

22. NPTKTSI 1998, 50–55. For recruitment materials and a list of official volunteers, see NPTKTSI 1998, 345–63. For comments from Paralympic volunteers about their experiences, see Wārudo yū Kawanakajima-chō yūsen hōsō 2001, 49–50, 55–56, 68–69 and 71–72. For details on the volunteer experiences of students from local universities, see Narusawa 1998; and Fujioka 1998.

23. The name comes from abbreviations for the Japanese versions of "Paralympic" and "volunteer." On NPBK see NPTKTSI 1998, 235 and 268–69. One of the group's leaders shared similar details about NPBK's origins and role, providing information on challenges involved in assisting spectators; see Ikeda Jun 1998.

24. *Para bora hiroba* 1996.

25. NPTKTSI 1998, 268–69. On snow wheelchairs, see *Shinano mainichi shimbun,* "Pararinpikku Pure Taikai kankyaku-yō 'setsujō kurumaisu' Nozawa de hatsu shiyō," February 13, 1997, digital edition, https://www.shinmai.co.jp/feature/olympic/para //1997/97021305.htm.

26. On the Athletes' Village, see NPTKTSI 1998, 89–92. See highlights of the village's accessibility in "Nagano Pararinpikku kaisai ni mukete: Pararinpikku Senshu Mura" 1998. On venues, see example of sledge hockey complex, NPTKTSI 1998, 120. On pre-Paralympic events and roles in evaluating accessibility, see "Nagano Pararinpikku kaisai ni mukete: 'Pure Pararinpikku' no kaisai" 1997.

27. On transport and onsite support, see NPTKTSI 1998, 129–31. For other details on transportation, see NPTKSI 1998, 172–77. On braille pamphlets, see NPTKTSI 1998, 38.

28. *Shinano mainichi shimbun,* "Gorin Pararinpikku mukaeru machidzukuri Hakuba songi shōgaisha no tachiba de genjō kakunin," October 14, 1995, digital edition, https:// www.shinmai.co.jp/feature/olympic/para//1995/95101404.htm.

29. For summary of participants and findings, see Ijima 1997, 1998.

30. "'Hito ni yasashii machidzukuri' o mezasu: Pararinpikku o kaisai shita Nagano no kōtsū kankyō o miru" 1998, 9–10.

31. Nagano-ken 1995.

32. Ogura 2015b, 67–68; see also references to barrier-free policies in the city in NPTKTSI 1998, 230; and to Nagano-ken law, in NPTKTSI 1998, 256. Details on financial support are vague—the ordinance itself only indicates that support will be available. Ogura (2015b, 42) mentions loans. Information on SME funds is in Ijima 1997, 36.

33. See for example, Ogura 2015b, 41–44.

34. On these earlier policies in Nagano, see Ijima 1997, 32–33; "'Hito ni yasashii machidzukuri' o mezasu" 1998, 8–10; and Ueno Shizuo 1998, 26.

35. On Ikeda's background, see Ikeda Jun 1998. See also an interview he gave in 2006: "Shōgai no aru hitotachi ga, machichū o kappo suru yo no naka ni shitai," Yuyuyu: shōgaisha kōreisha ni yakudatsu pōtaru saito, May 30, 2006, http://www.u-x3.jp /modules/tinyd113/index.php?id=123. On Human Net Nagano, see the official site: Hyūman netto Nagano 2017, http://w2.avis.ne.jp/~hynet/; for Ikeda's role see the organization's first newsletter: *Hyūman netto Nagano no sōkan* gō, 1998.

36. For an overview of these laws up through 1997, see Japanese Society for Rehabilitation of Disabled Persons 1997. For laws after 1997, see "Hōritsu gyōsei" 2016.

37. Headquarters for Promoting the Welfare of Disabled Persons, Prime Minister's Office 1995.

38. Heyer 2015, 151. On the disability rights movement, see also Hayashi and Okuhira 2001.

39. For one example, which includes calls for improved accessibility, see Keizai Kikakuchō 1982, 4 and 101–24. On the gendered nature of some of these changes, see Lock 1993.

40. Heyer 2015, 153–54 and 158.

41. See for example, Ueno Shizuo 1998, 26.

42. United Nations, Department of Economic and Social Affairs, n.d., "History of United Nations and Persons with Disabilities—United Nations Decade of Disabled Persons: 1983–1992," United Nations-Disability, accessed August 7, 2019, https://www.un.org/development/desa/disabilities/history-of-united-nations-and-persons-with-disabilities-united-nations-decade-of-disabled-persons-1983–1992.html.

43. United Nations General Assembly 1989.

44. Economic and Social Commission for Asia and the Pacific 1992.

45. Economic and Social Commission for Asia and the Pacific 2017, "History: Background of Disability-Inclusive Development in the Region," High-level Intergovernmental Meeting on the Midpoint Review of the Asian and Pacific Decade of Persons with Disabilities, 2013–2022, 2017, https://www.unescap.org/disabilityhighlevelmeeting2017/history.

46. See for instance, Kohrman 2005, especially 69–74; and Puar 2017, especially 63–93 and 189–90.

47. Heyer 2015, 144–47.

48. There is limited secondary scholarship on the Asian and Pacific Decades. Even Heyer's work overlooks this international campaign, which overlaps with her book's time frame. Further research is necessary, but it seems that Japan and Japanese activists have assumed a particularly prominent role in these regional decades. For Japan's official report, see Cabinet Office 2002.

49. As just one example, the official report does not mention social rehabilitation (*shakai fukki*) but highlights many of these other ideals in its first few pages; see NPTKTSI 1998, 6–7.

50. For instance, an article from a local NHK affiliate in Nagano described these Games as a "barometer" of Nagano's standing as an "international city": Kamo 1992, 28.

51. Shimazaki 1998, 1.

52. The "Heartful Building Law" was often criticized for its lack of enforcement provisions.

53. On barrier-creating fixes, see Akita 1998. For these criticisms, see Suzuki 1998, 52–53.

54. Suzuki (1998, 52–53) makes a distinction between points and lines, rather than hard and soft, but his point is similar.

55. Brittain 2010, 41.

56. See NPTKTSI 1998, 182 and 227.

57. For general relations with the IPC, see NPTKTSI 1998, 58–59; on antidoping measures, see NPTKTSI 1998, 182.

58. NPTKTSI 1998, 183–85.

59. NPTKTSI 1998, 21.

60. NPTKTSI 1998, 20.

61. This idea was actually raised in an article from a local NHK affiliate; see Kamo 1992, 28.

62. On this relationship, see NPTKTSI 1998, 228–29.

63. Quoted in Bailey 2008, 198. Original source of quotation is unclear.

64. *Yomiuri shimbun*, "Nagano Pararinpikku no yunihōmu JOC ga 'Gorin to onaji' kettei," August 13, 1997, p. 2.

65. Bailey 2008, 104. This statement was made specifically in relation to the Barcelona Games, but Bailey's account indicates that many in the movement shared this sentiment. For insights on how these developments affected athletes, see Howe 2008.

66. NPTKTSI 1998, 21.

67. Steadward 1998, 121.

68. NPTKTSI 1998, 6.

69. Quoted in Sugimoto 1997, 35.

70. NSSSK 1998, 33.

71. The phrase here comes from a member of the organizing staff who only realized that the Paralympics were truly competitive sports after seeing them in person. See comment from Satō Toshiaki, in Sugimoto 1997, 34–35.

72. Fujita 2013, 56–58.

73. Annual reports from these events are available in NSSSK 1985.

74. Fujita 2013, 58. For more detailed descriptions of the facilities in Osaka, see Takahashi Akira 2004, especially chapter 6.

75. Fujita 2013, 45–48 and 58–59.

76. Fujita 2013, 59–60.

77. Fujita 2013, 57.

78. Wakana 1998, 47–48.

79. Fujita 2013, 35; Ogura 2015b, 37.

80. NPTKTSI 1998, 256.

81. The official report cited these possibilities as explicit goals: NPTKTSI 1998.

82. NPTKTSI 1998, 28–29.

83. For the numbers of Japanese athletes at the various Games, see the official website for JPSA (formerly JSAD): Nihon Shōgaisha Supōtsu Kyōkai 2019, Japanese Para-Sports Association, 2019, http://www.jsad.or.jp/.

84. Medal counts available on the JPSA website: Nihon Shōgaisha Supōtsu Kyōkai 2019.

85. Saitō 1998, 114.

86. See chapter 5 for more on Tsuchida.

87. Shōgaisha Supōtsu ni Kansuru Kondankai Iin 1998.

88. Other forms of disability were added in later years, including mental illness and several internal disabilities such as heart or lung conditions and immunodeficiencies. On these changes and others, see Fujita 2013, 60–61.

89. Saitō 1998, 116–17; and Kotani 1998, 4.

90. Ogura 2015b, 37 and 66–67, note 17. For usage statistics and examples of current sports activities at affiliated sites, see Nagano-ken Shōgaisha Fukushi Sentā 2012, Sun Apple, 2012, http://www.avis.ne.jp/~sunapple/.

91. See the Nagano Prefecture organization's website: Nagano-ken Shōgaisha Supōtsu Kyōkai 2017, https://www.nsad.or.jp/. The city organization's website provides less details on the history of the organization: Nagano-shi Shōgaisha Supōtsu Kyōkai 2019, http://park10.wakwak.com/~n-city.p.sports/index.html. An email exchange with the city organization verified the connection between the founding and the Paralympics.

92. See 2005 nen Supesharu Orinpikku Tōki Sekai Taikai Nagano (SONA) 2005. Shriver is quoted on p. 8. The English version of the official report is very similar to the Japanese version.

93. NPTKTSI 1998, 6.

94. NPTKTSI 1998, 36–37.

95. In the months before and after the Games, there were multiple articles of this sort in *Kōsei*, *Nōmaraizēshon*, and *Rōdō jihō*.

96. NSSSK 1998.

97. "Hito to Shakai: Obinata Kuniko-san" 1998, 56.

98. "Nagano Orinpikku Pararinpikku to ken dzukuri" 1998, 62.

99. "Gendai supōtsu are kore: Nagano Pararinpikku" 1998. A sub-theme in the article was the support that the Olympic Committee (which would have been under the purview of the ministry) had provided for the Paralympics. For instance, the article cites the joint national uniforms as an example of collaboration, ignoring the earlier controversy.

100. Nakagawa 1998.

101. Yonekawa 1998.

102. NPTKTSI 1998, 6. Presumably much of this same language was included in promotional materials distributed before the Games.

103. Saitō 1998, 112–13.

104. Saitō 1998, 113.

105. Purdue and Howe 2012.

106. Schantz and Gilbert 2012, 363.

107. NSSSK 1998, 31.

108. On the historical relationship between sports and the media in Japan, see Frost 2010.

109. Fujita 2013, 54.

110. First published in Fujita 2016, 55.

111. Yamaguchi Ichirō, interview with author, Waseda University, Tokyo, June 29, 2017

112. Fujita describes many of these changes in his books; see Fujita 2013, 53–56; and Fujita 2016, 43 and 53–56.

113. Fujita 2016, 43. Fujita notes their establishment but not their dissolution. For commentary lamenting the elimination of these journals at the time, see "Henshū goki" 1998.

114. Araragi 2002a. There is another small jump in 1981 that may be linked to events associated with the UN International Year of the Disabled Person.

115. Sakita 2015.

116. Tsurushima 2017. NHK regularly published results of survey work related to the 2020 Games. For example, see Tsurushima and Saitō 2017.

117. NPTKTSI 1998, 155; see also Kotani 1998, 3.

118. Kondō Fumito 1998, 21. For all details on broadcasts for Nagano, see NPTKTSI 1998, 155–59.

119. Yamaha Hatsudōki Supōtsu Shinkō Zaidan 2017, especially 13–39.

120. On the live coverage of the marathon see chapter 3. While researching in Japan in 2017, I was at the airport one time waiting for a flight, and the television coverage was tuned to a disability sporting event.

121. On the joint work of the IPC and WOWOW to produce a series of documentaries on Paralympic athletes, see the WOWOW site, the bulk of which is in Japanese: WOWOW 2019, "Who I AM," WOWOW, 2019, https://www.wowow.co.jp/sports

/whoiam/. For English-language versions of NHK's animated series, see NHK 2019, "Animation x Paralympics: Who is Your Hero?" NHK World-Japan, 2019, https://www3.nhk.or.jp/nhkworld/en/ondemand/program/video/anipara/?type=tvEpisode&.

122. Yamaha Hatsudōki Supōtsu Shinkō Zaidan 2018. During my six-month stay in Japan in 2017, it was not unusual to "stumble" on television programming featuring such athletes.

123. For an English-language overview of recent surveys, see Ogura 2018, 580.

124. *Ōita gōdō shimbun*, "Shijūsō," June 2, 1975, p. 9.

125. Results are based on my survey of all available articles in the databases for all three newspapers. Keyword searches used several variations of the names for the event. In the final results, I excluded duplicate articles and those only tangentially related to FESPIC, such as several that only referenced athletes' previous participation in a FESPIC event.

126. References to coverage from these local newspapers are based on my surveys of microfilmed copies of papers from dates immediately before, during, and soon after events.

127. Results are based on my survey of all available articles in the databases for all three newspapers. Keyword searches used several variations of names for the event. In the final results, I excluded duplicate articles and those only tangentially related to the Ōita International Wheelchair Marathon, such as several that only referenced athletes' previous participation in the race.

128. Details on articles from *Ōita gōdō shimbun* are based on my surveys of coverage using microfilm copies of newspapers. I targeted periods immediately before, during, and after annual races, so it is possible that I missed articles before or after those points.

129. These observations are based on my analyses of content from national coverage in the three major dailies.

130. Watari 2018.

131. Yamaguchi, interview with author, 2017.

132. I encountered multiple articles featuring Kudō in *Ōita gōdō shimbun* over the years. He was also included in an edited volume on the marathon; see Nakamura and Ogata 2004, 71–72.

133. Yamada Kiyoshi 2016, 42.

134. There are several examples of critical reports from London. For one, see Brittain 2016.

135. Yamaguchi Ichirō highlights the potential impact of local reporting. Having started out covering disability sports mostly at the local level, he is—as of this writing—based in Tokyo and serves as a senior member of the Olympic/Paralympic Promotion Office for the *Mainichi* newspaper.

136. Sakita 2015, 79.

137. Fujita 2013, 55.

138. Yamaguchi, interview with author, 2017.

139. "Kanja tai shakaijin no tatakai datta: Pararinpikku ga Nihon jin ni oshieta mono" 1964. Notably none of the photos features Japanese athletes doing sports.

140. Watari 2010, 240.

141. Watari 2007.

142. Kodama 1998.

143. Saitō 1998, 113. Kondō Fumito's article cited earlier is an excellent example of what Saitō was critiquing. In multiple references to "inspiring" performances, Kondō Fumito (1998) is focused not on the performance itself but on how that performance defied his preconceived notions of athletes with disability. More recently, Watari has characterized coverage for Nagano as "ritual attention," a step forward from earlier media representation but one that remained problematic. This approach acknowledged the importance of disability sports and of those with disabilities, but the overwhelming focus on sports precluded the genuine acknowledgment of issues and challenges pertaining to disability. See Watari 2010, 240–241; neither Saitō nor Watari offered a detailed analysis of media coverage in support of their views.

144. Fujita 2013, 55–56.

145. Kondō Fumito 1998.

146. Fujita 2013, 55–56.

147. Articles on the Ōita International Wheelchair Marathon appeared on society pages as recently as 2016.

148. Kyōya Kazuyuki, interview with author, Chiba Disability Sports and Recreation Center, Chiba, June 14, 2011.

149. Yamaha Hatsudōki Supōtsu Shinkō Zaidan 2017, 29–30.

150. Reported in *Asahi shimbun*, "Kurumaisu marason o shingi," February 15, 2015, sec. Ōita Prefecture page.

151. Brittain 2010, 98.

152. On inspiration porn more generally, including several references to the Paralympics, see Grue 2016. On inspiration porn and connections to the "super-crip" stereotype, see Brittain 2017, 248–49.

153. Fujita 2002; Fujita 2013, 104–114.

154. Endō 2017.

155. Yamaha Hatsudōki Supōtsu Shinkō Zaidan 2017, 13–30.

156. For an essay offering highlights from the workshop, see Nakano Jun 2018, "Tōkyō Pararinpikku o mae ni 'nōryoku shugi' to dō tsukiau ka," NHK hāto netto, September 13, 2018, https://www.nhk.or.jp/heart-net/article/108/.

157. Yamaguchi, interview with author, 2017.

158. Bundon and Clarke 2015. Studies of new media and sports in general remain limited, too; on Olympics and new media, see Miah and Jones 2012.

159. For details on Nagano's website, including live streaming, see NPTKTSI 1998, 47–49; for additional details on processes and challenges for streaming, see Yoshii 1998.

160. Yoshii 1998.

161. The most extensive details on streaming are in Yoshii 1998.

162. On the IPC's streaming network, see Brittain 2017, 253–54.

163. On the history of STAND and its role, see NPO STAND 2015, "Dantai gaiyō," NPO hōjin STAND, 2015, https://npo-stand.jp/019.html. Itō details her involvement in her book promoting disability sports; see Itō 2012.

164. One of STAND's projects was Mobachū, live streaming of disability sports events using cellular phones. It involved cooperation with NEC, a partner with STAND for other projects. See NPO STAND 2010, "Mobachū to wa," NEC X STAND, 2010, http://pastellabo.co.jp/sponsor_for_stand/nec_stand/mobachoo.html.

165. NPO STAND 2019, Chōsenshatachi, June 2019, http://www.challengers.tv/.

166. For the Center's website and links to other new media feeds there, see Nippon Foundation Paralympic Support Center 2019, English homepage, 2019, https://www.parasapo.tokyo/en/. For Nagano City's group, the Facebook page appears to be updated more regularly than the official website: see Nagano-shi Shōgaisha Supōtsu Kyōkai 2016, "Nagano-shi Shōgaisha Supōtsu Kyōkai's Facebook Page," Facebook, April 2016, https://www.facebook.com/naganocity.para.sports/

167. See website: Shingo Kunieda 2015, http://shingokunieda.com/; and Kunieda Shingo 2013, "Shingo Kunieda's Facebook Page," April 2013, https://www.facebook.com/KuniedaShingo/

168. See website: Hajimu Ashida 2019, https ://ashida-hajimu.com/; Ashida Hajimu 2012, "Hajimu Ashida's Facebook Page," Facebook, February 2012, https://www.facebook.com/hajimu.ashida; Ashida Hajimu 2012, "Ashida Hajimu's Twitter Page," February 2012, https://twitter.com/ah_ws?lang=en.

169. My own Facebook feed is a case in point; it is filled daily with information about Paralympic-related sports, events, and athletes, but only because I have actively searched for the information and followed several pages. Without that initial effort, I would be unlikely to see such content.

5. Athletes First

1. Satō's speech has received repeated attention in both Japanese and English. Tokyo's winning bid and Satō's role in particular were featured on the IPC website as a highlight of the year; see "No. 9: Tokyo lands 2020 Paralympic Games" 2013, archived, Media Center for Official Website of the Paralympic Movement, December 23, 2013, https://web.archive.org/web/20140308195757/http://www.paralympic.org/feature/no-9-tokyo-lands-2020-paralympic-games. For a more recent example, see Teddy Katz, "This Paralympian's Story Helped Tokyo Land the 2020 Games," *CBC Sports*, August 14, 2019, https://www.cbc.ca/sports/paralympics/tokyo-2020-olympics-paralympics-1.5184563.

Reproductions of Satō's bid speech in English and Japanese are provided in a new edition of her autobiography: Satō 2014, 169–73.

2. See Bailey 2008, especially 225–63; Brittain 2010, 23–36; and Legg 2018.

3. Legg 2018, 161–63; Brittain 2010, 32–33.

4. Ōsaka Orinpikku Shōchi Iinkai 2001, 154–55; for a timeline of the bid process, see 300–04.

5. Yokohama-shi 1997, "Pararinpikku yūchi no rinen," archived, 2008 nen Yokohama Orinpikku Pararinpikku website, 1997, http://web.archive.org/web/20070316155343/http://www.city.yokohama.jp:80/ne/news/lib/dareo/p10.html.

6. The only detailed sections on the Paralympics are in Ōsaka Orinpikku Shōchi Iinkai 2001, 138–39 and 154–55.

7. Tōkyō Orinpikku Pararinpikku Shōchi Iinkai 2009, 265–79.

8. Tōkyō Orinpikku Pararinpikku Shōchi Honbu 2010, 297–99.

9. Tōkyō Orinpikku Pararinpikku Shōchi Honbu 2010, 568.

10. Tōkyō 2020 Orinpikku Pararinpikku Shōchi Iinkai 2013, preface. Page references to the candidature file here are to the English/French versions, which are close translations of the Japanese version.

11. Tōkyō 2020 Orinpikku Pararinpikku Shōchi Iinkai 2013, 64–84. Budgets are provided at the end of the subsection.

12. Tokyo Organising Committee of the Olympic and Paralympic Games 2019, Tokyo 2020, August 2019, https://tokyo2020.org/en/.

13. Tokyo Organising Committee of the Olympic and Paralympic Games 2019, "Tokyo 2020 Emblems: Selection Process," Tokyo 2020, August 2019, https://tokyo2020.org/en/games/emblem/archive/.

14. Tokyo Organising Committee of the Olympic and Paralympic Games 2019, "Mascot Profile," Tokyo 2020, August 2019, https://tokyo2020.org/en/special/mascot/.

15. Tokyo Organising Committee of the Olympic and Paralympic Games 2019, "Tokyo 2020 Organised and Joint Events," August 2019, https://tokyo2020.org/en/special/countdown/olympic_event/.

16. "Six Paralympians in Tokyo 2020 Athletes' Commission" 2014, Media Centre for Official Website of the Paralympic Movement, September 12, 2014, https://www.paralympic.org/news/six-paralympians-tokyo-2020-athletes-commission.

17. On the history of these legal shifts, see Heyer 2015, 188–202; for an English summary of Japan's legal changes in the last decade, see Shirasawa Mayumi, "The Long Road to Disability Rights in Japan," *Nippon.com*, October 2, 2014, https://www.nippon.com/en/currents/d00133/the-long-road-to-disability-rights-in-japan.html.

18. On these developments in disability sports, see Fujita 2016, 51–53.

19. On the origins of the PAJ, see Fujita 2016, 49–50. For the association's activities see the official website: Nihon Pararinpianzu Kyōkai 2019, Tsukinukero! We Can Make a **Para**digm Shift, 2019, https://www.paralympians.jp/.

20. "Tokyo 2020 Celebrates 50th Anniversary of Para-Sport in Japan" 2015, Media Centre for Official Website of the Paralympic Movement, May 27, 2015, https://www.paralympic.org/news/tokyo-2020-celebrates-50th-anniversary-para-sport-japan.

21. On changes in the JPSA, see Ogura 2018, 591–93; for additional information on sponsorships and JPSA activities see the association's homepage: Nihon Shōgaisha Supōtsu Kyōkai 2019, Japanese Para-Sports Association/Nihon Shōgaisha Supōtsu Kyōkai, 2019, http://www.jsad.or.jp/.

22. On a sampling of Nippon Foundation activities to support the Paralympics, see Nippon Foundation 2018, "Paralympic Support," https://www.nippon-foundation.or.jp/en/what/projects/paralympic.

23. "Opening Day of the Nippon Foundation Para Arena" 2018, News & Topics from the Nippon Foundation Paralympic Support Center, June 22, 2018, https://www.parasapo.tokyo/en/news/168/.

24. This "blade library" has received widespread media coverage; for example, see Minami Funakoshi, "Japan's 'Blade Library' Offers Joy of Blade Running to Amputees," *Reuters*, October 17, 2017, https://www.reuters.com/article/us-japan-prosthetics-runners/japans-blade-library-offers-joy-of-blade-running-to-amputees-idUSKBN1CM0SI.

25. Ogura 2018, 593.

26. Tahara Kazuhiro and Kobayashi Yuta, "Sports Agency to Channel Funds into Events Likely to Produce Olympic Medals," *The Mainichi*, January 1, 2019, English version of Japanese edition, https://mainichi.jp/english/articles/20190101/p2a/00m/0sp/022000c.

27. Watari 2018.

28. Ogura 2018, 581–82.

29. Brittain 2010, 32.

30. Legg 2018, 163–68; and Brittain and Dos Santos 2018, 545–48.

31. Tōkyō 2020 Orinpikku Pararinpikku Shōchi Iinkai 2013, especially 76–82.

32. Tōkyō 2020 Orinpikku Pararinpikku Shōchi Iinkai 2013, 66.

33. Darcy 2017.

34. Tokyo Organising Committee of the Olympic and Paralympic Games 2017, 1:1.

35. Tokyo 2020 Online Press Room 2018, "Tokyo 2020 Accelerates Preparations for the Paralympic Games," Press Release, August 22, 2018, pp. 2–3, https://fpcj.jp/wp/wp-content/uploads/2018/08/20188022_2YTG_Paralympic_pressrelease_ENG-web.pdf.

36. The Japanese title for the plan varies from the English translation. The English version is much less detailed, so references here are to the Japanese version. Tōkyō-to Seisaku Kikaku-kyoku Keikaku-bu Keikaku-ka 2016, especially 156–70.

37. The phrase is sometimes rendered as a "society of coexistence." I have encountered both translations. For the Prime Minister's Office's national action plan, which is only available in Japanese, see Shusō Kantei 2017, 1.

38. Details on hotel changes are noted in Tokyo 2020 Online Press Room 2018, "Tokyo 2020 Accelerates Preparations for the Paralympic Games," p. 3. The current requirement is only one room, so the actual increase in the number of accessible rooms may be limited.

39. Tokyo 2020 Online Press Room 2018, "Tokyo 2020 Accelerates Preparations for the Paralympic Games," p. 3. See also "Universal Tourism Promotion Committee" 2019, Accessible Japan: blog, 2019, https://www.accessible-japan.com/universal-tourism-promotion-committee/.

40. "New App to Help People with Disabilities Navigate Tokyo" 2018, Accessible Japan: blog, 2018, https://www.accessible-japan.com/new-app-to-help-people-with-disabilities-navigate-tokyo/.

41. "JPN TAXI" 2019, Toyota, 2019, https://global.toyota/en/jpntaxi/.

42. "Mobility for All" 2019, Toyota, 2019, https://www.mobilityforall.com/global/en/Mobility/.

43. "Find out about Us" 2019, Accessible Japan, 2019, https://www.accessible-japan.com/about/.

44. "Bmaps—An Award-Winning Accessibility Information App" 2016, Accessible Japan: blog, 2016, https://www.accessible-japan.com/bmaps-award-winning-accessibility-info-app-anyone-without-disability/; "WheeLog! An Accessibility App for Japan . . . and the World" 2017, Accessible Japan: blog, 2017, https://www.accessible-japan.com/wheelog-an-accessibility-app-for-japan-and-the-world/. Both apps have dedicated websites.

45. "IPC President Praises Japan's Adoption of Universal Design" 2017, Media Centre for Official Website of the Paralympic Movement, February 23, 2017, https://www.paralympic.org/news/ipc-president-praises-japan-s-adoption-universal-design.

46. "IPC President Praises Japan's Adoption of Universal Design"; and *Kyodo News*, "Koike Says 2020 Paralympics Will Determine Aging Tokyo's Fate," August 3, 2017, https://english.kyodonews.net/news/2017/08/de9f7f426aba-koike-says-2020-paralympics-will-determine-aging-tokyos-fate.html.

47. Yasushi Yamawaki 2014, "Yasushi Yamawaki: Tokyo 2020 Will Be Gateway to the Future," Media Centre for Official Website of the Paralympic Movement, November 12, 2014, https://www.paralympic.org/blog/yasushi-yamawaki-tokyo-2020-will-be-gateway-future.

48. Darcy 2017, 81–83.

49. Tokyo Organising Committee of the Olympic and Paralympic Games 2017, 1:3.

50. *The Mainichi*, "80% of Existing 2020 Olympic Venues Fail to Meet Wheelchair Space Criteria," April 6, 2017, https://mainichi.jp/english/articles/20170406/p2a/00m/0na/021000c.

51. *Nikkei sangyō shimbun*, "Bariafurī (5): Kyōgi kaijō, shōgaisha mesen de (yoku wakaru) shū," October 12, 2017, p. 2.

52. *Mainichi shimbun*, "Shasetsu: Gorin Para no tenji annai shōgaisha ni kakasenai," September 16, 2019, https://mainichi.jp/articles/20190916/ddm/005/070/063000c. For the English version, see *The Mainichi*, "Editorial: Tokyo 2020 Organizers Falling Short of 'Diversity & Harmony' Slogan," September 17, 2019, English edition, https://mainichi.jp/english/articles/20190917/p2a/00m/0na/013000c. On criticisms from an organization for the visually impaired that prompted the editorial, see Michael Gillan Peckitt 2019, "Disability Group Claims Olympic and Paralympic Ticket Vendors Inaccessible to the Blind, Violating Organizing Committee Guidelines," Barrier Free Japan, September 4, 2019, https://barrierfreejapan.com/2019/09/04/disability-group-claims-olympic-and-paralympic-ticket-vendors-inaccessible-to-the-blind-violating-organizing-committee-guidelines/?fbclid=IwAR35KVCFU7Qj5nJB3OupcVnfn9JEgPcDPmSxQA0sskiztyk7oVMDXjc__GY.

53. Tōkyō-to Seisaku Kikaku-kyoku Keikaku-bu Keikaku-ka 2016, 157.

54. *Nippon.com*, "Toyota to Improve Taxi for Wheelchair Passengers," February 4, 2019, https://www.nippon.com/en/news/yjj2019020400875/toyota-to-improve-taxi-for-wheelchair-passengers.html.

55. *The Mainichi*, "Tokyo Gov't Barrier Free Bylaws under Fire for Not Accommodating All Wheelchair Types," January 21, 2019, https://mainichi.jp/english/articles/20190121/p2a/00m/0fe/025000c; a follow-up article provided additional details: *The Mainichi*, "Tokyo's Barrier-Free Push Hits Snag for Wheelchair Users," February 18, 2019, https://mainichi.jp/english/articles/20190218/p2g/00m/0dm/074000c.

56. *Japan Times*, "Ordinance on Barrier-Free Hotel Rooms Takes Effect in Tokyo Ahead of 2020 Games," September 1, 2019, https://www.japantimes.co.jp/news/2019/09/01/national/ordinance-barrier-free-hotel-rooms-takes-effect-tokyo/#.XZE5T-dKiT8.

57. For an overview of reports soon after the killings in 2016, see Michael Peckitt 2016, "After the Sagamihara Attack," Accessible Japan: blog, 2016, https://www.accessible-japan.com/after-the-sagamihara-attack/; on forced sterilizations and victims' efforts seeking redress, see Elaine Lies, "Victims of Japan's Forced Sterilizations Demand Justice after Decades of Silence," *Reuters*, May 8, 2018, https://www.reuters.com/article/us-japan-sterilisations/victims-of-japans-forced-sterilizations-demand-justice-after-decades-of-silence-idUSKBN1I90MU.

58. For an insightful analysis of the employment controversy and the larger issues behind it, see Philip Brasor, "The Problem with Padding Employment Records in Japan," *Japan Times*, September 22, 2018, https://www.japantimes.co.jp/news/2018/09

/ 22 / national / media-national / problem-padding-employment-records-japan / # .XGRoSc9KiT8; as an example of some critiques, see *Yomiuri shimbun*, "Swiftly Create Environment Where Disabled People Can Work Stably," February 18, 2019, http:// the-japan-news.com/news/article/0005552021.

59. *Asahi shimbun*, "Paralympics Posters Ditched over 'Offensive' Expressions," October 17, 2018, http://www.asahi.com/ajw/articles/AJ201810170043.html.

60. A full accounting of Japan's ongoing accessibility campaigns and their impacts is beyond the scope of this chapter; fortunately, other studies addressing these issues are already underway: see Bookman 2018.

61. Tōkyō 2020 Orinpikku Pararinpikku Shōchi Iinkai 2013, 84.

62. The Japanese version of the official website includes much more detailed information on events than the foreign-language versions. Tokyo Organising Committee of the Olympic and Paralympic Games 2019, Tokyo 2020, August 2019, https:// tokyo2020.org/jp/.

63. The national government website for the host town program includes Japanese and English documents on the program; see Secretariat of the Headquarters for Tokyo 2020 Olympic and Paralympic Games 2019, "Host Town Initiative," Shusō Kantei, 2019, https://www.kantei.go.jp/jp/singi/tokyo2020_suishin_honbu/hosttown _suisin/index_e.html. For educational materials, see Tokyo Organising Committee of the Olympic and Paralympic Games 2019, Tokyo 2020 Education Programme, 2019, https://education.tokyo2020.org/en/.

64. International Paralympic Committee 2017, I'mPOSSIBLE, 2017, https:// im-possible.paralympic.org/.

65. Tokyo 2020 Online Press Room 2018, "Tokyo 2020 Accelerates Preparations for the Paralympic Games," p. 2.

66. The official Japanese website includes information on most past and future events: Tokyo Metropolitan Government 2018, NO LIMITS CHALLENGE, 2018, http://no-limits.tokyo/nlc/.

67. The official Japanese website includes details on the organization's purpose and activities: Tokyo Metropolitan Government 2016, TEAM BEYOND, 2016, https:// www.para-sports.tokyo/.

68. On the festival and sponsors, see the TEAM BEYOND website.

69. Nippon Foundation 2018, "Paralympic Support," Nippon Foundation, 2018.

70. "Official Opening of the Nippon Foundation Paralympic Support Center's New Office" 2015, Nippon Foundation: News, November 11, 2015, https://www.nippon -foundation.or.jp/en/news/articles/2015/20151111–20940.html.

71. Nippon Foundation Paralympic Support Center 2019, English homepage, 2019, https://www.parasapo.tokyo/en/. The Japanese version of the site has additional content.

72. Nippon Foundation Paralympic Support Center 2019. The magazines are available via the official Japanese website: Nippon Zaidan Pararinpikku Sapōto Sentā, 2019, https://www.parasapo.tokyo/gojournal/.

73. The newsletters can be downloaded from the official Japanese version of the site: Nippon Zaidan Pararinpikku Sapōto Sentā, 2019, https://www.parasapo.tokyo /topics/13042.

74. The most detailed information on past and future events is available on the Japanese version of the website.

75. See for example Suntory's CSR page: "Supporting Challenged Sports" 2018, Suntory, 2018, https://www.suntory.com/csr/activity/society/challenge/.

76. "Toyota no jūgyōin mo muchū! Shanai kara hirogaru 'botcha' no kanōsei" 2019, Pararinpikku sapōto sentā: nyūsu, February 25, 2019, https://www.parasapo.tokyo /topics/14147?fbclid=IwAR0HdA1s2RTcX9WW4azszbNAnYkbkCUtbr6gI4xwmosl z7O1-kNpaJKDRyI.

77. Tōkyō 2020 Orinpikku Pararinpikku Shōchi Iinkai 2013, 66 and 82.

78. In recounting Suzaki's story, unless otherwise noted, the following paragraphs draw primarily from our interview conducted at Taiyō no Ie, in Beppu on July, 14, 2017. Many of the details were similar to those from published interviews; see Sportiva 2016, "1964 nen no Nihon daihyō senshu wa 'Para shutsujō no jishin de kaotsuki mo kawatta,'" web Sportiva: Love Sports, September 7, 2016, https://sportiva.shueisha .co.jp/clm/othersports/para_sports/2016/09/07/1964_split/index.php. Sources providing unique details are cited separately.

79. "1964–2020: A Tour of the Past and the Future" 2014, Media Centre for Official Website of the Paralympic Movement, November 9, 2014, https://www.paralympic .org/news/1964-2020-tour-past-and-future.

80. Suzaki and other participants from the 1964 Paralympics have appeared in several recent newspaper articles, although few made the papers in 1964. See Iiyama Tarō, "1964 Tōkyō kara 2020 TOKYO e: dai 2 bu Pararinpikku no hajimari/ 3 gekai kikai no tane maku," *Mainichi shimbun*, March 13, 2014, p. 18; Iiyama Tarō, "1964 Tōkyō kara 2020 TOKYO e: dai 2 bu Pararinpikku no hajimari/ 5 tome jakusha ni yasashii shakai hasshin o," *Mainichi shimbun*, November 15, 2014, p. 17; Iiyama Tarō, "Kisha no hitori goto: Kokoro no baria furī /Tōkyō," *Mainichi shimbun*, March 13, 2016, pp. 28; and *Mainichi shimbun*, "Tōkyō Para: Hoteru riyō shiyasuku 64 nen no kin medarisuto," December 1, 2018, https://mainichi.jp/sportsspecial/articles/20180113/k00/00m/050 /095000c.

81. For Gamō's story, details in the following paragraphs were pieced together from a variety of sources, with the most information about her background provided by Kawakita Akira, "Hito: Gamō Akemi-san," *Mainichi shimbun*, October 24, 1986, p. 3; other sources with specific details are cited individually here.

82. *Asahi shimbun*, "Gamō Akemi-san shiryoku shōgai ni makezu Honoruru kansō (hito kinō kyō)," December 21, 1987, evening edition, p. 2.

83. Kōbe Rakueikai 2018, "Rakueikai nenpyō," http://www10.plala.or.jp/rakuei /nenpyo.html.

84. *Kōbe shimbun*, "Tabun naiteshimaisō," September 15, 1989, p. 26.

85. *Kōbe shimbun*, "Kin 'Akemi no yume' ima mankai," September 17, 1989, p. 23; *Kōbe shimbun*, "Gamō 4 shumoku ni kin medaru," September 19, 1989, p. 16.

86. Kōbe Rakueikai 2018, "Rakueikai nenpyō," Kōbe Rakueikai, 2018.

87. Kawakita Akira 1986, "Hito: Gamō Akemi-san," p. 3.

88. *Asahi shimbun*, "Nihon-kei to Tōkyō-kei de shikaku shōgaisha o shujinkō ni dorama tsukuri," January 12, 1990, evening edition, p. 10; *Yomiuri shimbun*, "Shitsumei josei ga marason kansō jitsuwa dorama ni Oginome Keiko ga idomu," January 12, 1990, evening edition, p. 7.

89. *Kōbe shimbun*, "Kin 'Akemi no yume' ima mankai," September 17, 1989, p. 23.

90. 1989NFKT 1989.

91. Kōbe Rakueikai 2018, "Rakueikai nenpyō," Kōbe Rakueikai, 2018.

92. This is the language used in the title for one of the articles on her completing the Honolulu Marathon: *Asahi shimbun*, "Gamō Akemi-san shiryoku shōgai ni makezu Honoruru kansō (hito kinō kyō)," December 21, 1987, evening edition, p. 2.

93. Kawakita Akira 1986, "Hito: Gamō Akemi-san," p. 3.

94. *Yomiuri shimbun*, "Shitsumei josei ga marason kansō jitsuwa dorama ni Oginome Keiko ga idomu," December 12, 1990, evening edition, p. 7.

95. For these quotations, see Hiromichi 2004, 6 and 10. Unless otherwise noted, the following details for Hiromichi's story are drawn primarily from this autobiographical work and from Akamine 2004. Details are similar in both accounts and overlap with other sources. Sources providing unique information are noted individually.

96. For the most updated information on his competition results, see his personal website at Hiromichi Jun 2018, JHiromichi wheelchair athlete, 2018, https://jhiromichi.com/.

97. On Hiromichi's sponsors at the time of this writing, see his personal website.

98. In 2018 the event was not held, but for information on Hiromichi's role in starting and maintaining the meet, see Ōita-ken Shōgaisha Supōtsu Shidōsha Kyōgikai 2017, "IPC kōnin Ōita Para rikujō repōto," Ōita-ken Shōgaisha Supōtsu Shidōsha Kyōgikai, May 18, 2017, https://ooitamejiro.jp/repo-201705oitapara.html.

99. For his activities, see Hiromichi Jun 2018, JHiromichi wheelchair athlete, 2018; on the early history of Sports of Heart events and Hiromichi's roles, see Itō 2012, 29–37 and 166–181; for details on Sports of Heart's past and future events, see official website: Sports of Heart 2019, https://s-heart.org/organization.

100. Talk titles listed on Hiromichi Jun 2018, JHiromichi wheelchair athlete, 2018; for a summary of earlier versions of such talks and selected student responses, see Akamine 2004, 91–94.

101. For details on these activities, see Hiromichi Jun 2018, JHiromichi wheelchair athlete, 2018.

102. Details that follow on Tsuchida are drawn primarily from Sasaki 2004, especially 51–92; and from Tsuchida's (2012) autobiographical work. Unique information from other sources is cited separately.

103. Tsuchida has a personal website where many of these accomplishments are recorded: Tsuchida Wakako 2015, http://www.tsuchidawakako.net/profile.html; however, the most updated results appear on her company's website: Yachiyo 2019, "Tsuchida Wakako senshu," https://www.yachiyo-ind.co.jp/wakako_tsuchida/.

104. Yachiyo 2019, "Tsuchida Wakako senshu."

105. For an example, see Sasaki 2004, 54–57.

106. Tsuchida 2010.

107. "Interview with Wakako Tsuchida, the Queen of Wheelchair Racing" 2012, Tamron, October 15, 2012, https://www.tamron.co.jp/en/special/athlete/tuchida1.html.

108. For an example of her role in the bid campaigns, see "Tokyo 2020 Games Will Be Built on Delivery, Celebration, Innovation: Tokyo 2020 Unveils Its Candidature File, Stresses Importance of Legacy" 2013, Tokyo 2020, January 8, 2013, https://tokyo2020.org/en/news/bid/20130108-02.html; on the Athletes' Commission, see "Six Paralympians in Tokyo 2020 Athletes' Commission" 2014, Media Centre for

Official Website of the Paralympic Movement, September 12, 2014, https://www
.paralympic.org/news/six-paralympians-tokyo-2020-athletes-commission.

109. Sasaki 2004; and Nakamura and Ogata 2004, 235–36.

110. Tsuchida 2012.

111. Tsuchida 2012, 171–72.

112. Tsuchida 2012, 3–4.

113. For Satō's case the following details are drawn largely from Sasaki 2004, especially 9–50; and from Sato's earliest autobiographical work, Satō 2013. Unique details
from these and other works are cited individually.

114. The fact that she was the first female with a prosthetic limb is specifically cited
in Satō 2012b, 84.

115. Details on her early talks and her award are from Sasaki 2004, 38–39.

116. See the company's CSR page: "Supporting Challenged Sports" 2018, Suntory,
2018, https://www.suntory.com/csr/activity/society/challenge/.

117. Sasaki 2004.

118. Satō 2013, 2014.

119. Satō 2012a, 2012b.

120. Satō 2012b, 115–24.

121. Kaz Nagatsuka, "Sato Shines as Role Model," *Japan Times*, October 4, 2014,
https://www.japantimes.co.jp/sports/2014/10/04/more-sports/track-field/sato
-shines-role-model/#.XJJP3RNKiT8.

122. Satō 2012b, 110–13.

123. Yoshii Taeko, "Tani Mami: Iron Paralympian with a Heart of Gold," *Nippon
.com*, March 29, 2018, https://www.nippon.com/en/views/b08902/tani-mami-iron
-paralympian-with-a-heart-of-gold.html.

124. For examples of press coverage on the situation, see Beppu Ikurō, "[Nichiyō
ni kaku] Amari ni zankoku de rifujin Tōkyō Para Tani Mami no fushutsujō wa kono
mama de ii no ka: ronsetsu iin," *Sankei nyūsu*, August 19, 2018, https://www.sankei
.com/column/news/180819/clm1808190004-n1.html; and Sakakibara Issei, "Tōkyō
Para no michi, ichido wa tozasare, tsui ni hiraita Tani Mami," *Asahi shimbun*, November 27, 2018, https://www.asahi.com/articles/ASLCM4TG2LCMUTQP00M.html.

125. Based on her publication history, it would not be surprising if a new or updated edition of her autobiography was published in connection with the Tokyo 2020
Games.

126. Ogura 2018, 585–86 and 591–93. Survey work related to these issues is ongoing in Japan.

127. Peers 2015, especially 104–20 and 176–225.

128. The first quotation refers to a statement from Satō's mother that she adopted
early on as the theme of her inspirational lectures; see Sasaki 2004, 38; the second is a
subheading from Tsuchida's autobiography (2012, 44).

129. Frost 2010, especially 10–11.

Coda

1. On legacy and the Paralympics more generally, see Misener 2017; and Pappous
and Brown 2018.

2. Fujita 2016, 181–82.

3. Ogura 2018, 588 and 592.

4. Fujita 2016, 187–88.

5. Fujita 2016, 182.

6. Fujita 2016, 184–87.

7. Ogura 2018, 592–93. Ogura notes that the feasibility of JPSA targets remain uncertain.

8. Fujita 2016, 185.

9. For example, *Kyodo News*, "Paralympics: Para Sports Gym Completed in Tokyo, to Provide Training Ahead of 2020," June 1, 2018, https://english.kyodonews.net /news/2018/06/8bb02d318188-paralympics-para-sports-gym-completed-to-provide -training-ahead-of-2020.html.

10. Fujita 2016, 183–84.

BIBLIOGRAPHY

Abbreviations Used in Notes

1989NFKT	1989 nen Fesupikku Kōbe Taikai Soshiki Iinkai
APC	Asian Paralympic Committee
D1KK	Dai 1 kai Kyokutō Minami Taiheiyō Shintai Shōgaisha Supōtsu Taikai Jikkō Iinkai
KSSSTUI	Kokusai Shintai Shōgaisha Supōtsu Taikai Un'ei Iinkai
NPTKTSI	Nagano Pararinpikku Tōki Kyōgi Taikai Soshiki Iinkai
NSSSK	Nihon Shintai Shōgaisha Supōtsu Kyōkai
NYD	Nakamura Yutaka Den Kankō Iinkai
OKKMTJ	Ōita Kokusai Kurumaisu Marason Taikai Jimukyoku

Published and Unpublished Sources

"2nd FESPIC Games Ended in Success." 1978. *FESPIC* 4 (1): 1.

"2nd Parramatta." 2006. *J.S.A.D. Sports* 28 (December): 15.

"3rd Hong Kong." 2006. *J.S.A.D. Sports* 28 (December): 17.

"4th Surakarta." 2006. *J.S.A.D. Sports* 28 (December): 19.

"6th Beijing." 2006. *J.S.A.D. Sports* 28 (December): 23.

"7th Bangkok." 2006. *J.S.A.D. Sports* 28 (December): 25.

"8th Busan." 2006. *J.S.A.D. Sports* 28 (December): 27.

"9th Kuala Lumpul [*sic*]." 2006. *J.S.A.D. Sports* 28 (December): 29.

1989 nen Fesupikku Kōbe Taikai Soshiki Iinkai. 1989. *Fesupikku Kōbe Taikai: FESPIC Kobe '89.* VCD of Japanese documentary film originally produced on videocassette. Kōbe: 1989 nen Fesupikku Kōbe Taikai Soshiki Iinkai with Tōkyō Fukuhara Firumusu.

——. 1990. *1989 nen Fesupikku Kōbe Taikai kōshiki hōkokusho.* Kōbe: 1989 nen Fesupikku Kōbe Taikai Soshiki Iinkai.

2005 nen Supesharu Orinpikku Tōki Sekai Taikai Nagano (SONA). 2005. *2005 nen Supesharu Orinpikku Tōki Sekai Taikai kōshiki hōkokusho.* Nagano: 2005 nen Supesharu Orinpikku Tōki Sekai Taikai Nagano (SONA).

Akamine Kazuo. 2004. "Kurumaisu marason wa tanoshii." In *Kurumaisu marason: Ōita kara sekai e no messēji*, edited by Nakamura Tarō and Ogata Hajime, 73–94. Tokyo: Iryō bunkasha.

Akita Shigeru. 1998. "Nagano Pararinpikku Tōki Kyōgi Taikai e no kakawari." *OT jānaru* 32 (June): 641–44.

Andranovich, Greg, Matthew J. Burbank, and Charles H. Heying. 2001. "Olympic Cities: Lessons Learned from Mega-Event Politics." *Journal of Urban Affairs* 23 (2): 113–31.

Anzai Kiyomi. 2006. "Dai 4 kai taikai ni sanka shite." *J.S.A.D. Sports* 28 (December): 20.

Aoki, Michiko Yamaguchi. 1997. *Records of Wind and Earth: A Translation of Fudoki, with Introduction and Commentaries.* Ann Arbor, MI: Association for Asian Studies.

Araragi Kazuma. 2002a. "Shōgaisha supōtsu no hōdō ni kan suru kenkyū—1945 nen-1999 nen no *Asahi shimbun* no kiji bunseki." *Kyōiku igaku* 47 (5): 374–80.

——. 2002b. "Tōkyō Pararinpikku to shōgaisha supōtsu." *Tōkai Joshi Daigaku kiyō* 22: 13–23.

Asian Paralympic Committee. 2015. "Strategic Plan, 2015–2018." http://www .asianparalympic.org/apc-strategic-plan-2015–2018.

Asō, Manabu. 2010. "Introduction: The Infinite Possibility of Sports and Future." In *FESPIC Movement: Sports for People with Disabilities in the Far East & South Pacific,* edited by Silas T. C. Chiang, 12–22. Hong Kong: Commercial Press.

"Background and Point of Consideration on Merger between FESPIC and APC." 2004. *FESPIC* 38 (August): 2–3.

Bailey, Steve. 2008. *Athlete First: A History of the Paralympic Movement.* West Sussex: John Wiley & Sons.

Beppu-shi Kyōikukai. 1933. *Beppu-shi shi.* Beppu: Beppu-shi Kyōikukai.

Beppu-shi Kyōiku Iinkai. 2012. "Bunkateki keikan: Beppu no yukemuri keikan hozon keikaku." Beppu-shi. https://www.city.beppu.Ōita.jp/pdf/gakusyuu /bunkazai/yukemuri_keikan/02_04.pdf.

Bookman, Mark. 2018. "Politics, Prosthesis, and the Popular Imagination: 100 Years of Disability in Japan." PhD diss. prospectus, University of Pennsylvania, Philadelphia. https://bookmanresearch.com/dissertation -prospectus/.

Bourke, John. 2010. "Perspective of an Official from the Australian Team: The 4th FESPIC Games in Surakarta, Indonesia (1986)." In *FESPIC Movement: Sports for People with Disabilities in the Far East & South Pacific,* edited by Silas T. C. Chiang, 79–83. Hong Kong: Commercial Press.

Braye, Stuart, Kevin Dixon, and Tom Gibbons. 2013. "'A Mockery of Equality': An Exploratory Investigation into Disabled Activists' Views of the Paralympic Games." *Disability & Society* 28 (7): 984–96. https://doi.org/10.1080 /09687599.2012.748648.

Brittain, Ian. 2010. *The Paralympic Games Explained.* London: Routledge.

——. 2014. *From Stoke Mandeville to Sochi: A History of the Summer and Winter Paralympic Games.* Champaign, IL: Common Ground.

——. 2016. "A Critical Perspective on the Legacy of the London 2012 Paralympic Games." *Nippon Zaidan Pararinpikku Kenkyūkai Kiyō* 5 (April): 23–42.

——. 2017. "Communicating and Managing the Message: Media and Media Representation of Disability and Paralympic Sport." In *Managing the Paralympics,* edited by Simon Darcy, Stephen Frawley, and Daryl Adair, 241–62. London: Palgrave Macmillan.

Brittain, Ian, and Aaron Beacom, eds. 2018. *The Palgrave Handbook of Paralympic Studies.* London: Palgrave Macmillan.

Brittain, Ian, and Leonardo Jose Mataruna Dos Santos. 2018. "The Rio 2016 Paralympic Games." In *The Palgrave Handbook of Paralympic Studies*, edited by Ian Brittain and Aaron Beacom, 531–53. London: Palgrave Macmillan.

Bruce, Toni. 2014. "Us and Them: The Influence of Discourses of Nationalism on Media Coverage of the Paralympics." *Disability & Society* 29 (9): 1443–59. https://doi.org/10.1080/09687599.2013.816624.

Bundon, Andrea, and Laura Hurd Clarke. 2015. "Unless You Go Online You Are on Your Own: Blogging as a Bridge in Para-Sport." *Disability & Society* 30 (2): 185–98. https://doi.org/10.1080/09687599.2014.973477.

Busan FESPIC Games Organizing Committee. 2003. *2002 Busan FESPIC Games Official Report.* Busan: Busan FESPIC Games Organizing Committee.

Cabinet Office. 2002. *Country Report on the Achievement of the Government Measures for Persons with Disabilities during the Asian and Pacific Decade of Disabled Persons, 1993–2002: Japan.* Tokyo: Cabinet Office. https://www8.cao.go.jp/shougai /english/ootsureport/mokuji.html.

Chiang, Silas T. C., ed. 2010a. *FESPIC Movement: Sports for People with Disabilities in the Far East & South Pacific.* Hong Kong: Commercial Press.

——. 2010b. "Vision of One and Passion of All: The 3rd FESPIC Games in Shatin, Hong Kong (1982)." In *FESPIC Movement: Sports for People with Disabilities in the Far East & South Pacific*, edited by Silas T. C. Chiang, 61–78. Hong Kong: Commercial Press.

Dai 1 kai Kyokutō Minami Taiheiyō Shintai Shōgaisha Supōtsu Taikai Jikkō Iinkai. 1975. *FESPIC '75.* Ōita: Dai 1 kai Kyokutō Minami Taiheiyō Shintai Shōgaisha Supōtsu Taikai Jikkō Iinkai.

Dai 30 kai kinen Ōita Kokusai Kurumaisu Marason Taikai kinen jigyō. 2010. *Shōgaisha supōtsu shashinten odekake wākushoppu: Dai 30 kai kinen Ōita Kokusai Kurumaisu Marason Taikai kinen jigyō kinenshi.* Beppu: Mitsubishi Shōji Taiyō kabushiki gaisha.

Dai 49 kai Nihon Rihabiritēshon Igakkai Gakujutsu Shūkai. 2012. "Nihon Rihabiritēshon Igakkai 50 shūnen kinen jigyō tokubetsu kiga: 'Kyūshū ni okeru rihabiritēshon no ayumi.'" Kitakyūshū-shi. http://kyureha.umin.ne.jp /img/jarm2012_50th_anniversary.pdf.

Darcy, Simon. 2017. "Accessibility as a Key Management Component of the Paralympics." In *Managing the Paralympics*, edited by Simon Darcy, Stephen Frawley, and Daryl Adair, 49–92. London: Palgrave Macmillan.

Darcy, Simon, Stephen Frawley, and Daryl Adair, eds. 2017. *Managing the Paralympics.* London: Palgrave Macmillan.

Dickson, Tracey J., Angela M. Benson, and Deborah A. Blackman. 2011. "Developing a Framework for Evaluating Olympic and Paralympic Legacies." *Journal of Sport & Tourism* 16 (4): 285–302. https://doi.org/10.1080/14775085.2011.635014.

Dunstan, George. 1995. "Relationship between FESPIC and IPC." *FESPIC* 25 (August): 3.

——. 2010. "All Difficulties in the Beginning Years: The 2nd FESPIC Games in Parramatta, Australia (1977)." In *FESPIC Movement: Sports for People with Disabilities in the Far East & South Pacific*, edited by Silas T. C. Chiang, 56–60. Hong Kong: Commercial Press.

Economic and Social Commission for Asia and the Pacific. 1992. *ESCAP Resolution: 48/3, Asian and Pacific Decade of Disabled Persons, 1993–2002.* http://www.dinf .ne.jp/doc/english/intl/apddp/8.html.

"Editorial." 1987. *FESPIC* 12 (March): 2.

Elgin, Don, and Kevin Moloney. 2015. *One Foot on the Podium.* Unpublished manuscript.

Endō Hanae. 2017. "Rio de Janeiro Pararinpikku Taikai ni kan suru shimbun hōdō no keikō bunseki to ichikōsatsu." *Nippon Zaidan Pararinpikku Kenkyūkai kiyō* 7 (April): 31–40.

FESPIC. 1990. 16 (January): 1–7.

"FESPIC and APC Agreed to Form a Task Force for the Purpose of Merge." 2004. *FESPIC* 38 (August): 1.

Festschrift: Internationales Versehrten-Sportfest Linz 1963. 1963. Linz: 15 Jahre Oberös-terreichischer Versehrten-Sportverband.

"FRF to be Enlarged." 1978. *FESPIC* 4 (1): 1.

"From the Secretariat." 1990. *FESPIC* 17 (December): 4.

"From the Secretariat." 1998. *FESPIC* 29 (February): 4.

Frost, Dennis J. 2010. *Seeing Stars: Sports Celebrity, Identity, and Body Culture in Modern Japan.* Harvard East Asian Monographs 331. Cambridge, MA: Harvard University Asia Center.

Fujioka Tomoko. 1998. "Watashi no naka no Pararinpikku." *Kango kyōiku* 39 (7): 570–72.

Fujita Motoaki. 2002. "Shōgaisha supōtsu to media." In *Gendai media supōtsu ron,* edited by Hashimoto Junichi, 197–217. Tokyo: Seikai shishō sha.

——. 2013. *Shōgaisha supōtsu no kankyō to kanōsei.* Tokyo: Sōbun kikaku.

——. 2016. *Pararinpikku no tanoshimikata.* Tokyo: Shōgakukan.

Fujiwara Shinichirō. 2006. "FESPIC Kyōgi Taikai o furikaette." *J.S.A.D. Sports* 28 (December): 10.

——. 2010. "Looking Back on FESPIC Events: The 5th FESPIC Games in Kobe, Japan (1989)." In *FESPIC Movement: Sports for People with Disabilities in the Far East & South Pacific,* edited by Silas T. C. Chiang, 84–89. Hong Kong: Commercial Press.

"Gendai supōtsu are kore: Nagano Pararinpikku." 1998. *Monbu jihō* 1456 (February): 74–75.

Gilbert, Keith, and Otto J. Schantz, eds. 2008. *The Paralympic Games: Empowerment or Side Show?* Disability & Sport. New York: Meyer & Meyer.

Grant, John M. F. 2006. "The History of the FESPIC Games." *J.S.A.D. Sports* 28 (December): 9.

——. 2010. "Prologue: The Founding Era." In *FESPIC Movement: Sports for People with Disabilities in the Far East & South Pacific,* edited by Silas T. C. Chiang, 24–28. Hong Kong: Commercial Press.

Grue, Jan. 2016. "The Problem with Inspiration Porn: A Tentative Definition and a Provisional Critique." *Disability & Society* 31 (6): 839–49. https://doi.org/10 .1080/09687599.2016.1205473.

Guttmann, Allen, and Lee Thompson. 2001. *Japanese Sports: A History.* Honolulu: University of Hawai'i Press.

Hagiwara Sadasuke. 1914. *Beppu onsenshi.* Beppu: Hagiwaragō.

Han, Min Kyu. 2010. "The Year of Another Big Strive: Development of Sports in Korea: The 8th FESPIC Games in Busan, Korea (2002)." In *FESPIC Movement: Sports for People with Disabilities in the Far East & South Pacific*, edited by Silas T. C. Chiang, 109–15. Hong Kong: Commercial Press.

Hargreaves, Jean Ann, and Brent Hardin. 2009. "Women Wheelchair Athletes: Competing against Media Stereotypes." *Disability Studies Quarterly* 29 (2). https://doi.org/10.18061/dsq.v29i2.920.

Hatada Kazuo. 1998. "Fesupikku Renmei (Kyokutō Minami Taiheiyō Shintai Shōgaisha Supōtsu Renmei) no dōkō." *Rinshō supōtsu igaku* 15 (2): 127–32.

——. 2010a. "Foreword." In *FESPIC Movement: Sports for People with Disabilities in the Far East & South Pacific*, edited by Silas T. C. Chiang, 8–11. Hong Kong: Commercial Press.

——. 2010b. "Recollections of the Past 33 Years: From the 1st FESPIC Games in Oita, Japan (1975) to Others." In *FESPIC Movement: Sports for People with Disabilities in the Far East & South Pacific*, edited by Silas T. C. Chiang, 29–55. Hong Kong: Commercial Press.

Hatta Aki. 1964. "Genshi bakudan hibakusha Beppu onsen riyō kenkyūjo no tōji seiseki." *Hiroshima igaku* 17 (7): 104–108.

Hayashi, Reiko, and Masako Okuhira. 2001. "The Disability Rights Movement in Japan: Past, Present and Future." *Disability & Society* 16 (6): 855–69. https://doi.org/10.1080/09687590120083994.

Headquarters for Promoting the Welfare of Disabled Persons, Prime Minister's Office. 1995. "The Government Action Plan for Persons with Disabilities: A Seven-Year Normalization Strategy." http://www.dinf.ne.jp/doc/japanese/law/archives.html.

Hemmi Masaaki. 1982. "Shōigunjin shōgakkō kyōin yōseijo no setsuritsu." *Hokkaidō Daigaku Kyōiku Gakubu kiyō* 40 (March): 1–29.

"Henshū goki." 1998. *Hyūman netto Nagano kikan-shi* 2 (October): 8. http://hynet.webcrow.jp/magazine.html.

Heyer, Katharina. 2015. *Rights Enabled: The Disability Revolution, from the US, to Germany and Japan, to the United Nations*. Ann Arbor: University of Michigan Press.

Hiramatsu Morihiko. 1984. "Ashita he no chōsen: Ōita Kokusai Kurumaisu Mara-son." *Todōfuken tenbō* 12 (315): 2–3.

Hiromichi Jun. 2004. *Dōse, ikiru nara: kurumaisu asurīto no akarui tatakai*. Tokyo: Jitsugyō no Nihonsha.

"'Hito ni yasashii machidzukuri' o mezasu: Pararinpikku o kaisai shita Nagano no kōtsū kankyō o miru." 1998. *JAMAGAZINE* 32 (5): 9–13.

"Hito to shakai: Obinata Kuniko-san." 1998. *Kōsei* 53 (6): 55–57.

Hori Tōkichirō. 1966. *Beppu onsen rekishi ryaku nenpyō*. Beppu: Asō shoten.

"Hōritsu gyōsei." 2016. Disability Information Resources. 2016. http://www.dinf.ne.jp/doc/japanese/law/archives.html.

Howe, P. David. 2008. *The Cultural Politics of the Paralympic Movement*. Routledge Critical Studies in Sport. London: Routledge.

Howe, P. David, and Andrew Parker. 2012. "Celebrating Imperfection: Sport, Disability and Celebrity Culture." *Celebrity Studies* 3 (3): 270–82. https://doi.org/10.1080/19392397.2012.717745.

Ibusuki Tadaaki. 1987. "Dai 4 kai Kyokutō Minami Taiheiyō Shintai Shōgaisha Supōtsu Taikai o oete." *Taiiku no kagaku* 37 (1): 82–86.

Ide, M., H. Ogata, M. Kobayashi, F. Tajima, and K. Hatada. 1994. "Anthropometric Features of Wheelchair Marathon Race Competitors with Spinal Cord Injuries." *Paraplegia* 32 (3): 174–79. https://doi.org/10.1038/sc.1994.31.

Ijima Eiichi. 1997. "Nagano Orinipikku Pararinpikku ni muketa machidzukuri taiō: Nagano-shi hito ni yasashii machidzukuri suishin jigyō purojekuto ni tsuite." *Kōtsū kōgaku* 32 (6): 32–38.

——. 1998. "Nagano Orinipikku Pararinpikku ni muketa yasashii machidzukuri purojekuto." *Nōmaraizēshon* 18 (2): 72–74.

Ikeda Jun. 1998. "Kandō o arigatō: Nagano Para Bora no Kai." *JD jānaru* 18 (2): 20.

Ikeda Taka. 2006. "Bankoku Taikai o furikaete." *J.S.A.D. Sports* 28 (December): 26.

"Impressions of the 4th FESPIC." 1987. *FESPIC* 12 (March): 1–2.

Itō Kazuko. 2012. *Yōkoso, shōgaisha supōtsu e.* Tokyo: Kōsaidō.

Jackson, Daniel, Caroline Hodges, Mike Molesworth, and Richard Scullion, eds. 2015. *Reframing Disability: Media, (Dis)Empowerment and Voice in the 2012 Paralympic Games.* Abingdon: Routledge.

Japan Sports Association for the Disabled. 2006. *J.S.A.D. SPORTS: sōryoku tokushū: Fesupikku Kyōgi Taikai* 28 (December).

Japanese Society for Rehabilitation of Disabled Persons. 1997. *The 30 Selected Japanese Laws Related to Persons with Disabilities.* Tokyo: Japanese Society for Rehabilitation of Disabled Persons. http://www.dinf.ne.jp/doc/english/law/japan/30select.html.

Johnson, Craig. 2012. *As the Crow Flies.* New York: Viking.

Kamo Akira. 1992. "Mō hitotsu no Nagano Gorin 'Pararinpikku.'" *Chōsa geppō* 371 (March): 28.

"Kanja tai shakaijin no tatakai datta: Pararinpikku ga Nihon jin ni oshieta mono." 1964. *Shukan yomiuri* 23 (49): 28–32.

Kanō Kazuhisa. 2000. "Chihōchō topikkusu: (Ōita-ken) Ōita Kokusai Kurumaisu Marason Taikai." *Shūkan shakai hoshō* 54 (2104): 57.

Kasai Yoshisuke. 1964a. "Aragaki Hideo rensai taidan: toki no sugao 68: Kasai Yoshisuke." *Shūkan asahi* 69 (46): 34–37.

——. 1964b. "Pararinpikku." *Niigata kenjin* 129 (November): 7.

——. 1964c. "Pararinpikku no koto." *Kōsei* 19 (12): 16–19.

Kayama, Misa, and Wendy L. Haight. 2014. *Disability, Culture, and Development: A Case Study of Japanese Children at School.* Oxford: Oxford University Press.

Keizai Kikakuchō, ed. 1982. *2000 nen no Nihon: kokusaika, kōreika, seijukuka ni sonaete.* Tokyo: Ōkurashō insatsu kyoku.

Kelly, William W. 2019. *The Sportsworld of the Hanshin Tigers: Professional Baseball in Modern Japan.* Oakland: University of California Press.

Kietlinski, Robin. 2011. *Japanese Women and Sport: Beyond Baseball and Sumo.* London: Bloomsbury Academic.

"Kigyō no 'kanmuri' senryaku nau dai 1 kai: shinshōsha ni supōtsu no rin o: Ōita Kokusai Kurumaisu Marason—Omuron." 1991. *Jitsugyō no Nihon* 94 (1): 123–25.

Kobayashi Junichi. 2006. "Dai 9 kai Fesupikku Kyōgi Taikai hōkoku." *J.S.A.D. Sports* 28 (December): 31–32.

Kodama Kazuhiko. 1998. "Shinbun hōdō ni miru 'shōgaisha supōtsu' mondai: Nagano Pararinpikku ga tōikaketa koto." *Rinshō supōtsu igaku* 15 (10): 1190–93.

Koga Jirō. 1985. "Tokushū: jijitai no imējidsukuri repōto: Ōita Kokusai Kurumaisu Marason Taikai." *Jiji kenshū* 305 (August): 38–42.

Kōhō Bukai. 1964. "Paralympic Tokyo 1964: Pararinpikku Kokusai Shintai Shōgaisha Supōtsu Taikai." Kokusai Shintai Shōgaisha Supōtsu Taikai Un'ei Iinkai. Seikyū bangō: "bunkan-01 039-00 Hei 3 sō-00964-100" (Kenmei bangō: 30). National Archives of Japan: Kokuritsu kōbun shokan shozō.

Kohrman, Matthew. 2005. *Bodies of Difference: Experiences of Disability and Institutional Advocacy in the Making of Modern China*. Berkeley: University of California Press.

Koike Masashi. 1998. "Shimin borantea ga tsukuri ageta 'Āto Pararinpikku Nagano' kaisai hōkoku." *Gekkan fukushi* 81 (6): 68–73.

"Kokusai Shintai Shōgaisha Supōtsu Taikai no kaisai ni tsuite." 1964. In *Kakugi hōkoku*. October 23, 1964. Seikyū bangō: "bunkan-01 039-00 Hei 3 sō-00964-100" (Kenmei bangō: 30). National Archives of Japan: Kokuritsu kōbun shokan shozō.

Kokusai Shintai Shōgaisha Supōtsu Taikai Un'ei Iinkai. 1963. "Kokusai Shintai Shōgaisha Supōtsu Taikai (kaisetsu)." Kokusai Shintai Shōgaisha Supōtsu Taikai Un'ei Iinkai. Seikyū bangō: "bunkan-01 039-00 Hei 3 sō-00964-100" (Kenmei bangō: 30). National Archives of Japan: Kokuritsu kōbun shokan shozō.

——. 1964. "Leaflet: Pararinpikku: Kokusai Shintai Shōgaisha Supōtsu Taikai." Kokusai Shintai Shōgaisha Supōtsu Taikai Un'ei Iinkai. Seikyū bangō: "bunkan-01 039-00 Hei 3 sō-00964-100" (Kenmei bangō: 30). National Archives of Japan: Kokuritsu kōbun shokan shozō.

——. 1965a. *Pararinpikku Tōkyō Taikai hōkokusho*. Tokyo: Kokusai Shintai Shōgaisha Supōtsu Taikai Un'ei Iinkai.

——. 1965b. *Tōkyō Pararinpikku: Kokusai Shintai Shōgaisha Supōtsu Taikai shashinshū*. Tokyo: Kokusai Shintai Shōgaisha Supōtsu Taikai Un'ei Iinkai.

Komori Masaichi. 1998. "Chihōchō topikkusu: (Ōita ken) Ōita Kokusai Kurumaisu Marason Taikai." *Shūkan shakai hoshō* 52 (2002): 57.

Kondō Fumito. 1998. "Hajimete no honkakuteki hōsō." *JD jānaru* 18 (2): 21.

Kondō Kazuo. 2006. "FESPIC Kōbe Taikai no omoide." *J.S.A.D Sports* 28 (December): 22.

Kōseishō Gojūnenshi Henshū Iinkai. 1988. *Kōseishō gojūnenshi*. Tokyo: Kōsei Mondai Kenkyūkai.

Kotani Naomichi. 1998. "Nagano Pararinpikku no seika to kadai." *Rihabiritēshon* 403 (May): 3–4.

Le Clair, Jill M. 2011. "Transformed Identity: From Disabled Person to Global Paralympian." *Sport in Society* 14 (9): 1116–30. https://doi.org/10.1080/17430437.2011.614768.

Legg, David. 2018. "Development of the IPC and Relations with the IOC and Other Stakeholders." In *The Palgrave Handbook of Paralympic Studies*, edited by Ian Brittain and Aaron Beacom, 151–72. London: Palgrave Macmillan.

Lock, Margaret. 1993. "Ideology, Female Midlife, and the Greying of Japan." *Journal of Japanese Studies* 19 (1): 43–78. https://doi.org/10.2307/132864.

"Mae e: dai 30 kai Ōita Kokusai Kurumaisu Marason: bangai hen 5." 2010. In *Dai 30 kai kinen Ōita Kokusai Kurumaisu Marason Taikai kinen shi*, Ōita Kokusai Kurumaisu Marason Taikai Jimukyoku, 116. Ōita: Ōita-ken.

"Mae e: dai 30 kai Ōita Kokusai Kurumaisu Marason: dai 2 bu: ishizue 2." 2010. In *Dai 30 kai kinen Ōita Kokusai Kurumaisu Marason Taikai kinen shi*, Ōita Kokusai Kurumaisu Marason Taikai Jimukyoku, 105. Ōita: Ōita-ken.

Maharaj, Jagdish C. 2011. "Living Disability and Restructuring International Paralympic Committee Sport in Oceania: The Challenge of Perceptions, Spatial Dispersal and Limited Resources." *Sport in Society* 14 (9): 1211–26.

Manurung, P. 1985. "The 4th FESPIC Games 1986 in Indonesia." *FESPIC* 10 (June): 2–4.

——. 1986. "The 4th FESPIC Games in Surakarta-Indonesia." *FESPIC* 11 (June): 1–2.

Mao, Ailin, and Shuhan Sun. 2018. "The Rise of China as a Paralympic Super Power." In *The Palgrave Handbook of Paralympic Studies*, edited by Ian Brittain and Aaron Beacom, 295–320. London: Palgrave Macmillan.

Markus, Andrew L. 1985. "The Carnival of Edo: Misemono Spectacles from Contemporary Accounts." *Harvard Journal of Asiatic Studies* 45 (2): 499. https://doi.org/10.2307/2718971.

Maruta Tsutomu. 1998. "Borantea de hajimari borantea de owaranai '98 Āto Pararinpikku Nagano." *Kenchiku to machidzukuri* 260 (November): 16–19.

Masuda Yatarō. 1965. "Pararinpikku no kaimaku made." *Taiiku no kagaku* 15 (1): 7–9.

Matanle, Peter. 2017. "Towards an Asia-Pacific 'Depopulation Dividend' in the 21st Century: Regional Growth and Shrinkage in Japan and New Zealand." *Asia-Pacific Journal: Japan Focus* 15.6 (5). https://apjjf.org/2017/06/Matanle.html.

Matsumoto Koji. 2008. "Shōgaisha supōtsu ibento no māketingu: Ōita Kokusai Kurumaisu Marason no manejimento jirei." *Yamaguchi Kenritsu Daigaku Shakai Fukushi Gakubu kiyō* 14 (March): 87–96.

Matsuo Masao. 1989. "1989 nen Fesupikku Kōbe Taikai." *Toshi seisaku* 56 (July): 124–40.

Miah, Andy, and Jennifer Jones. 2012. "The Olympic Movement's New Media Revolution: Monetisation, Open Media and Intellectual Property." In *The Palgrave Handbook of Olympic Studies*, edited by Helen Jefferson Lenskyj and Stephen Wagg, 274–88. London: Palgrave Macmillan.

Miller, Aaron L. 2013. *Discourses of Discipline: An Anthropology of Corporal Punishment in Japan's Schools and Sports*. Japan Research Monograph 17. Berkeley, CA: Institute of East Asian Studies.

Misener, Laura. 2015. "Leveraging Parasport Events for Community Participation: Development of a Theoretical Framework." *European Sport Management Quarterly* 15 (1): 132–53. https://doi.org/10.1080/16184742.2014.997773.

——. 2017. "Managing Legacy and the Paralympic Games." In *Managing the Paralympics*, edited by Simon Darcy, Stephen Frawley, and Daryl Adair, 93–111. London: Palgrave Macmillan.

"Nagano Orinpikku Pararinpikku to ken dzukuri." 1998. *Hito to kokudo* 23 (5): 59–63.

"Nagano Pararinpikku kaisai ni mukete: 'Bunka Puroguramu' tte nani?" 1997. *Nōmaraizēhon* 17 (9): 60–61.

"Nagano Pararinpikku kaisai ni mukete: Nagano Pararinpikku seika rirē no rirē chīmu boshū ni tsuite." 1997. *Nōmaraizēshon* 17 (10): 62–63.

"Nagano Pararinpikku kaisai ni mukete: nyūjō-ken ga hanbai saremasu." 1997. *Nōmaraizēshon* 17 (5): 54–55.

"Nagano Pararinpikku kaisai ni mukete: Pararinpikku Senshu Mura." 1998. *Nōmaraizēshon* 18 (1): 58–59.

"Nagano Pararinpikku kaisai ni mukete: 'Pure Pararinpikku' no kaisai." 1997. *Nōmaraizēshon* 17 (6): 60–61.

Nagano Pararinpikku Tōki Kyōgi Taikai Soshiki Iinkai. 1998. *Nagano Pararinpikku Tōki Kyōgi Taikai kōshiki hōkokusho*. Nagano: Nagano Pararinpikku Tōki Kyōgi Taikai Soshiki Iinkai.

Nagano-ken. 1995. *Nagano-ken no fukushi no machidzukuri jōrei*. March 31, 1995. Amended December 17, 2015. https://www.pref.nagano.lg.jp/kenchiku/kurashi/sumai/shisaku/machizukuri/shikokisoku/kijun.html.

Nagano-shi Kōchō Kai. 1999. *'98 Nagano Orinpikku·Pararinpikku Tōki Kyōgi Taikai: sekai no hito to tomo ni ikiru: Ikkō Ikkoku kōryū katsudō no kiroku*. Nagano: Nagano-shi Kyōiku Iinkai.

Nakagawa Kazuhiko. 1975. "FESPIC Games ni sanka shite." *Sōgō rihabiritēshon* 3 (11): 51–53.

——. 1978. "Shinshōsha no tame no supōtsu: FESPIC Games." *Taiiku no kagaku* 28 (3): 199–204.

——. 1998. "Tokushū Orinpikku gakkō taiiku: Pararinpikku no kyōiku teki igi." *Gakkō taiiku* 51 (1): 25–27.

——. 2006. "Dai 2 kai FESPIC Paramatta Taikai." *J.S.A.D. Sports* 28 (December): 16.

Nakamura, Karen. 2006. *Deaf in Japan: Signing and the Politics of Identity*. Ithaca: Cornell University Press.

——. 2013. *A Disability of the Soul: An Ethnography of Schizophrenia and Mental Illness in Contemporary Japan*. Ithaca: Cornell University Press.

Nakamura Tarō. 2002. *Pararinpikku e no shōtai: chōsen suru asurītotachi*. Tokyo: Iwanami shoten.

Nakamura Tarō, Nakamura Eijirō, Asō Kuniichi, Masumi Shōgo, and Hatada Kazuo. 1995. "Kako 13 kai Ōita Kokusai Kurumaisu Marason ni okeru hōkatsuteki igaku chōsa: sono genjō to mondaiten." *Rinshō supōtsu igaku* 12 (8): 923–27.

Nakamura Tarō, and Ogata Hajime, eds. 2004. *Kurumaisu marason: Ōita kara sekai e no messēji*. Tokyo: Iryō bunkasha.

Nakamura Yutaka. 1964. "Sekizui sonshōsha no Orinpikku." *Nihon Ishikai zasshi* 52 (9): 867–70.

——. 1965. "Kokusai Shintai Shōgaisha Supōtsu Taikai o owarite." *Seikei gaika* 16 (5): 459–79.

——. 1975. *Taiyō no nakamatachi yo*. Tokyo: Kōdansha.

——. 1978. "Kaigai repōto: Fesupikku." *Hataraku hiroba* 5 (February): 22–24.

Nakamura Yutaka Den Kankō Iinkai. 1988. *Nakamura Yutaka den*. Ōita: Nakamura Yutaka Den Kankō Iinkai.

Namikoshi Nobuo, and Tomita Yukihiro, eds. 1999. *Supōtsu gyōsei seisaku manyuaru*. Tokyo: Bunkashobō hakubunsha.

Narusawa Kazuko. 1998. "Nagano Pararinpikku borantea o taiken shite." *Kango kyōiku* 39 (7): 568–69.

NHK Kōsei Bunka Jigyōdan. 1965. *8–14 November 1964, Tōkyō, Yoyogi Senshu Mura ato*. VCD of documentary film produced in cooperation with NHK. Tokyo: NHK Kōsei Bunka Jigyōdan.

Nihon Kurumaisu Supōtsu Kenkyūkai. 1991. *Kurumaisu marason: Ōita Kokusai Kurumaisu Marason no 10 nen o kaerimite: chōsa kenkyū hōkokusho.* Tokyo: Nihon Shintai Shōgaisha Supōtsu Kyōkai.

Nihon Pararinpikku Iinkai. 2007. *Fesupikku Kuararunpūru Taikai hōkokusho.* Tokyo: Nihon Shōgaisha Supōtsu Kyōkai.

Nihon Shintai Shōgaisha Supōtsu Kyōkai. 1985. *Sōritsu 20 nen shi.* Tokyo: Nihon Shintai Shōgaisha Supōtsu Kyōkai.

——. 1998. *1998 Nagano Pararinpikku Nihon senshu meikan.* Tokyo: Chūō hōki shuppan.

Nihon Shōi Gunjinkai. 1967. *Nihon Shōi Gunjinkai 15 nen shi.* Tokyo: Senshō byōsha kaikan.

Nojiri, Yoshitaka. 1985. "Report of the Inspection Tour in Indonesia." *FESPIC* 10 (June): 4.

Ogoura Kazuo. 2015. "1964 Tōkyō Pararinpikku ga nokoshita mono." *Nippon Zaidan Pararinpikku Kenkyūkai kiyō* 1 (January): 5–23.

Ogura, Kazuo. 2015a. "The 'Legacy' of the 1964 Tokyo Paralympics." *Nippon Zaidan Pararinpikku Kenkyūkai kiyō* 1: 24–43.

——. 2015b. "The Legacy of the 1998 Winter Paralympics in Nagano." *Nippon Zaidan Pararinpikku Kenkyūkai kiyō* 3: 33–71.

——. 2018. "Visions of the Legacy of the Tokyo 2020 Paralympic Games." In *The Palgrave Handbook of Paralympic Studies*, edited by Ian Brittain and Aaron Beacom, 579–601. London: Palgrave Macmillan.

"Ōita Kokusai Kurumaisu Marason Taikai." 1996. *Kōsei* 51 (12): 35.

Ōita Kokusai Kurumaisu Marason Taikai Jimukyoku. 1988. *Dai hachi kai Ōita Kokusai Kurumaisu Marason Taikai kinenshi.* Ōita: Ōita-ken.

——. 2003. *Dai 23 kai Ōita Kokusai Kurumaisu Marason Taikai.* Ōita: Ōita-ken.

——. 2004. *Dai 24 kai Ōita Kokusai Kurumaisu Marason Taikai kinenshi.* Ōita: Ōita-ken.

——. 2010. *Dai 30 kai kinen Ōita Kokusai Kurumaisu Marason Taikai kinenshi.* Ōita: Ōita-ken.

——. 2015a. "Dai 35 kai Ōita Kokusai Kurumaisu Marason Taikai." Ōita.

——. 2015b. "Ōita Kokusai Kurumaisu Marason Taikai: dai 34 kai taikai no kekka." Ōita.

——. 2015c. "Ōita Kokusai Kurumaisu Marason Taikai no rekishi." Ōita.

——. 2015d. "Dai 35 kai Ōita Kokusai Kurumaisu Marason Taikai Jikkō Iinkai." June 19, 2015. Ōita.

——. 2016a. "Dai 36 kai Ōita Kokusai Kurumaisu Marason Taikai: kansen gaido." Ōita.

——. 2016b. *Dai 36 kai Ōita Kokusai Kurumaisu Marason Taikai: taikai kinenshi.* Ōita: Ōita-ken.

Ōita-ken. 1982. *Tobe kurumaisu: dai 1 kai Ōita Kokusai Kurumaisu Marason Taikai.* Ōita: Ōita-ken.

——. 2018. "Ōita-ken 2018: kensei gaiyō." Ōita-ken Kikaku Shinkō-bu Seisaku Kikaku-ka. http://www.pref.oita.jp/uploaded/attachment/2024867.pdf.

Ōita-ken Fukushi Hokenbu Shōgai Fukushika. 2000. "Tokushū 2: Shōgaisha supōtsu no shinkō to kore kara no supōtsu kankyō: Ōita Kokusai Kurumaisu Marason Taikai no torikumi." *Supōtsu to kenkō* 32 (1): 41–44.

Ōita-ken Kinkyū Gyōzaisei Kaikaku Honbu. 2004. "Ōita-ken gyōzaisei kaikaku puran." Ōita-ken. http://www.pref.oita.jp/uploaded/attachment/1001954.pdf.

Ōita-ken Sōmubu Sōmuka. 1984. *Ōita-ken shi: kindai hen*, Vol. 1. Ōita: Ōita-ken.

———. 1986. *Ōita-ken shi: kindai hen*, Vol. 2. Ōita: Ōita-ken.

———. 1988. *Ōita-ken shi: kindai hen*, Vol. 4. Ōita: Ōita-ken.

———. 1989. *Ōita-ken shi: chishi hen*. Ōita: Ōita-ken.

———. 1991. *Ōita-ken shi: gendai hen*, Vol. 2. Ōita: Ōita-ken.

Ōkura Yoshio. 1976. "Fesupikku Dai ikkai Taikai to sono dezain ni tsuite." *Ōita Kenritsu Geijutsu Tanki Daigaku kenkyū kiyō* 13 (March): 53–56.

Organizing Committee. 1994. "Fespic Beijing '94 Official Report." Beijing: Organizing Committee, 6th Far East and South Pacific Games for the Disabled.

Ōsaka Orinpikku Shōchi Iinkai. 2001. *2008 nen Orinpikku Kyōgi Taikai Shōchi katsudō hōkokusho*. Osaka: Ōsaka Orinpikku Shōchi Iinkai.

Pappous, Athanasios (Sakis), and Christopher Brown. 2018. "Paralympic Legacies: A Critical Perspective." In *The Palgrave Handbook of Paralympic Studies*, edited by Ian Brittain and Aaron Beacom, 647–64. London: Palgrave Macmillan.

Para bora hiroba. 1996. 7: 1–6.

Park, Chang Il. 2010. "Epilogue: The End of FESPIC but the Beginning of APC." In *FESPIC Movement: Sports for People with Disabilities in the Far East & South Pacific*, edited by Silas T. C. Chiang, 124–30. Hong Kong: Commercial Press.

Peers, Danielle. 2015. "From Eugenics to Paralympics: Inspirational Disability, Physical Fitness, and the White Canadian Nation." PhD diss., University of Alberta, Edmonton, Alberta, Canada.

Pennington, Lee. 2015. *Casualties of History: Wounded Japanese Servicemen and the Second World War*. Studies of the Weatherhead East Asian Institute, Columbia University. Ithaca: Cornell University Press.

"President Report, 1999–2001." 2001. *FESPIC* 32 (April): 3.

Puar, Jasbir K. 2017. *The Right to Maim: Debility, Capacity, Disability*. Anima. Durham, NC: Duke University Press.

Purdue, David E. J., and P. David Howe. 2012. "See the Sport, Not the Disability: Exploring the Paralympic Paradox." *Qualitative Research in Sport, Exercise and Health* 4 (2): 189–205.

Saitō Yoshihiko. 1998. "Nagano Pararinpikku kara mita Nihon no shōgaisha supōtsu." *Sportsmedicine Quarterly* 10 (2): 112–17.

Sakita Yoshihiro. 2015. "Tōkyō Pararinpikku Taikai (1964) ni kansuru terebi hōsō— NHK de terebi hōsō sareta eizō ni chakumoku shite." *Supōtsu shi kenkyū* 28: 71–83.

Sasaki Hanako. 2004. *Pararinpikku ga kureta okurimono*. Tokyo: Media fakutorī.

Satō Mami. 2012a. *Yume o tobu: Pararinpikku asurīto no chōsen*, 3rd ed. Tokyo: Iwanami shoten.

———. 2012b. *Tobu! Yume ni mukatte: Rondon Pararinpikku rikujō Nihon daihyō Satō Mami monogatari*. Tokyo: Gakken kyōiku shuppan.

———. 2013. *Rakkī gāru*, 2nd ed. Tokyo: Shūeisha.

———. 2014. *Rakki gāru*, 3rd ed. Tokyo: Shūeisha bunko.

Schantz, Otto J., and Keith Gilbert. 2012. "The Paralympic Movement: Empowerment or Disempowerment for People with Disabilities?" In *The Palgrave Handbook of Olympic Studies*, edited by Helen Jefferson Lenskyj and Stephen Wagg, 358–80. London: Palgrave Macmillan.

Secretariat of the FESPIC Bangkok '99. 1999. *FESPIC Bangkok '99*. Bangkok: Secretariat of the FESPIC Bangkok.

Shimazaki Kiyoshi. 1998. "Shibaraku wa 'yūgen jikkō' de." *Hyūman netto Nagano kikan shi* 3 (December): 1.

Shinano kyōiku. 1999. 1346 (January).

"Shōgaisha shakai sanka ibento hanazakari." 1994. *Kōsei* 49 (12): 38–39.

Shōgaisha Supōtsu ni Kansuru Kondankai Iin. 1998. "Shōgaisha Supōtsu ni Kansuru Kondan Kai hōkoku." Tokyo. https://www.mhlw.go.jp/www1/shingi/s9806/s0629-1.html.

Shusō Kantei. 2017. *Yunibāsaru dezain 2020 kōdō keikaku*. Shusō Kantei. https://www.kantei.go.jp/jp/singi/tokyo2020_suishin_honbu/ud2020kkkaigi/.

Steadward, Robert D. 1992. "IPC President Visits China." *FESPIC* 20 (August): 4–5.

———. 1998. "Pararinpikku katsudō: senshuken takai no shoraizo (yoyaku)." Translated by Hatsuyama Yasuhiro. *Rinshō supōtsu igaku* 15 (2): 121–25.

Stevens, Carolyn S. 2013. *Disability in Japan*. Japan Anthropology Workshop Series. Hoboken, NJ: Taylor & Francis.

Sugimoto Masamitsu. 1997. "Nagano Pararinpikku de towareru borantia no arikata." *ASHITA* 16 (2): 34–35.

Suzuki Masato. 1998. "Pararinpikku no kaisai de Nagano no 'machi' ga kawatta mono." *Nōmaraizēshon*, June, 52–54.

Tagsold, Christian. 2009. "The 1964 Tokyo Olympics as Political Games." *Asia-Pacific Journal: Japan Focus* 23 (3–09). https://apjjf.org/-Christian-Tagsold/3165/article.html.

Taiyō no Ie Shintai Shōgaisha Shokunō Kaihatsu Sentā Kaihatsuka. 1975. "Taiyō no Ie jūnen no rekishi." Beppu: Taiyō no Ie. www.taiyonoie.or.jp/wp-content/themes/original/pdf/file3.pdf.

Takahashi Akira. 2004. *Shōgaisha to supōtsu*. Tokyo: Iwanami Shoten.

Takahashi Hiroshi. 2006. "Dai ikkai Taikai o furikaette." *J.S.A.D. Sports* 28 (December): 14.

Takamine, Jenny. 2010. "Tremendous Impetus to the Development of Sports for People with Disabilities in Thailand: The 7th FESPIC Games in Bangkok, Thailand (1999)." In *FESPIC Movement: Sports for People with Disabilities in the Far East & South Pacific*, edited by Silas T. C. Chiang, 104–8. Hong Kong: Commercial Press.

Takano Shoji. 1986. "Dai 4 kai Kyokutō Minami Taiheiyō Shintai Shōgaisha Supōtsu Taikai." *Rinshō supōtsu igaku* 3 (11): 1174–76.

Takemae, Eiji. 2003. *The Allied Occupation of Japan*. Translated by Robert Ricketts and Sebastian Swan. New York: Continuum.

Tan, Wei Yu Wayne. 2019. "Disability, Text, and Performance: The Significance of One Blind Musician's Career in Tokugawa Japan." *Journal of Japanese Studies* 45 (1): 91–119. https://doi.org/10.1353/jjs.2019.0004.

"Technical Seminar." 1987. *FESPIC* 13 (December): 2.

Terada Muneyoshi. 1965. "Pararinpikku kobore hanashi." *Kōsei* 20 (1): 36–38.

"Third FESPIC Games in Hong Kong." 1983. *FESPIC* 9 (1): 1.

"The Thirteenth International Stoke Mandeville Games for the Paralysed." 1964. Official English-Language Program. Tokyo. November 8, 1964.

Thomas, Nigel, and Andy Smith. 2009. *Disability, Sport, and Society: An Introduction*. London: Routledge.

Tōkyō 2020 Orinpikku Pararinpikku Shōchi Iinkai. 2013. *Tokyo 2020 Candidate City*, Vol. 1. Tokyo: Tōkyō 2020 Orinpikku Pararinpikku Shōchi Iinkai.

Tokyo Organising Committee of the Olympic and Paralympic Games. 2017. *Tokyo 2020 Accessibility Guidelines*. Tokyo: Tokyo Organising Committee of the Olympic and Paralympic Games.

Tōkyō Orinpikku Pararinpikku Shōchi Honbu. 2010. *2016 nen Orinpikku Pararinpikku Kyōgi Taikai shōchi katsudō hōkokusho*. Tokyo: Tōkyō Orinpikku Pararinpikku Shōchi Honbu.

Tōkyō Orinpikku Pararinpikku Shōchi Iinkai. 2009. *Tokyo 2016: Candidate City: Rikkōho fairu*, Vol. 2. Tokyo: Tōkyō Orinpikku Pararinpikku Shōchi Iinkai.

Tōkyō-to Edo Tōkyō Hakubutsukan. 2014. *Tōkyō Orinpikku to shinkansen*. Kyoto: Seigensha.

Tōkyō-to Seisaku Kikaku-kyoku Keikaku-bu Keikaku-ka. 2016. *Tomin fāsuto de tsukuru "Atarashii Tōkyō": 2020 nen nu muketa jikkō puran*. Tokyo: Tōkyō-to Seisaku Kikaku-kyoku Keikaku-bu Keikaku-ka.

Tongsiri, Sirinart, and Ratana Taweesangsuksakul. 1999. "Sports for the Person with a Disability: The 7th FESPIC Games in Bangkok, Thailand." *Asia and Pacific Journal on Disability* 2 (1). http://www.dinf.ne.jp/doc/english/asia/resource/z00ap/004/z00ap00401.html#.

Toyosawa, Nobuko. 2008. "The Cartography of Epistemology: The Production of 'National' Space in Late 19th Century Japan." PhD diss., University of Illinois at Urbana-Champaign. https://www.ideals.illinois.edu/handle/2142/87209.

Tsuchida Wakako. 2010. *Shintai shōgaisha supōtsu kanzen gaido: Pararinpian kara no messēji*. Tokyo: Tōhō shuppan.

———. 2012. *Ima o ukeire, ima o koeru: kurumaisu marason sekai kiroku hojisha no "mae ni susumu kotoba."* Tokyo: Tokoma shoten.

Tsurushima Mizuho. 2017. "Tōkyō 2020 Orinpikku Pararinpikku e bunken yoron chōsa de sagaru Tōkyō 2020 e no kitai to ishiki." Presented at the NHK bunken fōramu. http://www.nhk.or.jp/bunken/forum/2017/docs.html.

Tsurushima Mizuho, and Saitō Takanobu. 2017. "2020 nen Tōkyō Orinpikku Pararinpikku e no kitai to ishiki: '2016 nen 10 gatsu Tōkyō Orinpikku Pararinpikku ni kansuru yoron chōsa' no kekka kara." *Hōsō kenkyū to chōsa* (November): 2–29.

Tynedal, Jeremy, and Gregor Wolbring. 2013. "Paralympics and Its Athletes through the Lens of the *New York Times*." *Sports* 1 (1): 13–36. https://doi.org/10.3390/sports1010013.

Ueda Sakiko. 2013. "Kokuritsu shintai shōgaisha kōsei shidōjo no nyūsho jijō: shōi gunjin no shogun o chūshin ni." *Shintennōji Daigaku Daigakuin kenkyū ronshū* 8: 107–30.

———. 2016. "Shōigunjin shokugyō hogo taisaku ni seikei geka i ga hatashita yaku-wari." *Kōbe Iryō Fukushi Daigaku kiyō* 17 (1): 1–18.

Ueno Kazuya. 1920. *Beppu onsen annai: sento*. Beppu-chō: Asakino shōten.

Ueno Shizuo. 1998. "Nagano Orinpikku Pararinpikku ni muketa machidzukuri." *Rihabiri* 407 (October): 26–29.

Ujiie Kaoru. 1975. "Dai ikkai Kyokutō Minami Taiheiyō Shintai Shōgaisha Supōtsu Taikai o kaerimite." *Kōsei* 30 (8): 17–22.

United Nations General Assembly. 1989. *A/RES/44/70: Implementation of the World Programme of Action Concerning Disabled Persons and the United Nations Decade of Disabled Persons.* http://www.un.org/documents/ga/res/44/a44r070.htm.

Wakana Tsunenobu. 1998. "Nagano Pararinpikku ga owatte." *Seishōnen mondai* 45 (12): 46–49.

Wārudo yū Kawanakajima-chō yūsen hōsō. 2001. *Kusa no ne borantea kenbun roku: Nagano Tōki Orinpikku Pararinpikku o sasaeta hitobito.* Nagano: Hōzuki shoseki.

Watanabe Hanako. 1964a. "Pararinpikku ni miru rōdō taisaku no danmen." *Shūkan rōdō nyūsu*, November, p. 4.

——. 1964b. "Pararinpikku wa itaitashikunai ka." *Fujin no tomo* 58 (12): 173–74.

——. 1965. "Kango rōdō no kachikan o takameru mono: Tokyo Pararinpikku ni tsudzugu." *Kango* 17 (1): 3–9.

Watanabe Kimio, dir. 1965. *Tōkyō Pararinpikku: ai to eikō no saiten.* DCP of Japanese documentary film originally produced by Daiei Eiga. Tōkyō: Kadokawa Eiga.

Watari Tadashi. 2007. "Shōgaisha supōtsu ni yoru girei teki kanshin no kōchiku: 1970 nendai no 'undō' to Pararinpikku no hyōshō." *Chiba Daigaku Nihon bunka ronsō* 8: 92–106.

——. 2010. "Pararinpikku no hyōshō jissen to girei teki kanshin." In *Supōtsu kansen gaku: nekkyō no sutēji no kōzō to imi*, edited by Hashimoto Junichi, 230–51. Tokyo: Sekai shisō sha.

——. 2012. *Shōgaisha supōtsu no rinkaiten.* Tokyo: Shinhyōron.

——. 2018. "Pararinpikku ni okeru nashonarizumu: Pararinpian ni mukerareru nashonarizumu no yōtai." Unpublished manuscript shared with author.

Yamada Kiyoshi. 2016. "Shōgaisha supōtsu to hōsō: Tōkyō 2020 Pararinpikku o misuete." *Hōsō kenkyū to chōsa*, December, 30–48.

Yamada Yukihiko. 1999. "Watashi no aidea: 'Nagano Pararinpikku' he no torikumi." *Shinano kyōiku* 1346 (January): 62–63.

Yamaguchi Yasuo. 1993. "'Shōgai supōtsu' no ibento nyūmon 15: Ōita Kokusai Kurumaisu Marason Taikai." *Taiikuka kyōiku* 41 (8): 65–68.

Yamaha Hatsudōki Supōtsu Shinkō Zaidan. 2017. *2016 (Heisei 28) nendo shōgaisha supōtsu no shinkō to kyōka ni kansuru chōsa kenkyū hōkokusho: terebi hōsō, senshu ninchido, daigaku ni yoru shien ni chūmoku shite.* Iwata-shi: Yamaha Hatsudōki Supōtsu Shinkō Zaidan. http://www.ymfs.jp/project/culture/survey/008/.

——. 2018. *2017 (Heisei 29) nendo shōgaisha supōtsu no shinkō to kyōka ni kansuru chōsa kenkyū hōkokusho: terebi CF, daigaku no senshin-teki torikukmi, chiiki genba no jittai ni chūmoku shite.* Iwata-shi: Yamaha Hatsudōki Supōtsu Shinkō Zaidan. https://www.ymfs.jp/project/culture/survey/010/.

Yamashita Shin. 2006. "Fesupikku Pekin Taikai no omoide." *J.S.A.D. Sports* 28 (December): 25.

Yamazaki Noboru. 2006. "Fesupikku Honkon Taikai ni sanka shite." *J.S.A.D. Sports* 28 (December): 18.

Yonekawa Kōji. 1998. "'Kandō ga hirogaru, tsutawaru, wakiagaru' mō hitotsu no Orinpikku: Nagano Pararinpikku Tōki Kyōgi Taikai." *Shōroku kyōiku gijutsu* 50 (13): 26–27.

Yong, Jia. 2010. "The Rise of [a] Giant in Sports for People with Disabilities: The 6th FESPIC Games in Beijing, China (1994)." In *FESPIC Movement: Sports for People with Disabilities in the Far East & South Pacific*, edited by Silas T. C. Chiang, 90–103. Hong Kong: Commercial Press.

Yoshii Isamu. 1998. "Intānetto raibu chūkei ga hatsu no kōshiki media to natta Nagano Pararinpikku Tōki Taikai." *New Media* 16 (6): 82–83.

Yoshinaga Eiji. 2006. "Fesupikku Taikai ni omou." *J.S.A.D. Sports* 28 (December): 13.

Zarin, Dato' Zainal Abu. 2010. "Hope to Change the Asian Scenario towards Disabled to a Better One: The 9th FESPIC Games in Kuala Lumpur, Malaysia (2006)." In *FESPIC Movement: Sports for People with Disabilities in the Far East & South Pacific*, edited by Silas T. C. Chiang, 116–23. Hong Kong: Commercial Press.

INDEX

Figures are indicated by an *"f"* after the page number.

Abbott World Marathon Majors Wheelchair Race Series, 127, 139

Abe Shinzo, 213

ableism, 6, 37, 39, 141, 190, 196. *See also* super-crip stereotype

Abu Zarin, Dato Zainal, 96

accessibility: of FESPIC Games, 62, 75; in Kobe, 86; Nagano Winter Paralympics and, 152–155, 161–162, 165; in Ōita, 133–134; post–Tokyo Paralympics and, 33; of sports facilities, 208; Tokyo Summer Paralympic Games and, 202, 210–217; universal design, 212, 216. *See also* infrastructure

Accessible Japan website, 213

activism: Independent Living Movement, 158–159; Japan's disability rights movement and, 157, 159; Nagano Games and changes to, 144; by people with disabilities, 6

Acton, Norman, 18, 22

admission fees, for Nagano Paralympics, 149, 166

Agitos Foundation, 218

akarui (bright), 252n124. *See also* bright life and brightness

Akihito, Crown Prince: on disability sports as rehabilitation, 40; on Japan's treatment of individuals with disabilities, 46; at Ōita FESPIC Games, 66; Tokyo Paralympics and, 24, 30–31, 32, 50

Akiyama Chieko, 70

All Nippon Airways (ANA), 64

Andō Tokuji, 36

antidiscrimination laws, 206

Aono Shigeo, 31, 45

Araragi Kazuma, 181

arcade districts, 127, 264n75

Art Paralympics Nagano, 151

Asahi shimbun (newspaper): disability sports, role in emergence of, 22; disability sports coverage, 179, 179f, 180f, 181; FESPIC Games coverage, 184–187, 185f, 186f; International Stoke Mandeville Games, coverage of, 24; International Stoke Mandeville Games, support for Japanese team at, 30; Ōita International Wheelchair Marathon coverage, 187–190, 188f, 189f

Asahi Shimbun Newspaper Company, as Tokyo Paralympics guarantor, 24

Asahi Shimbun Social Welfare Organization, 21, 22, 249–250n36

Asahi Weekly, Kasai Yoshisuke interview in, 41, 45

Ashida Hajimu, 199

Asian and Pacific Decade of Disabled Persons, 158–159, 270n48

Asian Para Games, 52, 99–100

Asian Paralympic Committee (APC), 52–53, 90, 98–100

Asian Paralympic Council (APC), 52, 96, 97

Asō Manabu, 238, 239, 243, 259n151

Association for the Promotion of Sports for the Disabled, 20

Association of Green Grass (Aoi Shiba no Kai), 6

athletes: bright life and, 44–49; disability classifications of, 134–135, 136–137, 140, 190–191, 235; disability sports, initial exposure to and resources for, 236; elite performances, emphasis on, 98–99, 140–141, 144, 168, 171, 185, 209, 241; impact of disability sports on, 43; with intellectual disabilities, 89, 90, 168, 169, 172; invited, at Ōita International Wheelchair Marathon, travel support for, 127, 139; participation in Olympic and

inspirational discourses of, 195–196;
Japan, disability sports in, 167–170; in
Japan, changes to, 167–170; legal changes'
impact on, 206–207; multi-disability
sports events, 22–23, 60–61, 65;
newspaper articles on, 179–181, 179f,
180f; normalization of, 170–173;
representations of, 14, 209; research on,
6–11; triathlons, 136. *See also* athletes;
bidding process; Far East and South
Pacific (FESPIC) Federation . . . ; Ōita
International Wheelchair Marathon;
Paralympics and disability sports;
rehabilitation
disability sports specialists, 167–168, 244
Disability Winter Sports Promotion Project
(Nagano Prefecture), 169
Don, Robert, 56
doping and anti-doping, 83, 136, 163

Edo-Tokyo Museum, 223
elite performance, emphasis on, 98,
140–141, 144, 168, 171, 185, 209, 241
employment (of people with disabilities): of
athletes at Tokyo Paralympics, 46, 49;
employment rates, 8; laws and policies
on, 206, 216–217; Nakamura and, 68, 116;
Ōita Prefecture plans on, 124. *See also*
rehabilitation; Taiyō no Ie
exhibition sports, at Kobe FESPIC Games, 76
expenses. *See* financing

Fang, Harry S. Y., 73, 93
Far East and South Pacific (FESPIC)
Federation and FESPIC Games for the
Disabled, 52–103; early games, 71–74;
FESPIC Federation, initial constitution
of, 58–59; FESPIC Information Center for
the Disabled, 68, 128; FESPIC Information System (FINS), 83–84; FESPIC
Movement, 54–63, 71, 98, 102; FESPIC
Rehabilitation Fund, 68, 71, 72; forgotten
legacy of, 100–103; funding for, 62–63,
68–71; Games as mega-events, 87–91;
impact of, 240, 241; IPC, merger with,
91–100; Kobe games, 74–87; media
attention to, 178, 184–187, 186f, 189–191;
Ōita, inaugural FESPIC games in, 55,
64–71
financing: IOC-IPC relationship and, 95, 203;
from Japan's central government, 168; of
Kobe FESPIC Games, 76, 79, 80–81; of
Nagano Winter Paralympics, 148–149,

150; from Nippon Foundation, 218,
220–221, 243; of Ōita FESPIC Games,
68–69, 70, 71; of Ōita International
Wheelchair Marathon, 124, 127; for
participation in FESPIC Games, 57, 62–63,
90, 120; of Tokyo Paralympics, 24, 25–26
FINS (FESPIC Information System), 83–84
First International Sports Festival for the
Disabled (Linz, Austria), 18
Frei, Heinz, 104, 126, 138, 228
Freund, Georg, 122
Frost, Dennis J.: Ōita, visit to, 265n92;
Paralympics in Japan, interest in, 7–8
Fujita Motoaki: newspaper coverage of
disability sports, analysis of, 179, 180, 181,
185, 187, 193, 194, 196; on pre–Nagano
Games periods, 167–168; on 2021
problem, 243–245
Fujiwara, Shinichiro, 87
Fundamental Law for Disabled Persons, 156

Gakkō taiiku (School Sports) journal, disability
sports article, 175
Games Co-operation Agreement, 203–204
Gamō Akemi, 226–227, 236
gender differences, in prizes, 140
General Assembly (on disability sports
organizations), 93, 94
GO Journal (Paralympic Support Center), 221
Goffman, Erving, 193–194
Goh, C., 56
Government Action Plan for Persons with
Disabilities (1995), 156, 157, 159
Grant, John, 56, 61, 63, 93–94
graying of Japan, 157–158
Grisdale, Josh, 213
Ground Self-Defense Forces, at Ōita FESPIC
Games, 69
Guangzhou, China, Asian Para Games in, 98
Guttmann, Ludwig: discussion of, 15–18; on
living with disabilities, 41; on multiple
disability sports, 61; Nakamura and, 16,
28, 56, 61; at Ōita FESPIC Games, 66;
Okino and, 20; on Tokyo Paralympics, 12

Hakuba village, accessibility in, 153–154
Hashimoto Tomisaburō, 64
Hatada Kazuo, 61, 66, 73–74, 88, 89, 96
Hawkins, Peter, 138
Heartful Building Law (Law for Buildings
Accessible to and Usable by the Elderly
and Physically Disabled Persons), 156,
157–158